Architecture as **Built** Criticism

Architecture as Built Criticism

Yasmin Shariff Tosin Oshinowo
Rasmus Wærn Mengfei Pan
Büşra Köroğlu Juhani Pallasmaa
Luísa Augusta Gabriela Teixeira Gonçalves
Jaime Silva Xiang Ren
Naomi Mehta / Priyanka Salunkhe
Algimantas Grigas Eliyahu Keller
Ricardo Leitão Luiz Recamán / Mariana Wilderom
Patrizia Mello Trenton Sexton
Yifei Zhang Maria Valeria Bernabei
Al Borde – David Barragán, Pascual Gangotena,
Maríaluisa Borja, and Esteban Benavides
Jin Qiuye / Chang Tao Wang Shu

Editors Li Xiangning and Wilfried Wang

PARK BOOKS

TONGJI UNIVERSITY CAUP

Credits

This book is published following the International Conference on

Architecture as Built Criticism

held on October 14, 15, 21, and 22, 2023 at Tongji University, CAUP, Shanghai.

Scientific Committee	Carlos Eduardo Comas, UFRGS, Porto Alegre Elias Constantopoulos, University of Patras, Hellenic Institute of Architecture Manuel Cuadra, Frankfurt am Main/Lima Fernando Diez, Di Tella University, Buenos Aires Jasna Galjer, University of Zagreb, Croatia Berna Göl, Yeditepe University, Istanbul Hélène Jannière, Université Rennes 2 Morten Birk Jørgensen, Royal Academy, Copenhagen Li Xiangning, Tongji University Robert McCarter, Washington University, St. Louis Valerio Paolo Mosco, IUAV, Venice Louise Noelle Gras, UNAM, Mexico CdMx Şengül Öymen Gür, Beykent Üniversitesi, Istanbul José Manuel Pozo Municio, ETSAUN, Pamplona Xing Ruan, Shanghai Jiao Tong University Paolo Scrivano, Politecnico di Milano Jaime Solares, Escola da Cidade, São Paulo Ana Tostões, CiTUA-Instituto Técnico, Lisbon Ruth Verde Zein, U. Presbiteriana Mackenzie, São Paulo
Supporting Institutions	CICA International Committee of Architectural Critics Beykent Üniversitesi, Istanbul Hellenic Institute of Architecture, Athens Instituto Superior Técnico, Lisbon Istituto Universitario Architettura Venezia, Venice Jiao Tong University, Shanghai Tongji University, Shanghai Universidad de Navarra, Pamplona Universidade Presbiteriana Mackenzie, São Paulo IIEs Universidad Nacional Autónoma de México Universidad Nacional de Ingeniería Lima University of Patras Washington University, St. Louis
Sponsorship	Tongji University, Shanghai
Editors	Li Xiangning and Wilfried Wang
Copy Editor	Dean Drake
Proofreader	Ian McDonald
Graphic Design	Sabine Hahn, www.sh-gd.de
Image Processing, Printing and Binding	DZA Druckerei zu Altenburg GmbH, Thuringia

Park Books is being supported by the Federal Office of Culture with a general subsidy for the years 2021–2025.

Park Books AG, Niederdorfstrasse 54, 8001 Zurich. Switzerland, www.park-books.com, T +41 44 262 16 62, E info@park-books.com

Product safety: Responsible person pursuant to EU Regulation 2023/988 (GPSR): GVA Gemeinsame Verlagsauslieferung Göttingen GmbH & Co. KG, Post Box 2021, 37010 Göttingen, Germany, T +49 551 384 200 0, E info@gva-verlage.de

ISBN 978-3-03860-423-5

Table of Contents

Introduction

Architecture as Built Criticism
Introduction

Li Xiangning / Wilfried Wang

The built environment structures people's lives, gives societies meaning, and forms part of their enduring cultural legacy. At a domestic level, whether it be apartments or single-family houses, typological organization and patterns of use speak about individual value systems. Often, the place where food is prepared is the heart of the home and an intensively used space for eating and conversing, while a formal area for guests is treated respectfully, like a shrine. Of course, such usage patterns vary across regions and time. During the nineteenth and twentieth centuries, the upheavals in domestic typologies were wide-ranging: millions of people moving from rural areas to urban centers to work in industries found minimal accommodation, often without sanitation and running water. This urbanization process, parallel to suburban sprawl, continues in many regions around the world. Over centuries, political goals, development companies, and design teams have sought to adapt and evolve unit types, together with settlement layouts and configurational typologies. The compendium of realized changes at all these levels of design is effectively the accumulated critique of housing and lifestyles. Architects have had a major impact on the search for improved solutions in housing design, whether it be at the conceptual level of how best to gather large communities of residents while respecting their individual privacy, or at the contructional level, etc. Major and minor improvements at the larger and smaller scales are constructive critiques that, when realized, become Built Criticism.

Realizing any instance of Built Criticism requires a consensus between the commissioning organization and the design team. Following World War I, the renewal of housing typologies in Europe was primarily instigated by committed politicians, resulting in public housing being constructed on an unprecedented scale. However, especially with the post–World War II generation of public housing, the design logic of these developments produced social crises when their overwhelming scale greatly diminished the possibility of social cohesion and identifiability. Some of these housing schemes only lasted for a couple of decades, such as the Pruitt–Igoe development in St. Louis, Missouri, USA (completed 1955, demolished 1976), whose destruction was to become synonymous with the supposed end of modernism. What was to be an instrument of social innovation and liberation through a broadly accessible architecture had turned into the opposite: a means of uprooting and disaggregating people. What had started as a constructive form of Built Criticism had degenerated into a rationalistic model devoid of place-making and sociocultural ambitions. The aftermath of this failed housing policy continues to be felt on the outskirts of some of the world's most civilized cities, such as Paris or Stockholm.

At the level of individual buildings, the Philharmonie Berlin (1959–63) by Hans Scharoun is a Built Criticism at every imaginable level of architecture. The commissioning agent, Berlin's politicians, decided to resite Scharoun's winning scheme on Albert Speer's infamous North–South Axis, as if to say that Hitler's vision for Germania as the new Nazi capital of the conquered world could be exorcized by a democratic alternative. Scharoun chose to characterize the concert hall as a tent-like configuration, where the profile of the drooping ceilings would be translated to that of the roof, as a direct inversion of Speer's domed Hall of the People. Scharoun's concept for the auditorium is more radical still in its critique of conventional audience–orchestra arrangements: in the Philharmonie, music is at the center and the audience is distributed in distinctly unequal groups around the performers. The spatial and formal language is openly multifaceted, the structural system polygonal, and the construction directly expressed: what you see is what it is. The Philharmonie is about as diametrically opposed to Albert Speer's neoclassicism as possible. It is a dramatic assertion of a Built Criticism.

Half a century earlier, Adolf Loos's commercial building on Vienna's Michaelerplatz for the gentlemen's outfitters of Goldman & Salatsch (1909–11) caused public controversies during its construction phase, as it became evident to conservative observers that it would be devoid of then conventional plaster decoration. Loos's critique of ornament went far, but did not exclude the installation of real marble columns that were so subtle a critique of the plaster pilasters on the facades of the neighboring imperial palace, the church, and the contemporary historicist buildings that they could not compensate for the more barren surfaces of the upper office floors.

Over centuries, clients and architects have sought to address a series of issues in their Built Criticism, whether these relate to ethical (healthcare facilities), aesthetic (museums), social (schools), cultural (conservation and local identities), functional (kitchen layouts), constructional (high-tech or crafts), environmental (use of regenerative materials), formal (esoteric games or minimalism), or political (official government buildings) concerns. Depending on the ideological–political bases on which Built Criticisms are founded and on the points of view from which built objects are read, what appear as affirmative critiques to some observers are negative critiques to others.

Following the first two international conferences held by CICA, the International Committee of Architectural Critics ("On the Duty and Power of Architectural Criticism" in 2021[1] and "Defining Architectural Quality" in 2022[2]), the topic of the third conference was "Architecture as Built Criticism." The College of Architecture and Urban Planning (CAUP) of Tongji University together with the Tongji Architectural Design (Group) Co., Ltd. sponsored the hybrid conference, which was held at the Tongji University CAUP in October 2023.[3] The papers presented at the conference are gathered in this volume, beginning with the six keynote lectures: **Yasmin Shariff's** call for a planetary perspective on the climate crisis and its consequences for architecture; **Juhani Pallasmaa's** brilliant analysis of Alvar Aalto's Villa Mairea as an ethical counter to the inadequacies of industrial modernism; **Tosin Oshinowo's** global review of critiques of modernity by local initiatives that ingeniously bridge the gap between needs and resources; **Al Borde's** exemplary collective approach in realizing appealing architectural designs to solve social and environmental challenges and **Jin Qiuye** and **Chang Tao's** unfolding of Chinese architecture's reconnection with historical garden architecture that introduced **Wang Shu's** construction-based Built Criticism, which is an innovative and fresh counter to the absence of cultural roots and values in the conventional building industry. The six keynote lectures constitute a general as well as a detailed alternative body of knowledge to dominant conceptions of architectural design and construction.

Following the conference call, a number of abstracts on individual cases were selected for the four conference sessions and the publication. The Built Criticisms originate from three continents—Asia, the Americas, and Europe—with the earliest being completed in 1910. **Rasmus Wærn** offers a reflection on the way Carl Westman's Museum of Arts and Crafts in Gothenburg engaged in the timeless topic of asserting an individual's interpretation of what should be considered appropriate vis-à-vis the dominant Zeitgeist. Similarly, **Büşra Köroğlu** reveals two architects' search for the appropriate relation to history and context in the early years of Kemal Atatürk's Turkey: the one, the Austrian-Swiss Ernst Egli, whose sensibilities and respect for his adopted home infuse his earlier modernist orthodoxy, while the other, the Turk Sedad Hakki Eldem, distills his profound knowledge of traditional Turkish architecture in an essentializing process without losing its roots. **Mengfei Pan** provides a paradigmatic example of an uncompromising competition entry (1931) that was submitted in the knowledge that, while it would stir controversy, it would never be realized: Kunio Maekawa's proposal for a national museum in Tokyo nevertheless inscribed itself

1 Wilfried Wang, *On the Duty and Power of Architectural Criticism* (Zurich: Park Books, 2022).

2 José Manuel Pozo Municio and Wilfried Wang, *Defining Architectural Quality* (Zurich: Park Books, 2024).

3 The unedited video recordings are freely available at https://cicarchitecture.org/international-conference-on-architecture-as-built-criticism-sessions-1-3-4/.

indelibly in the minds of subsequent generations of architects for its indefatigable critique of academic architecture.

Of lasting success is **Luísa Augusta Gabriela Teixeira Gonçalves's** case of the São Bento Subway Station in São Paulo by the Brazilian architect Marcelo Fragelli and his team, who proved that it is possible to design public infrastructure as a celebration of the quotidian. At the other end of the scale of architecture, two family houses realized by the same person, in this case the architect, historian, and critic Peter Blundell Jones, can be understood as personal manifestos; **Xiang Ren** compares these houses with Blundell Jones's writings on the organic tradition in architecture. As an instance of a Built Criticism in public housing, **Jaime Silva** examines Taller de Arquitectura's radically open design for Walden 7 at Sant Just Desvern (1975) against the then dominant Francoist family ideal.

If the aforementioned Built Criticisms experienced countercriticisms, these pale by comparison with what Raimund Abraham's competition entry (1992) for the Austrian Cultural Forum in New York (2002) received; **Eliyahu Keller** recounts the turbulent international response to the miniature high-rise that was considered by some to be a forward-pointing critique of the bland capitalist development machine called New York City. Of regional relevance is the winning scheme, with its abstracted rationalist design, for the Estonian Embassy (1998) in Vilnius by 3+1 architects; **Algimantas Grigas** shows how the embassy's cultural message has influenced the architectural discourse in both Estonia and Lithuania. In the case of Giorgio Grassi's classicizing rationalist architecture, **Ricardo Leitão** traces the Italian architect's unerring insistence on a contemporary classical order that is developed from the logic of construction for a bank in Florence, thereby overcoming "fashionable" "expressionism."

Trenton Sexton deciphers Hiroshi Sambuichi Architects' Inujima Seirensho Art Museum (2008) on Seto Inland Sea as a wholly integrated work of architecture that is critical of its dominant cultural context and that is capable at the same time of setting an exceptionally high standard as a sustainable building in function and culture. Similarly, **Luiz Recamán** and **Mariana Wilderom** evaluate the Antonio Derka School by Obranegra Arquitectos in Medellín (2008) as part of a political goal for architecture to not only serve to educate every child but also elevate the schoolchildren literally and metaphorically. For the sustainable public school at Lo Zárate in Chile, **Maria Valeria Bernabei** shows how Al Borde's team spirit inspired the collaborative realization of a building complex that uses part of a previous building together with a variety of recycled components to become a comprehensive paradigm of a sustainable architecture. In a similar vein, **Patrizia Mello's** case of the competition-winning design by the Dutch architects MVRDV uses elements of a former shopping center to become a revitalized part of Tainan's downtown (2020). Working in the privileged context of a private university with the corresponding traditional architectural self-respect, Thomas Phifer and Partners' sleek abstracted temple of white-painted steel, Brochstein Pavilion, is analyzed by **Yifei Zhang** in regard to how it manages to counter the traditional reclusive character of the doubly academic campus of Rice University, while still exuding an elite air of the sublime.

Priyanka Salunkhe and **Naomi Mehta's** paper from the conference on "Defining Architectural Quality" is included in this publication, since its approach of critically reviewing Antonin Raymond's Golconde and Charles Correa's Kanchanjunga Apartments in Bombay (now Mumbai) is the starting point for their Architecture as Critical Redesign, showing how important works of architecture could benefit from detailed improvement given the freedom of unrestrained criticism.

As the joint organizers and editors of the conference and publication, our thanks go to the sponsoring institutions, Tongji University College of Architecture and Urban Planning and Tongji Architectural Design (Group) Co., Ltd., and to the many members of the Scientific Committee who reviewed the numerous submissions and who participated in the chairing of individual conference sessions; we are grateful to the CICA, particularly to Louise Noelle Gras, chair of the CICA Board, and Manuel Cuadra, CICA general secretary, for their guidance—and to the numerous supporting universities around the world. Li Xiangning and Wilfried Wang are particularly grateful to the many advisors who recommended the keynote lecturers and to Thomas Kramer and his team at Park Books, Zurich, for their uncompromising and continued support in enabling this book to come into being, including Dean Drake for copyediting the texts. We thank Sabine Hahn for her dedicated, faithful, and engaging graphic design. Our final thanks go to the keynote lecturers and the authors for their unstinting work. May the readers find answers to their intellectual curiosity with the help of the essays assembled herein.

Biographies

Li Xiangning

Born in Nanjing, Li Xiangning is director of the Division of Planning and Academic Development of Tongji University; professor in history, theory, and criticism, former dean of Tongji University CAUP; and editor-in-chief of *Architecture China*. In addition, he is a member of the Board of Directors of CICA and author of numerous essays on contemporary Chinese architecture and urbanism. He has served as a visiting scholar and professor at various institutions, such as MIT and Harvard GSD, and has curated numerous exhibitions, including the China Pavilion at the 16th Venice Architecture Biennale; *Towards a Critical Pragmatism: Contemporary Architecture in China* at Harvard GSD; and Shanghai Urban Space Art Season 2015, 2017, and 2023. Li Xiangning has been working with international museums and exhibitions, including the Museum of Modern Art and the Milan Triennale, and has been a jury member on international awards and competitions, such as the Mies van der Rohe Award.

Wilfried Wang

Born in Hamburg, he studied architecture in London and founded Hoidn Wang Partner in Berlin with Barbara Hoidn. He taught at the PNL, UCL, ETH Zurich, Harvard University, UT Austin, and Universidade de Navarra, and is currently professor of architecture at Tongji University CAUP, as well as being president of CICA. Wilfried Wang is a foreign member of Kungliga Konstakademien, Stockholm; a member of the Akademie der Künste, Berlin; an honorary member of the Ordem dos Arquitectos, Portugal; has an honorary doctorate from the KTH Stockholm; and is Changjiang Distinguished Scholar, Ministry of Education, China.

David Barragán photographing Pudong from the Bund, Shanghai, 2023.
Photo: Wilfried Wang.

Architecture as Built Criticism: A Planetary Perspective

Yasmin Shariff

Architecture as Built Criticism is flashing red lights and sounding emergency sirens. With cities mushrooming, biodiversity diminishing, inequality increasing, resources depleting, and greenhouse gas emissions causing havoc, we have been catapulted into the Anthropocene.[1] This is an era rooted in postwar consumerism, where human activity is making a dramatic impact on planet Earth.[2] We are under attack: fires, floods, droughts, bombings, riots, and plagues are all confronting the world. This rate of destruction and loss is unsustainable. Architecture as Built Criticism is pivotal in the Anthropocene, because most of humanity now lives in cities.[3] The design of our built environment and the way it shapes our lifestyle and lifestyle choices directly impacts planetary systems.[4]

Architecture as Built Criticism cannot be divorced from the political and economic forces that control and shape cities and the societies that inhabit them.[5] The 2023 International Union of Architects (UIA) Congress in Copenhagen focused on the UN Sustainable Development Goals, which have at their core most of the critical issues we face on planet Earth: climate change, the depletion/pollution of resources, the loss of biodiversity, and social inequality.[6] It was recognized that there is a need for architects to deliver on these goals, but without critical analysis of the built environment we are in danger of preserving the status quo and empowering the empowered. The main keynote speeches by city architects at the UIA Congress were silent on the issues of poverty, homelessness, and migration. Their urban transformations pander to the short-term ambitions of their political masters by showcasing green open spaces, bike lanes, and pedestrianization.[7]

The spatial expression of the ambitions of those who control resources and decide how they are to be deployed has always been the framework in which architects operate,

1 "Anthropocene," National Geographic Society, accessed January 31, 2024, https://education.nationalgeographic.org/resource/anthropocene/.

2 Dipesh Chakrabarty, "Humans Are a Geological Force," interview by Shiraz Sidhva, UNESCO, March 27, 2018, https://courier.unesco.org/en/articles/humans-are-geological-force.

3 Anna Kajumulo Tibaijuka, Jos Maseland, and Jay Moor, "Our Urban Future: Making a Home for 'Homo Urbanus,'" *The Brown Journal of World Affairs* 11, no. 2 (Winter/Spring 2005): 57–67, http://www.jstor.org/stable/24590546.

4 Stuart Capstick, Radhika Khosla, and Susie Wang, "Bridging the Gap—The Role of Equitable Low-Carbon Lifestyles," in *Emissions Gap Report 2020* (United Nations Environment Programme, January 2021), 62–75, https://www.un-ilibrary.org/content/books/9789280738124c010/read.

5 Anja Eickelberg, Kathrin Zeller, and Marco Contardi, "Making Cities Part of the Global Solution—Overcoming Obstacles, Exploring Opportunities," G20 Germany 2017, accessed August 28, 2024, https://www.global-solutions-initiative.org/wp-content/uploads/2022/11/10_Agenda-2030_Making-Cities.pdf.

6 UIA World Congress of Architects Copenhagen, July 2–6, 2023, accessed January 31, 2024, https://uia2023cph.org/.

7 UIA, "The Long-Term Creative: Rob Adams and the City of Melbourne," 2023, YouTube video, accessed January 31, 2024, https://www.youtube.com/watch?v=Y-saffWwZ7k.

but the critical voice active in the postwar decades of the twentieth century has been neutered. For the first time in the history of the UIA the international independent critics, CICA, were denied a place in the program at the UIA Congress, but more worrying is that the lack of a critical voice was not even noticed.

In the complex web of big data economics and social and ecosystem analysis, the role of the profession, ironically, is increasingly caricatured by starchitects and what buildings look like. Recognition of architects working with the powerless is often focused on the developing world, epitomized at the congress by Yasmeen Lari.[8] Her complex, nuanced, diverse approach serves the needs of thousands, but the impact on global climate change is limited as it is the wealthy and not the poor who are wrecking our planet. G20 countries represent 85 percent of global GDP, 75 percent of international trade, 59 percent of the world's population, and 52 percent of the world's habitable land area,[9] and are responsible for 78 percent of planetary emissions.[10] It is in G20 countries where most of the world's resources are consumed and where most of the greenhouse gases are emitted.[11] Architecture as Built Criticism, not just policymakers, has the potential to empower decision-makers to morph resource-hungry cities from gas-guzzling engines of consumption to eco-planetary balanced environments.

[8] UIA, "Sustainable Communities with Yasmeen Lari: Rehabilitation of Climate Migrants," Realdania Talks, 2023, YouTube video, accessed January 31, 2024, https://www.youtube.com/watch?v=eKEP9xwaYsc.

[9] "Member States of the G20—Group of Twenty," WorldData.info, accessed January 31, 2024, https://www.worlddata.info/alliances/g20-group-of-twenty.php.

[10] Oxfam International, "G20 Countries Failing by Big Margins to Cut Greenhouse Gas Emissions to below 'Catastrophic' Levels," 2023, accessed January 31, 2024, https://www.oxfam.org/en/press-releases/g20-countries-failing-big-margins-cut-greenhouse-gas-emissions-below-catastrophic.

[11] UIA, "Keynote Dialogue with Bjarke Ingels & Margrethe Vestager: The EU Goes Green," 2023, YouTube video, accessed January 31, 2024, https://www.youtube.com/watch?v=JdR5miyrozo.

keywords:

climate change, Anthropocene, lifestyle, Huizhen High School, Floating Forest School, Reyhanlı Refugee Centre, G20 Cities World Architecture Festival, Spaceship Earth, Buckminster Fuller, Soleri, Whole Earth Catalog, Habitat Safdie, UNEP

Introduction

Architecture as Built Criticism is urgently needed from a planetary perspective to tackle humanity's main issues: climate change, resource depletion/pollution, and inequality. Nothing else matters.[12] The current oversimplistic stylistic or technical architectural debate is puerile and serves little purpose. The mere "look" of a building or its LEED (Leadership in Energy and Environmental Design)/carbon rating deemed to be architecture's current USP is irrelevant without a critique on its planetary impact.

Planetary Perspective Origins

Our modern planetary perspective has its origins in 1966, when Stewart Brand, the editor of the *Whole Earth Catalog*,[13] thought that seeing an image of the whole Earth would change how we think about the planet and ourselves. Brand's view was that the overarching project of humankind was about living interactively within natural systems. He campaigned to get NASA to release the then rumored satellite image of Earth. During his campaign, Brand met Richard Buckminster Fuller, who offered to help. NASA released the first full disc color photograph of Earth, taken by the satellite ATS-3 on November 10, 1967, which was subsequently used on the cover of Brand's *Whole Earth Catalog* and changed our perspective of planet Earth forever. Vitruvian man suddenly became a tiny speck of dust on Earth's blue horizon.

[12] World Commission on Environment and Development, *Report of the World Commission on Environment and Development: Our Common Future*, United Nations General Assembly document A/43/427 (1987), accessed January 31, 2024, https://sustainabledevelopment.un.org/content/documents/5987our-common-future.pdf.

[13] Carole Cadwalladr, "Stewart Brand's *Whole Earth Catalog*, the Book That Changed the World," *Guardian*, May 5, 2013, https://www.theguardian.com/books/2013/may/05/stewart-brand-whole-earth-catalog.

Inhabiting Spaceship Earth

At the fiftieth annual convention of the American Planning Association on October 16, 1967, Fuller addressed his audience on the "Operating Manual for Spaceship Earth," and published a book of the same title the following year.[14] Fuller's core message was that "Spaceship Earth" has a finite number of resources and cannot be resupplied. His ideas for the design of cities and the vision for the future of our planet were showcased at Expo 67, "Man and His World," held in Montreal. Habitat was the major theme of the expo, and Fuller and Moshe Safdie demonstrated two very different ways forward. Fuller's giant geodesic dome created its own world within a world: the biosphere. In contrast, Safdie's landmark demonstration project at the expo, Habitat, pioneered a vision for prefabricated urban housing integrating humans with nature, which included open spaces, vital neighborhoods, and garden terraces.[15]

Environmental Action

Following Expo 67, concerns about development and the environment were mounting, and the UN Conference on the Human Environment held in Stockholm in 1972[16] led to the creation of UNEP (the UN's Environmental Programme) in 1976 and the first UN Conference on Human Settlements, Habitat I, was held in Vancouver on May 31–June 11, 1976.[17] The cornerstones of the current UN-Habitat mandate were set by the Vancouver Declaration and by the Vancouver Action Plan.[18] The declaration was a recognition of the need to provide solutions for world problems and create an international community based on equity, justice, and solidarity. The approach towards urbanization was holistic and global, linking political, spatial, social, cultural, economic, and environmental issues. Countries needed to reconcile economic development with environmental protection, and the primary concern was "over the extremely serious condition of human settlements, particularly that which prevails in developing countries."[19]

Developing Destruction

Subsequent conferences included the 1992 Earth Summit in Rio de Janeiro, which led to the Rio Declaration[20] adopting the findings of the 1987 Brundtland Report[21] and in particular the concept of sustainable development. The focus on the state of the planet's degrading environment in the form of floods, fires, plastics in oceans, and the loss of habitat, resources, and species overshadowed the central cause of the problem—essentially, that our cities are not fit for purpose. The design of our cities and the lifestyles they shape are on the agenda of global stakeholders, but policymakers play a more significant role than architects and architectural critics. Even at the 1996 UN Conference on Human Settlements: Habitat II,[22] popularly called the "City Summit," held in Istanbul, there were few professional practitioners or experimental projects demonstrating how to create more ecological and equitable cities. To UN policymakers it appears that the solution for better planetary living is more effective policy. This in turn is leading to a plethora of reports, targets, and design guides with tick-box compliance and ratings, but clearly this is not enough: the planet is getting hotter, emissions are increasing, and resources are diminishing.[23]

A Rich Man's World

The UN's *Emissions Gap Report 2020* identified that the richest 1 percent of people account for more than twice the emissions of the poorest 50 percent.[24] The glittering centers of power and privilege lighting up our planet on satellite images and causing havoc with our ecosystem are being obscured by concerns about poverty and

[14] R. Buckminster Fuller, *Operating Manual for Spaceship Earth*, New York: E.P. Dutton & Co., 1963.

[15] Maude-Emmanuelle Lambert, "Expo 67," *Encyclopedia Britannica*, 2023, accessed January 31, 2024, https://www.britannica.com/event/Expo-67.

[16] Lance N. Antrim, "The United Nations Conference on Environment and Development," in *The Diplomatic Record 1992–1993*, ed. Allan Goodman (New York: Routledge, 2019), 189–210.

[17] UN, United Nations Conference on Human Settlements: Habitat I, Vancouver, May 31–June 11, 1976, accessed January 31, 2024, https://www.un.org/en/conferences/habitat/vancouver1976.

[18] UN General Assembly, "The_Vancouver_Declaration_1976," United Nations Conference on Human Settlements: Habitat, December 16, 1976, A/RES/31/109, accessed January 31, 2024, https://www.refworld.org/docid/3b00f03758.html.

[19] Significantly, the emphasis was on developing countries and not the real culprits who are causing havoc to the planet, namely the G20 countries. Patronizing colonial attitudes are embedded in global initiatives. While slum dwellers need housing, they also need the G20 to stop depleting the Earth's resources and polluting the planet.

[20] UN, *Report of the United Nations Conference on Environment and Development*, Rio de Janeiro, June 3–14, 1992, https://www.un.org/en/development/desa/population/migration/generalassembly/docs/globalcompact/A_CONF.151_26_Vol.I_Declaration.pdf.

[21] World Commission on Environment and Development, *Our Common Future*.

[22] UN, *Report of the United Nations Conference on Human Settlements: Habitat II*, Istanbul, June 3–14, 1996, accessed January 31, 2024, https://documents-dds-ny.un.org/doc/UNDOC/GEN/G96/025/00/PDF/G9602500.pdf?OpenElement.

[23] UNEP, *Emissions Gap Report 2022* (2022), accessed January 31, 2024, https://www.unep.org/resources/emissions-gap-report-2022.

[24] UNEP, *Emissions Gap Report 2020* (2020), accessed January 31, 2024, https://www.unep.org/resources/emissions-gap-report-2020.

development in developing countries. The design of the built environment that shapes the lifestyle of these city dwellers in G20 countries that are responsible for over 78 percent of emissions has yet to be tackled in an effective manner. Powerful models of transformation are being overlooked because of the image-obsessed, uncritical culture of social media. Architects pandering to policymakers and neoliberal forces in the public and private sectors have left a trail of homelessness, disease, and poverty in their wake.

Architecture Is Politics

The design of our cities shapes the way we live and is delivered through and used by political structures. Michael Sorkin was one of the few architectural critics brave enough to stand up to powerful political forces, stating that "Architecture is never not political, given both its economic stakes and its commitment to setting social life."[25] The politics of access to land, infrastructure, public spaces, building codes, etc. generates everything from the suburban United States to the Middle Eastern skyscrapers. G20 cities emit most of the greenhouse gases, devour the greatest amount of the planet's resources, and rapidly reduce the planet's biodiversity; their politicians have both the responsibility and the potential to engage the minds of those working in the built environment to reverse these trends and create environmentally sustainable and equitable cities for the benefit of all humanity and the planet's ecosystem. As Sorkin points out, ". . . the main issues confronting the planet are distributive – the apportionment of resources and equity."[26]

Global Impact: We Are Not Alone

The political impact on the built environment is plain to see from satellite images, where national boundaries, especially those in the G20, are easy to spot. What happens in the suburban United States and skyscraper Dubai impacts the planet. The dynamic and nuanced nature of the built environment defies the tick-box response to policy compliance; the built environment is always in flux. From 9/11 to Covid-19, the repercussions on the built environment are global and architecture as criticism from a planetary perspective is urgently needed to empower architects and architectural critics as agents of change.

Developing World Politics

The UIA partnered with the UN for the first time in 2023 to focus on global issues. The theme of the UIA Congress, "Sustainable Futures—Leave No One Behind,"[27] gave participants an opportunity to showcase their work in the context of the UN's planetary perspective. The highlight of the congress was a presentation by the Pakistani architect Yasmeen Lari. Her privileged position and passion for public works result in a remarkable series of achievements helping thousands of women and communities across the Indian subcontinent.[28] These initiatives are transformative in bringing families out of poverty but do little to impact global emissions or resource use in the G20 countries that are causing such devastation. More relevant were presentations by city architects from Copenhagen, Melbourne, and Malmö but at times it was difficult to separate the greenwash and gentrification from any genuine concern for the environment and its poor, homeless, or migrant inhabitants.[29] Seductive images and energy ratings mask a Pandora's box of power and privilege.

Sorkin advocates for the critic's role to assess and promote the positive effects of architecture on society and the wider world: "The greatest minds of my generation diddling themselves on behalf of money and acting as if they have progressive politics. This is the architecture of neo-liberalism, driven by a market to which it offers

[25] Michael Sorkin, "Critical Mass: Why Architectural Criticism Matters," *Architectural Review*, May 28, 2014, https://www.architectural-review.com/essays/critical-mass-why-architectural-criticism-matters.
[26] Sorkin, "Critical Mass."
[27] UIA World Congress of Architects—CPH 2023, accessed January 31, 2024, https://uia2023cph.org/.
[28] UIA, "Sustainable Communities with Yasmeen Lari."
[29] UIA, "Conversation with Jan Gehl & Rob Adams: Cities for People—50 Years Later," 2023, YouTube video, accessed January 31, 2024, https://www.youtube.com/watch?v=Z7T8g-cRrILM.

not the slightest resistance . . . . But the question to be asked is whose interests are served and, especially, how particular interests shape relevant ideas of the good. Thus, a political criticism is urgently needed for a planet that is clearly going to hell in a handcart."[30]

Capital Decisions

It is unclear how the UN is going to pursue its goals following the UIA Congress, although there was a clear understanding that architects were needed. Few political entities are willing to take the risk of engaging architects to do innovative projects. The capital investment required is often prohibitive and needs a long-term view at odds with short-term political cycles. The idea that architecture is about a process and is constantly in flux and not just a physical product is difficult and risky for decision-makers accountable to corporations and the public purse. Perhaps the next step for the UN is to participate in the World Architecture Festival (WAF),[31] where architects from all over the planet showcase their latest works. Outside the UIA there is no other global stage for the profession. Held a few months after the UIA Congress, WAF23 had many winning projects that demonstrated the vital contribution architects can make.[32] Two projects that stood out because of their partnerships with political stakeholders were a refugee center in Reyhanlı, Turkey, and a school in Ningbo, China.[33]

Nature and Nurture

The Huizhen High School in Ningbo—poetically referred to as the Floating Forest School—is remarkable in the simplicity of its concept. Persuading government authorities to spend additional money on an idea that gave no additional classrooms or formal sports space but just somewhere for kids to "hang out" was probably not so

[30] Sorkin, "Critical Mass."
[31] The WAF is an annual event that is the brainchild of Paul Finch and does not receive public funding.
[32] WAF, World Architecture Festival—WINNERS 2023, accessed January 31, 2024, https://worldarchitecturefestival.com/worldarchitecturefestival2024/en/page/winners-2023.
[33] WAF, World Architecture Festival.

fig. 1-3
Huizhen High School Floating Forest. Credit: Qingshan Wu.

simple. The architects, Approach Design Studio/Zhejiang University of Technology Engineering Design Group, managed to persuade the local authority in Ningbo to invest in a radically different approach to education. The concept is to make the school 100 percent efficient by transforming playtime into learning time, that is, creating an environment where students learn even when they are "hanging out." The floating forest links the more conventual classroom blocks to the sports arena and its hanging spaces evoke the concept of birds' nests or tree houses. Rooftops and atria are green spaces providing children with a variety of places to play, rest, and just be in a landscape setting. The designers have created calm, exciting, and fun places—places that promote well-being and learning diametrically opposed to the more traditional Victorian "factory" style of education where children learn by rote rather than creative exploration. The planetary approach to Architecture as Built Criticism of this school moves the perspective from the classroom to the floating forest and global horizons. It is a local response with global repercussions, in contrast to the Reyhanlı Refugee Centre, which is a global response to a local problem of helping refugees.

Citizens of the World

The Reyhanlı Refugee Centre on the border between Syria and Turkey was initiated by Chen-Yu Chiu (Cho), an architect from Taiwan teaching at Bilkent University in Turkey. He was so moved by the plight of Syrian refugees that he persuaded the Taiwanese government to donate funds to design a center which would stimulate sociocultural, economic, and political integration and inclusion between the Syrian refugees and the local Turkish residents. The town of Reyhanlı's population had grown from 120,000 to 270,000, and following recent earthquakes in the area there were an estimated 200,000 environmental refugees also seeking shelter. "This is a place for everyone,"

principal architect and center director Chen-Yu Chiu (Cho) explains, "it is not a refugee centre per se, but a community centre. . . . This is where you help the community, and the community helps you."[34]

The center is built of reappropriated materials—concrete highway barriers provide a base for corrugated metal roofing, creating pointed arches. The structure probably does not meet any of the LEED criteria or tick any boxes of the policy design guides, but this scheme is an example of Architecture as Built Criticism that answers Sorkin's question about who it serves. The project responds to urgent needs and conditions of crisis—it is a bazaar, a mosque, a home, a workshop, a political gesture, and a technical complex all at the same time. It houses a plethora of activities, including learning, handicraft, and weaving workshops, and it has a cinema, a library, a vegetable garden, a laundry, an art gallery, PET bottle recycling, solar energy, biowaste, and much more.

Cho speaks of the experience of working for many years with the Taiwanese architect Ying-Chun Hsieh, who is firmly committed to architecture as a means of influencing social change and on projects focusing on post-disaster reconstruction and cooperation involving local and/or indigenous communities with remote, displaced, deprived, and traumatized conditions. The architecture of the Reyhanlı Refugee Centre is a demonstration of solidarity from a place that concerns itself with citizens beyond national boundaries, and their rights and responsibilities towards one another. The project would not have come about had it not been for a socially committed architect, political will, and global cooperation. It is truly a remarkable achievement and gives hope for the future.

[34] Doreen Bernath, "Taiwan-Reyhanlı Centre for World Citizens, Reyhanlı, Turkey," The Twentieth Century Society, September 2022, accessed January 31, 2024, https://c20society.org.uk/https://c20society.org.uk/building-of-the-month/taiwan-reyhanli-centre-for-world-citizens-reyhanli-turkey.

fig. 4, 5
Reyhanlı Refugee Centre.
Credit: Reyhanlı Refugee Centre.

Conclusion

Looking at Architecture as Built Criticism from a planetary perspective gives a picture of the Anthropocene. What we see is destruction and disrupted ecosystems. Our way of inhabiting the planet is suicidal, and urgent action is required. We can see the hot spots illuminated on satellite images; it is not difficult to pinpoint the main sources of the problems we face. The problems are not in the developing world but primarily in the G20. As city dwellers we cannot afford to continue to be reliant on informal growth—cities are complex, and to gain efficient use of resources we need skilled professionals able to integrate the social, economic, and environmental requirements in nuanced and equitable ways so that we can all live on Earth equitably. Our consumer lifestyle and reliance on policy and targets are not delivering the transformation we need to survive on planet Earth. The initiatives shown at WAF demonstrate how architects can make a difference, *and they can* make a difference in the G20 where it really matters.

Biography
Yasmin Shariff is director of Dennis Sharp Architects and has lectured extensively on the subject of environment and equity in the built environment. As a student she apprenticed with Paolo Soleri in Arcosanti, learning about architecture and ecology, and won an EU Thermie Award to research sustainable exemplars in Europe. Yasmin was a member of the UK Government's Round Table for Sustainable Development and initiated Equinox 2000, the RIBA's (Royal Institute of British Architects) first conference on sustainable development, in March 2000.

Local versus Global: A Critique of Modernity

Tosin Oshinowo

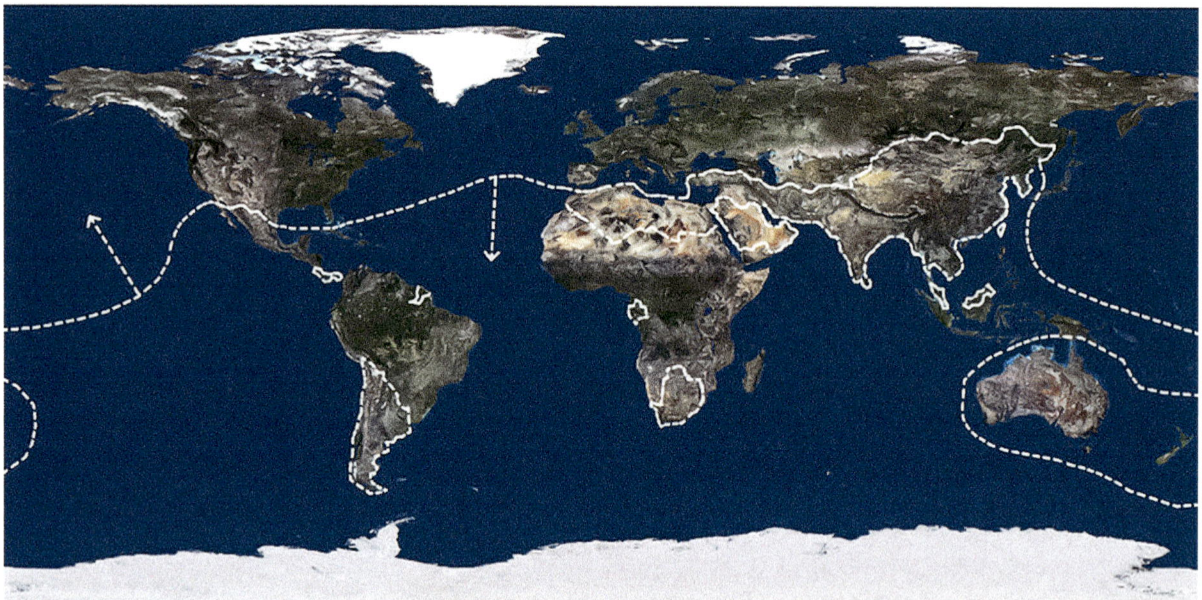

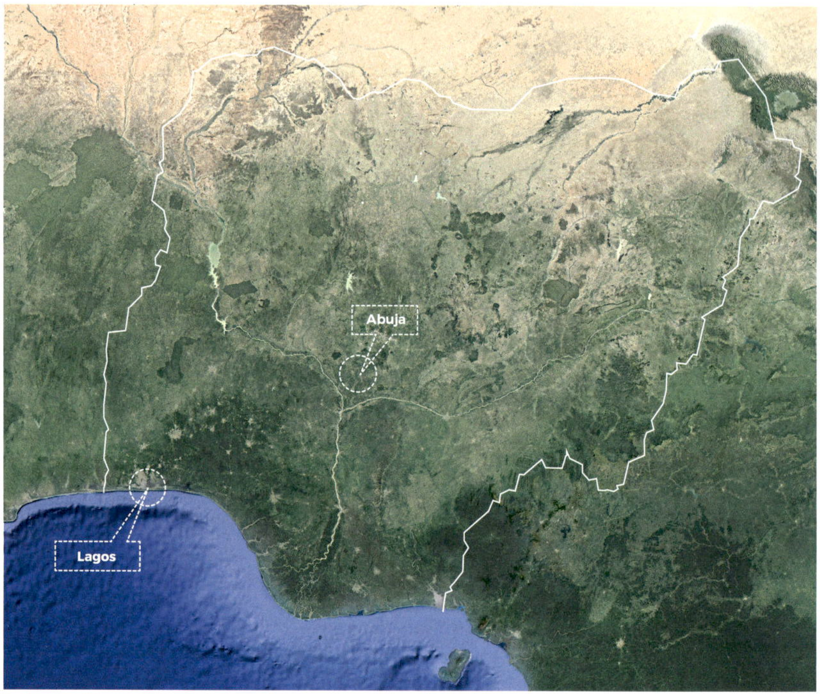

fig. 1
Global map showing diagram representation of Global North and Global South.

fig. 2
Satellite image of Nigeria, with Lagos and Abuja labeled.

The title *Beauty of Impermanence: An Architecture of Adaptability* for the second Sharjah Architecture Triennial, held in the United Arab Emirates (UAE), is a metaphor drawing attention to the built environment's design and technological innovations visible in the Global South. These solutions are born out of conditions of scarcity; that is to say, it is important to work within the limitations of the available resources. And here, as the triennial's curator, I find myself drawing new narratives from this position. In contrast, the last four hundred years have seen the Global North exercise an approach to scarcity through cornucopianism.

keywords:

local vs. global, Global South, impermanence, adaptability, invention through scarcity

Cornucopianism[1] is a principle in economics that stems from the optimism that our natural resources, though limited, can be extended indefinitely. The Global North, through land conquest, slavery, resource extraction, and technological advancement—all supported by mythological and religious beliefs—has encouraged the position that humanity has been ordained to multiply infinitely with dominion over all things ***(fig. 1)***.

My interest in this topic stems from my childhood growing up in 1980s Lagos. I wanted to understand the deep-rooted challenges of the self-organizing systems surrounding me. Lagos had humble beginnings as a fishing town that became an important policing point for the British navy in their efforts to enforce the abolition of the slave trade. It eventually became a colony in 1862 and then the capital of the protectorate of Nigeria in 1914. However, the region already had a long interaction with the British since the 1800s through the Royal Niger Company. In 1976, the decision was made to move the capital of Nigeria to Abuja, a more geographically central location in the country, and in 1991, this change was formalized ***(fig. 2)***. By then, Lagos had been crippled by a population increase that had led to services becoming oversubscribed. During the 1980s, the progressive infrastructure developments of the 1970s had stalled and, like in much of Africa, the prosperity delivered by independence had failed to live up to the promise.[2] ***(fig. 3)*** The lack of regional infrastructure development has continued to encourage rural-to-urban migration without the infrastructure of the city being upgraded to sustain this increasing densification. The postcolonial African city—a proposed model of progress—was crippled under the weight of the postcolonial state. Scarcity, once regarded as primarily a condition for pre-industrialization, was now the basis of existence. The 1990s and the 2000s saw self-propagating bottom-up initiatives come to the fore as a way of coping in modernity.

Oshodi is a naturally occurring geographical convergence point in Lagos. It originated as a market during the slave trade and remains a prominent intersection for motor vehicle and train traffic ***(fig. 4)***. Oshodi is famous for its informal market, growing and receding daily with the intensity of people's movement. It is also the primary access route connecting the only airport to the city. In the 1990s, autonomous networks and structures almost crippled its transient function. These challenges called for interventions by the state to modernize the node. Lagos has since progressed from this position thanks to policy initiatives by successive state administrations. However, during this progress, sadly, a uniqueness has been lost. Oshodi still struggles with the complexities of an organizing system for a dense postcolonial African city ***(fig. 5)***.

1 Fredrik Albritton Jonsson and Carl Wennerlind, *Scarcity: A History from the Origins of Capitalism to the Climate Crisis* (Cambridge, MA: Harvard University Press 2023), Chapter 2, especially 47, 70, and 73.

2 Lukasz Stanek, *Architecture in Global Socialism: Eastern Europe, West Africa, and the Middle East in the Cold War* (Princeton, NJ: Princeton University Press 2020), Chapter 3, especially 99.

Considering the details of the initiatives' implementation, certain things need to change to better suit the structures and the cultures Oshodi must now accommodate. The ultramodern Oshodi Bus Terminal replaced a natural intersection. However, since completion in 2019, the facility has yet to be fully commissioned, as the more comprehensive transport network infrastructure required to sustain this intervention has been slow to be implemented. Oshodi is a fascinating place; the principles found there partly inspired the concept for the triennial.

The second edition of the Sharjah Architecture Triennial, held in 2023, brought together the work of twenty-nine participants from twenty-six countries. These participants explored what happens when we provide solutions more consciously and empathetically in our built environment. The exhibition opened a discourse on how we live, how we can build better, and how we can achieve harmony with our environment.

Returning to Lagos, where scarcity is a prominent condition, innovative autonomous design finds itself in the foreground of existence in modernity. Nifemi Marcus-Bello, one of the triennial participants, presented a project called A Designer's Utopia[3] that catalogs the collective contemporary knowledge of products brought about by socioeconomic conditions. Here, communities, through open-source and collaborative approaches, create contextual solutions to solve contextual issues ***(fig. 6)***. It raises the question: What does it mean to work within limits and in proximity to materiality and need? The work of these practices explores and encourages empathetic initiatives that promote social sustainability, a consciousness of materiality, and a respectful acknowledgment of the environment. These can also be great propagators of climate-conducive initiatives.

However, when we speak about architecture and the built environment, we talk about the architect, a dictation brought about by experience and training that encourages

fig. 3
Aerial overview of Lagos. Photo: Andrew Esiedo.

fig. 4
Oshodi. Photo: Edgar Cleijne (first published in *Mutations*, 2000, by Rem Koolhaas, Stefano Boeri, Sanford Kwnter, Nadia Tazi, and Hans Ulrich Obrist).

fig. 5
Satellite images of Oshodi, 2003 and 2022. © Google Earth.

[3] https://nmbello.com/Africa-A-Designer-s-Utopia.

2003
bus terminal/train station/market place
road to the airport
train track

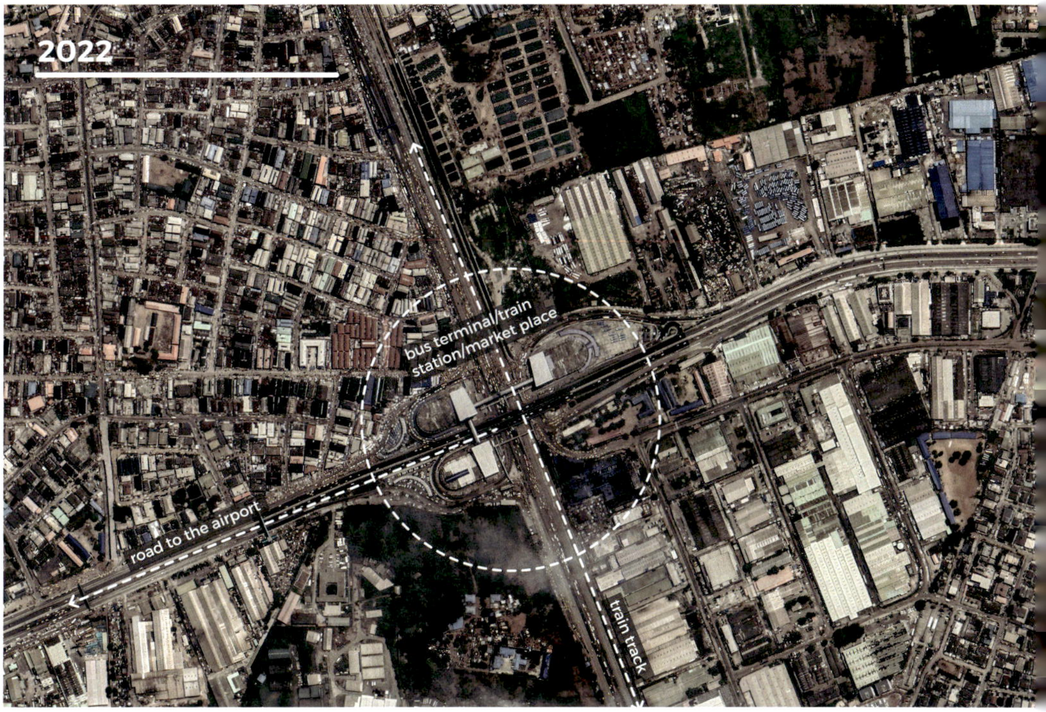
2022
bus terminal/train station/market place
road to the airport
train track

a personalized perspective and, in many cases, an aesthetic language. How do we address the implications of this perspective? What do Vitruvius's three principles of *Firmitas*, *Utilitas*, and *Venustas* for well-designed buildings[4] mean to us as architects/designers when we leave our commissions to end users?

One of the exhibits at the triennial, by the Art and Culture Development Foundation of the Republic of Uzbekistan (ACDF),[5] presented a brilliant case to support the argument that modernism can be seen as a set of historical styles informed by local traditions rather than a uniform, globally oriented trend. What can we learn from a specific example of modernist architecture introduced by a centralized program of Soviet urban development on a territory that had an entirely different aesthetic experience? The ACDF exhibit presented three projects designed and built in the postwar modernist era; their research documents the aesthetic adaptations of buildings over the years ***(fig. 7)***.

The architectural heritage of Uzbekistan reveals a blend of Persian, Islamic, and Central Asian influences brought together and enriched by the Silk Road. Modern architecture from the Soviet era proposed a language of forms and materials that aimed to communicate ideas of progress and renewal, seemingly applicable across places and cultural contexts. What does this adaptation of the architect's top-down design approach mean? For example, these designs manifest strong nationalist and modernist statements celebrating the materiality and tectonics of built-in elements that are exemplary of the technologies of the modern era—in this case, concrete. This material completely detaches itself from the contextuality of place but ideally constitutes a nationalist identity that all citizens should rally to. So when buildings are adapted to another narrative, what does this say about our intentions as expressed through architecture?

Similarly, there are many instances across the African continent where nationalist structures have been aesthetically adapted over time. What does this say about our approach as architects to building aesthetics? What can we learn from the balance between traditional and modern in the past decades? What influences and causes these shifts? What does this mean in relation to the social constructs surrounding

fig. 6
A Designer's Utopia by Nifemi Marcus-Bello.

fig. 7
State Museum of Arts: view of the original facade juxtaposed with the transformation. The building is currently undergoing restoration. Source Waiwai Design.

fig. 8
Sharjah Mall, located in Sharjah, UAE. Source: Danko Stjepanovic.

fig. 9
Super Limbo, at Sharjah Mall. Installation by Limbo Accra for Sharjah Architecture Triennial 2023. Source: Edmund Sumner

fig. 10
Independence House. Photo: Gaelen Pinnock.

[4] Marcus Vitruvius Pollio, *De architectura*, trans. Luciano Migotto.

[5] Tashkent: Appropriating Modernism by the Art and Culture Development Foundation of the Republic of Uzbekistan (ACDF) for the second Sharjah Architecture Triennial.

these buildings and the materials used to produce them? What can we learn from these modernist structures when they are in their liminal state?

As many buildings are adapted aesthetically, many more are in a liminal state. For the triennial, Limbo Accra occupied the Sharjah Mall ***(fig. 8)***. With its estimated 64,753 square meters of retail, entertainment, and culinary space, the Sharjah Mall is one of the largest uncompleted building projects in the UAE. Limbo Accra's practice emerges from research, interdisciplinary engagement, and experimentation with the aesthetics and cultural significance of unfinished, decaying concrete structures in West African cities. Limbo Accra draws attention to the liminality of large-scale buildings. Far from their intended programs, the structures have an autonomy of occupation and adaptability. Their alternative use provides a more humanist narrative than the intended grandeur of their predecessors ***(fig. 9)***.

The 2019 Lagos Biennial, which I co-curated, was in a similar vein to the Sharjah Architecture Triennial. It occupied four of the twenty-five floors of the abandoned

MISSISSIPPI

Independence House on Lagos Island. The building was gifted to Nigeria by the British as a gesture of goodwill to support independence in 1960 ***(fig. 10)***. In 1993, portions of it caught fire, and following the incident the building was left in a state of disrepair. Titled "How to Build a Lagoon with Just a Bottle of Wine?," the biennial brought together artworks and architectural projects by forty-two individuals and collectives working in a range of mediums. Inspired by the writing of Nigerian poet Akeem Lasisi, the title speaks partly to how societies, especially in the Global South, can mobilize vernacular knowledge and skills to realize meaningfully ambitious creative and social projects despite inadequate economic resources and state support ***(figs. 11-13)***.

fig. 11
Sandra Poulson, Plastic Broken Chairs, Juxtaposed, for Lagos Biennial 2019.

fig. 12
Ndidi Dike, A History of a City in a Box, for Lagos Biennial 2019.

fig. 13
Pedro Pires, Container/Invisibility, for Lagos Biennial 2019.

Our occupation of the building was only made possible by squatters—most likely recent immigrants to the city. Though initially cautious, our interaction brought the realization that we had common goals of coexistence—living together in ways that were mutually beneficial and productive. One of the many residents at the site who was instrumental to our success was Mr. Ben Abuze, whom we hired to assist in cleaning, painting, and securing the site ***(fig. 14)***. Mr. Abuze is from Benin, a neighboring country; he speaks fluent English, French, and Yoruba and is a trained painter. He also became our link to the broader community of residents in and near the building. In between the numerous challenges of delivering an event unfamiliar to its host environment, the many volunteers who offered their time did so for the opportunity to lend their voices to a cause.

Thomas Heatherwick made an equally interesting argument for the importance of emotions as a building design requirement. Unlike the premise of the triennial, which amplifies the materiality of context, Heatherwick pointed to the importance of materiality and contextuality in the creation of place and their role in eliciting conscious and subconscious emotions, thereby establishing the well-being of people. Heatherwick supported this argument for emotive building with a series of design elements.[6] In particular, he drew attention to the importance of curvaceous structures in stark contrast to the brutalist structures of the modernist era—buildings with earth colors and an emphasis on the use of natural materials like wood that retain softness and the human factor. These are elements not far from many of our more traditional architectures that contextualize place. Heatherwick's suggestions are part of a global narrative that creates a unified understanding of place, and I am drawn to this argument because it also supports the rationale concerning the contextuality of place.

I relate this to my experiences designing a resettlement town for a community in northern Nigeria displaced by the Boko Haram insurgency ***(figs. 15-16)***. Here, color was an important contextualizing and localizing part of the intervention. At one of my early meetings with the community, I asked the Bale (community head) what color preferences they had for their homes. Color plays an essential role in our experience of space. As we sat under a Nime tree, he pointed to a color on the wall known locally as Abuja brown. During my research regarding traditional technologies, I realized that this was the color of the traditional walls made using local earth. In fact, the community yearned for the familiar. In this project, no paint was used on the exterior. We achieved this color and textured render through a combination of local soil— sourced from down the road—cement, and a bonding agent ***(fig. 17)***. The long-term goal is for the intervention to foster development of the community, providing a sustainable platform for economic growth and, most importantly, giving the people dignity by offering homes that provide the community with a sense of pride.

This takes me back to the reflections from the triennial and the importance of the contextuality of place. My curatorial interests and practice concern cultural (contextual) representation in architecture and the question "What is an African building?" This research has led me to the understanding that visually, tradition is based on the

[6] Thomas Heatherwick, *Humanise: A Maker's Guide to Building Our World* (New York: Viking Press, 2023).

fig. 14
Co-curators Antawan Byrd, Oyinda Fakeye and Tosin Oshinowo with Mr. Ben Abuze, Lagos Biennial 2019.

fig. 15
Ngarannam, a resettlement village in Borno for UNDP Nigeria. Architects: Oshinowo Studio. Source: Tolu Sansusi & JB Multimedia Studios.

aesthetics of the place. The buildings' materiality is dependent on their location, and their location defines the available materials. Thus, material context determines crafts, constructional techniques, and tectonics, combined with and composed through social norms and daily practice. Together, these influences produce an aesthetic language and a building identity based on the context of a place. Take, for example, the great Benin Kingdom of 1180 to 1897 ***(fig. 18)***. It is an excellent example of how most pre-industrialization mobility was determined by pedestrian movement. With services and supplies concentrated in city centers, the development radius from the city's heart was limited to about one mile—roughly the distance that a person can walk in thirty minutes. This meant most of the building materials would have been sourced locally. In our modern age, how do we encourage innovation through the contextual use of building materials? With this in mind, how can we retain the cultural relevance of place and identity? How do we unite contextual materiality with the industrialized world's need for "speed and scale"?

During seasonal renovation works to a palace in Kano, a city in northern Nigeria, a final layer of a waterproof plaster called *makuba* was applied to the walls ***(figs. 19-20)***. This contextuality has a natural cycle of life, like the human body, that also requires a process of replenishment and renewal. In pre-industrial times, innovation occurred through contextual materiality, creating an architecture of place that embodied the local identity and was culturally relevant. How do we address and reproduce these principles today in our globalized world? Reflecting on this, how can we retain the cultural relevance of place and identity? Here, the Republic of Uzbekistan's exhibit at the triennial provides an example of how modern buildings can be transformed in the age of modernity through a cultural intervention.

What lessons can be learned from these autonomous systems that work within the limitations of the available natural resources? Can these systems be scaled to address our densification and potentially curb carbon emissions and alleviate our planetary scarcity?[7] Some of the participants' exhibits for the triennial converged on the topic of "renewed contextual," paying homage to the pre-industrialized societies that were in better balance with the natural world. These practices rethink tradition

[7] Jonsson and Wennerlind, *Scarcity*, Chapter 8.

and holistically engage with the concepts of upcycling and recycling, championing the reuse of materials and positing gentler versions of modernity. Globalization affords us a context where everything is within reach, easily acquired from anywhere, and is fueled by a capitalist developmental process that has eroded local identity to the extent of destroying historic neighborhoods. This raises the fundamental question: What does it mean to be local? The theory and practice of another participant, Al Borde from Ecuador, inhabit the territory of questioning where certainties about what architecture should or should not be are under constant reevaluation. From ideas of making and precision to detail on site, they promote local development, social innovation, and sustainability in their projects. For their structure, Al Borde used wood supplied by the Sharjah Electricity, Water, and Gas Authority (SEWA), which had commenced the replacement of wooden utility poles with metal ones. The shades for the structure are composed of palm tree mats, widely available regionally and used in various ways ***(fig. 21)***. This approach resulted in a raw and tactile intervention crafted with natural materials and allowing for intimate and direct discourse with the surroundings.

Globalization has led us to scale down everything from our cultural preferences to aesthetic connotations, with our attention focused on the northern hemisphere. We are finding ourselves in a world in which the monotony and homogeneity of progress are determined by the Global North setting the precedents that the Global South follows. What has been the trade-off from this prosperity? We must look at how the regions of the Global South have dealt with limited resources as a model for alleviating the strain placed on our planet's limited capacity to neutralize pollution. What is wrong with our current global value system? Why does our acknowledgment of progress negate the use of passive and naturally occurring phenomena; for example, clinically

fig. 16
Homeowner at Ngarannam, a resettlement village in Borno for UNDP Nigeria.
Architects: Oshinowo Studio.

fig. 17
Application of tyrolean render to the exterior wall at Ngarannam, a resettlement village in Borno for UNDP Nigeria. Architects: Oshinowo Studio.

fig. 18
Street activity in the Royal Quarter of Benin City around 1897. © The Trustees of the British Museum.

fig. 19
Kano, 1970, showing the final layer of a waterproof plaster called *makuba* being applied to the walls. *An Introduction to Nigerian Traditional Architecture*, Volume 1: Northern Nigeria.

fig. 20
Kano, 1970, showing the completed domed and flat roofs. *An Introduction to Nigerian Traditional Architecture*, Volume 1: Northern Nigeria.

sealed hard surfaces in preference to natural, unsealed ground or air-conditioning instead of passive cooling and ventilation? After all, when these notions of progress and convenience are scaled, they significantly harm our natural environment.

The cornucopian model is now unsustainable; using the Chinese ivory puzzle ball as a metaphor, the industrial revolution and subsequent great technological acceleration have propelled us into an unnatural run on our natural resources and direct conflict with the globe's ecological balance. The examples of works exhibited at the second Sharjah Triennial speak to both an "alternative materiality" and a change in our "occupation of space." Merely replacing our construction materials alone will be insufficient in addressing our climate crisis. Today, it is more critical to reevaluate the consequences of modernity's convenience not as an option but as an imperative and to design the necessary solutions for the ways we could live.

fig. 21
Raw Threshold, at Al Qasimiyah School. Recycled wooden utility poles and palm tree mats for Sharjah Architecture Triennial 2023. Source: Danko Stjepanovic.

Biography
Tosin Oshinowo is a Lagos-based Nigerian architect and designer, and the principal and founder of Oshinowo Studio, established in 2013. She has a BA in Architecture from Kingston University London, an MSc in Development and Planning: Building and Urban Design in Development from University College London, an AA Diploma from the Architecture Association London, and a master's in Business for Architecture and Design from IE University Madrid. She is also a 2025 Harvard University Loeb Fellow.

She has worked on a number of civic, commercial, and residential projects throughout Nigeria and is renowned for her socially responsive approach to architecture, design, and urbanism. Oshinowo's key designs include the Maryland Mall in Lagos and a project with the United Nations Development Programme to build a new community in northern Nigeria for a village displaced by Boko Haram. Her work demonstrates a strong interest in architectural history while embodying a contemporary perspective on African design and innovation. She partnered with Lexus on a conceptual design exploration for Design Miami 2020; she co-curated the second Lagos Biennial in 2019 and curated the second Sharjah Architecture Triennial in 2023.

Oshinowo is a registered architect in the Federal Republic of Nigeria and a member of the Royal Institute of British Architects. Before founding Oshinowo Studio, she worked in the offices of Skidmore, Owings & Merrill in London and the Office of Metropolitan Architecture in Rotterdam, where she was part of the team that designed the 4th Mainland Bridge proposal in 2008. Returning to Lagos, she practiced at James Cubitt Architects and led notable projects, including the corporate head office building for Nigeria LNG in Port Harcourt.

Early Critiques

Architecture in Opposition: Carl Westman's Critical Attitude

Rasmus Wærn

fig. 1
Competition entry for an arts and crafts museum in Gothenburg by Charles Lindholm in 1901. Facade towards Vasagatan. Illustration from *Arkitektur* 8 (1901). Even though the area was urbanizing rapidly, Lindholm presented his winning proposal as being surrounded by trees and hills. The competition also included a school on the back of the museum. Its facade was similar to the museum's.

Carl Westman's concern was for the future. While not the first architect in Sweden to write critiques on the state of Swedish architecture, he was a pioneer in considering modernity to be obsolete. His tirade against meaningless repetitions of antiquated forms was the first of its kind in the Swedish press.[1] Presentations of domestic or international contemporary buildings were not rare in the late nineteenth-century Swedish press, but in the 1890s Westman spearheaded a critical discussion on future conditions for architecture. Though not a frequent writer, he managed to transform his polemics into a constructive critique that changed the direction of contemporary architecture in Sweden. His design for the Röhsska Museum provided an alternative future based on atmosphere, heritage, and human presence.

keywords:
Carl Westman, Röhhska Museum, Heimatstil, Swedish Arts and Crafts

The criticism, in words and in buildings, that Westman delivered was personal and devoted. He was a polemic writer, akin to Adolf Loos. Of the same generation, the two also shared an admiration for contemporary North American architecture. Both left Europe in 1893 to spend a few years in the United States, but its plutocratic society filled Westman with despair.

His response to the superficiality of contemporary architecture was opposite to Loos's. Whereas Loos regarded the Heimatstil as a problem, Westman saw it as a way forward. His built statement from 1906, the headquarters for the Swedish Society of Medicine, was also an acclaimed manifesto, stylistically contrary to Loos's controversial Goldman and Salatsch building from 1911.

Westman did not have to resist overloaded expressions of a declining empire; he was fatigued with civilization. He channeled his interest to primary states of existence and to history at the dawn of modern civilization. A clean and matter-of-fact architecture related to a domestic architectural heritage became a mobilizing idea with which to oppose the cultural pressure from a troubled outside world. The Röhsska Museum for arts and crafts in Gothenburg, Sweden, became a bulwark against the anonymity of industrialization. The building, designed in 1909 and inaugurated in 1916, was essentially a critique of its times. It was designed to transform established notions.

Such a critical attitude ensured Westman's success as an architect. He established his ethos with critical comments on contemporary architecture in *Dagens Nyheter*, Stockholm's major daily newspaper:

> If you pay attention to our modern architecture here at home, to the shapes in which it appears, you will ask yourself the question: is this architecture, considered as art, a true expression of our time? Do you find the character and mood of our time in these forms? No, this architecture, with styles borrowed from past periods, into which our new needs are more or less happily squeezed, cannot be said to stand as an expression of the spiritual position of our time. The character of our present-day society is so widely separated from that of ancient centuries, that it can hardly be considered expressed in these old forms. We see it in other areas such as painting, sculpture, literature, but not in architecture. It gives the impression of a masquerade, in which costumes of all times except our own appear. Where are the trousers, the work shirt and the tailcoat?[2]

1 The national media database at Kungliga biblioteket, browsed in November 2023.

2 Carl Westman, "Är vår moderna arkitektur modern?," *Dagens Nyheter*, April 19, 1893.

The text stimulated a vivid discussion within as well as outside the profession. Hjalmar Sandberg, the arts editor of *Svenska Dagbladet*, the rival conservative daily newspaper of the liberal *Dagens Nyheter*, claimed that if the architects did not want to adopt a more contemporary costume like the arts already had, they only had themselves to blame.[3] Westman's text was also discussed at a meeting of the Architects' Association in Stockholm.[4] The response was very polarized, but Westman did not take the discussion further. He left Sweden for the United States three weeks later and did not return until 1895.

This was years before his career as an independent architect developed, but the critical writing turned into a manifesto. Westman distrusted the traditional way of designing architecture by studying ancient monuments. The energy in Westman's later architecture was drawn from his resistance to conventions. Or, according to his own words, the methodology where the architect "doesn't try to give the content a significant form but takes a form into which he squeezes the content."[5]

Carl Westman was born in 1866 and died in 1936. He was a prolific architect with influential designs for private houses and large institutions, such as the seminal headquarters for the Swedish Society of Medicine (1904–6), the Stockholm Courthouse (1911–15); numerous hospitals; and, as his most significant demonstration of critical thinking in architecture, the Röhsska Museum. His criticism was more emotional than analytical. His reaction against a building culture of hollow ambitions was in line with John Ruskin's. Westman's interpretation of modernism was, if anything, closely related to the British tradition. Later, with the 1930 Stockholm Exhibition, the language of Swedish modernism became attached to the developments in Germany, where modern architecture had established itself in the early 1920s. James Stirling's apocryphal remark "Let's face it, William Morris was a Swede"[6] expressed a young, frustrated generation's view of welfare state architecture but could also be interpreted the other way around: Westman's brick buildings were an attempt to bring architecture back to the citizens. But his appetite for disputes waned as the commissions grew. Even as a promoter of humanistic values, Westman became part of the unrhetorical tradition of "silent" Scandinavian architects.[7]

Background

The Röhsska Museum is Sweden's first, and so far only, museum for arts, crafts, and design. The initiators were the local councilor and culture enthusiast Wilhelm Berg and the Gnistan Society, a cultural association with members from Gothenburg's bourgeoisie. By creating a modern collection of rule models, they wanted to strengthen the city's industrial design abilities. Preserving and bringing history to life was not a primary goal.[8] The city was focused on expansion and renewal. This was the era of "The Opponents" art movement (Opponenterna), who made Gothenburg Sweden's leading city for art in the 1880s. The Gnistan Society turned to Gothenburg's handicraft association with the proposal for a museum, and the result was that both the museum and the handicraft association's new school came to be planned at the same time and on the same site. The museum and the collection were financed through donations, but from the very beginning they were owned and run by the municipality. A small collection existed before the museum came into being, but it was never displayed. In principle, the building came first and the collection later. While this was a necessary progression, it stood in direct contrast to Westman's statement from 1893. Large parts of the collection were brought from Germany and France, but numerous purchases and even raids were made in the Far East.[9]

3 Hjalmar Sandberg, "Svenska konstnärernas förening. Arkitekturutställningen," *Svenska Dagbladet*, May 5, 1893.

4 *Dagens Nyheter*, "Är vår moderna arkitektur modern?," April 26, 1893.

5 Westman, "Är vår moderna arkitektur modern?"

6 Reyner Banham, *The New Brutalism: Ethic or Aesthetic?* (New York: Reinhold, 1966): 16.

7 Wilfried Wang, "Epilogue," in *Nordic Architects Write*, ed. Michael Asgaard Andersen (New York: Routledge, 2008).

8 Hans-Olof Boström, "Röhsska konstslöjdmuseets tillkomst och första donatorer," *Konsthistorisk tidskrift* 57, no. 3/4 (1988): 112–18.

9 Promemoria angående Konstindustrimuseum mm by Hans Hedlund, c.1900, Inkommande och utkommande skrivelser, Röhsska museet B2, Gothenburg City Archive.

Plans for a museum had existed since the 1880s, parallel to emerging industrial museums around Europe, such as those in Copenhagen, Helsinki, Oslo, Bergen, Hamburg, Vienna, Berlin, and Paris. All of these were modeled on the Victoria and Albert Museum in London. In January 1901, the estate of Wilhelm Röhss handed over 250,000 Swedish kronor to the city to be used for an arts and crafts museum. By May of the same year, the building committee had adopted the building program and the conditions for an architectural competition. Two architects and one accountant had been involved in the rapid preparation of these, but none with museum know-how; this led to a lot of time and effort being wasted on a project with no future.[10] A competition for two buildings—a museum and a crafts school—was announced, with a submission deadline in October 1901. Nineteen proposals were received, from which the jury awarded three prizes.

fig. 2
Development of Lindholm's proposal made by Yngve Rasmussen in 1902. After the competition, Rasmussen was asked to develop the winning entry, which he did very thoroughly. Source: Röhsska Museum.

One of the jury members was Professor Isak Gustaf Clason, the architect of the Nordic Museum in Stockholm, whose opinion carried weight. The jury was unreservedly positive about all competition proposals.[11] The local architect Charles Lindholm won the competition with his proposal named Blue Bird ***(fig. 1)***. The facade was simple and conventional, but the proposal convinced the jury mainly because of its economical layout. Lindholm was well versed in museum issues as he had been the director of the Nordic Museum's drawing office. After the competition, however, the more experienced architects Yngve Rasmussen and Hans Hedlund were entrusted with developing the winning proposal, where the former would work on the museum and the latter on the school ***(fig. 2)***.

Rasmussen adhered to a design that was only held back by the meager finances until the superintendent of the king's collections, Dr. John Böttiger, sharply criticized the proposal from an exhibition technical point of view. But Rasmussen plucked up courage and revised his drawings. However, following an assessment from the superintendent at the Nordic Museum, Axel Nilsson, the revised proposal was scuppered. Nilsson stated that "it would irreparably damage the interests that the museum building had to represent, were the current project to lay the basis for an arts and crafts museum in Gothenburg even only using the design's main features."[12]

The controversies mirrored the wider situation that architecture faced at the turn of the century. The nineteenth-century approach of using historical references to direct the emerging institutions was no longer relevant. But contemporary architecture lacked a theory, and without such an intellectual basis architects were operating on weak foundations. Westman's critical manifesto, then, gave him a roadmap that proved to be reliable.

[10] City architect Carl Fahlström, architect C. F. Eberling, and accountant Wilhelm Berg.

[11] The jury was especially fond of the proposal from Torben Grut. He did not receive a prize, but agreement on the qualities of his proposal seems to have been unanimous. Its only flaw was that it was too expensive, a fate that later befell all proposals. Grut's facades bring to mind seventeenth-century palaces. With their monumental power, they are not without parallels to Westman's work eight years later.

[12] Axel Nilsson, Assessment (1902), Röhsska Museum Archive.

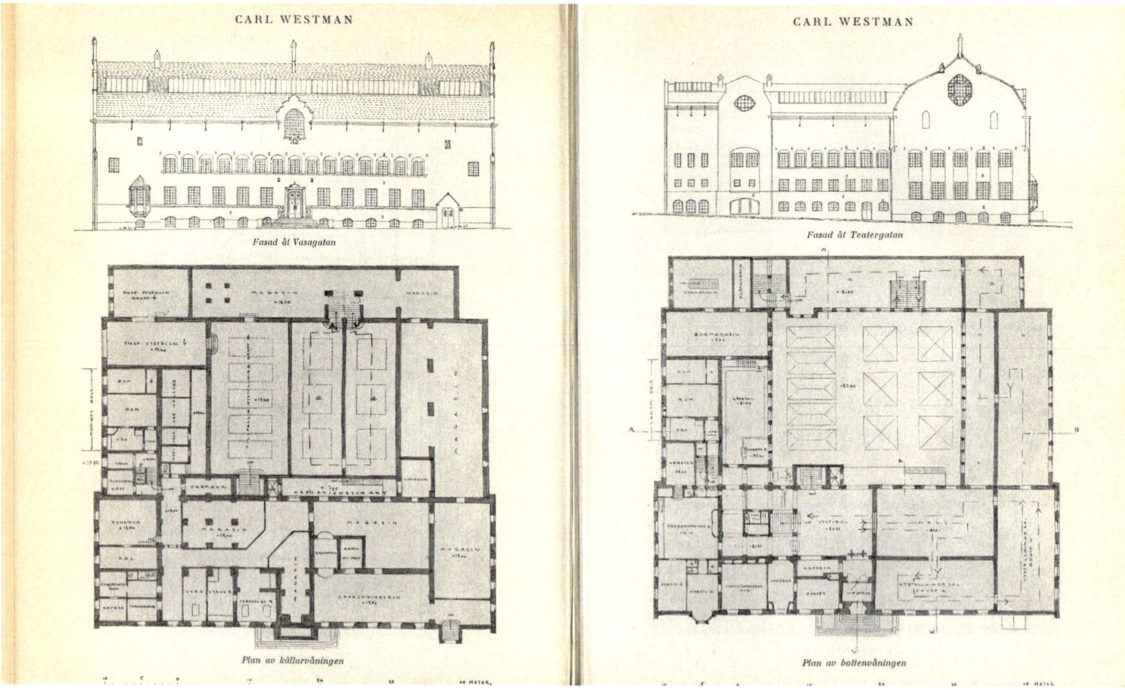

fig. 3
Competition entry for an arts and crafts museum in Gothenburg by Carl Westman in 1910. He proposed to build the entire block and connect the museum to the school behind. Source: "Röhsska konstslöjdmuseet i Göteborg. Årstryck" (1928).

When it became clear that a completely new proposal was required, the building committee charged the newly formed museum board with drafting a new building program according to Nilsson's intentions. Following the invited competition in the spring of 1910, Carl Westman received the first prize.[13] While admittedly more expensive than the designs by both Lindholm and Rasmussen, his was architecturally superior[14] ***(fig. 3)***.

Axel Nilsson and Carl Westman

After the competition, Westman designed the museum in close dialogue with Axel Nilsson. Nilsson (1872–1924) was interested in architecture and a close friend of Westman. They probably met in 1901 when Nilsson came to Stockholm. Nilsson and Westman both had a taste for the robust and jovial, and Nilsson's interest in old Swedish wooden construction art probably influenced Westman.[15] From 1904 to 1915 Nilsson taught wooden building construction at the Institute of Technology in Stockholm.[16] In 1910, Nilsson was elected to the technology association's department for building, for which Westman had served as a board member since 1906 and for which he became vice-chairman from 1909 to 1917. Westman, six years older than Nilsson, was at the peak of his career at the time of the construction of the Röhsska Museum.

He was invited to the competition while in the middle of the largest job of his life, the Stockholm Courthouse, which commissioned him in installments from 1904 to 1915, of which the last five or six years must have been the most intensive. When faced with a new problem, he did not consider it his task to create a new form, but rather a character. Or, in his own words of 1893: "You want to see a personality behind a work of architecture."[17] Westman never had a large office, but for the courthouse he gathered a group of young architects, several of whom continued to work with him on the museum's interior design.[18]

[13] Besides Westman, the architects Sigfrid Ericson, Charles Lindholm, Yngve Rasmussen, and Ragnar Östberg had also been invited. The jury consisted of Dr. Bernhard Salin, Axel Nilsson, Prof. Erik Lallerstedt, architect Hans Hedlund, and Hjalmar Wijk. Rasmussen was a former colleague of Hedlund, Lindholm was a former employee, and Westman was one of Nilsson's and Lallerstedt's best friends. However, Westman's victory should not be undermined by suspicions of favoritism. (Röhsska konstlöjdmuseet i Göteborg, 1928).

[14] Cost estimation from C. Olsson addressed to Hjalmar Wijk 1910-05-20, Gothenburg City Archive.

[15] Bertil Palm, *Arkitekten Carl Westman* (Konsthistoriska institutionen, Lunds universitet, 1954).

[16] Axel Nilsson's application for the commission at the Röhsska Museum, Gothenburg City Archive.

[17] Westman, "Är vår moderna arkitektur modern?"

[18] The team included Erik Friberger (twenty-five years old in 1914), who, among other things, designed the wood and metal fixtures, an experience he brought with him from the courthouse. Conny Nyqvist (twenty-eight) and Arvid Fuhre (twenty-nine)

The Site and the Building

The site for the new museum and school was undulating and had poor soil conditions on the south side. For some time, the surrounding area had already been a cultural center in Gothenburg. The Valand School of Fine Art was located at the corner of Vasagatan and Kungsportsavenyen, a building that the Gnistan Society had also encouraged. The art association had its permanent exhibition there. Of decisive significance was the proximity to the Chalmers Institute of Technology, which at the time was located right across the street. However, the site itself was anything but monumental. Since 1907, the institute had been enthroned further up the street, but the immediate surroundings themselves seemed banal and brackish to Westman.[19] Three of Westman's most significant buildings—the headquarters for the Swedish Society of Medicine, the Stockholm Courthouse, and the Röhsska Museum—were all located on low-lying and inconspicuous plots.

The museum was constructed as a solid brick building of a kind that Gothenburg had not seen since the Kronhuset (the royal granary) was completed in 1654. While it appears intent on mastering its surroundings, it is prevented from doing so due to the dense neighborhood pattern, a contradiction that local critics mentioned. The facades elicited reactions from both professional journals and columnists. It was likened to a large warehouse, and a local opinion accused the red brick of having a lack of contextual connection.

Westman immediately met the criticism.[20] He justified the use of the brick by saying that the handicraft association's new school next door had red brick. It was probably an afterthought. The fact that the building became an oddball in the city did not worry him. He was eager for cities to be shaped uniformly and remarked that a violation of the surroundings "was not in and of itself necessary," but the urban typology, the perimeter block, was now more important than the place. He showed no expectations that the neighborhood would one day consist of red brick perimeter blocks, given that the museum was drawn as a freestanding object. While the desire for uniformity in a Parisian tradition was common, for Westman the "personality" of the architecture was paramount.

His generation of architects was the first to use mass media to propagate their ideas. The *Swedish Review of Architecture* was dominated by architects who shared Westman's values. These were warmly received by the narrow cultural elite of the time, and were passed on in newspapers and magazines by, among others, Sixten Strömbom, one of the museum's first amanuenses and the person who wrote the main criticism of the building in the magazines *Ord och Bild* and *Hvar 8 dag*.

Although Westman rarely commented on his own buildings, writing gave him the interpretive privilege to expound on his own architecture. Research on Westman and his era, by returning to the forums that were used for rhetorical purposes, has confirmed the view of the early twentieth century as a period of strong correlation between form and content—what contemporaries called honesty. Such honesty was revealed in the choice of materials, where granite and the rustic, handmade brick were considered "real" materials, as opposed to plaster, which was considered inauthentic. A facade that reflected the underlying plan was also "honest." In practice, however, Westman did not put these ideals above contemporary requirements and technological achievements. When devising his plans, Westman was pragmatic and cost-conscious.

The ideal was a basis for the design he used to manage demands of economy and buildability. As long as the vision was alive, the structures also became expressive. His austerity was a reaction to the exuberant post-eclecticism of the turn of the

had also participated in the courthouse project, where Nyqvist worked on facade designs in lime and granite and Fuhre was engaged in wrought iron grates and sculptural decorations. The painter Brocke Blückert, who, together with Olle Nordmark, painted the trefoil vault in the so-called Architecture Hall, a large exhibition space in the center of the building, as well as in the museum's central hallway, also worked on the courthouse. New names were Hugo Jahnke, Carl A. Nilsson, and Carl Berger.

19 Palm, *Arkitekten Carl Westman*.

20 Carl Westman, "Röhsska konstlöjdsmuseet i Göteborg," *Arkitektur*, no. 2 (1917): 15–17.

century. When he designed the museum in what he himself called "Wasa style," it was not for the style's specific suitability but for the saturation of the building with associations. Freedom in the choice of technique, style, and materials was the particular prerogative of the modern architect. Idealism and realism met in the craft. The architect should control the form of the products, a wish that the brick industry was among the first to obey.

The Program

After a study trip to foreign museums in 1910, Axel Nilsson put forward a precise building program. It was strikingly progressive and specified both desired surfaces and spatial relationships: "The exhibition premises should therefore bound as little as possible by the architecture, so that they are left the greatest possible freedom to be adapted for different purposes. No partitions other than those absolutely necessary should be installed, that also applies to windows, doors, floors, ceilings or other details. There should only be right-angled four-sided windows with the smallest possible sash, no window and door linings or frames, whether stone or wood, no vaulted ceilings and so on (except possibly in skylit halls)."[21]

The finished building, however, received extensive door linings as well as a vaulted roof, and as far as the glazing is concerned, the technique readily allowed the windows to be made of single panes instead of the many subdivisions that Westman promoted. He adhered to the program as far as it corresponded with his own ideas. Nilsson's pragmatic attitude was balanced in the competition jury above all by Erik Lallerstedt. In a letter to Hjalmar Wijk, Hans Hedlund expressed his concern about Nilsson's reluctance to let his artistry play a role in the assessment of the proposals.[22]

Before the launch of the competition, Nilsson had traveled around Europe on behalf of the museum's board to study new examples. Hamburg was certainly an important destination. There was both the Museum für Kunst und Gewerbe (Museum for Arts and Crafts), from 1877, and the Kunsthalle, where Alfred Lichtwark had established the first museum pedagogy. Now, museum operations were no longer just about exhibiting objects. The museum would also serve to educate the public. Nilsson's experience from his previous workplace, the Nordic Museum, certainly had a great impact on the program. It was Europe's newest museum of artifacts, created to save the traces of a disappearing culture. The Röhsska Museum followed a modern concept; it aimed to change and not preserve. This preference was also expressed in its architecture.

Remodeling

Westman's winning proposal differs in several respects from the finished building. In addition to the published competition proposal from May 1910, three sets of drawings have been preserved in the museum's archive: December 1910, July 1911, and August 1912. However, the competition proposal is the only one that is markedly different from the other versions. First, the volume was much larger—3,251 square meters for the museum part, about 1,000 square meters more than what was built. From having been a rectangular body around a closed yard, it became two volumes at an angle. The competition proposal was heavier in its expression compared with the finished building. This was mainly because the gables were not thinned out and the wings reached almost as high as the main building. The roof also had a peculiar shape. By bending in two directions, it had a contradictory effect of heaviness and lightness. The original idea was later refined into a slight concavity. However, the key features of the facade facing Vasagatan were clear. The changes that occurred mostly in plan

[21] "Museets byggnadshistoria" in *Röhsska konstlöjdmuseet i Göteborg, Årstryck* (1928).

[22] Letter dated 1910-05-15. In Röhsska Museum archive, Gothenburg City Archive, volume B1:1.

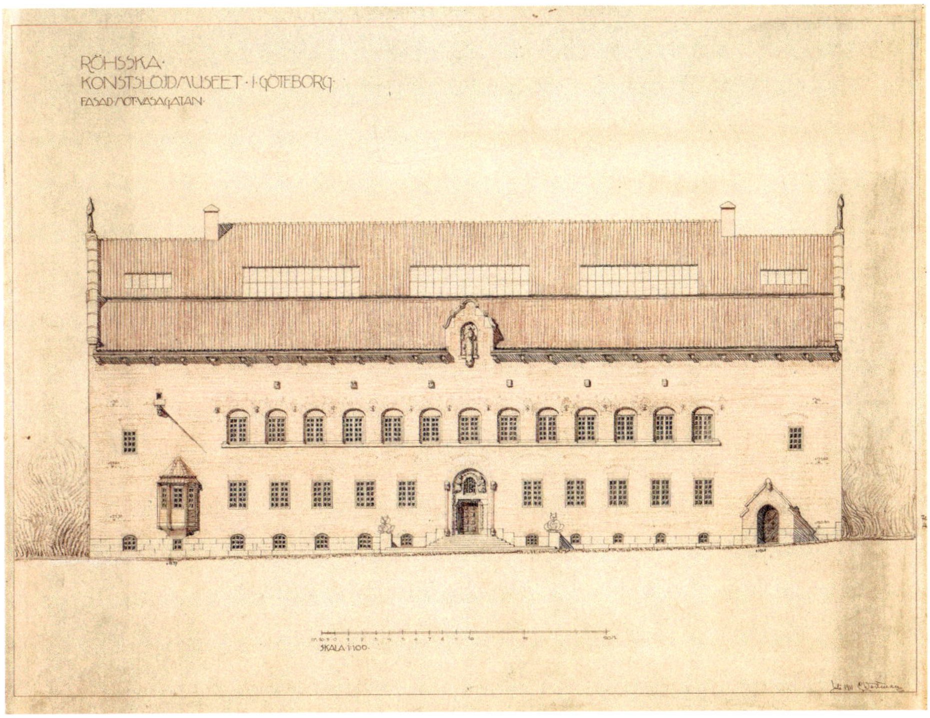

fig. 4
Facade of the museum by Carl Westman in July 1911. Note the small creatures on the plinths next to the stairs. The Chinese lions that were placed here later became an emblem for the museum. Source: Röhsska Museum.

were probably the result of practical rather than aesthetic decisions. In the drawing of December 1910, the volume was reduced but the floor plan was not changed. It was only with the 1911 drawing that the stairs and the reading room were moved and the number of windows facing Vasagatan was reduced from fifteen to thirteen. By then, the building was largely complete. All construction details experienced reductions. The sculptures on the gables and the ridge disappeared, as did the sculpture on the front fireplace. The portal, which in the sketches was rather richly sculpted, was given a clearer character in its masonry and carpentry. The Chinese lions in front of the gate, which have become the museum's symbol, are included as a humorous cartoon in the 1911 drawing ***(fig. 4).*** Perhaps they had just then arrived in Gothenburg. The lions were items purchased by Thorild Wulff on the museum's trip to Asia. The museum lacks the typical tower of a monumental building. Instead, Westman emphasized the horizontality of the building and gathered the facades' gravity towards the center. The statues on the roof ridge, originally proposed in the competition, disappeared in the design of December 1910.

Facades and Plans

The bricks with their small decorations have become one of the museum's most recognizable details. The small carvings serve as messages from the past. Yet it was not only the craftsmanship but also the colors of the bricks that were remarkable. In a posthumous column, Westman's friend Lallerstedt expressed his surprise that he chose this "ordinary bright red brick" and not Gothenburg's traditional yellow one. At the same time, however, he conceded that his colleague had the right to choose.[23] The bricks were pressed into the mold by hand, a method that naturally gave rise to some variation and made it easy to mark each piece.

[23] Erik Lallerstedt, "Carl Westman. En oppositionsman från sekelskiftet," in *Trettiotalets byggnadskonst i Sverige*, ed. Hans Brunnberg, Hans-Fredrik Neumüller, and Inga Mari Lönnroth (Stockholm: SAR, 1943).

fig. 5
The Röhsska Museum in 2024. The front of the building is much the same as when it was built. Photo: Rasmus Wærn.

Modern technology was used in places where it was not visible, such as in the glass roof, which was laid so that as little as possible was seen from the outside, and in the joists, which were made of reinforced concrete. John Ruskin's ethical demand for correspondence between form and content was not Westman's. The cast-iron I-beams were plastered to resemble wooden beams. Westman never sought the limits of a material or a method of construction but worked within what he perceived as the natural conditions. This also contributed to his building having modest production costs.

After the design of the courthouse, Westman seemed liberated from a compelling idea of reviving lost architectural values. With the Röhsska Museum, he left that notion behind and achieved something new, something of his own, of a level of quality that he never reached again.

The facades are principally experienced at an angle. The adaptation of the design to the oblique perspective is underlined by the simultaneous perception of the gables and the north facade ***(fig. 5)***. It is deliberately difficult to get an idea of the main depth of the building. The main wing is configured as a whole and indivisible volume. It is the overall effect of the facade that demands attention, not the details. The massive walls contrast with shallow recesses that hardly cast any shadows. The eaves are minimal, and overhangs are completely missing. The ground-floor windows are set completely flush with the brick wall, while the windows of the upper floor and the gables are recessed into shallow niches. Together with the expansive wall surfaces at the ends of the main facade, the observer's view is drawn towards the center. The dense concentration of windows, underlined with a common sill, holds this central part of the facade. With more windows on the second floor than on the first, there is no columnar effect in the facade, thereby intensifying the idea of the building as a massive block, from which openings have been carved from the inside. The apertures are small and clustered, as if the wall had offered resistance. Even the gables have more windows on the upper floors than on the ground floor. This composition, too, emphasizes both the center and the solid brick corners. This compositional approach was a step towards a free facade design that younger architects like Erik Gunnar Asplund later came to develop.

The projecting blocks of stone some ten meters up the brick wall at either end of the front facade are vestiges of sculptures that had been proposed in the competition entry. In the design development from December 1910, they were transformed into large reliefs—the one at the center could be imagined as a boat motif. Right up to the final construction drawings, these granite blocks were apparently intended to be decorated. In the end, it was only the brackets under the eaves and the coping of the gables that were sculpted. There, each stone was treated individually; each sculpture appears as a demonstration of free will, in line with Ruskin's ideas about the repetitive elements of antiquity being expressions of a slave society as opposed to the free, medieval "savage" art.

In the undecorated appearance of the blocks of stone, which are also found in the porch, Westman demonstrated a possible approach to the development of an architectural language. It was here that his sense of the inherent beauty and power of natural materials found its most consistent expression. While Westman began to play with facade elements—here completely freed from the Beaux-Arts' requirements for both horizontal and vertical alignment—he let the materials carry their own expression. This is most clearly visible in the stone above the hatch. The absence of a scope promotes the stone's expressive effect. The material alone has had to fill the emblematic role that was intended for a female figure. The stone is a cap, which closes an opening and increases the feeling that the building is a casket cradling valuable treasures. Westman may have been inspired by a book by the Finnish philosopher Yrjö Hirn. *The Sacred Shrine* (*Det heliga skrinet*, 1909) deals with the poetry and art of the Catholic Church. "The Catholic Church," says Hirn, "is a medieval reminiscence that survived until the twentieth century." In the introduction, the German mystic Angelus Silesius is quoted: "Die Seel' ist ein Kristall, die Gottheit ist ihr Schein. Der Leib in dem Du lebst, ist ihrer beiden Schrein" (The soul is a crystal, and divinity its shine. The body in which you live, is the shrine of them both).[24] Could that thought have crossed Westman's mind when he designed the Röhsska Museum that very year? More than anything else, the house can be compared to a jewelry box, in form as well as content.

Built Criticism

Westman was critical of the addition of motifs in contemporary architecture. Compiling elements defined architecture as a choice of details. He sought a design guided by the architect's dialogue with his sketch, to obviate conventional drawing board products. This ambition was critical without being subversive. Westman had no intention to break with all notions of what a building should look like. It was rather a matter of restoring lost codes.

A shift in levels between the exhibition spaces (to the right side of the entrance) and the offices (to the left) made it possible to keep an even line of windows on the ground floor as well as an appropriate window height on the interior ***(fig. 6)***. The variation in content (offices to the left, exhibitions to the right) could have been expressed in the facade, but Westman avoided this in favor of a composition based on juxtapositions. The complexity of the facade (in, for example, the compressed fenestration) occurred in relation to the city, not as a consequence of internal solutions.

Westman's critical thinking started off with a call for an architecture dressed in "trousers [and a] work shirt." With the Röhsska Museum he demonstrated what this

[24] Yrjö Hirn, *Det heliga skrinet. Studier i den katolska kyrkans poesi och konst* (Stockholm: Wahlström & Widstrand, 1909).

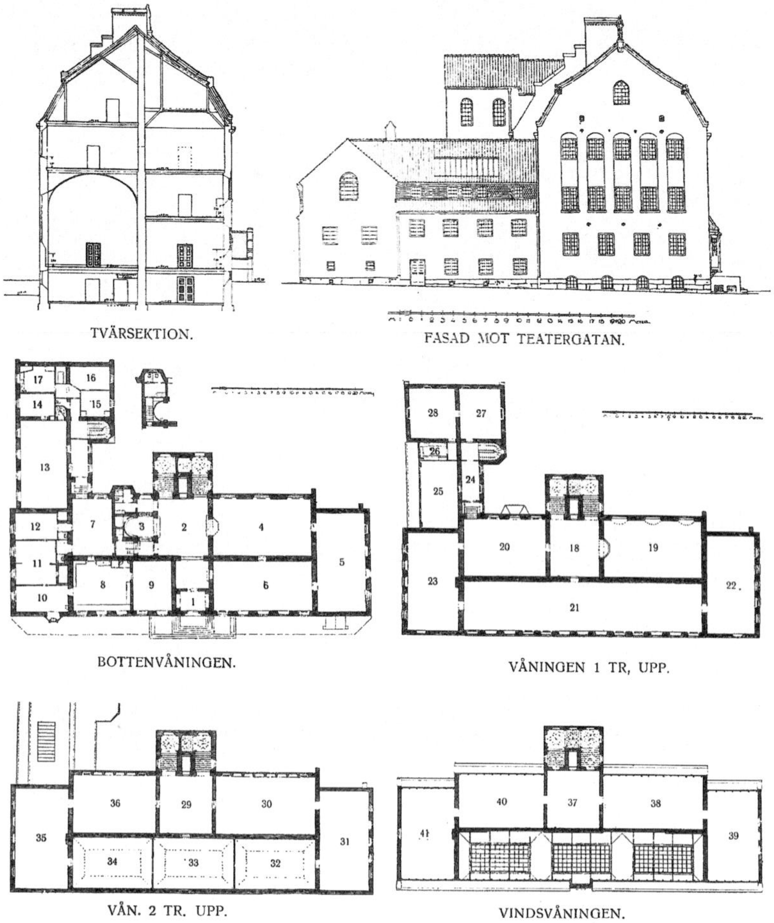

fig. 6
Plan of the building. Behind the symmetrical facade, a diverse plan with a mix of public and administrative areas takes advantage of the multiple levels. Source: Stockholm: *Arkitektur*, 1917, 2.

could be. The dress was not prêt-à-porter; the rustic fashion with handmade bricks had to be carefully designed ***(fig. 7)***. There was no tradition to employ. The plan and section were not mirrored in the facades, nor the facades on the interior. Later this was regarded as a defeat. But architecture is experienced, not cross-checked.

Westman belonged to the last branches of nineteenth-century idealism, a plant with roots in many, partly contradictory values. One of these consisted of an emotional view of nature, with an emphasis on individualism and an idealization of folk culture. The motif of loneliness was strongly developed in art and literature towards the end of the nineteenth century. In the Röhsska Museum, we encounter several motifs that can be traced back to this concept, such as the singularity of the building in the city. Another part of nineteenth-century idealism was connected to criticism. Westman's critique of 1893 anticipated Hermann Muthesius's *Stilarchitektur und Baukunst*, which became a huge success when it was published in 1902. In 1910, the year of the competition for the Röhsska Museum, a Swedish edition was released. The criticism on which Westman built his vision was now an established paradigm. That Westman's architecture found its energy in contempt of its precedents does not explain its artistic strength, but does declare the seminal effect of critical thinking.

fig. 7
The handmade bricks are decorated with simple images. This brick features the building and the initials of the architect. Photo: Rasmus Wærn, 2024.

The architects of the early twentieth century applied three different attitudes as they approached a new task. The *critical* had an ambition to change established conceptions. Some of them expressed their thoughts in writing, but architectural competitions offered an opportunity to visualize their ideas. As well as Westman, renowned architects such as Gunnar Asplund and Carl Bergsten are examples of this attitude.

The *intuitive* architects, on the other hand, had no desire to manifest their thoughts in programs. They focused on the problem as such. Sigurd Lewerentz is the most prominent example of this attitude. Finally, the *skilled* applied all their knowledge of how similar tasks had previously been solved. In the competition for the Röhsska Museum, Charles Lindholm is an example of this approach. All methods were ways to a professional outcome, and none of them could guarantee a sensitive and buildable solution. But it is significant that within the wide range of approaches, the standard was largely respectable.[25]

[25] Rasmus Wærn, *Tävlingarnas tid. Arkitekttävlingarnas betydelse i borgerlighetens Sverige* (Stockholm: Arkitektur förlag, 1996), 118.

Biography
Rasmus Wærn is an independent architectural critic and architect. He has been writing on architecture and urbanism for Swedish and international press since the 1980s, and is also author of numerous books on architecture such as *What is Architecture?* and (in Swedish) *Buildings and Feuds* and *Stone architecture*. He has received the CICA Pierre Vago Journalism Award and been laureated for the film *An Other City*. Wærn has curated exhibitions and has been an editor of the *Swedish Review of Architecture*. He is the author and curator of a book and exhibition on regional Swedish architecture. See www.nordicarchitecture.com for a full CV.

Unbuilt Architectural Criticism: Revaluing Kunio Maekawa's 1931 Museum Proposal

Mengfei Pan

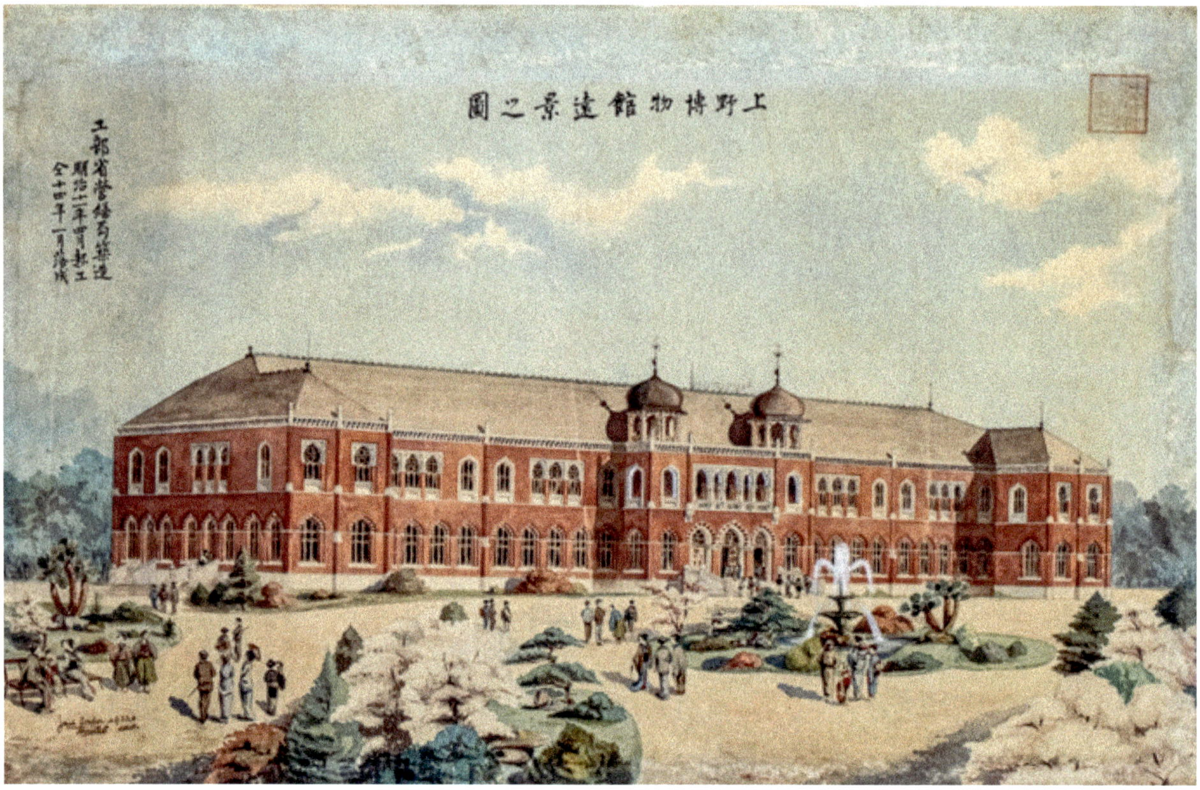

fig. 1
Drawing of the Ueno Museum by Josiah Conder, late nineteenth century.
Collection of Tokyo National Museum. Image source: TNM Image Archives.

Kunio Maekawa's (1905–86) proposal for the Tokyo Imperial Household Museum Competition (1931) challenged the architectural world by questioning the parameters of the competition, which limited architects' freedom of expression, leading young modernist architects to refrain from participating. As Maekawa rejected the competition guidelines, his entry was not selected by the jury and was therefore not realized. However, this unbuilt project was an architectural criticism that not only presented his modernist and urbanist visions of museum architecture but also revealed how he challenged the practices of the time and defined "authentic architecture" as prioritizing function, showing integrity between the exterior and interior and between material and structure, and connecting with its surrounding environment. This case attracted attention with the aid of newspapers and emerging architectural journals, and mediated the personal propositions of Maekawa and his supporters in wider society. Maekawa's unbuilt architectural criticism provoked reflections on the meaning of defeat and encouraged debates on competitions, conventions, and the social responsibility of architects.

Ueno Museum: Manifesting Meiji Aesthetics

In 1931, Maekawa was among the 273 applicants who proposed a new museum building for Ueno Park, Tokyo.[1] From its inception during the mid-Meiji period (1868–1912), this museum, as an idea, architecture, and institution, had been a monumental project in the domestic context. Its monumentality was amplified by its geographic location, architectural style, and a tie with the Imperial Household. Ueno is located in the northeast of the city of Edo (or Tokyo after 1868) and features a highland area adjacent to an alluvial plain in the east and south.[2] This topography affords the southern tip of the upland another name, "Ueno Hill." With the belief that evil enters from the northeast, the ruling Tokugawa shogunate in the Edo period (1603–1868) established a magnificent temple, Kan'ei-ji, atop the hill in 1625. The temple carried political and social significance as it held the funeral of the third shogun, Tokugawa Iemitsu (1604–51), and entombed six of fifteen successive shoguns.

The Meiji Restoration of 1868 marked the transfer of political authority from the Edo Bakufu to the Meiji government, leading to significant social consequences. In 1868, Ueno Hill was the site of the only battle in Edo between the forces loyal to the Tokugawa shogunate and the new government's army. The battle saw the grand edifices of Kan'ei-ji burned to the ground. However, Ueno Hill maintained its role as a symbolic place of political authority, becoming a showcase of modernity and demonstrating the new government's ambition to emulate and rival the West. The Meiji government strategically appropriated the precinct of Tokugawa to install its new "exhibition complex" upon the Kan'ei-ji's ruins.[3] Ueno Hill was transformed into one of the first parks in the country, hosting numerous exhibitions and housing modern institutions such as museums, libraries, and schools.

keywords:

Tokyo Imperial Household Museum, architectural competition, architectural criticism, modernism architecture in Japan, Ueno Park

1 The total number was 281, with eight submitted late and rejected, see Tokyo Imperial Household Museum, *Tokyo teishitsu hakubutsukan kenchiku sekkei kenshō ōbō zuan shinsa hōkoku*, 1931. The museum, currently called the Tokyo National Museum, was first established by the Ministry of Education in 1872 and moved to Ueno in 1882. It was renamed, reorganized, and underwent changes in its administrative positioning and social meaning, see Tokyo National Museum, *Tokyo kokuritsu hakubutsukan hyakunenshi honpen*, 1973.

2 The city of Edo became the new capital and was renamed Tokyo in 1868.

3 Ian Jared Miller, *The Nature of the Beasts: Empire and Exhibition at the Tokyo Imperial Zoo* (Berkeley, CA, and London: University of California Press, 2013), 37.

fig. 2
Hyōkei-kan. Photo: Mengfei Pan.

The museum in Ueno epitomized the modernization process occurring in the new capital and presented a new architectural expression promoted by the Meiji government. Its first building was designed by the English architect Josiah Conder (1850–1920) and completed in 1881 ***(fig. 1)***. Conder was hired by the Ministry of Public Works to teach at the newly established Imperial College of Engineering. He is remembered and credited as the father of modern Japanese architecture who nurtured the first generation of local architects, including Tōkuma Katayama (1854–1917) and Kingo Tatsuno (1854–1919). The design of the Ueno Museum was his first public work in Japan.

This Western two-story brick building adorned with Islamic decorations was constructed over the site of the main hall of Kan'ei-ji, manifesting the eradication of Tokugawa memory. During the 1881 Second Domestic Industrial Exhibition held in Ueno, its first floor functioned as an art gallery. The following year, the building became the new home of Hakubutsukan, a museum that had been founded in central Tokyo in 1872. As the architectural historian Alice Tseng observed, the Ueno Museum established the precedent of monumentality of both scale and style, "served as the archetype for institutional building," and played a significant role in shaping the public face of the government and in developing "the idea of expressing the nation's identity through ornamental forms and fragments."[4] The Meiji emperor's attendance at the opening ceremony added to its grandeur.

In the late 1890s, the Ueno Museum underwent imperialization. The political agenda was to enhance a national polity centering on the Imperial Household. In 1889, the official name of the museum was changed to Teikoku hakubutsukan (Imperial Museum), and in 1900, it became Tokyo Teishitsu hakubutsukan (Tokyo Imperial Household Museum). A new building, emblematic of the strengthened ties with the Imperial Household, was added. Standing to the southwest of Conder's building, the neobaroque Hyōkei-kan, designed by Conder's student Katayama, was built to celebrate the marriage of the crown prince Yoshihito (1879–1926; the later Taishō emperor) and opened to the public in 1909 ***(fig. 2)***. While Hyōkei-kan survived the 1923 Great Kantō Earthquake, Conder's building was damaged ***(fig. 3)***. This catastrophe triggered

[4] Alice Y. Tseng, *The Imperial Museums of Meiji Japan: Architecture and the Art of the Nation* (Seattle: University of Washington Press, 2008), 81.

[5] Hideo Seki, *Hakubutsukan no tanjō: Machida Hisanari to Tōkyō teishitsu hakubutsukan* (Tokyo: Iwanami shinsho, 2005), 172–79.

[6] Kiyoyuki Shigematsu, *Tairei Tokyo teishitsu hakubutsukan fukkō yosankai tekiyō* (Tokyo: Shigematsu Kiyoyuki, 1928), 4–5.

[7] Jacqueline Eve Kestenbaum, "Modernism and Tradition in Japanese Architectural Ideology, 1931–1955" (PhD thesis, Columbia University, 1996), 45.

[8] The jury members were renowned art historians, architectural historians, and bureaucrats, including the architect and architectural historian Chūta Itō (1867–1954) and the art historian Sei'ichi Taki (1873–1945). See Takeshi Kawata, "Keitai kettei no purosesu nitsuite," in *Showa shoki no hakubutsukan kenchiku: Tōkyō hakubutsukan to Tōkyō teishutsu hakubutsukan*, ed. Hakubutsukan kenchiku kenkyūkai (Tokyo: Tokai University Press, 2007), 98–125, and Hiroshi Matsukuma, "Tōkyō teishitsu hakubutsukan no imi," *Kenchiku jānaru* 1207 (2013): 50–53, for details of discussions among the committee members, and Mengfei Pan, "Whose is the Museum? A Case Study of The Tokyo Imperial Household Museum Competition in 1931," *Proceedings of 11th International Symposium on Architectural Interchanges in Asia* (2016), 920–25, for a timeline and details of the establishment of the jury. As Hashitera and Kawamichi point out, the definition of "*nihon shumi*" was vague and diverse, and the awarded

fig. 3
Conder's building, damaged after the 1923 Great Kantō Earthquake. Collection of Tokyo National Museum.
Image source: ColBase (https://colbase.nich.go.jp/).

the museum's transformation from one focused on industry to one devoted to fine art and history. In 1924, it transferred its natural and industrial collection to the Tokyo Museum (now the National Museum of Nature and Science, Tokyo) and restructured its collection into two departments: fine arts and history. In the same year, Ueno Park was bestowed by the Imperial Household to the metropolitan government of Tokyo and renamed Ueno Imperial Gift Park (Ueno onshi kōen). The Tokyo Imperial Household Museum was expected to serve as a shrine displaying the essence of the national polity—the fine arts—and to visualize and symbolize the taste of the Imperial Household at this site imbued with historical and political implications.[5]

The Tokyo Imperial Household Museum Competition of 1931

The aftermath of the earthquake offered an opportunity to revise Meiji aesthetics through architecture and erect another monument at Ueno Hill. A competition was held between December 1930 and April 1931 for a new building to replace Conder's structure. The new construction was seen as a "national commemorative project" that would build a museum for ancient art to extol both the nation and the Imperial Household.[6]

The competition was the "catalyst for an historic debate on the direction of Japanese architecture" and a focal point of emerging architectural criticism.[7] The competition committee required the style of the building to be "East Asian based on Japanese taste" (*nihon shumi wo kichō to suru tōyō shiki*), to match its content of ancient art from the region.[8] An interior plan was included in the competition brief, suggesting that the competitor was expected to design the exterior based on this plan.

The architectural criticism was directed against the architectural style that had been favored by previous competitions and likely this 1931 one as well. The Nihon Intānashonaru kenchiku-kai (Japan International Architectural Association), established by young architects inspired by modernism in the Kansai region in 1927, fiercely opposed the competition. At the beginning of 1931, the group announced that they would not participate.[9] In an article in the newspaper *Yomiuri shimbun*, Kikuji Ishimoto (1894–1963), a member of Nihon Intānashonaru kenchiku-kai, expressed the group's opinion

competition designs helped develop the social understanding of "*nihon shumi*" architecture (Tomoko Hashitera and Rintaro Kawamichi, "On the Manner for Representing 'nihon-shumi [Japan taste]' Argued at the End of Meiji Era," *Journal of Architecture, Planning and Environmental Engineering* 444 [1993]: 149–56).

9 Nihon Intānashonaru kenchiku-kai, "Seimei," *Intānashonaru kenchiku* 3, no. 2 (1931): 11–12.

10 In this article, Chūta Itō defended the jury's position and explained that the style requirement was imposed so the exterior would match the content of the museum, see "Teishitsu hakubutsukan shinchiku ni kurai kage," *Yomiuri shimbun*, January 25, 1931, 7. However, Nihon Intānashonaru kenchiku-kai continued to denounce

fig. 4
Perspective drawing, Kenjirō Maeda's design for the Kyoto Art Museum.
Image source: Yō Takatori, *Nihon shumi* (Osaka: Nihon kenchiku kyōkai, 1931), 25.

that the style requirement was merely reflecting the jury's confined personal taste, and requested that the "senior masters" overcome the limits of the old conventions.[10]

The favored style, or "personal taste" of the jurors as held by Nihon Intānashonaru kenchiku-kai, consisted of roofs that embrace motifs of traditional Japanese architecture. This style, called "Imperial Crown Style" (*teikan yōshiki*) by later architectural historians, was popular in the late 1920s and 1930s. As historian Shōichi Inoue observed, the style of having a tiled-and-gabled roof on an altered classical body had originated in the early 1910s with thesis designs at the architectural department of the Imperial University.[11] He further explicated that its actualization from the late 1920s had various impetuses, including students' emergence as mature architects, architects' struggles to raise their wages by demonstrating their ability to design decorative details, and intentions to cater to popular tastes and foreign tourists.[12]

Members of Nihon Intānashonaru kenchiku-kai and the architect Masami Makino (1903–83), who worked at Le Corbusier's (1887–1965) atelier in 1928, were among many who attacked this style in the 1930s. They associated it with "hearses" (*sōgi jidōsha*) topped by flamboyant but unnecessary architectural decorations.[13] Makino even condemned this style as a "national disgrace."[14]

Competitions' style requirement and their winners' answering with tiled-and-gabled roofs took precedence. In 1930, the competition for a new museum in Kyoto celebrating the Shōwa emperor's enthronement asked for "Japanese taste" (*nihon shumi*). The winning design by Kenjirō Maeda (1892–1975) had a gabled roof on top of a reinforced-concrete structure ***(fig. 4)***.[15] Tiled-and-gabled roofs and a mix of traditional motifs and modern structures became established as winning approaches. The design book *Nihon shumi wo kichō to seru saikin kenchiku kenshō zushū* (Design collection of recent architectural competition based on Japanese taste) was published in 1931. Compiling the winning designs of four competitions held in 1930 and 1931, it suggests a widespread need for a design book featuring "Japanese taste" and a concretization of architectural paradigms of such a taste, with particular emphasis on the roof.[16]

the style requirement and express their distrust of the jurors in the February 1931 issue of their journal, *Intānashonaru kenchiku*. In addition to the modernists and those supporting Asian/Japanese styles, another opinion was that both approaches were wrong and harmony with Hōkei-kan and the garden should be prioritized, see Tari Moriguchi, "Hakubutsukan no shinsekkei no tameni," *Kenchiku shinchō* 12, no. 1 (1931): 1–4.

11 Currently the University of Tokyo. Shōichi Inoue, *Senjika nihon no kenchikuka: Āt, kicchu, Japanesuku* (Tokyo: Asahi shimbunsha, 1995), 50–101.

12 Inoue, *Senjika nihon no kenchikuka*, 50–101.

13 S. T. Sei, "Saikin no kenchiku sekkei zuan kenshō kyōgi ni kansuru ichi hihan," *Intānashonaru kenchiku* 3, no. 2 (1931): 13; Masami Makino, "Kokusui teki kenchiku ka kokujoku teki kenchikuka: gendai kenchiku sesō hihan (1)," *Kokusai kenchiku* 7, no. 2 (1931): 5. According to Shōichi Inoue, these hearses started to appear in Osaka from the late 1920s (Inoue, *Senjika nihon no kenchikuka*, 80).

14 Makino, "Kokusui teki kenchiku ka kokujoku teki kenchikuka (1)" and Masami Makino, "Kokusui teki kenchiku ka kokujoku teki kenchikuka: gendai kenchiku sesō hihan (2)," *Kokusai kenchiku* 7, no. 3 (1931): 1–5.

15 The museum was initially named Tairei kinen Kyōtō bijutsukan (Kyoto Enthronement Memorial Museum of Art), then renamed as Kyoto City Museum in 1952, and further as Kyoto City KYOCERA Museum of Art in 2020.

Maekawa's Unbuilt Architecture as Criticism

Nihon Intānashonaru kenchiku-kai's suspicion that the jury would prefer this particular style turned out to be correct. The winning applicants all answered the requirements in a similar way. The various roof designs were almost the only distinguishing features, while little attention was paid to the inside, as many competitors simply followed the interior plan attached to the competition brief. Jin Watanabe's (1887–1973) Imperial Crown design won first place ***(fig. 5)***.[17] As the critic Fumio Tanaka satirized after the release of the results, the competition only wanted "roof designers" (*yaneya*).[18]

fig. 5
Jin Watanabe's winning proposal for the Ueno Museum.
Image source: Yō Takatori, *Nihon shumi* (Osaka: Nihon kenchiku kyōkai, 1931), 1.

Kunio Maekawa, however, refused to be merely a "roof designer." Born to a former samurai warrior family, with his father serving as an engineer-bureaucrat in the new government, Maekawa was educated at the architectural department of the Imperial University, followed by a two-year apprenticeship at Le Corbusier's atelier in Paris. In 1930, he returned to Japan and soon joined Antonin Raymond's (1888–1976) office. His museum proposal became one of his first designs during this time.

Maekawa submitted a proposal disparate from those of the winners. His design consisted of connected parallelepiped configurations, pilotis at the center, long horizontal windows, flat roofs, and a distinctive H-shaped plan ***(figs. 6-9)***. The architectural historian Jonathan M. Reynolds has shown that this configuration resembles Le Corbusier's proposal for the League of Nations of 1927.[19] Maekawa rearranged his master's design by emphasizing the axiality of the building and adding a large pavilion atop the pilotis.

The most distinctive gesture was the connection between the proposed building and its environment; thus, his proposal extended beyond the building to the museum premises and Ueno Park. He suggested underground connections between the competition building, Hyōkei-kan, and an E-shaped annex located in the northwest of the museum premises that he proposed as a potential expansion, highlighting his attention to inter-building accessibility ***(fig. 10)***.

Maekawa foresaw a society increasingly reliant on automobiles. For the park, he widened and straightened the roads in front of the building and added a traffic circle at the southwest end, thus providing direct automobile access to the museum entrances. The arrows in the park design indicate organized traffic routes for automobiles, thereby enhancing access not only to the main building of the Tokyo Imperial Household Museum but also to Hyōkei-kan and the two other museums flanking the park.[20] This would solve the issue of difficult access to the museum that art historian and critic Tari Moriguchi (1892–1984) raised in early 1931.[21] Maekawa might also have been aware of the plaza next to the Ueno railway station, which was being modified to smooth the flow of automobile traffic. Although Ueno Station was not mapped in his "block plan," the proposal clearly takes into consideration the flow between the station and the park.

Automobile traffic grew rapidly after the 1923 earthquake. In 1927, the number of automobiles in Japan reached 51,862, nearly doubling that of 1924.[22]

16 Yō Takatori, *Nihon shumi wo kichō to seru saikin kenchiku kenshō zushū* (Osaka: Nihon kenchiku kyōkai,1931). In addition to the two museum competitions, the other two are the 1930 Gunjin Kaikan (Reservists' Association Hall; currently Kudan kaikan) competition, which asked for *kokusui no kihin* (nationalistic elegance), and the Nihon seimei-kan (currently Takashima-ya department store in Nihonbashi) competition of the same year, which stipulated a modern architectural design based on East Asian taste.

17 Watanabe's design was actualized with significant alternations by Takumi-ryō (Bureau of Construction, Ministry of Imperial Household) and became the present-day main building.

18 Fumio Tanaka, "Hakubutsukan no konpechishon," *Kenchiku sekai* 25, no. 6 (1931): 12.

19 Jonathan M. Reynolds, *Maekawa Kunio and the Emergence of Japanese Modernist Architecture* (Oakland: University of California Press, 2001), 97.

20 The two museums were the Tokyo Prefectural Museum of Art (currently Tokyo Metropolitan Art Museum) and Tokyo Science Museum (currently National Museum of Nature and Science, Tokyo).

21 Tari Moriguchi, "Futatabi atarashii hakubutsukan no tameni," *Kenchiku shinchō* 12, no. 2 (1931): 1–5.

22 Ryōzō Yanagida, *Jidōsha sanjūnen shi* (Tokyo: Sansui-sha, 1944), 5.

fig. 8

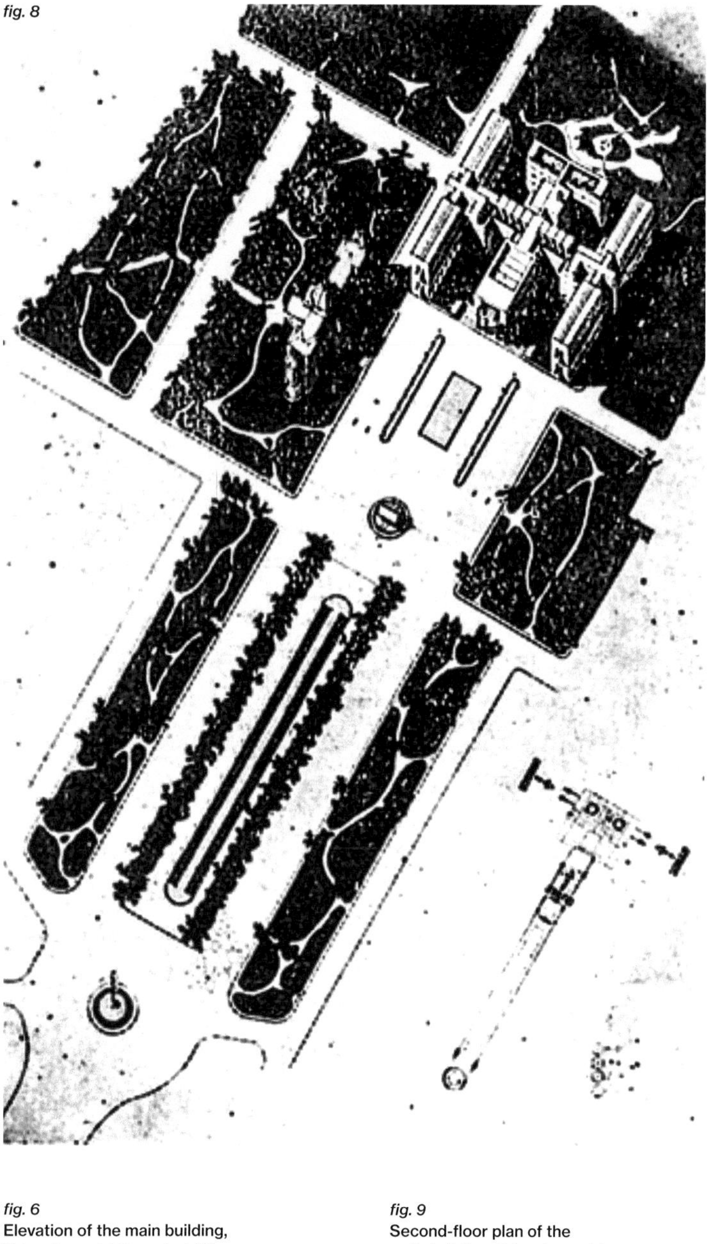

fig. 6

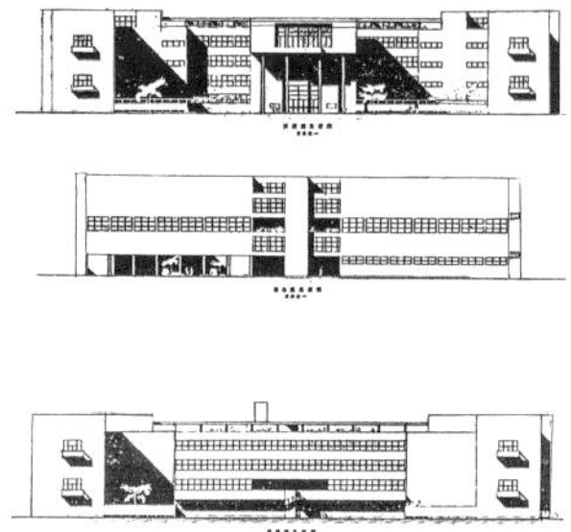

fig. 7

fig. 9

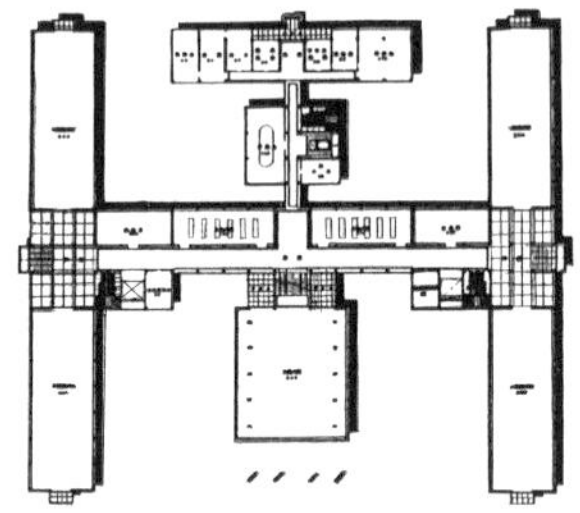

fig. 10

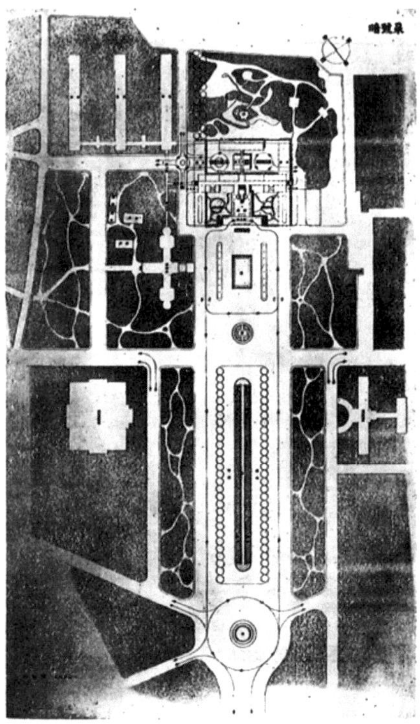

fig. 6
Elevation of the main building, Tokyo Imperial Household Museum proposal, by Kunio Maekawa. Image source: *Kokusai kenchiku* 7, no. 6 (1931): 7.

fig. 7
Perspective of the main building, Tokyo Imperial Household Museum proposal, by Kunio Maekawa. Image source: *Kokusai kenchiku* 7, no. 6 (1931): 4.

fig. 8
Axonometric of Ueno Park, Tokyo Imperial Household Museum proposal, by Kunio Maekawa. Image source: *Kokusai kenchiku* 7, no. 6 (1931): 4.

fig. 9
Second-floor plan of the main building, Tokyo Imperial Household Museum proposal, by Kunio Maekawa. Image source: *Kokusai kenchiku* 7, no. 6 (1931): 5.

fig. 10
Block plan, Tokyo Imperial Household Museum proposal, by Kunio Maekawa. Image source: *Kokusai kenchiku* 7, no. 6 (1931): 3.

Regulations regarding driving licenses, laws of automobile transportation business, and roads for automobiles were established. Maekawa's father, Kan'ichi (1873–1955), who was working as the chief of the engineering section at the Home Ministry, wrote an article on road infrastructure in 1931, emphasizing the need for exclusive roads for automobiles.[23]

The younger Maekawa's plan would have accentuated the park's monumentality. Compared with the preexisting park ***(fig. 11)***, his proposal stressed symmetry, adding grandeur to the front of the museum and the park. Experience gathered in Paris, which has a famous axial route between the Arc de triomphe de l'Étoile and the Louvre, may have influenced his understanding of a museum park symbolizing a modern city and nation, and thus he created a "miniature version of that famous Parisian vista with a Corbusian structure as its apex."[24]

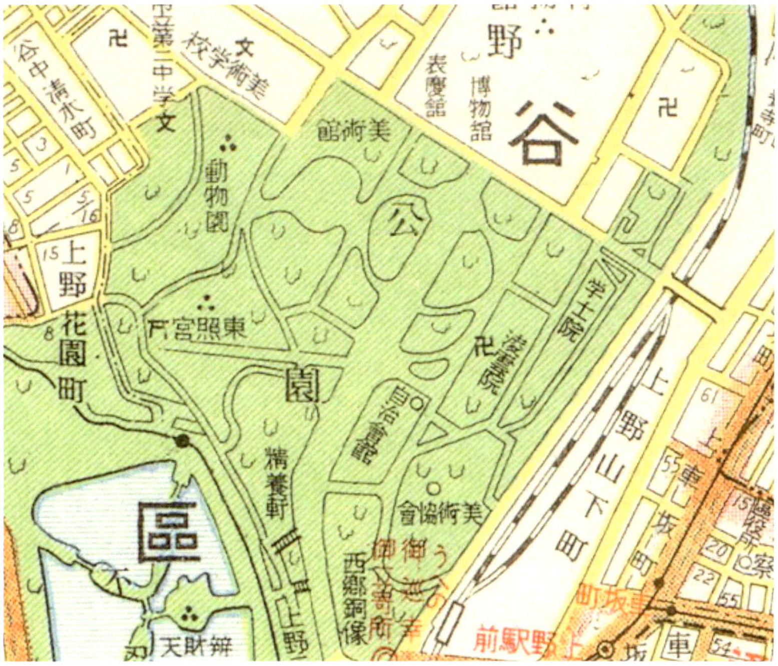

fig. 11
Roads in Ueno Park, part of "Tokyo city map commemorating the completion of revitalization," appendix of *Tokyo Nichinichi Shimbun*.
Collection and Image source: International Research Center for Japanese Studies.

Criticism through Writings

Although not awarded a prize, Maekawa's competition entry attracted considerable attention from newspapers and architectural journals. The architectural editor and critic Yoshihisa Miyauchi observed that in Japan the modernist movement and journalism supported each other from the 1920s onwards.[25] Soon after returning from France, Maekawa joined this movement and engaged in journalistic activity. In October 1930, he delivered a speech entitled "3+3+3=3×3" for Sōusha, a group of young modernist draftsmen.[26] The transcript was later published in the journal *Kokusai kenchiku* (International architecture).[27] As the title suggests, the speech argued that various approaches can lead to the same results, revealing Maekawa's disagreement with the idea of linking architecture to art or ideology. He criticized the nationalistic architecture represented by Nagoya City Hall, and the modernist groups as elites barricading themselves in an ivory tower, and thus advocated freedom of choice.[28]

Maekawa's view of architecture and his critical attitude remained unchanged when he participated in the Tokyo Imperial Household Museum Competition the following year. Regarding the museum proposal, Maekawa published two essays in *Kokusai kenchiku* after the competition: one is an excerpt of the explanatory text (*setsumeisho*) submitted to the competition, and the other is titled "The defeated are rebels" ("Makereba zokugun"). Architectural historian and critic Hajime Yatsuka posits that it was Maekawa's text, rather than the design, that constituted a polemic against "Japanese taste."[29] In contrast to Chikatada Kurata (1895–1966), who also submitted a modernist design to the competition but wrote his *setsumeisho* in a calm and objective tone, Maekawa's essays were literary and passionate.[30] Maekawa's *setsumeisho* drew connections between the Parthenon, Japanese shrines, and other architectural monuments, and traced the tradition of cohering structure and material back to the

[23] Kan'ichi Maekawa, "Dōro gijutsu saikin no shinpo," *Kōsei* 137 (1931).
[24] Kestenbaum, "Japanese Architectural Ideology," 72.
[25] Yoshihisa Miyauchi, *Shōsuha kenchiku ron: Ichi henshūsha no shōgen* (Tokyo: Inoue shoten, 1974), 273.
[26] Sōusha was established in 1923 with a majority of its members coming from the Telecommunications Ministry.
[27] *Kokusai kenchiku* was founded in 1928 by young modernist architects and introduced Le Corbusier's works as early as 1929.
[28] Kunio Maekawa, "3+3+3=3×3," *Kokusai kenchiku* 6, no. 12 (1930). The Nagoya City Hall competition was held in 1929, to which Maekawa submitted a modernist design from Paris. The winning and executed design by Kingo Hirabayashi (1894–1980) included a tower on the rooftop, modeled on the Nagoya Castle keep.
[29] Hajime Yatsuka, *Shisō toshite no nihon kindai kenchiku* (Tokyo: Iwanami shoten, 2005), 394–95.
[30] Chikatada Kurata, "Tōkyō teishitsu hakutsukan keikaku: setsumeisho bassui," *Kokusai kenchiku* 7, no. 6 (1931): 3.

mythical foundation of Japan 2,591 years earlier.[31]

His "Makereba zokugun" essay has been celebrated as a symbol of his courage and resistance to predominant aesthetics and conventions.[32] The title stemmed from a saying in the Meiji period, "the winners are the official army and the defeated are rebels" (*kateba kanbun, makereba zokugun*), lamenting the misfortune of those who aligned with the failing Tokugawa shogunate during the civil war in 1868–69 and the vanity of success.[33] This self-labeling as *zokugun* mobilized a sympathy for losers, which is rooted in Japanese culture, to justify his design.

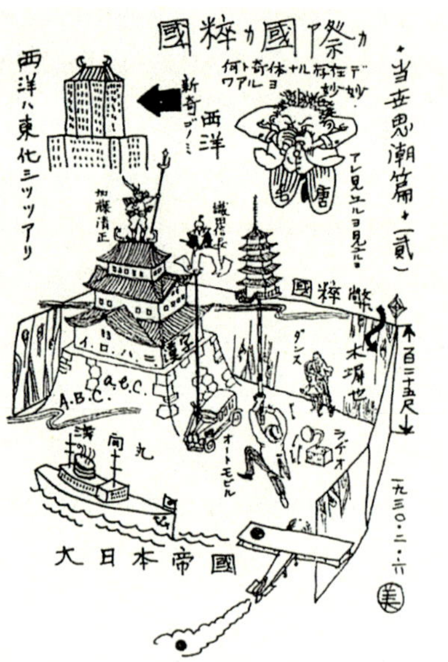

fig. 12
***Tōsei shichō hen (2)* (Contemporary Thinking Trend), by Yoshi Niwa. Image source: *Kokusai kenchiku* 6, no. 5 (1930): 31.**

fig. 13
***Doku Maekawa Kunio-kun* (Reading Maekawa Kunio), by Yoshi Niwa. Image source: *Kokusai kenchiku* 7, no. 8 (1931): 29.**

Maekawa's proposal challenged the definition of the "architecture of Japanese taste" and called for all architects to be conscious members of a collective community. He rejected gabled roofs as "fake" (*ese*) Japanese architecture and offered another interpretation of "Japanese taste" that was determined by updated materials and technology.[34] He believed that his design "best presents Japanese characteristics" (*mottomo nihon teki narumono*).[35] He also emphasized the "joint responsibility" (*kyōdō sekimu*) of architects.[36] Maekawa viewed the nonparticipation of young architects as regrettable and insisted that competitions were the only battlefield on which an architect could challenge "wrong" (*jadō*) architecture.[37] As Reynolds pointed out, Maekawa's public protest echoed Le Corbusier's media campaign after his defeat in the competition for the Palace of the League of Nations in 1927.[38]

Maekawa succeeded in rallying support. Two articles of the newspaper *Asahi shimbun*, one in the readers' column and one by the art critic Bōshin Kuroda (1885–1967), as well as an editorial in the professional journal *Kenchiku sekai* (Architectural world), expressed their sympathy for a work that did not follow the Japanese style requirement but displayed rational thinking.[39] Excerpts from Maekawa's *setsumeisho* were circulated in two other journals in addition to *Kokusai kenchiku*: *Shin kenchiku* (New architecture) and *Kenchiku sekai*.[40] The former was accompanied by an editorial comment praising Maekawa's design as a scientific solution for museum architecture. The latter was quoted at the end of Fumio Tanaka's criticism of competition practices that require adherence to reference plans. Tanaka, who considered Maekawa a respectful friend (*iyū*), approved his original layout, lighting, and circulation design, and highlighted the proposal as the most economic, progressive, and Japanese in character.[41] Architect Renshichirō Kawakita (1902–75), in an essay published next to Maekawa's "Makereba zokugun" in *Kokusai kenchiku*, also paid respect to Maekawa, noting that while his work made no compromises, many others showed little effort as architects.[42]

Yoshi Niwa's cartoons also strike a chord. Niwa drew cartoons for *Kokusai kenchiku* between 1928 and 1932 and had caricatured architecture of "Japanese taste" in 1930 ***(fig. 12)***. Soon after the competition result was released, he created a one-page cartoon praising Maekawa ***(fig. 13)***. It includes the first four lines of Chinese literati Zhang

31 Kunio Maekawa, "Tōkyō teishitsu hakutsukan keikaku: setsumeisho bassui," *Kokusai kenchiku* 7, no. 6 (1931): 1–2.

32 Miyauchi's biography (Yoshihisa Miyauchi, *Maekawa kunio: zokugun no shō* [Tokyo: Shōbunsha, 2005]) is one example, calling Maekawa a "marshal of zokugun."

33 See also Ivan Morris, *The Nobility of Failure: Tragic Heroes in the History of Japan* (Tokyo: Kurodahan Press, [1975] 2013) and Masao Yamaguchi, *"Haisha" no seishin shi* (Tokyo: Iwanami shoten, 1995) for discussions on the Japanese predilection for failed heroes and the labeling of losers in Japanese culture, respectively. Although the feudal lords of Oumi and Hirosaki that Maekawa's parents served were on the winning side of the Meiji government during the final battles with the Tokugawa troops, the family experience of civil war would likely have influenced Maekawa's thoughts on success and defeat.

34 Kunio Maekawa, "Makereba zokugun," *Kokusai kenchiku* 7, no. 6 (1931): 1.

35 Maekawa, "Tōkyō teishitsu hakutsukan keikaku," 2.

36 Maekawa, "Tōkyō teishitsu hakutsukan keikaku," and Maekawa, "Makereba zokugun."

37 Maekawa, "Tōkyō teishitsu hakutsukan keikaku," 2.

38 Reynolds, *Maekawa Kunio*, 99. See also the inclusion of media reports on the controversial competition results

Jiuling's (678–740) poem "Gan yu" (Sad thoughts) and German labels.[43] Zhang is known as an official of integrity but with the ill fortune of serving the government. In the poem, Zhang sees himself as a lone swan and the court that failed to recognize the upcoming dangers as complacent kingfishers. Niwa compares Maekawa to the swan, carrying a modernist broadcasting tower, and the advocates of Japanese taste to kingfishers, thus emphasizing the contrast.[44] The seventh line, "Meifu huan renzhi" (Extravagant clothes are accused), which is not quoted in the cartoon, makes a strong denunciation.

Conclusion

Reviewing Maekawa's 1931 museum proposal and the subsequent discourse demonstrates how deliberate defeat expresses criticism. The lone swan Maekawa failed to win the 1931 museum competition but succeeded in evoking public and professional reflections, praise for resistance, and the rise of modernist architecture. The modernist design and park proposal concretized his visions for a future architecture and for the profession of an architect, and embodied criticism against the conventional architectural world. His publications turned him into an icon for the architectural movement. Yoshihisa Miyauchi argued that this museum proposal marked the start of Maekawa's career, becoming a symbol of his life.[45] Architectural historian Hiroshi Matsukuma saw its significance in boosting Maekawa's reputation.[46] While the winning designs might have enforced a cultural identity that catered to the time and the jurors' preferences, Maekawa proposed an alternative, leaving an enduring influence.

This case sets a precedent for criticism through unbuilt architecture in Japan. A significant example is Arata Isozaki's (1931–2022) proposal for a new Tokyo Metropolitan Government Building in 1985.[47] Whereas all other architects, including Maekawa Kunio Associates and Kenzō Tange (1913–2005), submitted super high-rises, Isozaki proposed a high medium-rise design that contained a great hall.[48] Tange's tower has now become a landmark in the Western Shinjuku area, while Isozaki's design, in various forms such as prints, models made of wood, and photography, captures the imagination of an alternative. Immediately after the release of the competition results, one of the competition jurors, architectural critic Teiji Itō (1922–2010), mentioned to Isozaki that his proposal reminded him of Maekawa's Ueno Museum from half a century earlier.[49] The unrealized Tokyo Metropolitan Government Building became one inspiration for Isozaki to cultivate the "unbuilt," projects that are never to be realized, coming ahead of their time, that even in their unbuilt status nevertheless become crucial in making architectural history.[50] These instances of unbuilt criticisms shed light on how architects endeavor to seek alternatives, rail against prevalent practices, and reflect upon their social responsibility.

Biography
Mengfei Pan is an assistant professor at Faculty of Tourism and Community Development, Kokugakuin University, Japan. She earned her PhD degree with a thesis on the art networks in the Ueno area in the Meiji period from the University of Tokyo. Major publications include "Tōkyō Shitaya Negishi Oyobi Kinbō-zu and the Symbolism of Community Mapping in the Late Meiji Period", *Japan Review: Journal of the International Research Center for Japanese Studies*. Her primary research interests lie in the relationship between art and place, as well as in cross-cultural negotiations and exchanges, with a particular focus on the localities of Japan and the East Asian region.

in Le Corbusier's *Une Maison - Un Palais*, published in 1928.

39 "Shinsain muchi," *Asahi shimbun*, May 24, 1931, 3, Tokyo edition; Bōshin Kuroda, "Teishitsu hakubutsukan sekkei zuan shokan," *Asahi shimbun*, June 5, 1931, 9; "Kakon wo sare," *Kenchiku sekai* 25, no. 6 (1931): 1–2. None of the three articles mentioned Maekawa's name. The youngest juror and professor at the Imperial University, Hideto Kishida (1899–1966), had been supportive of Maekawa's design. It is said that he showed the design to his class at the university and expressed his pity, see Arata Isozaki, *Kenchiku no 1930 nendai: keifu to myakuraku* (Tokyo: Kajima shuppankai, 1978), 171.

40 Kunio Maekawa, "Tōkyō teishitsu hakutsukan keikaku setsumeisho," *Shin kenchiku* 7, no. 7 (1931): 251–55; Tanaka, "Hakubutsukan no konpechishon." Sutemi Horiguchi (1895–1984) also quotes Maekawa's *setsumeisho* to argue what should be the correct "nihon shumi" in his article published the following year, see "Gendai kenchiku ni arahareta nihon shumi nitsuite," *Shisō* 116 (1932): 83. The published versions of Maekawa's *setsumeisho* are identical to the text part of the full version that is in the collection of one of the competition jurors, Yoshikazu Uchida (1885–1972), at the Tokyo Metropolitan Archives.

41 Tanaka, "Hakubutsukan no konpechishon," 13.

42 Renshichirō Kawakita, "Teishitsu hakutsukan konpechishon," *Kokusai kenchiku* 7, no. 6 (1931): 20.

43 Yoshi Niwa, "Doku Maekawa Kunio kun," *Kokusai kenchiku* 7, no. 8 (1931): 29. See also Reynolds, *Maekawa Kunio*, 100 for a discussion on this cartoon. Niwa's early works caricature the office buildings and department stores that incorporate superficial Japanese forms but are built upon Western and modernist foundations, see Yoshi Niwa, "Tōsei shisōhen: Kokusui ka kokusai ka (1)–(3)," *Kokusai kenchiku* 6, no. 5 (1930): 30–32.

44 Niwa is referring to the broadcasting tower design that Maekawa submitted as his university graduation work.

45 Miyauchi, *Maekawa kunio*, 39.

46 Hiroshi Matsukuma, ed., *Kenchikuka Maekawa Kunio no shigoto* (Tokyo: Bijutsu shuppansha, 2006), 79.

47 The project was also called Tokyo City Hall at the time of the competition.

48 There is a master-and-pupil relationship between Maekawa, Tange, and Isozaki. Tange worked at Maekawa's office between 1938 and 1942 and Isozaki worked under Tange in the 1960s.

49 Tsuyoshi Hiramatsu, *Isozaki Arata no "Tochō": Sengo no nihon saidai no konpe* (Tokyo: Bungei shunshū, 2008), 444.

50 Arata Isozaki, *Han kenchiku-shi* (Tokyo: TOTO Publishing, 2001), 102.

Two Houses and Their Ineluctable Criticisms of Modernity: On the Introduction of a New Style in Turkey

Büşra Köroğlu

fig. 1
Gazi school project, Mimar Kemalettin, Ankara, 1926–30.

The Turkish architectural discourse of the early twentieth century was marked by significant transformations and critical dialogues within the profession as the country transitioned towards modernity. Two influential architects, the Austrian-Swiss Ernst Egli (1893–1974) and the Turk Sedad Hakki Eldem (1908–98), played pivotal roles in shaping this evolution. Ernst Egli, initially a proponent of the Western International Style, later shifted his focus to emphasize vernacular values. Significantly, Sedad Hakki Eldem, who studied abroad, developed a profound interest in traditional Turkish architecture, notably houses. He synthesized local Turkish architecture with modern approaches, incorporating familiar features of traditional Turkish houses, such as overhanging eaves, the sofa, and the cumba. As Walter Benjamin stated: "Criticism is a matter of correct distancing."[1] With this perspective in mind, this essay explores how Egli and Eldem held their critical distances to both tradition and innovation in their respective architectural endeavors.

keywords:

Sedad Hakki Eldem, Ernst Egli, internationalism vs. nationalism, interpreting Turkish vernacular

Introduction

The comparative analysis of two houses, one of them called Villa Ragip Devres by Ernst Egli and the other the Summerhouse of Fethi Okyar by Sedad Hakki Eldem, built during the 1930s in Istanbul will reveal the significant differences in the architectural approaches and the respective norms that were generated. These two edifices exemplify the critically conscious architecture of their time, with one of them resisting the self-confirming and nonnegotiable dominant culture while remaining connected to the characteristics of its place and period, and the other reluctantly detaching itself from the preexisting genealogy. Until the 1930s, architecture in Turkey was self-evident and had no need for external explanations; thus, there were no critics until the introduction of modernism. This naturally fostered a fresh comprehension of architecture within a new framework, where numerous local architects were in need of expertise.The key question that the two architects had to address was this: How does a building demonstrate its critical perspective when it is deeply entangled with the culture it serves? A building expresses ideas of a specific cultural attitude by means of its structure, elements, and style even without input from an architect. So how do architects communicate their reflected intentions in a realized work? And which position do they take in the larger quest for modernization?

Irony in the Critical Position

Similarly to other countries, Turkey was being confronted with a binary choice between tradition and modernity in the first half of the twentieth century. With the proclamation of the new Turkish republic, traditional housing was viewed by an imported Eurocentric ideology as an artifact from the past.This led to a robust dialogue that greatly influenced future generations, as many professions were engaged by the new republic to reform Turkish society in general and architecture's social and cultural norms in particular. New dominant construction programs were introduced by the Turkish government, expressly intended to suppress traditional architecture. Abstract geometric

[1] Walter Benjamin, *Reflections: Essays, Aphorisms, Autobiographical Writings*, ed. Peter Demetz, trans. Edmund Jephcott (New York: Harcourt Brace Jovanovich, 1978), 85.

architecture was very much appreciated and demanded by the upper middle class; its characteristic elements were flat roofs, extensive terraces, and simple external forms without ornament. Between 1924 and 1942, approximately forty architects and urban planners from Germany, Austria, France, and Switzerland were personally invited by President Mustafa Kemal Atatürk (1883–1938) to participate in the efforts to modernize Turkey. Among them was Ernst Arnold Egli, who had previously assisted Clemens Holzmeister at the Academy of Fine Arts in Vienna. On his recommendation, Egli was appointed chief architect in the building department of the Turkish Ministry of Education in Ankara in 1927. He was one of the earliest "architectural experts" appointed by the Kemalist state to work in Turkey. At the same time, he was appointed as the head of the architecture faculty at the Academy of Fine Arts in Istanbul.[2] His role, similar to that of an ambassador, was to steer the Turkish state in a more modern and progressive direction by means of its architecture, thus fostering a Westernized identity for Turkey.[3] Upon his arrival, Egli was asked to assist on several ongoing projects in Ankara. He was first commissioned to oversee the Gazi school project, which had already been designed by the architect Mimar Kemalettin (1870–1927) ***(fig. 1)***. Egli recommended simplifications such as removing the pointed arches from the windows, changing the size of the entrance, and reducing the size of the dome.[4]

This effect of Egli's criticism was summarized in an article by another colleague, Mehmet Emin, as follows:

> **In the Minister of Education Necati Bey's room, there was an ongoing conversation about the renewal of Ankara Teacher's School, and they were arguing about removing the arches of the windows, and making the entrance simpler. Suddenly, he turned around, advancing towards the door of the room in a manner that concealed his face. We came face-to-face. I saw two tear drops! He could no longer hide his excitement from me; in a voice that seemed as if he were crying, he said, "I have dedicated thirty years of my life to ensuring that Turkish aesthetic taste lives on in architectural works. For thirty years, I have strived for Turkish cities, like every civilized city, to reflect a taste unique to our nation. Now, they call this style tomb or mosque architecture."**[5]

In the end, the work of Aptullah Ziya was built with very minimal alterations ***(see fig. 1)***. This example highlights the importance of architects being open to constructive feedback from colleagues and embracing the opportunity for their work to be evaluated by peers. While most thoughtful creators, thinkers, and architects engaged with the world through their openness to external critique, some local architects felt threatened by the opinions of their foreign counterparts. For many, their Zeitgeist was still entangled with the pre-modern practice of imitation. After Ernst Egli made these observations, he immersed himself in Turkish culture, insisting that, as a foreigner, he would respect the values of the local architecture in its achievement of engaging with its geography and climate, and that he would also seek to reinterpret traditional values in modern terms. Egli's first encounter with an unknown region and culture made him open his eyes and mind. He was expected to bring his knowledge from a different Zeitgeist and to implement this new approach in his new surroundings. Over time, however, he began to develop an appreciation for the regional architecture he had been tasked with criticizing and transforming into a style more suitable for a modern nation. In his essay published in the magazine *Schweizerische Bauzeitung* with the title "Das Türkische Wohnhaus" ***(see fig. 2)***, Egli summarized his impressions of Turkey.

[2] https://www.architektenlexikon.at/de/101.htm#Pernliche-Daten.

[3] Oya Atalay Franck, *Architektur und Politik: Ernst Egli und die türkische Moderne 1927–1940* (Zurich: GTA Verlag 2012), 37.

[4] Umut Şumnu, "Between Being and Becoming: Identity, Question of Foreignness and the Case of the Turkish House" (PhD diss., Department of Interior Architecture and Environmental Design İhsan Doğramacı Bilkent University Ankara, January 2012).

[5] Mehmet Emin, "On the Occasion of the 50th Anniversary of the Death of Architect Kemalettin," *Arkitekt*, no. 3 (1977): 123.

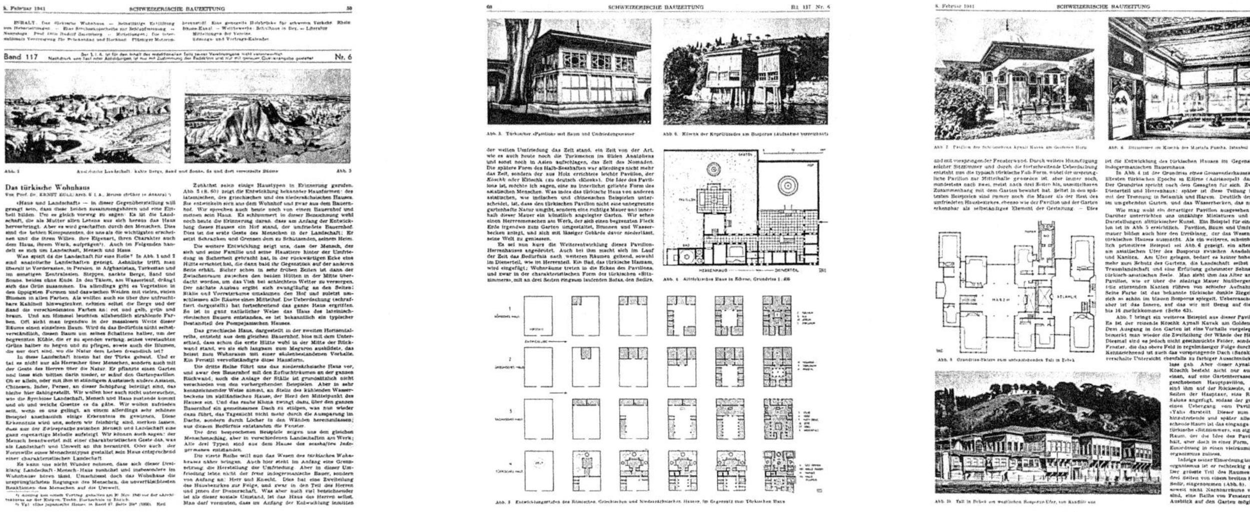

60 SCHWEIZERISCHE BAUZEITUNG Bd. 117 Nr. 6

Abb. 5. Türkischer «Pavillon» mit Baum und Umfriedungsmauer

Abb. 6. Köschk der Köprülüzades am Bosporus (Aufnahme verzeichnet)

With beautiful examples, he provided insights such as how the interaction between humans and their landscape generates a unique harmony. He posited that human responses to the environment are marked by characteristic gestures and that architectural choices made by humans are shaped by distinct landscape features. Turkish people have built within this landscape not only as rulers over inhabitants but also as masters over nature. They have planted gardens and settled in them, creating garden pavilions.

Egli analyzed the pavilion of the Aynali Kavak Palace ***(see fig. 3)*** situated on the Golden Horn, stating that it no longer needs a high wall to protect the garden, that the setting itself is a dream landscape and a fulfilment of the most secret longing of the Turkish-Asian soul. With this frame of mind, he started to look at the existing structures in Istanbul, reevaluating what had long been considered unimportant or secondary. With this article, he replenished the speculative power of Turkish architecture and pointed out how landscape and buildings need to coexist.

fig. 2
Article on Turkish houses ("Das Türkische Wohnhaus") in *Schweizerische Bauzeitung*, 1941.[6]
fig. 3
(Left) Pavilion of the Aynali Kavak Palace on the Golden Horn. (Right) Palace of Köprülüzade on the Bosporus.[7]

[6] Ernst A. Egli, "Das Türkische Wohnhaus," *Schweizerische Bauzeitung* 117/118 (1941): 59–61.
[7] Egli, "Das Türkische Wohnhaus," 60.

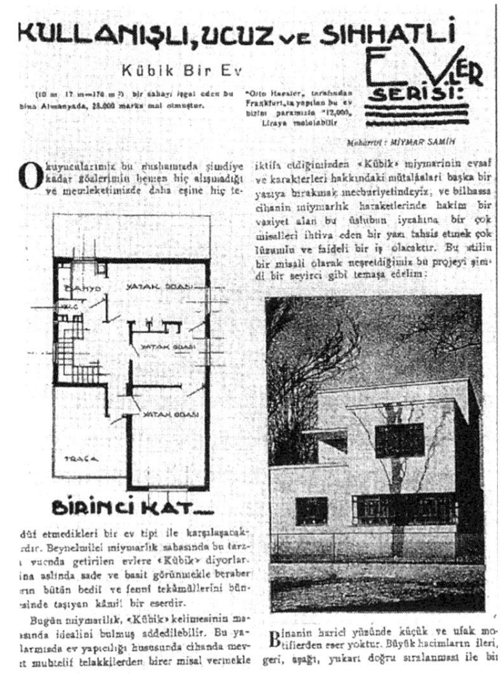

KULLANIŞLI, UCUZ ve SIHHATLI EVLER SERİSİ:

Kübik Bir Ev

(10 m. 17 m=170 m²) bir sahayı işgal eden bu bina Almanyada, 25.000 marka mal olmuştur.

"Otto Haesler" tarafından Frankfurt'ta yapılan bu ev bizim paramızla "12,000" Liraya malolabilir

Muharriri: MİYMAR SAMİH

Okuyucularımız bu mushamızda şimdiye kadar gözlerimin hemen hiç alışmadığı ve memleketimizde daha eşine hiç tedüf etmedikleri bir ev tipi ile karşılaşacaklardır. Beynelmilel miymarlık sahasında bu tarzda vucuda getirilen evlere «Kübik» diyorlar. ina aslında sade ve basit görünmekle beraber ın bütün bedii ve fenni tekâmüllerini bünsinde taşıyan kâmil bir eserdir.

Bugün miymarilık, «Kübik» kelimesinin masında idealini bulmuş addedilebilir. Bu yalarmızda ev yapıcılığı hususunda cihanda mevt muhtelif telakkilerden birer misal vermekle iktifa ettiğimizden «Kübik» miymarinin evsaf ve karakterleri hakkındaki mütalâaları başka bir yazıya bırakmak mecburiyetindeyiz, ve bilhassa cihanin miymarlık hareketlerinde hakim bir vaziyet alan bu üslubun iyzahına bir çok misalleri ihtiva eden bir yazı tahsis etmek çok lüzumlu ve faideli bir iş olacaktır. Bu stilin bir misali olarak neşrettiğimiz bu projeyi şimdi bir seyirci gibi temaşa edelim:

YATAK ODASI

YATAK ODASI

YATAK ODASI

TRACA

BİRİNCİ KAT

Binanin harici yüzünde küçük ve ufak motiflerden eser yoktur. Büyük hacimların ileri, geri, aşağı, yukarı doğru sıralanması ile bi

At the same time, there was a rising demand within Turkish society for modern houses, so architects reluctantly were obliged to serve this desire for a transition to a Western lifestyle. A radical change in society and a profound transformation in terms of modes of living and uses of furniture was occurring in Turkey. For many, being modern meant being innovative and radical, despite criticism from the traditionalists. The push for change was supported by publications in local magazines, showing various examples of modern living conditions with headlines like "Practical, Economical and Healthy Houses" in *Muhit* magazine ***(see fig. 4)***.

Another journal that engaged in publishing examples of modern architecture was the magazine *Arkitekt*, founded in 1931 by the architects Zeki Sayar, Abidin Mortaş, and Aptullah Ziya Kozanoğlu. The journal explored the question of Turkey's modernization process by reviewing various local and external references. In the first edition of *Arkitekt* in 1931, Aptullah Ziya Kozanoğlu articulated his views on the architect's role in his text called "Architect in the Building," making the case that architects bear responsibility not only for the exterior but also for the interior of a building. The magazine featured images of interiors ***(see fig. 5)*** that were analyzed in terms of their functions, such as guest rooms, dining rooms, and bedrooms—functions not typically found in traditional Turkish houses. Conventional interior furnishings such as sofas, storage cupboards, floor mattresses, oil lamps, and hearths were replaced with modern Western-style furniture and amenities, including sets of armchairs, chairs, beds, lamps, and electrical appliances.

Ernst Egli was known for his house designs and was commissioned by the engineer Ragip Devres for a project site in Bebek, Istanbul, in 1932/33. The main characteristics of the resulting house were its pure box-like configuration, light balcony structures, and white-painted modernist windows of steel and glass. The owners made many design decisions themselves during the construction of the house, being acutely

fig. 4
Small house project for the workers of the state railroad. Architect: Bekir Ihsan, 1933.[8]

fig. 5
Sketches of the modern way of living by Aptullah Ziya, 1931.[9]

fig. 6
Front facade of Weyrgasse 5, Vienna, designed by Walter Raschka and Ernst Egli. © Büşra Köroğlu.

[8] Sibel Bozdoğan, *Modernism and Building Turkish Architectural Culture in the early Republic* (Seattle: University of Washington Press, 2001), 204.

[9] Aptullah Ziya, "Binanin içinde Mimar" [Architect in the building], *Arkitekt* 1 (1931): 16–18.

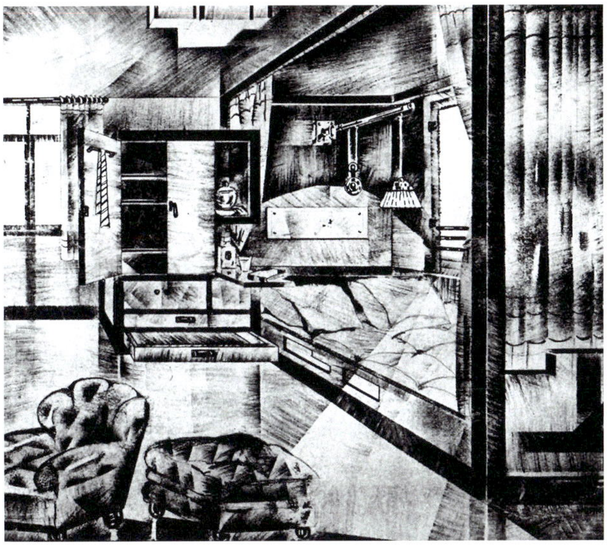

aware of their desire for a modern house that contrasted with the traditional Turkish house. In fact, at the time of the construction of the Villa Ragip Devres, there was little in the way of an advanced construction industry in Turkey; thus, the streamlined machine aesthetic had still not been introduced to the country. According to an explanation by the current owner, many construction materials and elements for the house were imported, such as Carrara marble from Italy and the door handles, the roller blinds, and the glass for the windows from Germany. Concrete and wood were supplied locally. However, from Ernst Egli's own memoirs and from what the edifice expresses, it appears that he translated his architectural approach in a contradictory way. His dilemma lay in that he was the foreign architect of an edifice that was disconnected from the norms and social structures of Turkey but he still wanted to defend the culture to which he was foreign:

> **Above all, it was the Turkish house, so peculiar in its building idea and overall conception, so surprising in its spatial arrangement, mostly delightful in its details, that I wanted to protect against the importation of cheap, run-of-the-mill houses that were being built at the time. It was enough to imitate foreign examples or to have them erected by developers. The "villa" unfortunately became the dominant element in urban and rural development. I found support from my assistant Sedad H. Eldem, who at that time was recording and preserving examples of good dwellings and had them documented.**[10]

[10] Franck, *Architektur und Politik*, 134–35.

Architecture's perennial difficulty is to resolve the wishes of both client and architect. As Philip Johnson put it in his lecture "The Seven Crutches of Modern Architecture":

"You can escape all the criticism if you can say: well, the client wanted it that way."[11] In the case of the Villa Ragip Devres, Egli was closely interpreting the client's wishes in his architecture but was not fulfilling Turkish social and architectural standards. This explains the fundamental difference between the outside and inside of the villa, the separation of private from social life. The exterior facade is a mask; on the interior, wooden panels line the inner walls. Visitors entering the house are met with a completely different ambiance to that of the exterior, in which the private space of the house gains an exhibition-like quality. The challenge of synthesizing the contemporary with the timeless, the regional with the international, had occupied Egli ever since his studies in Vienna. Earlier in Vienna, Egli had applied this approach to the functionality and representation of an apartment building. The edifice on Weyrgasse 5 and Geusaugasse (designed with Walter Raschka, Vienna, 1925; **see fig. 6**) is located within the urban fabric of late eighteenth- and early nineteenth-century architecture. Raschka and Egli developed terracotta-colored profiles for facade openings, including balconies, loggias, and bay windows. These details deviated from the typical design of the time for communal buildings and show Raschka and Egli's response to the context.

fig. 7
Residence in the manner of the British Arts and Crafts movement, before Sedad Hakki Eldem's architectural studies. © Salt Galata Research, collection of Eldem.

fig. 8
Sketch of a "National Assembly," reminiscent of Erich Mendelsohn. © Salt Galata Research, collection of Eldem.

Two Architects and Their Edifices

Sedad Hakki Eldem and Ernst Egli met on the occasion of the Milli Mimari (National Architecture) seminar at the Academy of Arts in Istanbul 1930.[12] The course aimed to explore the formal and aesthetic values of Turkish vernacular architecture, seeking to

fig. 9
Sedad Hakki Eldem, exterior views of the Summerhouse of Fethi Okyar on Princess Island. © Büşra Köroğlu.

find a new language that was not solely reliant on either modernism or traditional architecture. From this academic research, an analytical matrix of drawings of preserved vernacular houses in Turkey was generated by the students and published in three volumes by Eldem with the title *Türk Evi* (The Turkish house).[13] There must have been a reason for Eldem to dedicate his academic career to this research, when the reality of the built environment on the outskirts of the university consisted entirely of buildings that were of a very different type. Eldem sought to teach the students in his studio traditional architectural principles, such as pitched roofs, long overhanging eaves, narrow vertical 1:2 proportions, and the use of stone and brick as materials, to foster an awareness of their national identity and values. However, many graduate students struggled to integrate this knowledge into their own work due to their Westernized lifestyles.[14] Eldem, on the other hand, was a pioneer in the consistent application of his research to his own architecture. Nevertheless, he did not abandon the rational and functional principles of modernism, having gained experience from them. As illustrated in ***fig. 7 and 8***, the transformation of his ideas is visible when the sketches he produced on his trips abroad before he built in Turkey are compared with those from trips taken after.[15]

One of Eldem's extant edifices is the summerhouse constructed for Fethi Okyar on Princess Islands (1936–37). Unlike Egli, Eldem was fortunate in designing houses for his relatives; in this case the clients were his sister and brother-in-law, who expressed their wish for the house to be inspired by Japanese architecture, with particular emphasis on structural lightness and organic materials. The design is based on the enlargement of an existing country house in Viranbağ in Büyükada. In response to the clients' request, Eldem added a large semicircular hall to one side complete with a generous veranda on wooden pillars that surrounds the house on three sides. The house consists of two parts: the first is the old vineyard structure with storerooms,

[11] Philip Johnson, "The Seven Crutches of Modern Architecture," *Perspecta* 3 (1955): 43.
[12] Sibel Bozdogan, Süha Özkan, and Engin Yenal, eds., *Echoes of Sedad Eldem* (Singapore: Concept Media, 1987), 15.
[13] Franck, *Architektur und Politik*, 134–35.
[14] Bozdogan, Özkan, and Yenal, *Echoes of Sedad Eldem*, 16.
[15] Akcan Esra, *Architecture in Translation* (Durham, NC: Duke University Press, 2012), 133.

cistern, and kitchen on the lower floor and living room, bedrooms, bathroom, and toilet on the upper floor; the other is the large hall serving as the main room that is attached to the original structure ***(fig. 9)***. Eldem regarded the floor plan rather than any external views as the fundamental means to capture his ideas for the volumetric composition of the edifice; he expressed this as follows:

> **It is a striking fact that houses that are separated by hundreds of miles from each other, that have been built under greatly differing conditions, have a floor plan that, in its basic organization, is the same for all. Accordingly, we may say that the chief factor of unity and conformity in the different types of the Turkish house is their plan . . . The plan is therefore a subject of first importance in the study of the house.[16]**

The Villa Ragip Devres by Egli and the Summerhouse of Fethi Okyar by Eldem are characterized by their respective modernist expressions. Eldem did not advocate the abandonment of traditional architecture; instead, he aimed to reinterpret it in modern terms. In Egli's case, his clients shared the admiration that many upper-class families had for the machine aesthetic, with its association to clean, hygienic surfaces and social progress. Egli was concerned with reforming Turkish architecture not only by adopting sparse cubic configurations on the exterior but also by including divans as the classic ottoman type of seating, as well as the low *tabla* (table). Comparing the sketch of a room with *à la turka* hearth and divan by Eldem with a photograph of Villa Ragip Devres ***(see figs. 10-11)*** unveils a compelling similarity, indicating Egli's deliberate efforts to incorporate Turkish living styles into his architectural design.

fig. 10
Ernst Egli, Villa Ragip Devres, 1935. © Salt Galata Research, collection of Eldem.

fig. 11
Sedad Hakki Eldem, room with *à la turka* hearth and divan, sketch from early notebook, 1927. © Salt Galata Research, collection of Eldem.

[16] Sedad Eldem, *Türk Evi Plan Tipleri* [Turkish house types] (Pulhan Matbaası, 1954), 216.

Internationalism vs. Nationalism

In Turkey during the 1930s, the use of characteristic elements of vernacular architecture changed from pitched to flat roofs and from vertical windows with a 1:2 ratio to horizontal strip windows across the facade. Their application might be seen to be out of place. Yet not only key elements of a style but also its underlying ideology, its architects from Europe, and a range of building materials like roofing sheets, plaster, and tiles were imported to the country. Despite their high cost and concerns about their quality, these materials were preferred over local products. Eldem criticized the disregard for Turkey's economic structure and the trend towards Westernization that resulted in buildings ignoring reliable construction methods and regional cultural characteristics. In Turkey during the 1920s, flat roof tiles had to be imported from the West. Subsequently, from 1931 onwards, a new roofing system known by the trade name Ksilolit[17] was widely used.[18] There were few complaints about the roof shape, though the cost of importing construction material from abroad was an economical issue. More importantly, Eldem was defending visual unity to avoid disorder in the formal language of buildings. He was teaching about houses with pitched roofs, as illustrated from the archive in his studio at the Academy of Arts ***(see fig. 12)***: wide overhanging eaves, and narrow vertical windows.

Meanwhile Egli, following the path from German modernity visible in the Villa Ragip Devres ***(see fig. 13)***, favored the flat roof in his horizontal expression. Another significant difference between Egli and Eldem was that Egli prioritized the functionality and practicality of a building with respect to factors like climate and zoning, whereas Eldem focused on the formal and typological aspects of his work by using local materials, structural systems, and architectural elements.

[17] Ksilolit was the Turkish spelling for xylolite. In the mid-twentieth century, xylolite flooring technology was widely used for floors, but also for stairs, etc. The basis of "xylolite screed" is ground magnesium oxide (e.g., suitably burnt magnesite) and magnesium chloride solution with the addition of fine-grained, mostly organic, fillers and dyes. It was mainly used for jointless floors, as a base for linoleum, for coating walls and stairs in interiors, etc. The material was applied to the underlying concrete, then to the brick substrate or to the wooden floor. The substrate must always be completely dry and must not contain lime components. The lower xylolite base layer of natural color was laid 15–20 mm thick, on top of which the upper xylolite layer (natural or colored) was laid 5–12 mm thick after proper drying (it had to be loadbearing). The surface was treated with xylolite oil and polished with special waxes. Xylolite floors were essentially the forerunners of today's poured floors. See original Czech description at https://www.devasro.cz/xylolit.php.

[18] İnci Aslanoglu, "Evaluation of Architectural Developments in Turkey Within the Socio-economic and Cultural Framework of the 1923–38 Period," *O.D.T.Ü. Mimarlık Fakültesi Dergisi Cilt* 7, no. 2 (1986): 23.

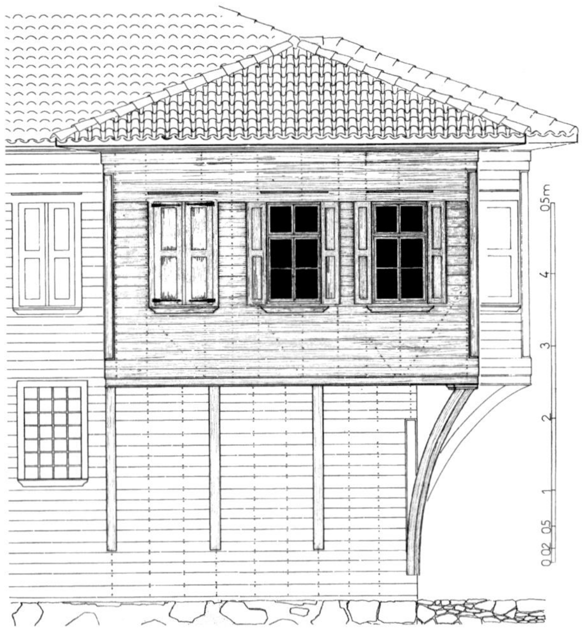

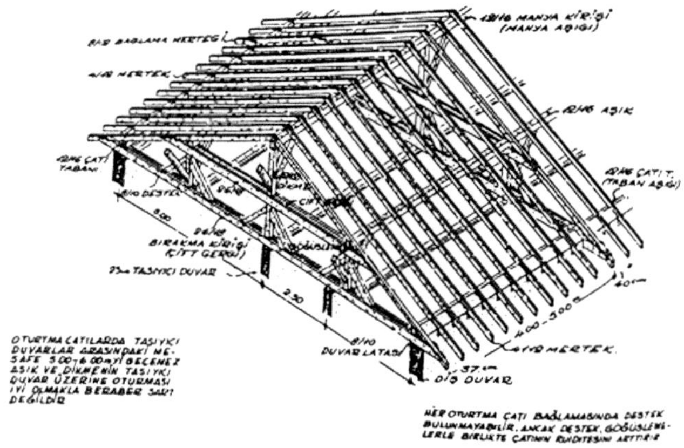

fig. 12
Research of vernacular architecture drawn by students of Sedad Hakki Eldem.[19]

Epilogue

The two villa designs reveal the challenge posed to Turkish architecture at a time when change was decreed by both the political leadership and the architectural profession. Architecture in Turkey was to be liberated from its traditional origins to reset the present in modern, foreign terms. However, the two architects struggled in a way reminiscent of the mythical Tower of Babel: despite the common aim of building a unified architecture, all ended in a confusion of multiple languages. Metaphorically, Turkey found itself in a similar situation. In a period of ideological turbulence, many ideas were imported and were expected to be captured and applied in architecture.

The examples of the Villa Ragip Devres and the Summerhouse of Fethi Okyar demonstrate the architect's influence on the critical potential of architectural types. For the summerhouse, Eldem aimed to strike a balance by preserving continuity with vernacular traditions while introducing elements of formal unity. His approach can be described as amenable, wherein he criticized the unreserved adoption of architectural modernism without completely rejecting it. Eldem emphasized a floor plan–based approach using existing Turkish house types by resynthesizing them with modern characteristics. He perceived the floor plan as a fundamental base for his ideas, instead of the facade view or the volume of the edifice. In contrast to this, Egli exhibited a sensitivity to both the physical and the cultural context, taking into account factors such as climate, zoning, and function. Egli's work was founded on technical and practical issues; he ultimately sought the timeless essence of the architectural heritage of a people or nation. While these qualities are latent in the Villa Ragip Devres, this villa also embodies an antithesis to Turkish tradition with its enveloping balconies, steel posts, flat roof, and panoramic windows, symbolizing the adoption of the Western way of life to which numerous people aspired. Eldem had copious exposure to Western lifestyles while he studied and worked abroad, gaining work experience under Hans Poelzig and Le Corbusier.

[19] Sedad Hakki Eldem, *Türk Evi Osmanlı Dönem*, 2 (Istanbul: Güzel Sanatlar Matbaası A.Ş., 1984), 237.

fig. 13
Villa Ragip Devres, built by Ernst Egli (1932–33). © Büşra Köroğlu.

His awareness transcended specific references; he displayed the selective intelligence of adopting what he considered to be appropriate, not looking too far but rather right in front of his eyes, recognizing the significance of the local, uncelebrated Turkish houses. Conversely, a foreign architect like Ernst Egli being invited to criticize the architectural production of Turkey before subsequently recognizing the potential within the nation's architecture and diverging from his initial mission is quite unexpected.

The comparative study of the two houses has revealed that architecture is a multifaceted art form, a manifestation of subjective perspectives. As John Gloag states: "Buildings cannot lie; they tell the truth directly or by implication about those who made or used them."[20] While over time buildings inevitably undergo processes of transformation for functional, aesthetic, and formal reasons, each edifice still articulates its fundamental essence and significance independent of any interventions made by its owner or by an architect, thereby affording objective analysis, proper evaluation, and fundamental criticism.

[20] John Gloag, *The Architectural Interpretation of History* (London: A & C Black, 1975), 1–2.

Biography

Büşra Köroğlu completed her bachelor's and master's degree in architecture at the Vienna University of Technology. Her diploma thesis dealt with the revitalization of a shipyard in Istanbul on the Golden Horn (2017). During and after her studies, she worked in different architectural offices: Tabanlioglu Architects (Istanbul), PLOV, AWG, and Roger Baumeister Architekten (Vienna). Since 2020, she has been working as a research assistant at the Institute Raum und Gestalt of TU Graz. Currently, she is working on her PhD, focusing on the advertisements for building materials published in the architectural magazine *Arkitekt* in Turkey.

The Ethical Dimension: Inner Criticality in Architecture

Juhani Pallasmaa

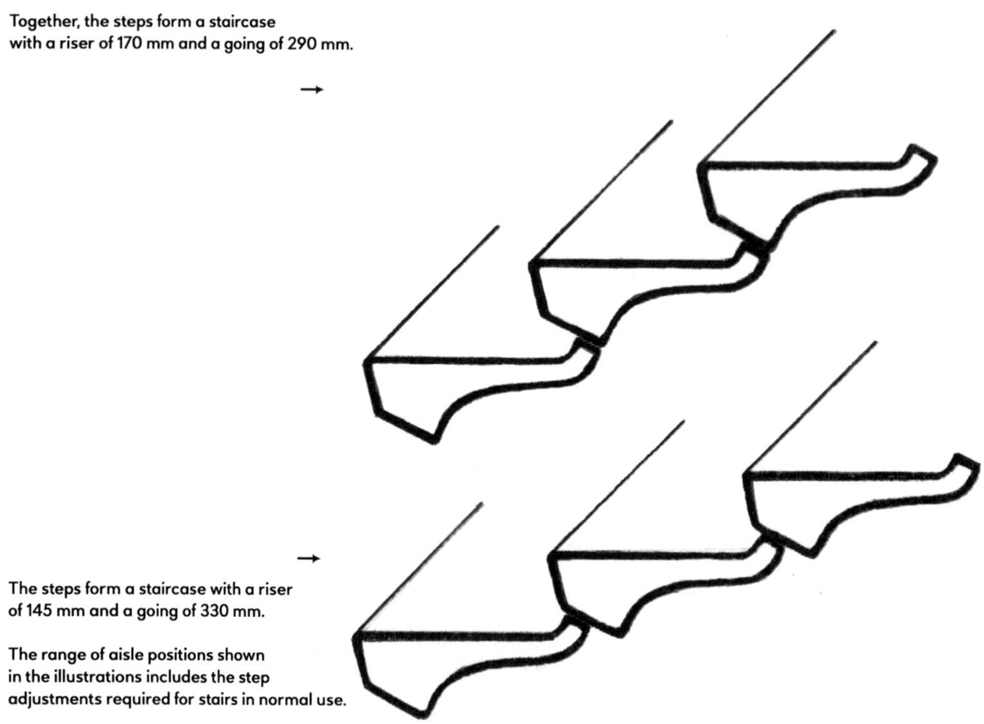

fig. 1
Alvar Aalto, proposal for "a flexible stair," theoretical project, 1940 (transcribed and translated).

Construction and criticism first appear as exclusive approaches: Doesn't engagement in a building project imply an accepting and supportive position of the given task? Isn't the act of building always grounded in the positive attitude of agreement, whereas the act of criticism implies evaluation, questioning, and a critical distance? Doesn't design work imply insideness, while criticism calls for outsideness? As a consequence of the inherently positive and accepting nature of the building task, Built Criticism, or critical building, is an a priori attitude in relation to the conditions, aims, and explicit or inherent values and consequences of the building task, while verbal architectural criticism is an a posteriori action.

In addition to the external criticism, there is a necessary internal ethical position of the architect in the design process itself—this is *The Ethical Function of Architecture* (1997), to quote the title of the significant book by philosopher Karsten Harries.[1]

keywords:

Alvar Aalto, critique of modernism, ethics, alternative traditions, extended rationalism, collage

The critical or ethical judgment also concerns the aesthetic and stylistic realms—this usually concerns "the truth" of the architectural expression. Here the categories of aesthetic and ethical interact. As the Nobel laureate poet Joseph Brodsky suggests: "Man is first an aesthetic creature before he is an ethical one. We are aesthetic beings before we become ethical beings."[2] During the past few years, the poet's suggestion of the primacy of the aesthetic criteria has gained new credibility from biological studies of the role of aesthetic qualities and judgments in mate selection among animals—an aesthetic choice seems to be part of the selective systems of nature to the degree that bowerbirds have been found to use false perspective in their constructions in order to strengthen the desired visual effect of their bowers.[3]

The interweaving of the aesthetic and the ethical in architectural thinking is exemplified by a statement of the architect and engineer Auguste Perret (1874–1954): "The builder who hides any part of the building's frame, abandons the only permissible, and at the same time, the most beautiful embellishment of architecture. The one who hides a loadbearing column makes a mistake. The one who builds a fake column commits a crime."[4] This ethical principle is an example of criticism internalized as an architect's moral code.

Projecting moral values on architecture may turn into crude moralist exaggerations, as in the case of Le Corbusier's manifesto on the implicit "moral" value of whiteness: "Whiteness is extremely moral. Let us assume that there would exist a decree that would require that all rooms in Paris must be white-washed. I claim that this would be a really notable police measure and a *tour de force* of high morality, a sign of a great people."[5]

The Interplay of the Aesthetic and the Ethic

Major stylistic shifts in the development of architecture and its stylistic codes have usually also had an ethical or moral grounding; that is, stylistic or aesthetic choices have frequently been supported by moral argumentation, as in the case of Le Corbusier above. In 1849, John Ruskin (1819–1900) was even concerned that the emphasis on

1 Karsten Harries, *The Ethical Function of Architecture* (Cambridge, MA, and London, UK: The MIT Press, 1997).
2 Joseph Brodsky, "An Immodest Proposal," in *On Grief and Reason* (New York: Farrar, Straus and Giroux, 1997), 208.
3 Richard O. Prum, *The Evolution of Beauty: How Darwin's Forgotten Theory of Mate Choice Shapes the Animal World—and Us* (New York: Anchor Books, 2018).
4 Auguste Perret, "Aineksia rakennustaiteen teoriaan" [Ingredients for a theory of architecture], *Arkkitehti*, 9/10 (1949): 29.
5 Le Corbusier, *L'Art décoratif d'aujourd'hui* (Paris: Edition Crès & Cie, 1925), 193.

individual genius destroyed the continuous fabric of cities: "A day never passes without our hearing our architects called upon to be original and to invent a new style."[6] In 1913, Adolf Loos (1870–1933) published an influential declaration entitled "Ornament and Crime" and even wrote against architectural invention and originality, seeing primary value in following the codes of traditions: "The best form is there already and no one should be afraid of using it, even if the basic idea for it came from someone else. Enough of geniuses and their originality."[7] In the cities of today, where new buildings compete hysterically for visibility and recognition at the cost of environmental integrity, we can understand the early concerns of both Ruskin and Loos. Individual expressions have historically been contextualized and harmonized by traditions and styles, and the rejection of a unifying style has reinforced the disappearance of environmental unity. The evolution of modernism, the postmodern counter-movement, and the later stylistic and individual artistic orientations have frequently been supported by moral and ethical arguments. The supporters of modern expression used these same arguments to criticize postmodernism.

Alternative Traditions

In his book *The Other Tradition of Modern Architecture: The Uncompleted Project* (1995),[8] Colin St John Wilson—an educator and the architect of the British Library, who was also one of the influential architectural writers of the end of the last century who had a clear ethical emphasis in his judgments and writings—presented Alvar Aalto, Hans Scharoun, Hugo Häring, and Frank Lloyd Wright as representatives of a contextually and psychologically oriented "resistance" within the modern movement. Wilson presents the work of these architects as a concrete, Built Criticism, or a modern counter-movement in relation to the prevailing International Style of the period. Häring and Scharoun did not actively take part in verbalized criticism, but in their frequent writings and lectures, Wright and Aalto explicitly presented their architectures as critical and synthetic ideologies against simplistic functionalism. Both connected their works with the rich and associative formality of the organic world. Regardless of the quality of their writings, their Built Criticisms are, however, even more convincing than their texts.

After having enthusiastically embraced functionalist ideology at the end of the 1920s with the main office of the *Turun Sanomat* newspaper in Turku, echoing contemporaneous works of Le Corbusier, Alvar Aalto produced one of the finest examples of functionalist design in the Paimio Sanatorium of 1929–32. Already in this early project, Aalto analyzed carefully the experiences and feelings of the users and began to develop an alternative modernism by fusing softer, more integrated, and formally more complex qualities in his work. This became even clearer a couple of years later in the fully integrated quality of the Viipuri Library of 1927–35, such as the shadowless natural illumination of the library hall and the undulating acoustical wooden ceiling of the lecture hall. By the mid-1930s, Aalto was already engaged in his contextually and historically grounded, environmentally conscious, and experientially and psychologically rooted multisensory architecture, conceived for "the little man"[9]—the anonymous user of the buildings.

In the revised edition of his canonical presentation of functionalism, *Space, Time and Architecture: The Growth of a New Tradition*,[10] Sigfried Giedion presents Aalto as the hero of the emergent organicist approach and celebrates the echoes of nature in his work, both in his architecture and in his product design. Instead of accepting the prevailing techno-rationalist approach, Aalto wanted to defend "the little man" against "the violence of technology,"[11] which was an opposing attitude to the prevailing uncritical enthusiasm for technology.

[6] John Ruskin, as quoted in Alain de Botton, *The Architecture of Happiness* (New York: Vintage Books, 2008), 183.
[7] Adolf Loos, as quoted in Botton, *Architecture of Happiness*, 183.
[8] Colin St John Wilson, *The Other Tradition of Modern Architecture: The Uncompleted Project* (London: Academy Editions, 1995).
[9] Alvar Aalto, "Speech at the Hundred-Year Jubilee of the Jyväskylä Lycée" (1958), in *Sketches: Alvar Aalto*, ed. Göran Schildt, trans. Stuart Wrede (Cambridge, MA, and London, UK: The MIT Press, 1985), 164.
[10] Sigfried Giedion, *Space, Time and Architecture: The Growth of a New Tradition* (Cambridge: MA: Harvard University Press, 1952).
[11] "The violence of technology." The source of this quotation is unknown.

Alvar Aalto's Extended Rationalism

Aalto was a rare architect, who developed his criticality of the International Style in both his design and his writings. "It is not the rationalization itself that was wrong in the first and now past period of modern architecture. The wrongness lies in the fact that the rationalization has not gone deep enough. Instead of fighting rational mentality, the newest phase of modern architecture tries to project rational methods from the technical field out to human and psychological fields . . . Technical Functionalism is correct only if enlarged to cover even the psychophysical field. That is the only way to humanize architecture,"[12] Aalto argued, continuing: "My aim was to show that the real Rationalism means dealing with all questions related to the object concerned, and to take a rational attitude also to demands that are often dismissed as vague issues of individual taste, but which are shown by more detailed analysis to be derived partly from neurophysiology and partly from psychology. Salvation can be achieved only or primarily via an extended concept of Rationalism."[13] In his significant book *Survival Through Design* of 1954, Richard Neutra (1892–1970) expanded architectural thinking to the new discipline of neuroscience. I found a letter from the mid-1950s in Aalto's correspondence, in which he acquired Neutra's address, but I have not found any indication that he would have actually contacted Neutra. Following the visions of Neutra and Aalto, the rational ground of understanding architecture has been meaningfully extended to neuroscience during the past couple of decades; this interaction has been advanced by the Academy of Neuroscience for Architecture (ANFA). It is an example of the "extended Rationalism" suggested by Aalto in the mid-1930s.

Aalto's numerous projects, built and unbuilt, are concrete examples of "Built Criticism" against the dehumanizing quasi-rational characteristics of the prevailing reductive practices in planning and construction. Aalto himself emphasized the value of his built projects and even wrote that what he has written or said could well be forgotten: "An architect is a man who has to deal with form and material, and what he says does not mean a damned thing. What counts is what he does. What I think of architecture you can see in my work, and what I say you can just forget."[14] This is an outright declaration for Built Criticism, which Aalto made in his lecture at the Architectural Association in London in 1950. Most often, however, Aalto provided a critical materialized work and a verbal, theoretically grounded criticism side by side. Also, his series of bent wood furniture arose in parallel with his sharp critique of the unergonomic hardness of the metal tube furniture that was fashionable among modernists. Aalto also demonstrated one of his favorite themes, "flexible standardization," both verbally and through a concrete design. One of his practical proposals was his idea of 1940 for a prefabricated unit for a standard "flexible stair," as a single prefabricated stair element could be used for all riser/tread breath variations.[15] This was Aalto's input towards the topical development of building standards and the establishment of the Finnish Institute of Standards during the war years.

Villa Mairea, Aalto's Demonstration of a New Architecture

In the Villa Mairea (1938–39), the second home for a wealthy and progressive industrialist and art collector couple in the countryside of Noormarkku, Western Finland, Aalto finally developed a unique synthesis, which fuses nature and artifice, anonymous traditions and modernity, and visuality and tactility, as well as art and architecture, in a uniquely sensory, sensuous, intimate, associative, and eroticized architecture. Sigfried Giedion, the ultimate spokesman and critic of modernism, visited the newly finalized house and underlined its unique sensuality and intimacy in his phone call from Villa Mairea to Aalto at his office in Helsinki: "Dear Alvar, this is not a house, this is a love poem."[16]

[12] Alvar Aalto, "The Humanizing of Architecture," in Schildt, *Sketches*, 77, 78.

[13] Schildt, *Sketches*, 50.

[14] Alvar Aalto, "Lecture at the Architectural Association, London, 20 June, 1950," in *Alvar Aalto in His Own Words*, ed. Göran Schildt (Helsinki: Otava, 1997), 184.

[15] The idea for the flexible stair was published as a sample sheet of standards for building components at the Standardization Institute of the Finnish Association of Architects. *Rakennustaide ja standardi: jälleenrakentamisen ydinkysymyksiä* [Architecture and standard: Core issues of reconstruction] (Helsinki, 1942).

[16] Kristian Gullichsen in conversation with the author, August 14, 1993.

fig. 2
Alvar Aalto, Villa Mairea, Noormarkku, 1938–39. Arrival view from south. Photo: Rauno Träskelin.

fig. 3
Alvar Aalto, Villa Mairea. The living room, main stair, and view of the sauna section and pool across the yard. Photo: Rauno Träskelin.

The Villa Mairea is an astonishingly rich tour de force of architectural and spatial composition, formal inventions, improvisations, detailing, and treatments of materials. The prosaic structural reality of black-painted steel columns on the ground floor, for instance, has been poetized by grouping them singly, doubly, and triply into a playful, haptic, and rhythmic articulation, varyingly tied by rattan bindings, to evoke a Japanese atmosphere; even structural elements turn into images of poetic narrative of theme and variation. There is even a single concrete column in the middle of the library without any structural or functional motivation. Aalto's main assistant in the project, the Swiss architect Paul Bernoulli, revealed to the current author that the construction work was almost finished when Aalto unexpectedly asked his assistant to purchase an extra steel column, which was placed at a skewed angle underneath the studio part without any structural function.[17] The motivation was clearly to complicate the structural reading of the facade and give a diagonal push to the overall image of the house; this could be seen as Aalto's comment to Auguste Perret's moral rule about a fake column. Practically all parts of the house have been elevated to an emotive and poetic role. The deliberate confusion of structural elements serves the purpose of emphasizing the continuity of spatial flow, abstracting and poetizing the construction elements beyond their prosaic functional or structural purposes.

This architecture is also in continuous dialogue or mirroring with the pine forest and the garden outdoors. The dense vertical grouping of wooden poles around the main stair in the corner of the living room effectively continues the accidental rhythms of the forest inside the house and projects an inviting and poetizing image of a gazebo. The oppositions of outdoors and indoors, objects and contexts, utility and poetry are eliminated. Several details, such as the free-form indentation in the corner of the fireplace, appear as products of natural processes rather than of human construction. This detail also seems to refer to the contemporaneous sculptures of Aalto's friend Hans Arp: the negative form appears as a mold for an imaginary Arp sculpture.

[17] Paul Bernoulli in conversation with the author, May 21, 1989.

Modernity was obsessed with a futuristic view of time. Numerous sketches of the design process reveal Aalto's desire to have creepers take over the house as a metaphor of time and duration, and the ultimate power of nature over man-made constructions. He was one of the modernist architects of the twentieth century who continued the tradition of building eroded ruins as stages of passing time, which was fashionable in the early nineteenth century. The overall experience of the Villa Mairea also resembles that of a walk in a forest, in which an immense number of stimuli and details are integrated into the embodied perception in movement; here again, the spatial experience is woven with a temporal suggestion. There is no given center point; the perceiver themself is the moving center of the experience, which unfolds as an unbroken flow of observations and encounters, much as one would experience a walk in a forest.

fig. 4a
Alvar Aalto, Villa Mairea. Corner of the fireplace. Photo: Rauno Träskelin.

fig. 4b
Hans Arp, physiognomic sculpture, 1936.

Aalto's Artist Friends and the Art of Collage

Aalto was a friend of several of the Continental masters in modern art: Fernand Léger, Hans Arp, Georges Braque, Constantin Brancusi, Max Ernst, László Moholy-Nagy, and Alexander Calder. Giedion makes a comment on Aalto's relationship with the arts: "Aalto recognizes modern art as a great reservoir which, though often invisible, provides the decisive power for his own creativeness."[18] In his project description of the Villa Mairea, Aalto himself refers to the inspiration that he has found in art: "It all began in art."[19] It is also significant to remember that Aalto painted all his life, although he did not want to exhibit his paintings independently of his architectural work. The Villa Mairea is very close in its compositional and emotive strategies, as well as in numerous details, to the art of collage; it could even be described as a collection of architectural collages. The tiny wooden gate next to the swimming pool is even a Duchampean "ready-made"; Aalto had the gate built in accordance with a sketch of a traditional Swiss farm gate with a wooden locking mechanism from the sketchbook of his Swiss assistant's father, Hans Bernoulli.

[18] Giedion, *Space, Time and Architecture*, 455.

[19] Göran Schildt, *Alvar Aalto kuvataiteilijana* [Alvar Aalto as a visual artist], exh. cat., ed. Juhani Pallasmaa (Noormarkku: Mairea-Säätiö, 1982), 8. In the project description of the Villa Mairea in *Arkkitehti* journal in 1939, Aalto confesses that the spatial idea of the house is grounded in ideas deriving from the art of painting.

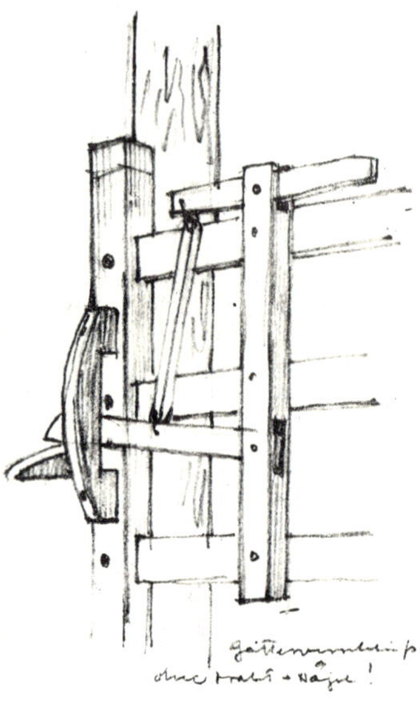

fig. 5a
Alvar Aalto, oil painting, 1945–47. Oil on canvas, 30 × 38 cm.

fig. 5b
Alvar Aalto, oil painting, 1945. Oil on canvas, 35.5 × 43.5 cm.

fig. 6a
Traditional locking mechanism of a Swiss farm gate. Drawing: Hans Bernoulli.

fig. 6b
Alvar Aalto, the garden gate at Villa Mairea next to the pool.

The collage idea does not stop at visual details, as the Villa Mairea also includes entire collaged scenes, and material treatments from Finnish vernacular (particularly in the sauna wing) and, quite surprisingly, from classical Japanese architecture. The Japanese influence becomes evident knowing that the Japanese ambassador to Finland in the 1930s and his wife were close friends of the Aaltos, and the couple donated several books on Japanese architecture to their architect friends. Aalto never visited Japan, but he received firsthand experiences of Japanese architecture in the Japanese teahouse Zui-Ki-Tei (The House of the Promising Light),[20] which was built in the gardens of the Museum of Ethnography in Stockholm in 1935 and became a deep influence for many of the leading Nordic architects. The postwar architecture in all Nordic countries, but especially in Denmark and Finland, was inspired by Japanese architecture; this influence lasted through the 1960s and was fused with a Miesian constructivism. For a few years before beginning to work on the Villa Mairea, Aalto had already been a member of the Finnish-Japanese Society, established in 1935, and spoke and wrote enthusiastically about the Japanese virtuosity in creating variety

[20] *Tehuset Zui-Ki-Tei, Det löftesrika ljusets boning* (The House of the Promising Light), Folkens Museum Etnografiska, Stockholm, 1996.

fig. 7a
Symbolic Japanese garden form with a miniature hillock.

fig. 7b
The northern end of the Villa Mairea fuses with the surrounding forest. The pool, sauna, gentle earth mound, and vegetation create a metaphoric miniature landscape. Photo: Rauno Träskelin.

within limited materials and forms. As a curious indication of his deep approval of Japanese aesthetics, Aalto even occasionally wore a red-brown kimono at his office in the mornings; the kimono was a gift from the Japanese ambassador couple.[21] Paul Bernoulli also testified to me that Aalto had brought Tetsuro Yoshida's book *Das Japanische Wohnhaus* of 1935[22] to the office to be consulted in the design of the Villa Mairea, especially the Japanese-influenced flower room and the diminutive landscape feature next to the swimming pool.

Whereas modernism generally aimed at a logical and unified elaboration of the main architectural idea, Aalto deliberately created discontinuities and fractures, and seemed to shift unexpectedly into new associations, keys, and rhythms. He kept juxtaposing opposites, such as: romantic/rational, modernist/vernacular, novel/traditional, Western/Japanese, natural/man-made, and free-form/geometric. Aalto suppressed simple logic and consistency of structure and articulation in order to evoke an air of adventure, poetic expectation, discovery, privacy, and secrecy. The Villa Mairea is subordinated into individual thematic entities in the same way as a play or a musical composition is divided into separate acts or movements—instead of continuity and unification, Aalto creates discontinuities and separations. There are late improvisations (akin to the extra diagonal steel column), such as the removable glass and wood modules between the ceiling and the top of the bookcases, to seal off the library acoustically from the living room; Mr. Gullichsen, the client, needed acoustic intimacy for his business conversations in the library, and that need was identified only after the house was already in use.

Aalto clearly questions the fundamental stylistic attitudes of modernity, such as clarity of gestalt, unambiguity, and the logic of thematic elaboration. He achieves this by creating "impure" collisions and juxtapositions, and by fusing items from different conceptual categories, such as combining a fireplace with a staircase on the terrace in the corner of the dining room, man-made and organic, modernistic and traditional. The sauna door divided into two halves, for instance, is covered by a pattern of wood splints, which makes one remember peasant splint baskets of the past. Deviating from the predictable and stylistic orthodoxy, he rejects the self-evident and gains a world of freshness and surprise. In his own words: "The goal was to avoid artificial architectural rhythm in the building."[23] Here the notion "artificial" seems to signify "forced" and imply simplistically rational and linear logic.

[21] Paul Bernoulli in conversation with the author, May 21, 1989.

[22] Tetsuro Yoshida, *Das Japanische Wohnhaus* (Tübingen: Verlag Ernst Wasmuth, 1935). Paul Bernoulli told the author about the use of this book as a source on May 21, 1989.

[23] Alvar Aalto, Villa Mairea, project description, *Arkkitehti*, 9, 193, as reprinted in *Alvar Aalto: Villa Mairea 1938–39* (Noormarkku: Mairea Foundation, 1998), 31.

House and Guitar: The Mentality of Play

The kidney-shaped swimming pool of the Villa Mairea has usually been interpreted as a metaphor of a Finnish forest lake. No doubt this is a pertinent reference for the shape, as the Finnish landscapes, lakes, and forests were important images in Aalto's work; his countless glass designs are also associated with the imagery of water. The design of his famous Finland Pavilion at the New York World's Fair of 1939 was based on the flowing imagery of the northern lights, or aurora borealis. But the shape of the pool is certainly also related to the frequent appearance of the amoeba shape in contemporary art, almost as a metaphor for the emancipation of architecture from its rigid rectangular framings and perspectival constructions. The shape has female connotations, too, and it is reminiscent of the characteristic form of the sound box of a string instrument—violin or guitar—in cubist paintings and collages. The bowl shape of the swimming pool also echoes the negative nest shape in the corner of the fireplace opposite the pool across the courtyard, which also appears as a mold for a fictitious Hans Arp sculpture.

The stringed instrument, with its soundboard, which became almost an obsession or fetish for the cubists, also evokes an image of the female body. The still lifes by Georges Braque and Pablo Picasso from the mid-1920s onwards repeatedly feature this image. A conspicuous detail in these images of stringed instruments is the representation of the strings as a distinct set of straight parallel lines. The overall plan of the Villa Mairea exhibits similarities to cubist still lifes with an image of a string instrument; the extended roof of the sauna being the fingerboard and the pool the soundboard. Underneath this terrace roof at the corner of the service wing there is a puzzling set of four horizontal, oval-sectioned bars, laboriously cast in concrete. When I asked about their function or meaning, Paul Bernoulli laughingly replied: "They are part of Alvar's play and poet's joy."[24] Indeed, they can be seen as the strings of Aalto's guitar collage

fig. 8
Zui-Ki-Tei, the Japanese teahouse built at the National Museum of Ethnography in Stockholm, 1935. The teahouse was destroyed by fire in 1969, but was rebuilt in 1990.

fig. 9
Alvar Aalto, Villa Mairea, the flower room. Note the "Japanese" suspended shelves behind the stair leading to the studio. Photo: Rauno Träskelin.

fig. 10
Alvar Aalto's first application of free form: the bandstand for the Itämeri Restaurant, Turku, 1929. The undulating profile became one of Aalto's recognizable images in designs ranging from glass vases to interiors of concert and opera houses.

fig. 11
Modular coordination of the Villa Mairea (study by Juhani Pallasmaa). Regardless of the general feeling of constant improvisation, the project is coordinated by a square modular grid. In the sauna section the grid has been shifted.

fig. 12
Villa Mairea, the sauna terrace with an air of traditional Finnish constructions. The juxtaposition of images of farming traditions and international modernism creates an essential emotive dialogue. Photo: Rauno Träskelin.

[24] Paul Bernoulli in conversation with the author, May 21, 1989.

[25] Alvar Aalto, "Experimental House, Muuratsalo," in Schildt, *Sketches*, 115.

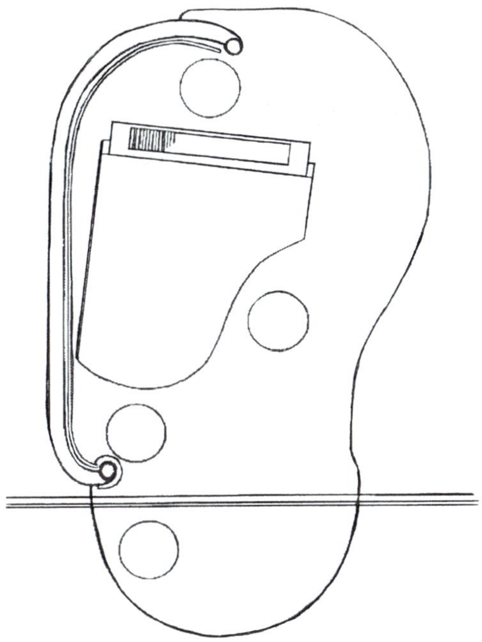

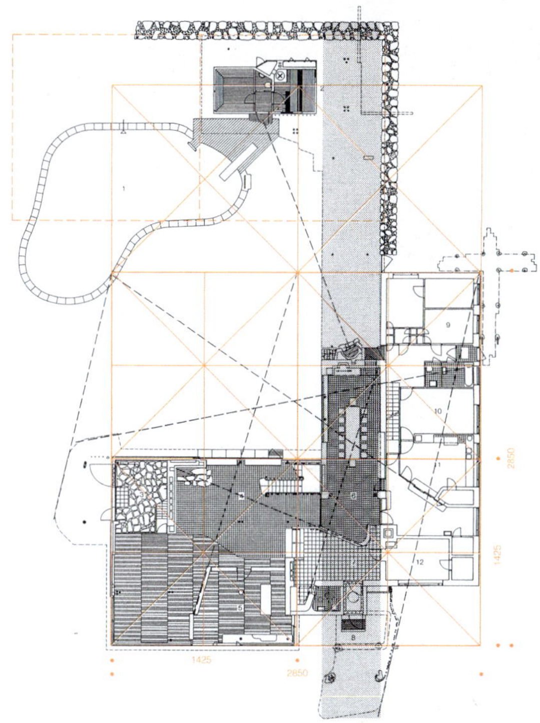

in his intellectual play with his cubist friends in Paris. Here Aalto also questions the usual seriousness of design and suggests a margin for play or even a joke. Aalto's humor can be compared with the sculptural joke by his friend Alexander Calder—a portrait of the architect made of a kitchen tool.

In fact, the strings cast in concrete had their origin in the tensioned cables shown in Aalto's drawing dated April 14, 1938, in which the entire terrace canopy is suspended from the corner of the service wing by a set of four steel cables. The real structural cables transformed into the metaphoric strings of a cubist guitar, cast in concrete.

The objective of this somewhat lighthearted paragraph of mine is to concretize Aalto's interest in play and his ties with Continental modern art. In one of his later articles, Aalto wrote about "the mentality of play" as an essential element of design in our calculating and utilitarian age: "Not until architecture's structural elements, the forms logically derived from them, and our empirical knowledge are modified by what we seriously can call play, or art, will we be proceeding in the right direction. Technology and economy must always be combined with life-enriching charm."[25] Regrettably, since the days of Alvar Aalto, architecture has lost its invigorating interaction with art and "the art of play." The distance between, or even separation of, architecture and art today underlines the seriousness of Aalto's playful built critique.

The Role of Play in Design

In his most brilliant essay "The Trout and the Mountain Stream" of 1947, Aalto reveals his use of subconscious sketches in his working process:

> **When I designed the city library of Viipuri . . . I pursued the solution with the help of primitive sketches. From some kind of fantastic mountain landscapes with cliffs lit up by suns in different positions, I gradually arrived at the concept for the library building . . . The childish sketches have only an indirect connection with the architectural conception, but they tied together the section and the plan with each other and created a kind of unity of horizontal and vertical structures . . . It is just an example of how my own instinctive belief has led me to the fact that architecture and art have a common source, which in certain sense is abstract, but which despite this is based on the knowledge and the data that we have stored in our subconscious.[26]**

Again, in our time, architecture has turned increasingly conscious, calculated, and rational, but here Aalto celebrates the freedoms of play, imagination, free association, and the unconscious.

Aalto's words on the Swedish architect Erik Gunnar Asplund—his early idol—and the architect's Skandia Cinema in Stockholm of 1923, apply directly to himself and the Villa Mairea:

> **I had the impression that this was an architecture where ordinary systems hadn't served as the parameters. Here the point of departure was man, with all the innumerable nuances of his emotional life and nature . . . Another architecture has arrived, which builds for man and essentially regards people as a social phenomenon, while at the same time taking science and research as the point of departure . . . But beyond that a newer architecture has made its appearance, one that continues to employ the tools of the social sciences, but also includes the study of psychological problems—"the unknown human" in his totality. The latter has proved that the art of architecture continues to have inexhaustible resources and means which flow directly from nature and the inexplicable reactions of human emotions.[27]**

Here, Aalto directly points at his own sources of inspiration.

In my sincere judgment, architecture is today in its deepest crises since the emergence of modernity. Architecture is losing its cultural and artistic dimensions, autonomy and societal authority, while turning increasingly into an uncritical technical, economic, and manipulatively aestheticized service. Today, architecture once again needs forceful, sincere, and independent criticality—built, unbuilt, as well as verbal. And we architects need to see our craft again, not as tasks to do uncritically what we have been asked to do, but to act as autonomous, critical, and ethical individuals. Our task is to reconnect architecture with the realities of the human experiential and existential life, and the emotive and poetic realm of the arts. Through the thinking and work of Alvar Aalto, I have given you an example of a master architect's simultaneously powerful and gentle Built Criticism.

I conclude with the reiteration of the essential statement from Alvar Aalto's essay "The Humanizing of Architecture" of 1940, during the time of World War II:

[26] Alvar Aalto, "The Trout and the Mountain Stream," in Schildt, *Sketches*, 97.
[27] Alvar Aalto, "E.G. Asplund in Memoriam," in Schildt, *Sketches*, 66.
[28] Aalto, "Humanizing of Architecture," 63.

As opposed to the view according to which using established forms and making new ones uniform are the only paths to architectural harmony and the successful control of construction technology, the purpose of everything I have said is to underline that variety and growth reminiscent of natural organic life are the very essence of architecture. I would like to say that this is ultimately the only true style in architecture.[28]

Biography

Juhani Pallasmaa (b. 1936), architect, professor emeritus, writer, lives in Helsinki. Architectural practice from 1962 to 2022; Rector of the Institute of Industrial Design, Director of the Museum of Finnish Architecture, Professor and Dean of the Faculty of Architecture, Helsinki University of Technology; several visiting professorships in the USA; teaching and lecturing at numerous universities in Europe, North and South America, Africa, Asia and Australia; member of countless juries, including the Pritzker Architecture Prize 2008–14.

Pallasmaa has published 75 books and 980 essays including: *Rootedness*, *The Embodied Image*, *The Thinking Hand*, *The Architecture of Image: existential space in cinema*, and *The Eyes of the Skin*. The writings have been translated into 36 languages.

Honorary member of SAFA, AIA and RIBA, and recipient of six honorary doctorates and numerous Finnish and international awards.

Early Paradigms

Transportation Architecture as Public Symbols: São Bento Subway Station in São Paulo, Brazil

Luísa Augusta Gabriela Teixeira Gonçalves

fig. 1
São Bento Station with the metallic pergola in front and São Bento Monastery behind. Source: Photo by Marcos Kiyoto, 2024.

The subway station of São Bento, located in the historical downtown area of São Paulo, is an exemplary public space and architectural design. It is an architecturally significant subway station with historical and cultural value, located near several important landmarks. The members of Marcello Fragelli's team designed the station beyond its basic function as a transit node and turned it into a public space. The station has five access points at different levels to the surroundings. The main access is from a large multi-level plaza that defines a remarkable excavated architectural space. It is surrounded by a concrete wall that can be used as a gallery with views below, revealing the metro entrance and creating a sunken plaza surrounded by gardens, small shops, and cafés. The configuration of the space offers numerous opportunities for public encounters, and, contrary to the many attempts at privatizing transit stations, it is a Built Criticism staking a claim for the public in public spaces.

keywords:

São Paulo's subway system, São Bento Station, urban design, public space, infrastructure architecture

Introduction

São Bento Subway Station is an example of how public transportation architecture could be considered as a Built Criticism that celebrates urban society's daily life. Everyday facilities such as subway stations, generally built by public entities for collective use, express the relative level of respect granted to common people by the authorities. Usually, transportation systems are part of urban planning policies addressing issues of accessibility and equality. In certain cases, they may convey a deep understanding of how to promote quality spaces for public use, contributing to enhancing the collective perception of places that pay respect to the public.

Subway stations are primarily designed as functional transportation nodes. They process a large number of people—especially in connecting stations and intermodal terminals— and they also present numerous interesting opportunities to define places for public encounters and further city engagement. This is the case with São Bento Station.

The station was designed for the first subway line in Brazil by the architect Marcello Fragelli and his team.[1] It is an architecturally significant subway station with historical and cultural value, located near several important landmarks, such as São Bento Monastery and "Sé" square, which is the central square of São Paulo. Fragelli's station designs for Line 1/Blue present several aspects that constitute their Architecture as Built Criticism. First, the stations are not merely a place for transit but public spaces, some of them configuring major squares. Second, Fragelli and his team opened the stations from their interior out, frequently bringing natural light to underground spaces and integrating gardens and fixed furniture, thereby allowing people to have a more pleasant and metropolitan spatial experience. Third, the stations demonstrate a deep appreciation for transportation architecture's potential for shaping the public realm and fostering critical conversations on the role of the built environment in society.

São Bento Station

São Bento Station is at the midpoint of Line 1/Blue of São Paulo's metro system. It is located near several important foundational landmarks, such as the Anhangabaú Valley (the indigenous name for the river crossing the area), São Bento Monastery, and

[1] Fragelli coordinated the projects for all stations along Line 1/Blue as part of Promon Engenharia. Promon itself was the civil engineering arm of Montreal, responsible for subway construction along with Hochtief and Deconsult, two German companies. Fragelli was directly responsible for the stations with public spaces, and the final team working on Line 1/Blue was composed of the following architects: Marcos Pelaes, João Batista Martinez Corrêa, Luiz Arnaldo Queiroz e Silva, Vasco de Mello, Ernani Mercadante, Luiz Antônio Vallandro Keating, Marcello Fragelli, Tito Livio Frascino, Luiz Gonzaga de Oliveira Camargo (Gonga), Flávio Raphael Soares Pastore, Silvio John Heilbut, Flavio Marcondes, Jorge Utimura, and Álvaro de Macedo Neto.

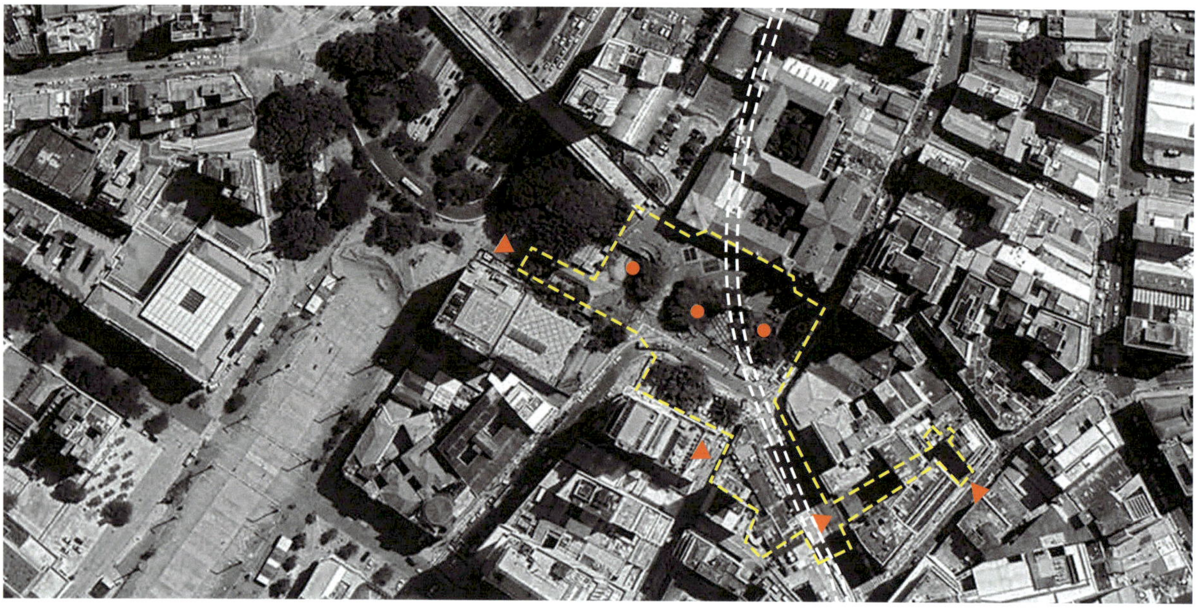

a major square called Sé (referring to the Catholic archbishop's seat), at the center of São Paulo. It is one of the twenty-three stations of Line 1/Blue and is used by an estimated forty thousand people during rush hour. In the 1980s, it hosted the city's initial slam and hip-hop gatherings until the movement expanded and relocated to bigger spaces. In 2019, the São Paulo Metro granted a license to the shopping mall company Patio to establish a commercial area inside the station, a function that was included as part of the initial design. After its installation, the original architecture was mostly preserved; a metallic pergola was added at the main plaza level ***(fig. 1)***.

Despite serving only one metro line, owing to its unique position in the city the station has five different access points ***(fig. 2)***. The foundational core of the city extends over a small triangular hill, surrounded and limited by three valleys, with each corner being marked by a different Catholic order: the Benedictines, the Franciscans, and the Jesuits. Even though São Bento Station's main entrance is from the plaza in front of the Benedictine monastery, it may be discreetly accessed from the surrounding streets. Each entrance is at a different topographic level, providing pedestrians with possible shortcuts to the irregular and steep surroundings.

The main access point is set in an excavated volume surrounded by a perimeter wall with an observation balcony that overlooks the large multi-level public space, revealing the metro entrance and creating a sunken plaza surrounded by small shops and cafés. All the architectural elements were carefully designed: the main staircase is defined by a monumental spiral in dialogue with circular-shaped gardens ***(fig. 3)***, offering the transient public a gradual transition between the upper street level and the underground station. The device of the sunken plaza ***(fig. 4)*** provides a monumentality without visually competing with the surrounding historical monuments. Furthermore, it consists of plateaus filled with gardens, benches, small bars, other commercial establishments, and different sitting opportunities for the enjoyment of the place. Beyond the plaza, there is the standard architecture of the subway, with sign systems leading the public to the ticket offices, stairs, escalators, trains, and platforms ***(figs. 5–6)***.

fig. 2
Map of the five access points (the three red dots refer to the plaza access). Source: Developed by Luísa Gonçalves, 2019.

fig. 3
Plan of São Bento Station at street level. Source: Companhia do Metropolitano de São Paulo – Metrô. *Terminais e estações da linha norte-sul do metrô.* São Paulo: Metrô, 1983.

fig. 4
fig. 4 Plan of São Bento Station at the level of the square. Source: Companhia do Metropolitano de São Paulo – Metrô. *Terminais e estações da linha norte-sul do metrô.* São Paulo: Metrô, 1983.

fig. 5
Plan of São Bento Station at the first of three underground levels of the square. Source: Companhia do Metropolitano de São Paulo – Metrô. *Terminais e estações da linha norte-sul do metrô.* São Paulo: Metrô, 1983.

fig. 6
Diagram of São Bento Station, with main vertical circulations highlighted. Source: Developed by Luísa Gonçalves, 2020.

[2] Marcello Fragelli, *Quarenta anos de prancheta* (São Paulo: Romano Guerra, 2010), 222–305.

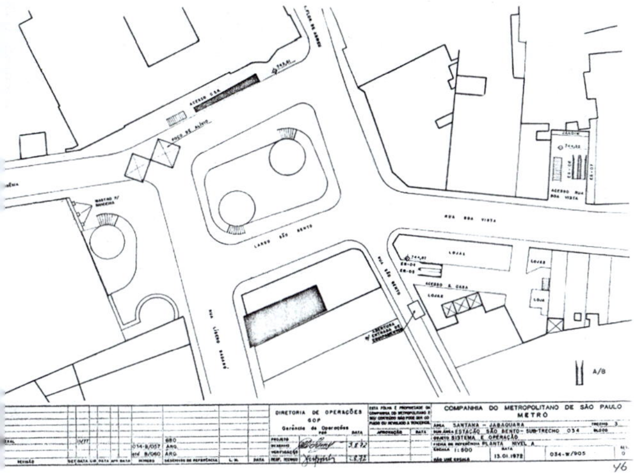

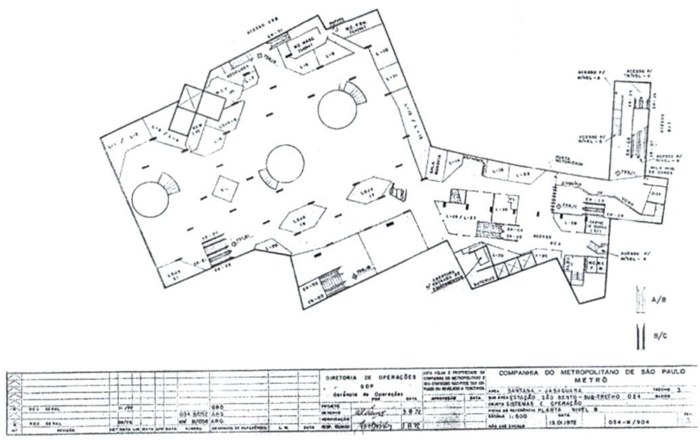

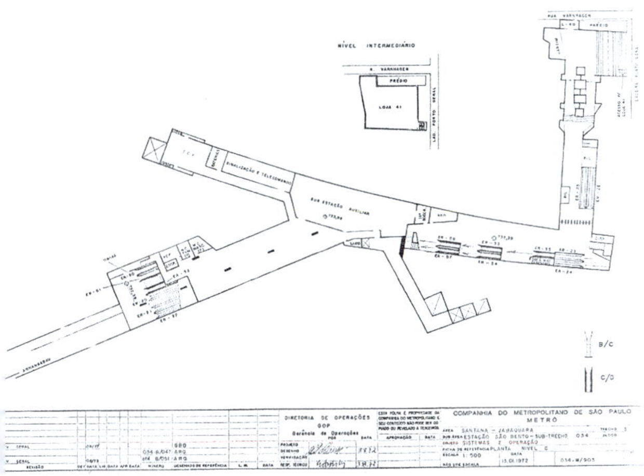

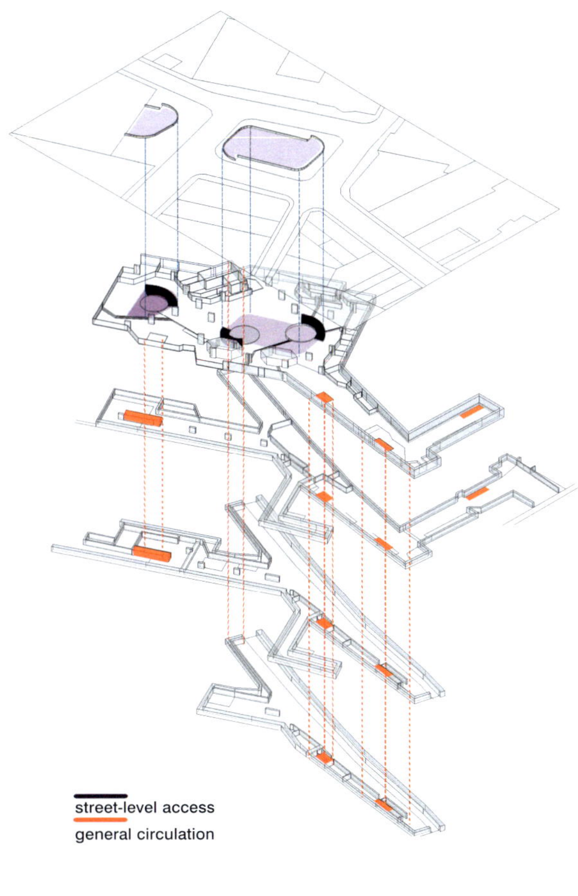

It is worth noting that the original design proposed a much larger square, as the metro company intended to build its headquarters there, facing the Anhangabaú Valley ***(fig. 7)***. In the end, this part of the design was dropped for financial reasons and due to its incompatibility with historic environmental protection directives.

The other entries to São Bento Station show a contrary design approach: they are small entrances assimilated in the urban landscape of the block's facades, posing like regular buildings but sheltering escalators and gates to the metro system. Although small, they are constructed with the same architectural elements as the main square: in situ concrete walls, skylights, and occasional gardens. This is the vocabulary employed by Marcello Fragelli and his team in revaluing architecture for public use.[2]

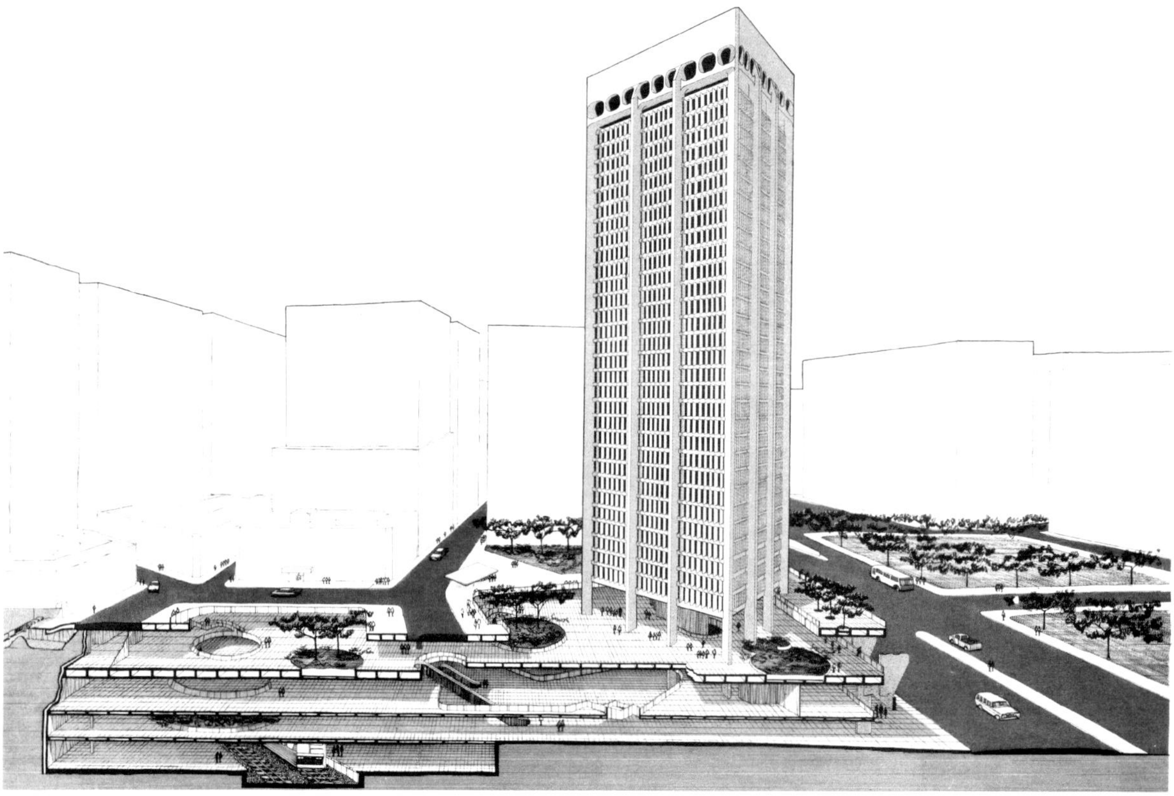

fig. 7
Sketch of the original design proposal with the metro headquarters building. Source: HOCHTIEF ; MONTREAL; DECONSULT–HMD. *Sistema Integrado de Transporte Rápido Coletivo da Cidade de São Paulo.* São Paulo: Companhia Litográphica Ypiranga, 1969.

Architecture for the Subway

Marcello Fragelli studied in Rio de Janeiro in the 1950s, a period of strong enthusiasm for modern Brazilian architecture. After practicing in Rio, he transferred to São Paulo and became a key figure in the development of Brazil's first subway line, which opened in 1974. By that point, São Paulo had already expanded into a huge metropolitan area. Throughout the state of São Paulo and the country as a whole, transportation infrastructure was being improved and urban mobility issues were being addressed, with the design participation of several important architects—for instance, the Central Bus Terminal in Brasília (1960) by Lucio Costa or the Interstate Bus Terminal (1973) in the city of Jaú by João Batista Villanova Artigas.

The infrastructure architecture of that period produced spaces for collective use that had a modern, monumental character. Resulting from close dialogues between the structural engineers and the architectural team, transportation infrastructures were thereby elevated into architectural and urban landmarks ***(fig. 8)***. As these were experimental works, Fragelli and his team felt the need to establish a set of principles. The design composition of the stations should display the structural elements in dialogue with the true nature of each material, not only as an aesthetic choice but also as a philosophical stance that would, in Fragelli's opinion, better define the public characteristic of the internal and external spaces. In other words, it was deemed inappropriate to clad the concrete elements—whether slabs, pillars, or beams—as these structural components were not to be understood as just being part of a regular interior space, but more directly as the underground guts of the city itself, where the supporting walls should convey the huge scale of the urban infrastructure.

Another principle was to illuminate with natural light as many of the underground levels as possible at each station. That would allow passengers to relate themselves to the time of the day and would soften the claustrophobic effect of the underground situation ***(fig. 9)***. Fragelli had visited the subway systems of some European cities and considered the long corridors connecting their interior spaces to be flawed, something to be avoided. So he wanted the stations in São Paulo to open up as much as possible to the exterior by subdividing the underground spaces into multiple levels and creating gradual transitions between interior and exterior, from street level to underground. Another principle was to introduce gardens inside the stations, an unusual design element in subways that were made possible thanks to the subtropical climate of São Paulo ***(figs. 10–11)***. The gardens were implemented not only at ground level or around

fig. 8
Armênia Station. Source: Photo by Marcos Kiyoto, 2024.

fig. 9
Santa Cecília Station. Source: Photo by Luísa Gonçalves, 2018.

fig. 10
Monumental stairs and gardens. Source: Photo by Marcos Kiyoto, 2024.

fig. 11
São Bento Station's access plaza, with pergola and gardens. Source: Photo by Luísa Gonçalves, 2019.

fig. 12
Sé Station. Source: Photo by Luísa Gonçalves, 2017.

the entrances of the stations but also in the ticket halls, mezzanines, and even along platforms, wherever possible. They were frequently surrounded by large concrete benches, inviting the public to sit next to them ***(fig. 12)***.

The combined application of these principles has rendered the station into a space of public permanence, beyond its simple use as a passage to the subway system. Fragelli and his team's work on Line 1/Blue of the São Paulo Metro system opened up the possibility of considering the stations as prominent public places and squares at a metropolitan scale. For the enormous number of people using São Paulo's subway system every day, the station plazas have become special opportunities for public encounters and engagement with the city, enriching the urban experience itself.

Public Transportation Architecture: A Metropolitan Problem

The metropolis requires a subway system. The design issues raised by São Bento Station are related to a scale that extends beyond the immediate surroundings of transport stations, as these inherently address in the same space the metropolis and the locality.[3] At the metropolitan scale, the station is a node in a network and therefore a space that always refers to a larger set of spaces, physically connected and part of an entire territory to which this network provides permeability, mobility, and also unity. The local dimension refers to how a specific station emerges from the network and opens up to a specific place in the city; this is achieved by its architectural and urban design. The design of a specific station addresses the metropolitan dimension, but not only that. That is to say, while the design of a specific station guides the passenger from the station's entrance to their train, it may not address all the opportunities or requirements that an urban mobility node might offer or need.[4] Such opportunities and requirements include the convergence of pedestrian flows, the creation or encouragement of urban centers, and the provision of public spaces for commercial, social, and civic use.

3 Luca Bertolini and Tejo Spit, *Cities on Rails: The Redevelopment of Railway Station Areas* (London: E&FN Spon, 1998).

4 Regina Meyer, "Atributos da metrópole moderna," *São Paulo em Perspectiva. Revista da Fundação SEADE*, vol. 14, no. 1 (São Paulo, 2000); and Luísa Gonçalves, "Arquitetura da infraestrutura e mobilidade urbana: uma análise sobre projeto, espaço público e metrópole através do metrô de São Paulo" (PhD thesis, Universidade de São Paulo, 2020).

fig. 13
São Bento Station's plaza access without gates. Source: Photo by Luísa Gonçalves, 2017.

fig. 14
São Bento Station's plaza access with gates. Source: Photo by Marcos Kiyoto, 2024.

The main problems facing public infrastructures are: (a) monofunctionality, or the prioritization of private vehicles over pedestrians and cyclists; (b) low-quality internal spaces, such as excessively long corridors, claustrophobic proportions, and lack of care in the choice of their materiality; (c) accesses connected to privatized and closed spaces instead of public and open spaces; and (d) accesses connected to public spaces that are inactive or poorly configured for permeability or sociability. There are several examples of these in São Paulo and other major Brazilian metropolises, such as the bridges over the Tietê and Pinheiros rivers (problem a); the long and complex passage connecting the Paulista and Consolação stations of Line 2/Red and Line 4/Yellow (problem b); the stations that are physically and commercially associated with shopping malls in Santa Cruz of Line 1/Blue and Tucuruvi of Line 2/Red (problem c); and the accesses to Faria Lima and Luz stations of Line 4/Yellow that are connected to Largo da Batata and Luz squares (problem d).

The reasons for the existence of these problems are complex and often go beyond the scope of architectural projects. They can include the administrative fragmentation of the entities responsible for project management and disputes over the allocation of income generated by the implementation of these works. In any case, they influence the designs. For Line 1/Blue, Fragelli's team developed a way of incorporating engineering elements into the infrastructure by using architectural techniques, from the structures of elevated stations that more prominently mark the urban landscape, as in the case of Armênia, to other important interventions such as the reorganization of the local topography, the urbanization of the surroundings, and the composition of buildings that integrate themselves with a plaza. São Bento Station is the paradigm for these architectural techniques at the levels of the station, plaza, and place.

The main design concept for São Bento Station is the displacement of the plaza to a lower level, thereby making the slope between platform level and street level more gradual. This configuration creates a new square that is outlined with concrete walls. To compensate for the aridity of exposed concrete, large flower beds were positioned near the stairs in such a way that they did not compromise the openness of the general circulation space. With this approach, the project manages to achieve a subtle combination of both monumentality and "anonymity" for this public space—"subtracted" from street level—without competing with the historical surroundings, and yet being generous in its spatiality. Projects with this characteristic of blending into their urban context are considered "urban objects."[5]

The square at São Bento Station functions as a communal space, showcasing the potential of architecture to shape the public sphere, fostering cultural and commercial exchanges, and even serving as a civic center.[6] The project endorses the metro's quality of converging flows of people and provides spaces for free movement, permanence, and collective gatherings. These encounters happen in both a spontaneous and an organized manner, as in the emblematic case of rap battles in the 1980s. With its plateaus and steps, the design of the square's topography stands out in the way that it contributes to the configuration of a "stage." While the architectural design successfully deals with the issues of monofunctionality and spatiality, the issues created by the private commercial spaces were almost a threat to this success. In 2019, the inauguration of the Patio shopping mall in the station brought some significant changes to its patterns of use. First, the station can no longer be accessed at all times. Gates were added to the stairs and are kept open in line with the metro's operating hours: from 4:40 a.m. to midnight on Sunday to Monday, and from 4:40 a.m. to 1:30 a.m. on Saturday ***(figs. 13–14)***. The hours are quite long, with the station being closed only during the early morning, but the addition of the gates is a noteworthy change.

Smets and Shannon have documented how the public character of transport stations and terminals has historically been losing ground to private and commercial dimensions, with significant European railway stations effectively being transformed into shopping malls.[7] However, the design of São Bento Station managed to circumvent this effect because retail units were envisaged in the original project by way of forming a normal public square. Thus, an urban-oriented building was configured to produce the logic of the street and public square, with commerce surrounding the area set aside for public circulation and occupation. For administrative and bureaucratic reasons, these units were not occupied from the time of the station's inauguration until 2019. The metal pergola, a prominent element in the mall's intervention, detracts from the materiality of the original concrete and from the vegetation, but neither touches the retaining walls of the square nor hinders ventilation and the admission of natural light, thus maintaining the presence of these features in the overall composition and respecting the crucial aspects of the original conception.

Public Architecture as Built Criticism

Considering urban mobility infrastructures, there are two important historical types: monofunctional road structures focused on vehicles (bridges, viaducts, highways, etc.), and stations for mass transportation networks (trains, subways, monorails, etc.). While large railway stations in developed countries have traditionally been recognized as "city gates" and halls for collective gatherings,[8,9] in Brazil those places have suffered from the deterioration of the rail network, whereas bus terminals have gained in importance. Regarding the subway, stations have been frequently interpreted as "non-places"; however, Marc Augé himself contradicts this idea in his book *Le métro*

5 Gonçalves, "Arquitetura da infraestrutura e mobilidade urbana."
6 Marcel Smets and Kelly Shannon, *The Landscape of Contemporary Infrastructure* (Rotterdam: NAI Publishers, 2010).
7 Smets and Shannon, *Landscape of Contemporary Infrastructure*.
8 Bertolini and Spit, *Cities on Rails*.
9 Smets and Shannon, *Landscape of Contemporary Infrastructure*.

revisité (The subway revisited).[10] The metro creates unique and, at the same time, common places with ambiguities—monumental and anonymous, quotidian and occasional, aboveground and underground. They are simultaneously open spaces and public buildings, representing the possibilities of modern metropolitan life.

The Built Criticism expressed in São Bento Station and the others of Line 1/Blue foregrounds their public potential and their role at the heart of metropolitan life: their open character permeates the city, they enable the convergence of a multitude of unknown people, they offer a variety of services, they are the new form of public space, of the public realm. However, when such facilities are poorly designed, which is unfortunately the case in many neglected urban peripheries, they convey the message that "public use" and thus the "public" itself are unimportant to society; the neoliberal city spends its scarce resources on the privatization of former public spaces and services.

São Bento Station demonstrates the alternative of a publicly meaningful approach to infrastructure architecture by exploring and realizing the entire breadth of possibilities of contemporary subway spaces: services, amenities, gardens, plazas, and a variety of places in which people can pause, rest, or transition from the rail network to urban life.

Biography
Luísa Gonçalves is a professor at the Faculty of Architecture and Urbanism at the Federal University of Rio de Janeiro (UFRJ), Brazil. She obtained her bachelor's degree in Architecture and Urbanism from the Federal Fluminense University (UFF), her master's degree from the Federal University of Rio de Janeiro (UFRJ), and her PhD from the University of São Paulo (USP). She has worked with and researched the relationship between architecture, infrastructure, and metropolises through urban mobility facilities, subway stations, and intermodal terminals.

[10] "To go further, we have to look at non-places (1992), which raises, upon a fresh look, the question of alienation from the social. In other words, to put it briefly (and I'm talking about the subway that I use every day—with its rush hour, its crowds, its stations, its homeless people, its advertisements, its corridors, its bizarre escalators, its stairs that are too wrinkled, its calls for anti-terrorist vigilance, its warnings against pickpockets, its soft announcements evoking, in the same tone, a social movement, whether it's the suicide of a passenger or the renovation of a station, its mixed smells, and its particular sounds), the metro is not a non-place. It is not a non-place, for me at least, nor for those who regularly make the same journey. They have memories, habits, recognize some faces, and maintain a kind of bodily intimacy with the space of certain stations that can be measured by the rhythm of the descent of the flight of stairs, by the precision of the gesture that feeds the ticket into the slot of the access gate, or by the acceleration of the walk when the arrival of the train at the edge of the platform is transmitted to the ear" (Marc Augé, *Le métro revisité* [Paris: Éditions du seuil, 2008]. Digital version, position 309. Translation by the author).

Housing the Gauche Divine: Tales of Franco, Family, and Walden 7

Jaime Silva

fig. 1
Ricardo Bofill Taller de Arquitectura, Walden 7, Sant Just Desvern, Spain, 1970–75.
Ricardo Bofill (second from the right) at the construction site. © Ricardo Bofill Taller de Arquitectura.

"Housing the Gauche Divine" aims to demonstrate the role of the Walden 7 housing project as a vehicle of social criticism against the Francoist regime. After identifying three of the main values associated with the dictatorship's conception of family and society, the essay proposes an interpretation of how the building managed to oppose them. Recognizing the powerful role of architecture in enabling and promoting new behaviors, it identifies the design solutions that managed to establish Walden 7 as a successful container for self-determination, multiple family associations, and the vision of communitarian life as a tool for individual improvement.

"Direct your eye right inward, and you'll find
A thousand regions in your mind Yet undiscovered.
Travel them, and be Expert in home-cosmography."
—Henry David Thoreau, *Walden or, Life in the Woods*

keywords:
collective housing, community, Francoism, Gauche Divine, Ricardo Bofill Taller de Arquitectura, Walden 7

Henry David Thoreau's (1817–62) words are a hymn to discovering the self. Thus, it is no surprise that the building that borrows its name from one of his works—Walden 7 (1970–75)—is grounded in the same idea. However, what is astonishing is the context from which it arises. Far from what might be assumed from its utopian outline, it was built during the Francoist regime, amid an arch-conservative social context. Walden 7 was a token of resistance against the dictatorship's traditional values that dared, against all odds, to give form to a new and more varied society—architecture as a vehicle for social criticism. Designed by a multidisciplinary team imbued with progressive ideals—the Ricardo Bofill Taller de Arquitectura—it was set to promote the rise of individual will—regardless of sex, orientation, or family composition—having the community as its supportive network. What then were the contested values and, more importantly, how did architecture shape this fight?

Family and Society in Franco's Regime

The word Francoism has been used to identify both the fascist regime of Spain led by *Generalíssimo* Francisco Franco (1892–1975)—also known as *El Caudillo*—and the historical period in which he ruled (1936–75).[1] Starting with a partially failed military coup in 1936, followed by a bloody civil war that lasted four long years (1936–39), the Francoist regime was initiated by the Nationalists, who defeated the Republicans and Communists previously in power.[2]

Nonetheless, contrary to what might be expected, the victorious political force lacked a cohesive and clear ideology, and instead consisted of several ideological threads, or values, roughly constant throughout the regime.[3] Given that its members came from distinct groups—mixing, among others, large landowners, the conservative bourgeoisie, and Catholic fundamentalists—their differences would merge into a kaleidoscope of "impure" dogma.[4] However, as highlighted by the historian Miguel Ángel Giménez Martínez, despite its "imprecise features, little originality, and a continuous mix between past and future—spiced with defensive ingredients against real and

1 José Luis Ibáñez Salas, *El franquismo*, e-book (Punto de Vista, 2013), 14.
2 Ibáñez Salas, *El franquismo*, 14.
3 Miguel Ángel Giménez Martínez, *El estado franquista: Fundamentos ideológicos, bases legales y sistema institucional* (Madrid: Centro de Estudios Políticos y Constitucionales, 2014), 63–65.
4 Giménez Martínez, *El estado franquista*, 65–66.

imaginary enemies—Franco's ideological conglomerate filled almost four decades of Spanish political life and served to fulfil its legitimizing function."[5]

From this conglomerate, the values that impact Walden 7—related to the conceptions of family and society—can be summarized in the following three ideas: *parts to the whole*, *the dream package*, and *the hierarchy of truth*.

Parts to the Whole

One of the strongest values associated with Francoism was the understanding of the Spanish people as a unified body, working collectively for the "good" of the nation.[6] That is to say: what mattered was not the individual, but solely the collective. In the game of who works for whom, the individual was to be seen as a tool for the determination of the collective. This was a vision that was applied not only to the relationship between citizens and the state but also to all the "natural entities of society": municipality; the syndicate; and, last but not least, the family.[7] Its members were not masters of their aspirations, but servants of a common will.

The Dream Package

Although the Catholic Church did not play an active role in the 1936 military coup, it was nevertheless relieved by its later success.[8] In truth, many of the winning party members were traditional Catholics and eager to reinstate the influence of religion in politics. Soon, the state and the Church were once again bound together by law, giving birth to what was called the *nacionalcatolicismo*.[9] In sum, to be Spanish was to be Catholic. Public morality, social behavior, education, cultural expression, and family had now to be submitted to ecclesiastic authority and norms.[10] Within this scheme, it meant that the only accepted and desired vision of the family was the one advocated by the Church: husband, wife, and their children. If one did not want to devote oneself entirely to God, one had better start searching for a partner recognizable to his eyes. Celibacy, if not in the name of God, was not cherished. Promiscuity and homosexuality were sins. There was only one acceptable type of family.

The Hierarchy of Truth

As the victorious faction, the Francoists saw themselves as the "good" side that had defeated the "evil" of Communism and Republicanism.[11] This messianic understanding consequently meant the faction's ruler—*El Caudillo*—was the bearer of the uncontested "truth," passed down to and managed by the head of each smaller group. The head of the family (that is, the husband), the teacher, and the boss were thus a modest emulation of Franco's "possession aura."[12] That is to say that the individual worked for the family, that the family should be a traditional Catholic one, and that if one was not the husband, then one was denied any say in one's life, as well as on the path to be taken as a group. Personal determination, with regard to the search for a tailored well-being—in its physical, mental, and social realms—and especially to pleasure and creativity, was to be eliminated.

Taller de Arquitectura's Walden 7

By the 1960s, challenges to the regime had grown, and this continued throughout the remaining years of Francoism.[13] Some of the members of the Church started to criticize it openly, students and workers demonstrated and went on strikes demanding freedom and better conditions, and the leftist liberals grew bolder in voicing their opinion, all despite the eminent fear of repression.[14] Barcelona's Gauche Divine—a group of intellectuals that gathered in the nightclub Boccaccio—belonged to the latter.

[5] ". . . con rasgos imprecisos, con escasa originalidad, con continuas mezclas de atención al pasado y llamadas al futuro, con muchos ingredientes de arma defensiva frente a enemigos reales o inventados, el conglomerado ideológico franquista llenó casi cuatro decenios de la vida política española y sirvió para cumplir su función legitimadora" (Giménez Martínez, *El estado franquista*, 66, translated to English by the author).

[6] Giménez Martínez, *El estado franquista*, 76.

[7] Giménez Martínez, *El estado franquista*, 76.

[8] Giménez Martínez, *El estado franquista*, 81.

[9] Ibáñez Salas, *El franquismo*, 88–149.

[10] Ibáñez Salas, *El franquismo*, 88.

[11] Giménez Martínez, *El estado franquista*, 70–73.

[12] Giménez Martínez, *El estado franquista*, 71.

[13] Ibáñez Salas, *El franquismo*, 189.

[14] See Ibáñez Salas, *El franquismo*; Giménez Martínez, *El estado franquista*.

[15] Raquel Álvarez Arce, Noelia Galván Desvaux, and José Manuel Martínez Rodríguez, "Taller de Arquitectura en Walden 7: el dibujo como lienzo de la imaginación / Taller de Arquitectura in Walden 7: The Drawing as Imagination's Canvas," in *Riflessioni: l'arte del disegno/il disegno dell'arte / Reflections: The Art of Drawing/The Drawing of Art* (41° Convegno internazionale dei docenti delle discipline della rappresentazione), ed. Paolo Belardi (Perugia: Gangemi, 2019), 1045, https://doi.org/10.36165/1024.

[16] At the completion of Walden 7, the team consisted of Ricardo Bofill, Anna Bofill (architect and his sister), Salvador Clotas (literary critic), Peter Hodgkinson (architect), Manolo Núñez Yanowsky, José Agustín Goytisolo (poet), and Ramon Collado. After its completion and coinciding with the Taller's shift to a more historicist approach, important members left—such as Anna Bofill, Manolo Núñez Yanowsky, and José Agustín Goytisolo. See Taller de Arquitectura, "Taller de Arquitectura," *L'Architecture d'aujourd'hui* 182 (1975): 57; Taller de Arquitectura, "Réaliser l'utopie," *Techniques & Architecture* 306 (1975): 88–96; Geoffrey Broadbent, "Bofill Taller de Arquitectura," *Architectural Design* XLV, no. 7 (1975): 402; Warren James, *Ricardo Bofill, Taller de Arquitectura: Buildings and Projects, 1960-1985* (New York: Rizzoli, 1988), 203; Raquel Álvarez Arce, "La última comunidad Walden (7). Taller de Arquitectura y la vivienda colectiva (1971–1978)" (PhD thesis, Universidad de Valladolid, 2021), 75–76, https://uvadoc.uva.es/handle/10324/51970.

fig. 2
Ricardo Bofill Taller de Arquitectura, Walden 7, Sant Just Desvern, Spain, 1970–75. Construction. © Ricardo Bofill Taller de Arquitectura.

fig. 3
Daniel Argimón, untitled and undated. Set of drawings for Walden 7's advertising materials depicting the transformation of a red spot, first into a human head, then into a vulva, and lastly into the building's geometric scheme. © Ricardo Bofill Taller de Arquitectura.

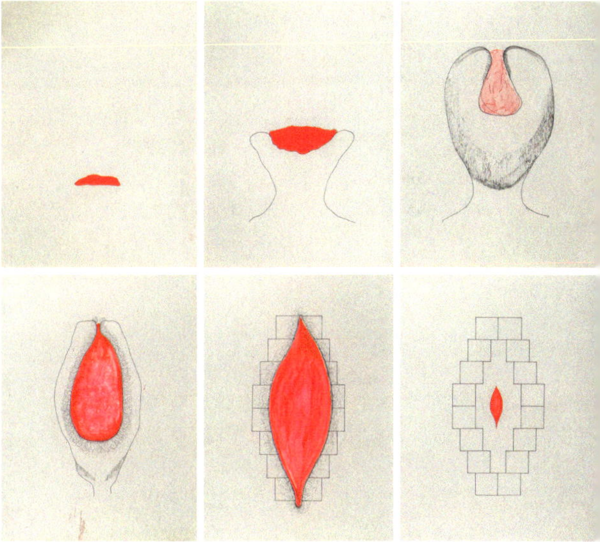

The architect Ricardo Bofill (1939–2022) was one of its members and a good representative of its intellectual fight against oppression.[15] Contradicting the regime's understanding of an uncontested hierarchical authority in the workplace, he created a multidisciplinary team[16] for the collective design and discussion of an architecture that could overrule the traditional approach: the "Ricardo Bofill Taller de Arquitectura," sometimes also identified, in the spirit of its mission, as the "Taller de Arquitectura," or just "Taller."[17]

Although Bofill's early projects were mainly characterized by a modernist approach with influences from vernacular Catalan architecture, by the mid-1960s, already working as a team, a more radical and utopian vision started to emerge. Project by project, there was a growing interest in rethinking the construction of housing for a new and more progressive society, adopting formal conceptions based on three-dimensional geometrical rules.[18] Walden 7 (1970–75), located in Sant Just Desvern, on the outskirts of Barcelona, was not only the last of this set of experiments but also the most mature.[19] How does the building's design relate to the three Francoist ideas previously mentioned?

The Equality of Truth

If Franco's regime was based on the idea that truth and determination were not individual idiosyncrasies but things incontestably handed down, the Taller valued self-will. For the design team, any individual had the right to search for one's well-being, to be at the center of one's life.[20] Given this conception, the first designs for Walden 7 were founded on the idea of the individual cell, an aspiration that was formally translated

[17] Broadbent, "Bofill Taller de Arquitectura," 402.
[18] From this list of projects, one can name: Barrio Gaudí (1964–68, Reus); Castillo de Kafka (1966–68, Sant Pere de Ribes); Xanadú (1966–68, Calpe); Ciudad en el Espacio (1968–70, Moratalaz; unbuilt); La Muralla Roja (1969–75, Calpe); and Walden 7 (1970–75, Sant Just Desvern).
[19] James, *Ricardo Bofill*, 44.
[20] Ricardo Bofill, *L'architecture d'un homme: entretiens avec François Hébert-Stevens*, ed. François Hébert-Stevens (Paris: Arthaud, 1978), 54.

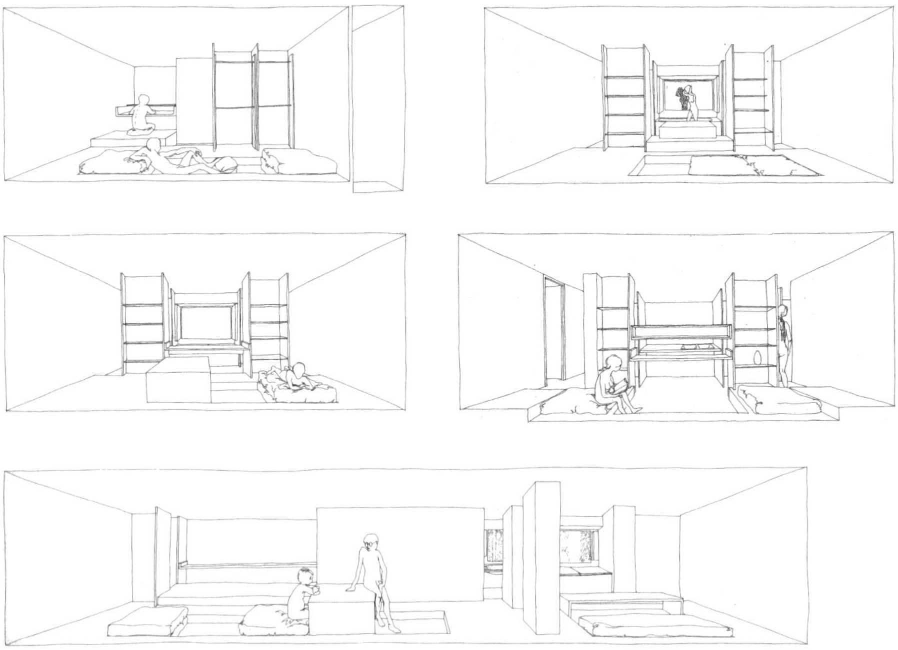

fig. 4
Ricardo Bofill Taller de Arquitectura, Walden 7, Sant Just Desvern, Spain, 1970–75. Views of different apartment typologies. © Ricardo Bofill Taller de Arquitectura.

fig. 5
Ricardo Bofill Taller de Arquitectura, Walden 7, Sant Just Desvern, Spain, 1970–75. Different apartment plans: top left – studio apartment; top right – three-room apartment; bottom – four-room duplex (left – first floor; right – second floor). © Ricardo Bofill Taller de Arquitectura.

fig. 6
Ricardo Bofill Taller de Arquitectura, Walden 7, Sant Just Desvern, Spain, 1970–75. Apartment interior. © Ricardo Bofill Taller de Arquitectura.

fig. 7
Ricardo Bofill Taller de Arquitectura, Walden 7, Sant Just Desvern, Spain, 1970–75. Ground-floor plan. The shops are located in the outer perimeter of the plan (dark gray) and can be accessed from both the exterior and the interior of the building. The rest of the plan is made up of circulation areas, courtyards, and multipurpose open-air spaces. © Ricardo Bofill Taller de Arquitectura.

through the thousandfold repetition of a basic unit—a cube with an area of thirty square meters—equivalent to the space for one person.[21] Continuing the previous experiments on the distribution of volumes in space, the team devised a geometrical system for the oblique stacking of cubes, almost like an ancient Mayan arch, creating womb-like openings ***(fig. 2)***. In sum, it was a grand and imposing "monument" composed of multiple experimental containers for the cultivation of the self.

On this matter, it is important to highlight Catalan artist Daniel Argimón's (1929–96) set of drawings for Walden 7's advertising materials[22] ***(fig. 3)***. In the form of a sequential narrative, Argimón controversially depicted a vibrant red spot first transforming into a faceless human head, then into a vulva, and finally into the geometric principle that determined the building. A potential buyer looking at these drawings would surely understand two messages: first, that this was not yet another undifferentiated building but a vibrant impactful idea orchestrated by the human mind and possessing the power to create a new reality; second, that the architecture and its community emerged from a pixelated vulva—that is, from a maternal womb composed of multiple individual cells. Here, Walden 7 was both the literal and the figurative result of the emancipated self.

The Dreamt Packages

Even though the formal conceptual base was the individual cell, that did not mean that the final proposed utopia excluded the desire to associate with other community members.[23] Developing the design, the team planned multiple combinations between cubic cells to establish a large variety of household types.[24] They had in mind not only the "traditional" family but also other types of association that people might choose: living alone, living with friends, or living with a partner, regardless of sex or orientation.[25] In order to achieve this vision, the apartments were not thought of in terms of traditional bourgeois configurations—living room, dining room, office, bedrooms, kitchen, bathrooms, etc.—but as the aggregation of several, almost equal, rooms for

[21] Taller de Arquitectura, "Réaliser l'utopie," 96.
[22] Álvarez Arce, "La última comunidad Walden (7)," 93–94.
[23] After partnering with Catalan bankers for the financing of the construction, the idea was altered to envision dwellings capable of housing more than one person or, using Bofill's words, "evolved bourgeois families." However, part of the idea of individual seclusion was adopted for the bedrooms. Bofill, *L'architecture d'un homme*.
[24] A total of 368 apartments divided into five main types—studio, studio atelier, and three-, four-, and five-room apartments—almost all of them subdivided into multiple variations. Taller de Arquitectura, "Walden 7," *L'Architecture d'aujourd'hui* 182 (1975): 70–71.
[25] Álvarez Arce, "La última comunidad Walden (7)," 112–13.

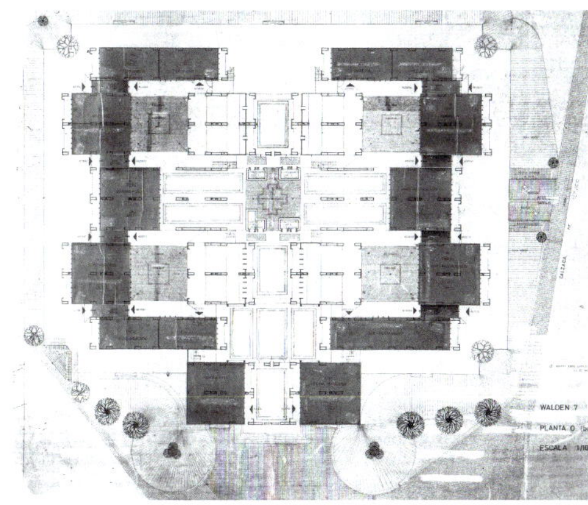

"being"[26] **(fig. 4)**. Bedrooms were larger and were also devised as places for individual leisure and work—almost as an independent cell—and living rooms gathered eating, working, and leisure in one space **(fig. 5)**. Another aspect of the design is that "service" spaces, such as bathrooms and kitchens, were not considered as individual rooms but as part of the rooms for "being."[27] Appliances and countertops were part of the living room. Bathtubs were placed within bedrooms.

Counteracting Spain's political isolation, this radical domestic vision testifies to the Taller's openness to international discourses. In fact, they were not only up to date with but also part of the most recent experiments being carried out internationally. As Walden 7's construction was about to start, MoMA's exhibition on Italian design—*Italy: The New Domestic Landscape* (1972)[28]—was proposing innovative solutions that were similar to those conceived by the Catalan office. Besides showcasing some of the most exceptional objects of the previous decade, the exhibition also presented a group of "environments" especially conceived and produced for the event.[29] Leading designers and architects, such as Gae Aulenti (1927–2012), Joe Colombo (1930–71), and Alberto Rosselli (1921–76), explored domestic environments similar in spirit to the ones put forward for Walden 7. For one, they privileged the "democratization" of the house by congregating in the given footprint of 4.8 by 4.8 meters, and in one single open space, most, if not all, domestic functions.[30] For another, in line with Le Corbusier's (1887–1965) proposal for the 1925 International Exhibition of Modern Decorative and Industrial Arts,[31] they thought of furniture not as isolated objects but as elements integrated into the overall architecture. Unfortunately, the Taller's *Gesamtkunstwerk*, with its carpeted conversation pits, would only see the light of day in a handful of apartments[32] **(fig. 6)**. Nonetheless, the democratic coincidence of domestic functions would be present in all of them.

[26] Taller de Arquitectura, "Réaliser l'utopie," 96.

[27] Taller de Arquitectura, "Réaliser l'utopie," 96.

[28] The exhibition *Italy: The New Domestic Landscape* was held at The Museum of Modern Art (MoMA), New York, from May 26 to September 11, 1972, and was curated by the architect Emilio Ambasz (b. 1943). Its content can be found in the corresponding catalog: Emilio Ambasz, ed., *Italy: The New Domestic Landscape. Achievements and Problems of Italian Design* (New York: The Museum of Modern Art, 1972).

[29] The Museum of Modern Art, "Italy: The New Domestic Landscape," press release, 1972, 3.

[30] See Ambasz, *Italy*, 137–210.

[31] On the occasion of the Exposition internationale des arts décoratifs et industriels modernes, held in Paris, between April and October 1925, Le Corbusier would come to design the Pavillion de l'esprit nouveau as an apartment prototype of his Immeuble-villas (1922, 1925). Within the exhibition's theme, this pavilion had a strong impact by "denying" the decorative arts and proposing furniture as an integrated element of architecture. Willy Boesiger and Oscar Stonorov, eds., *Le Corbusier et Pierre Jeanneret: Oeuvre Complète 1910-1929*, 9th ed., vol. 1, 8 vols. (Zurich: Girsberger, 1967 [1929]), 98–108.

[32] Álvarez Arce, "La última comunidad Walden (7)," 161.

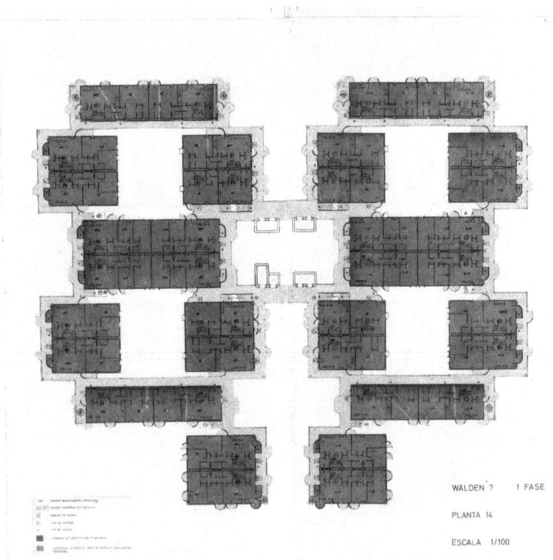

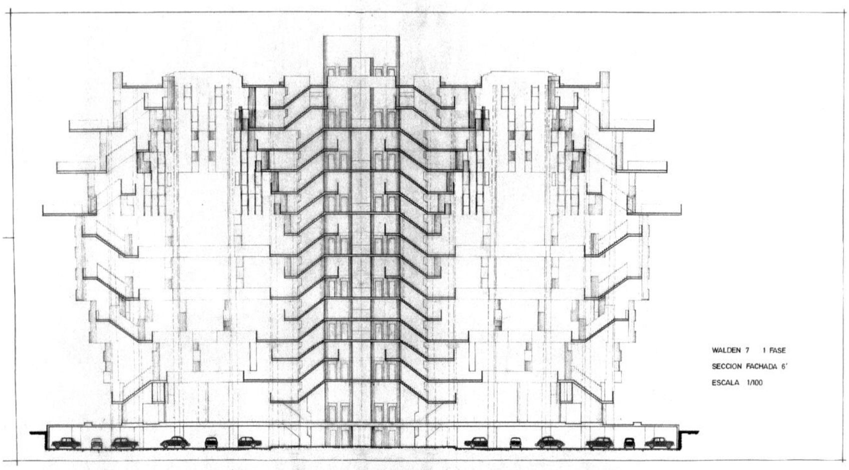

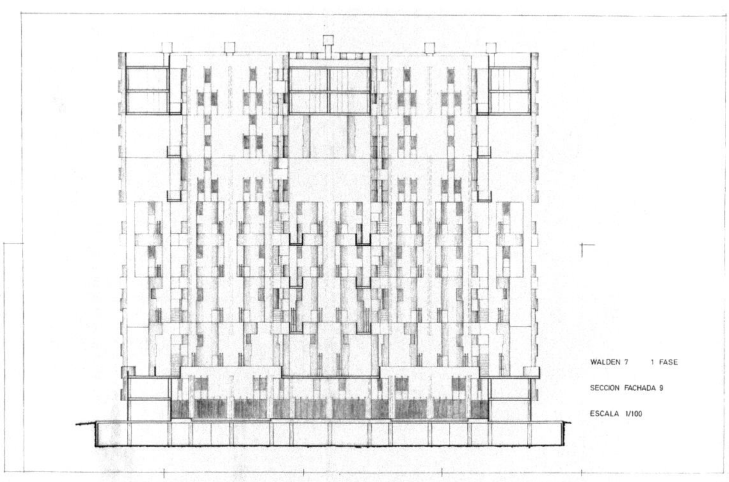

fig. 8
Ricardo Bofill Taller de Arquitectura, Walden 7, Sant Just Desvern, Spain, 1970–75. Fourteenth-floor plan. The circulation galleries swirl around the apartments and are punctuated with small dilatations for people to rest in, mimicking the street's spirit. © Ricardo Bofill Taller de Arquitectura.

fig. 9
Ricardo Bofill Taller de Arquitectura, Walden 7, Sant Just Desvern, Spain, 1970–75. Section through the elevators' landings. © Ricardo Bofill Taller de Arquitectura.

fig. 10
Ricardo Bofill Taller de Arquitectura, Walden 7, Sant Just Desvern, Spain, 1970–75. Section through the side courtyards. © Ricardo Bofill Taller de Arquitectura.

fig. 11
Ricardo Bofill Taller de Arquitectura, Walden 7, Sant Just Desvern, Spain, 1970–75. Rooftop pool. © Ricardo Bofill Taller de Arquitectura.

fig. 12
Ricardo Bofill Taller de Arquitectura, Walden 7, Sant Just Desvern, Spain, 1970–75. Circulation gallery. © Ricardo Bofill Taller de Arquitectura.

Whole to the Parts

At this design stage, it was clearer to the Taller than to the regime that the individual was not a tool for the collective but the other way around.[33] Furthermore, within the monumental megastructure, besides its innovative apartments, it is also possible to find a rich set of communitarian spaces, designed to cater to the inhabitants' well-being. On the ground floor, several retail spaces were planned—a restaurant, a coffee shop, a dry cleaner, a hairdresser, etc.—as well as communitarian open-air spaces for the collective use of residents ***(fig. 7)***.[34] On every residential level, intricate galleries with punctual dilatations not only give access to the apartments but also act as a collective threshold between the public and the private, creating the atmosphere of a street ***(figs 8–10)***. As for the rooftop—remembering Le Corbusier's Unité d'Habitation in Marseille (1945–52)—two swimming pools and several grassed solariums magically culminate the utopian dream under Barcelona's luminous sun[35] ***(fig. 11)***. As dreamt by the best-known modern architects of the interwar period, collectivity and seclusion could coexist.[36] The community could serve the self.

It is, therefore, no wonder that the building borrows its name—but not its full ideology[37]—from two books that dwell on different theories of human behavior: Henry David Thoreau's *Walden or, Life in the Woods* (1854) and Burrhus Frederic Skinner's (1904–90) *Walden Two* (1948). From the first comes a certain inspiration for the value of the self. Even though it delves into a form of existence that is antithetical to the building—the author recounts the benefits of his life in isolation and among nature, near the Walden Pond—it is an ode to the quest for one's individuality. As for the second book, it is undeniably a moderate analogy to the role of the community in one's service. In this science fiction novel, set in a utopian society named "Walden 2," individual happiness is achieved as part of a collective. Furthermore, it is also from this book that the number "7" arises. As the 6th Walden was already being built in Skinner's novel, the Taller's community would logically—but not without subversion—follow it.

33 "In an adult society, it is the individual that matters and that must be considered as the major element" (Bofill, *L'architecture d'un homme*, 54, translation by the author).

34 Taller de Arquitectura, "Walden 7," 70–71.

35 Taller de Arquitectura, "Walden 7," 70–71.

36 As an example, see the presentations given by both Le Corbusier and Walter Gropius, especially concerning the design of communitarian spaces inside housing schemes in order to optimize and improve the inhabitants' well-being (in these presentations the housing schemes were already thought of as being for slightly more progressive families): Carlo Aymonino, ed., *La vivienda racional: Ponencias de los congresos CIAM 1929-1930 [L'abitazione razionale: Atti dei congressi C.I.A.M. 1929-1930]* (Barcelona: Gustavo Gili, 1973 [1941]).

37 Although these books inspired the name, that does not mean that their respective radical ideologies were to be applied to the design. For one, the Taller did not try to establish a fully isolated existence among nature, as in Thoreau's recollections. For another, neither did they try to establish a utopian community, completely isolated from the surrounding reality, as in Skinner's novel. As highlighted in 1975 by the Taller: "The name Walden 7, even though inspired by Thoreau and Skinner's books on the theory of human behavior, does not follow their ideology; it designates a psycho-sociological conception of our urban environment, opposed to the purely technical and speculative threads that dominate most of the current operations" (Taller de Arquitectura, "Walden 7," 71, translation by the author).

Criticism *bis*: Rethinking the Past

Characteristic of the Taller's strong collective creativity, Walden 7 is not only a powerful take on housing design for a progressive society but also a reflection on both vernacular Catalan architecture and its consequent Catalan Modernism.[38] One example of this is Walden 7's design of streets in the air. Transcending the long and horizontal galleries of buildings such as Robin Hood Gardens (Alison and Peter Smithson, London, 1972), the team sought a deeper emulation of the traditional Mediterranean street. The galleries of Walden 7 are intentionally sinuous, full of dilatations and compressions, and open to the sky ***(fig. 12)***. There are direct parallels to the open-air passageways found along the traditional buildings of Barcelona. At Walden 7, entrances are also spaces for rest, where there are seats among a micro-oasis of plants. Another example is the abundant use of tiles—in multiple vibrant colors—as well as the expressive chimneys on the rooftop—distantly evoking Antoni Gaudí's Casa Milà (Barcelona, 1912)—which are a clear reinterpretation of the local cladding and detailing tradition, with its exponents in Catalan Modernism.[39]

Past, Present, and Future

Coincidence or not, the building was finished in the same year that the dictatorship ended, and could immediately start to be used quite openly as a place for self-determination; for multiple family associations; and, of course, for realizing the vision of communitarian life as a tool for individual improvement. However, one cannot help but wonder: What if the fascist regime had not fallen that year?

Even though Franco was no longer in good health, nobody could have predicted that he would die at that moment, or that the regime would immediately crumble after his death. Here lies the true audacity of the Taller. In truth, in the alternative scenario Walden 7 would most certainly have become—due to its DNA ***(fig. 13)***—a useful tool for protest. Not as a literal defensive barricade in a conflict, as in the case of Karl-Marx-Hof (Karl Ehn, Vienna, 1930),[40] but as a monumental statement of future possibilities:

fig. 13
Daniel Argimón, untitled and undated. Set of drawings for Walden 7's advertising materials depicting soldiers being transformed into the factory silos located on the plot. © Ricardo Bofill Taller de Arquitectura.

fig. 14
Ricardo Bofill Taller de Arquitectura, Walden 7, Sant Just Desvern, Spain, 1970–75. Circulation galleries. © Jaime Silva.

[38] Álvarez Arce, "La última comunidad Walden (7)."

[39] Álvarez Arce, "La última comunidad Walden (7)," 223–26.

[40] During the 1934 Austrian Civil War, the Karl-Marx-Hof housing complex in Vienna (which can also be considered as a megastructure) was used as a barricade by the Democratic and Communist faction fighting against the ruling Fascists. See Leonardo Benevolo, *Historia de la arquitectura moderna [Storia dell'architettura moderna]*, 5th ed. (Barcelona: Gustavo Gili, 1982 [1960]), 559–73.

the physical embodiment of a progressive and democratic society, built to shatter the blinds drawn by Francoist indoctrination. Perhaps some repression might have been imposed on its Gauche Divine inhabitants. However, sooner or later, the awareness of the qualities of its way of life would have reached the remaining population.

Having this in mind, it would be fair to claim that the building is a late child of 1960s' culture. When looking at Richard Avedon (1923–2004) or Doon Arbus's (1945) photographs and interviews,[41] the similarities between Walden 7 and the people depicted from that decade are striking. The latent desire for equality, freedom, and individuality—without fear to question authority—is present in both. The 1960s, here seen as a political and behavioral revolution,[42] were fully adapted and embraced by Bofill and his colleagues: while the political revolution is expressed in their intelligent contestation of the regime (aligning with the fight against racial segregation and the war in Vietnam), the behavioral revolution is mirrored in the definition of an architecture capable of housing "the refusal of frontiers and etiquettes, the absolute desire for authenticity, the will for a free and non-possessive sexuality, the love for art, music and the ecstatic states, the sense of community and sharing, the passion for leisure and freedom."[43] In sum, it is the "mods" from Carnaby Street, the Beatles, The Living Theatre, Andy Warhol, Martin Luther King Jr., and so many others, all encapsulated in one single building. Besides, it is also curious to notice that Walden 7 constitutes the end of an era in the Taller's work, precisely at the same time 1960s' culture slowly faded away.[44] Borrowing the introductory words of *Les Sixties: Années Utopies* on that glorious decade, it is credible that the Catalan building also stands in the Taller's path as "a luminous radiation of hopes, a [symbol] of a mythical and improbable time, [and perhaps] a lost paradise."[45]

When visiting Walden 7 today, it is impressive to see how many of its design solutions continue to be successful, especially the ones concerning its communitarian intentions. Although the interiors of many of the apartments have been changed, the communal spaces have retained their cherished aura. The ground-floor retail spaces are almost all in use. There are ping-pong tables in the multipurpose spaces. The streets in the air are full of plants and small coffee tables ***(fig. 14)***. The rooftop is pristine, with its scintillant pools and green grass. It seems that the Taller's vision for the future was not that far-fetched, and maybe is still fit for many years to come.

In the end, more than identifying the fascinating path that binds an idealized critique to a solid form, a wider reasoning takes shape in Walden 7: architecture can not only offer a system of internal critiques of its past devices but also serve as a powerful tool of social intervention. Through program and design, criticism can give birth to the never-before-accomplished but ever-more-desired home.[46]

Biography
Jaime Silva (Portugal, 1994) is an architect and PhD student currently conducting research on collective housing at IST-University of Lisbon (IST-UL) with a scholarship from FCT. He obtained his master's degree at IST-UL, complemented with an exchange program at EPFL. In 2019, he was awarded the Álvaro Machado Prize and in 2021, together with Manuel Alves Campos, he won a special mention in the ReUse Italy competition. He has worked as an architect in the office of Eduardo Souto de Moura and as a teaching assistant for the Theory of Architecture classes at IST-UL. He is a member of the CiTUA research group.

[41] See Richard Avedon and Doon Arbus, *The Sixties* (New York: Random House, 1999).

[42] Laurent Gervereau and David Mellor, eds., *Les sixties: années utopies* (Paris: Somogy Editions d'Art, 1996), 8.

[43] ". . . refus de frontières et des étiquettes, désir absolu d'authenticité, volonté d'une sexualité libre et non possessive, goût de l'art, de la musique, des états extatiques, sens de la communauté et du partage, passion de loisir et de liberté . . ." (translated to English by the author). Remark from Frank Musgrove (1922–2011) on 1960s youth, here taken, due to its similarities, to identify the behavioral aspirations envisioned in the Taller's designs for Walden 7. Cited in François Bédarida, *La Société anglaise du milieu du XIXe siècle à nos jours* (Paris: Le Seuil, 1990), 368–69.

[44] "Once a utopian idealist I have become rationalist and Cartesian, with a keen sense of paradox, realizing that every building cannot involve a return to the beginning nor the invention of a completely new aesthetic. During this period, a new and highly specialized group was constituted, inaugurating a second phase at the Taller [as opposed to the first phase, which ended with Walden 7]. . . . we have become involved with the concept of city, plaza, and street, with the industry of prefabricated construction, with concrete as an artificial stone, and with the history of architecture and art as a whole" (Ricardo Bofill, "Introduction," in *Ricardo Bofill, Taller de Arquitectura: Buildings and Projects, 1960-1985*, ed. Warren James [New York: Rizzoli, 1988], 14–15).

[45] ". . . une éclaircie radieuse d'espoirs, un temps mythique, improbable, paradis perdu . . ." (Gervereau and Mellor, *Les sixties*, 7, translated to English by the author).

[46] The author is highly thankful for the kind assistance Ricardo Bofill Taller de Arquitectura provided in the persons of Natalia Chiner (executive assistant to the chairman) and Ale Garzón (archivist). The shared knowledge and the consulted archives on Walden 7 have contributed significantly to a deeper understanding of the building and its context. The author is also immensely grateful to professors Robert McCarter and Wilfried Wang for their sagacious and valuable mentorship throughout the paper's development. This paper was written within the framework of the PhD research "Dwelling Utopias: Modern Collective Houses from the Post-War in England, France and Spain (1945–1975)," which is integrated in the Doctoral Program in Architecture of Instituto Superior Técnico—University of Lisbon (IST-UL) and is being developed at the Centre for Innovation in Territory, Urbanism, and Architecture (CiTUA), with financing from national funds through Fundação para a Ciência e Tecnologia (FCT), by the PhD research scholarship no. 2020.08517.BD, and by the project UIDB/05703/2020 from the research unit CiTUA.

The Built Heritage of Peter Blundell Jones: The Architectural Critic's Own Houses as Built Criticism[1]

Xiang Ren

fig. 1
The Round House seen from the enclosed garden. Photo: Peter Blundell Jones.
Source: Peter Blundell Jones Archive, University of Sheffield, 2023.

By tracing Peter Blundell Jones's architectural criticism and linking it to his two most important built works – the Round House of 1976 and Padley Mill of 1995 – the British architectural critic's contribution to architecture as a form of Built Criticism and his overall built heritage are analyzed, drawing out the internal capacity of architecture as both a discipline and a profession to reconcile the literal and the built discourses in a sustained and living tradition.

keywords:

Peter Blundell Jones, Round House, Padley Mill, design reinterpretation; Built Criticism

Introduction

The built heritage of the British architect, educator, and writer Peter Blundell Jones (1949–2016) is little known. While he had a prominent career as an internationally acclaimed architectural critic and academic, Blundell Jones completed just two synthetic buildings as lead architect: the Round House in Devon (1976) for his parents as his first built project, and Padley Mill in Grindleford (1995) for his own family as his last. For Peter Blundell Jones, architecture was a practical art based on use. Both houses are still in use, making a strong statement for the architectural critic's own design projects as an extended form of criticism—Built Criticism.[2]

Peter Blundell Jones's architectural journey, his position in architectural history, theory, and criticism—including his specific agenda on organic modernism, which was reflected and extended in his two buildings—is traced. Based on original illustrations and materials from the Peter Blundell Jones Archive at the University of Sheffield and an oral history of interviews with the architect, the Round House and Padley Mill are analyzed. The study of Padley Mill is also based on the author's experience of the house's digital preservation, as well as on numerous personal encounters and professional building visits.[3] The two case studies inform a critical reinterpretation of both Peter Blundell Jones's contribution to architecture as Built Criticism and his built heritage.

Peter Blundell Jones's Criticism

> "He could read a plan at 30 paces and spot bullshit at 60."
> —Jeremy Till, "Peter Blundell Jones: An Obituary"

Peter Blundell Jones was trained as an architect at the Architectural Association School of Architecture (AA) in London during the late 1960s by influential postwar architectural figures such as James Gowan, James Stirling's first partner. Orthodox modernism had reached a crisis as buildings were produced on the basis of economics and construction technology, with issues of context and meaning being ignored. Yet the rise of postmodernism failed to convince some of the younger generation of architects at the time, including Blundell Jones. Instead, he found and developed other sensibilities from pre-modern times, in particular sharing the values and positions of British Arts and Crafts heroes—John Ruskin, William Morris, William Richard Lethaby, et al.—with an appreciation of the everyday, the handmade, the human trace, the as-found, social commitment, and poetic production.[4] This laid the foundations for

1 The author would like to acknowledge Prof. Wilfried Wang for his encouragement, patience, and detailed edits of the draft; Prof. Jasna Galier from the University of Zagreb of Croatia and Prof. Ruth Verde Zein from Mackenzie Presbyterian University of Brazil for their advice on this paper, of which an earlier draft was presented at the International Conference on Architecture as Built Criticism on October 22, 2023; Mariam Yamin and Eleanor Mulkeen-Parker from Sheffield University Library for supplying the images from the Peter Blundell Jones Archive; finally, thanks to Chrissie Poulson, Timothy Blundell Jones, and Jan Woudstra for their long-standing support with continuing Peter Blundell Jones's intellectual legacy.

2 The term "Built Criticism" was first coined and used at the International Conference on Architecture as Built Criticism, organized by Prof. Wilfried Wang and hosted at the College of Architecture and Urban Planning at Tongji University, Shanghai, in October 2023.

3 The digital preservation of Padley Mill was initiated in 2023, with the first stage of physical survey and digital reproduction of drawings completed by architectural practice Studio Cloud, cofounded by the author, and the second stage of three-dimensional reality capture through scanning and photogrammetry completed by the author with research assistants Dr. Huriye Armagan Dogan and Omid Ebrahimbaysalami in May 2024.

4 Peter Blundell Jones, "Architecture as Mnemonic: The Accumulation of Memories around Morris's Red House," *Nineteenth-Century Contexts* 21, no. 4 (2000): 513–40; Peter Davey, "Home Ground," *The Architectural Review* 1253 (July 2001): 61–63.

Blundell Jones's intellectual position, setting him on his lifelong architectural journey that stood in opposition to academic classicism, including the so-called postmodern classicism. He revisited buildings from early modernist and even pre-industrial times, with their human-based, additive, and organic forms of settlements and their rich, inclusive, and diversified lifeworld.

While still surveying the architectural world as a young architect, and before and after his appointment by Colin St. John Wilson at the Cambridge University Department of Architecture as an assistant lecturer (1979–83), Peter Blundell Jones had demonstrated his energy and enthusiasm for architectural criticism by championing the cause of the alternative strands of modernism, including organic modernism.[5] After Cambridge, his absence from academia facilitated the launch of his extraordinary career as one of Britain's most prominent architectural critics, which included winning the International Committee of Architectural Critics (CICA) Award for "Best Periodical of the Last Three Years" for the June 1985 special issue of *The Architectural Review* and "Architectural Journalist of the Year 1992" for articles on Louis Kahn and authenticity published in the *Architects' Journal*.[6]

Through research, publications, and lectures, Peter Blundell Jones steadily and firmly discovered that there were and still are resilient alternatives to modern architecture that understand and respond to human needs and patterns more empathetically than dominant modernism, such as those positions taken by early European modern architects like Hugo Häring,[7] Hans Scharoun,[8] and Erik Gunnar Asplund.[9] Blundell Jones's theoretical analyses and criticisms of the work of these three architects have not been surpassed. He had a productive relationship with Peter Davey during the latter's long and influential editorship of *The Architectural Review*, on many occasions acting as a guest editor[10] and introducing the then younger generations of British architects such as Richard Rogers and David Lea to an international audience.

In one of his key articles, "From the Neo-Classical Axis to Aperspective Space," based on analyzing the works of Häring, Scharoun, and Asplund, Blundell Jones argued that there is a tacit persistence and continuity of the Western classical tradition in the modern movement that deserves deeper interpretation:

> **This tacit persistence of tradition helps explain the evident loss of quality between the work of pioneers and that of later generations trained only according to the impoverished programme of the post-war years. To recover and understand this tacit persistence it is necessary to reject the tabula rasa, and also the idea of Modernism as a kind of stable plateau, to see it rather in terms of continuous and continuing evolution. We need to look at all the familiar landmarks which were chosen to support the old thesis.**[11]

Blundell Jones was one of the leading contributors to the definition of the uncompleted project and the living tradition of modern architecture. He approached this via an alternative line, extending beyond the original discourse on organic architecture as defined by Bruno Zevi.[12] In his perspective, history had never really disappeared under the modernist paradigm, as tacit continuities in the works of many leading modernists showed. Time and place were the starting points of Blundell Jones's criticism. Furthermore, in his many articles,[13] in which he discussed a wide range of issues, such as building typologies, contexts, and methods, he kept asking questions about how we know and what we think we know.[14] Whether the topic is a rural cowshed or an urban complex, understanding the specificity of a place is key to his analysis: how

[5] According to the author's email correspondence with Dean Hawkes during the summer of 2021.

[6] Peter Blundell Jones, "Leader: Organic Response", in "Organic Architecture," special issue, *The Architectural Review* 1060 (June 1985): 23–24; Peter Blundell Jones, "In Search of Authenticity," *Architects' Journal* 19 (1991): 22–25.

[7] Peter Blundell Jones, *Hugo Häring: The Organic versus the Geometric* (Stuttgart: Menges, 1999), 8–12.

[8] Peter Blundell Jones, *Hans Scharoun* (London: Gordon Fraser, 1978); Peter Blundell Jones, *Hans Scharoun* (London: Phaidon, 1995); Peter Blundell Jones, "A Forty Year Encounter with Hans Scharoun" (PhD thesis, University of Sheffield, School of Architecture, 2013).

[9] Peter Blundell Jones, *Gunnar Asplund* (London: Phaidon, 2006), 5–19.

[10] Such as for the March 1988 issue "Organic: A Living Tradition." He also introduced new names from Germany and the rest of Europe, such as Günther Behnisch and the Stuttgart-based architect Peter Hübner.

[11] Peter Blundell Jones, "From the Neo-Classical Axis to Aperspective Space," in "Organic: A Living Tradition," special issue, *The Architectural Review* 1093 (March 1988): 18–51.

[12] See Zevi's early alternative architectural history *Towards an Organic Architecture* that focused on Lloyd Wright, Aalto, Mendelsohn, and a few others, including Häring.

[13] Over five hundred published in forty-seven journals spread across thirteen countries.

[14] A full list and most of the digital copy can be extracted from the Peter Blundell Jones Library, an open-access academic resource set up by the author in 2020 with support from the University of Sheffield. Available here: https://sites.google.com/sheffield.ac.uk/peterblundelljoneslibrary/.

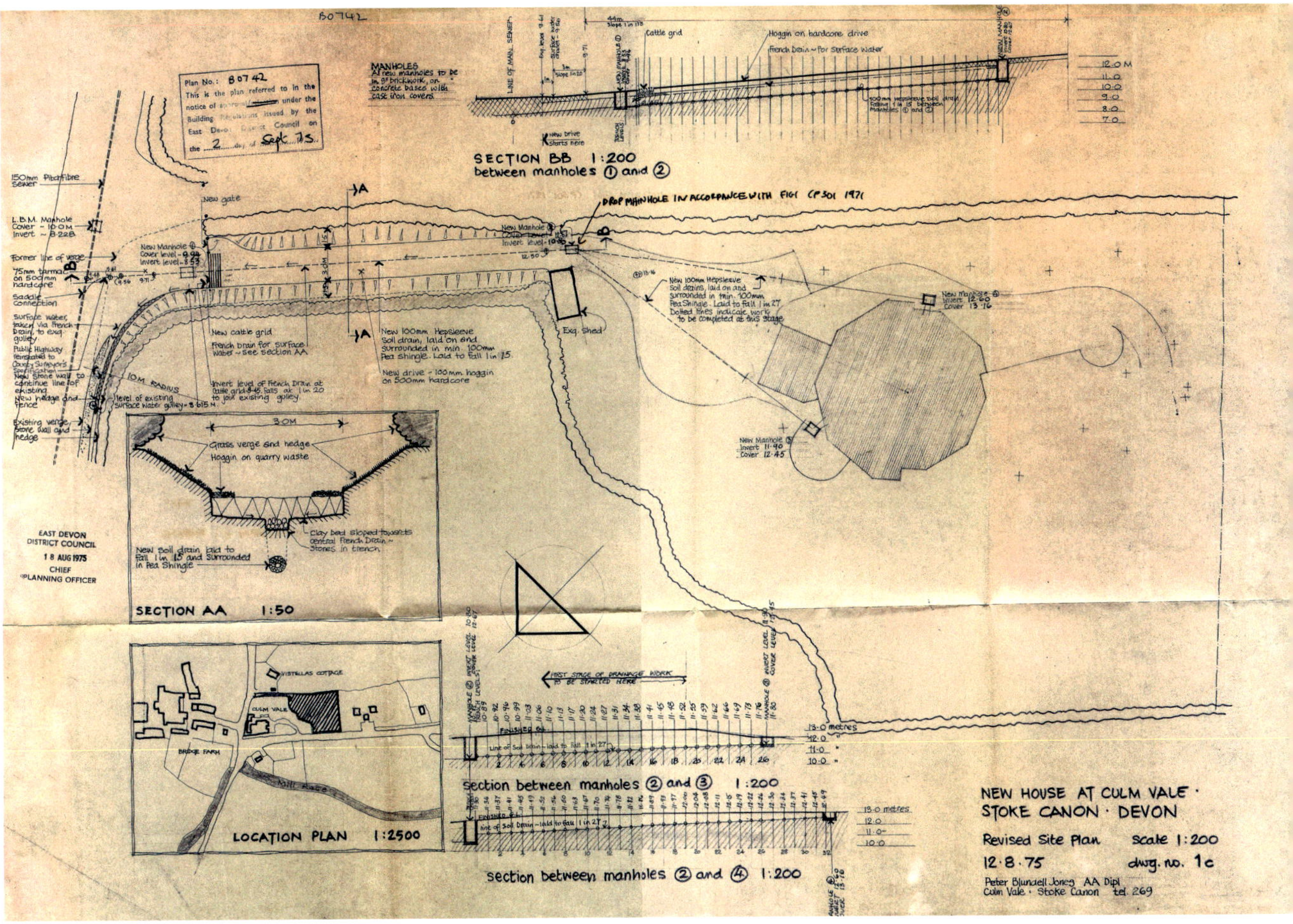

fig. 2
The Round House, site plan, 1:200. Drawing: Peter Blundell Jones. Source: Peter Blundell Jones Archive, University of Sheffield, 2023.

the place represents the point in history and the world in which it is situated; how the place reflects the users who dwell day to day in the world created by that place; how architecture makes a place and how it sets up a dialogue between individual people, the place, and society at large. With his thought penetrating the essence of architecture and with his uncovering of architecture's potential, Blundell Jones's architectural criticism was ahead of its time, particularly considering the context in which wider architectural criticism became part of the style wars that peaked in Britain with the then Prince Charles questioning modern architecture in favor of a return to classical architecture and the vernacular. In the twenty-first century, all that has been eclipsed with the growth of the internet and the collateral disappearance of professional journals, ushering in the demise of architectural criticism.

Peter Blundell Jones's Built Criticism via Two Houses

> "If he had not pursued an academic career, we would surely have enjoyed more Blundell Jones buildings."
> —David Lea, "Tributes Flood in for 'Irreplaceable' Tutor and Architectural Historian Peter Blundell Jones"

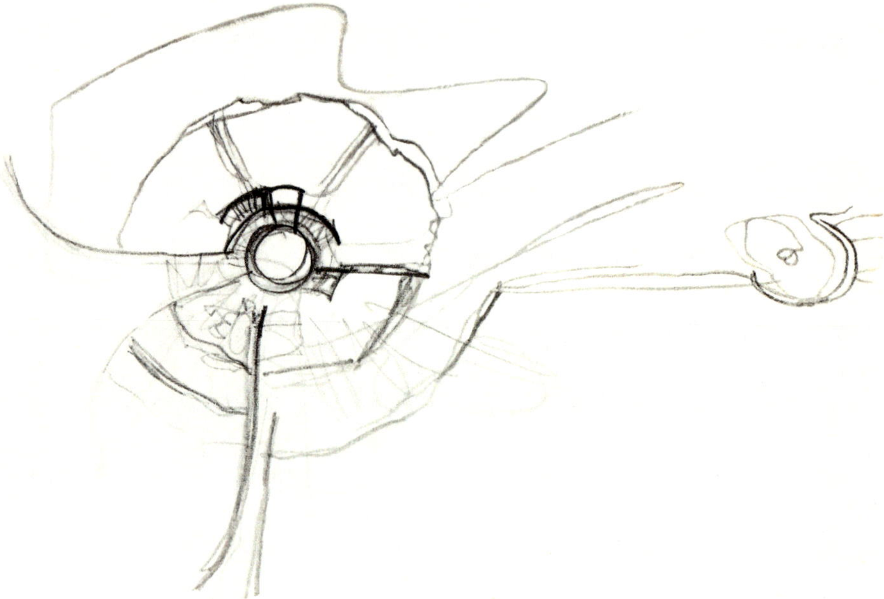

Practicing as an architect from the early 1970s until starting his full professorship at the University of Sheffield in the mid-1990s, Peter Blundell Jones designed quite a few buildings covering a variety of typologies from domestic to religious buildings. He often participated in the construction process.[15] His major works are the two family houses, not only because they were built and have been in active use but also because he was the designer, builder, and user, all three roles in one, allowing the architectural critic to connect different historical and theoretical aspects of architecture in an integrated design, construction, and criticism, and to examine it in real time and in situ as part of his family life.

fig. 3
The Round House, early sketch. Drawing: Peter Blundell Jones. Source: Peter Blundell Jones Archive, University of Sheffield, 2023.
fig. 4
The Round House, study model. Photo: Peter Blundell Jones. Source: Peter Blundell Jones Archive, University of Sheffield, 2023.
fig. 5
The Round House, floor plan. Drawing: Peter Blundell Jones. Source: Peter Blundell Jones Archive, University of Sheffield, 2023.
fig. 6
The space of transitions and the space of gathering of the Round House. Photo: Peter Blundell Jones. Source: Peter Blundell Jones Archive, University of Sheffield, 2023.

The Round House

In 1976, Peter Blundell Jones designed the Round House for his parents in Stoke Canon, a village in the county of Devon, southwest England ***(fig. 1)***. After completion, the building received a few minor awards and was even included in Nicholas Pevsner's *Buildings of England*. It can be seen as a first built prototype of Peter Blundell Jones's emerging Built Criticism of the then prevailing standardization of forms and layouts in British architecture.

Blundell Jones started by collecting information on the place, its history, and heritage. He was interested in how the ownership and use of the land, its landscape and settlement fabric, changed ***(fig. 2)***, and more importantly in how buildings meet the ground and construct their site. To balance the extensive level changes in the garden with the house's small footprint, a sense of center and orientation was needed in multiple directions to maximize the views to the immediate and distant surrounding landscape ***(figs. 3-4)***. Extending radial walls were chosen to divide each unit of the circular volume and to merge the house with the landscape, leaving the outer part of

[15] According to the author's interview with Peter Blundell Jones in April 2014.

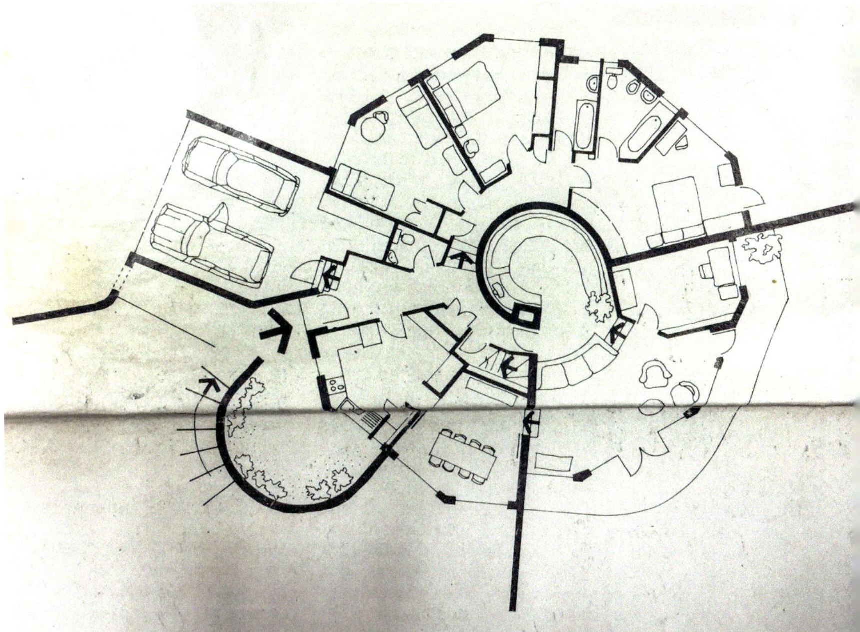

Plan showing pivotal living space with rooms wrapped around.

the garden to its own devices while the parts related to the living room and bedroom needed care and cultivation.

> **A room in the middle, heart and hearth, a family room where one can sit around the fire of a winter's evening: this is the dominant element to which all else relates . . . each room has a particular view, orientation, and relationship with the garden. . . . The geometry was broken, extended, shifted and modified to accommodate the various demands of internal and external pressures.[16]**

The circle or half-circle as the starting point of the Round House is the archetypal form for gathering, sharing communal events, and creating social space, as seen in the early choreographic documents on tribal dances. The spiraling movement of the circular plan pushes the individual units, bedrooms, toilets, and kitchen outwards, each with an intimately enclosed garden and a window with a view ***(fig. 5)***. Together they seem to fill the ground most conveniently, taking precisely the area available, while curating an internal circulation more like a medieval street spine than a modern corridor and leaving a series of spaces in between ***(fig. 6)***. At a smaller scale, they define thresholds as transitional spaces of encounter and liminality. The organic form of the Round House relates not only its geometry to the different outward views but also the internal spaces

[16] Peter Blundell Jones, "The Round House, Stoke Canon—Architect's Account" (unpublished, 1976), available at Peter Blundell Jones Archive, Sheffield University Library, and https://archives.shef.ac.uk/repositories/3/resources/433.

to their uses ***(fig. 7)***. Without the aid of a computer, Blundell Jones made every part specific, differentiating each room from the others in terms of filtered daylight and facilitated ventilation in this complex geometry of roofs and walls. Materials, detailing, and construction were subservient to the circular spatial ideas and were developed later to meet the limited budget and the construction techniques available locally.

The Round House is an earlier built testimony of Blundell Jones's first book, *Hans Scharoun*, developed from his AA thesis.[17] In this, he provided an alternative reading of modernism, revealing a freedom of design liberated from the need to use right angles and thereby recovering "the choice of direction." It brought home the need both to articulate "content to make recognizable territories" and to respond to site, neighbors, and terrain.[18] These were the guiding principles that determined the design of the Round House. The house also explores to its fullest the "tacit continuity" proposed by Blundell Jones around a decade later, between the architectural critic's key organic modernist protagonists and his specific belief about what a house means, namely the construction of a space for the family and a family of spaces. This involves a creative dialogue and a critical reinterpretation. The expression of the family's living space at the core of the Round House was not the most functionalist intention, but it centered on the collective archetype of human beings, from the primitive marking of a territory in a supernatural world to the purposeful marking of a territory in a modern world. The Round House manifests as a Built Criticism of the dominant industrial standardization in the building sector, which put ordinary people in uniform, by expressing Blundell Jones's view that architecture is a human discipline more concerned with how people come together through the built environment.[19]

fig. 7
The central family space of the Round House. Photo: Peter Blundell Jones. Source: Peter Blundell Jones Archive, University of Sheffield, 2023.

fig. 8
The main street frontage of Padley Mill. Photo: Peter Blundell Jones. Source: Peter Blundell Jones Archive, University of Sheffield, 2023.

[17] Blundell Jones, *Hans Scharoun* (1978).
[18] Jan Woudstra, "Peter Blundell Jones Obituary," *Guardian*, September 15, 2016, https://www.theguardian.com/artanddesign/2016/sep/15/peter-blundell-jones-obituary.
[19] Jeremy Till, "Peter Blundell Jones: An Obituary," October 2016, http://www.jeremytill.net/read/113/peter-blundell-jones-an-obituary.

Padley Mill

In 1995, a year after his professorial appointment at Sheffield and the same year he published his second monograph on Hans Scharoun,[20] Peter Blundell Jones was the architect, builder, and user of the conversion of an eighteenth-century ruined grit-stone water mill into his family home ***(fig. 8)***. It was to be his last building project.

In the 1990s, Sheffield was a thriving urban center with a strong legacy as a city of makers that was driving post-industrial regeneration and conservation of the nearby Peak District. Despite then prevailing perception in the UK of buildings as industrial products that were constructed with a high degree of control and precision, the pre-industrial rural landscape and fabric remains fundamental to how architecture works in the region. The project site is located in Grindleford, a picturesque Peak District village ***(fig. 9)***. The mill structure has been at the bottom of Padley Gorge since medieval times. In the mid-eighteenth century the building's core activity of milling determined its solid, rectangular form and volume. First a sawmill, then a café from the 1930s, later a house with a Grade II conservation listing from the 1960s, and subsequently derelict and deemed dangerous, without an interior structure, the mill was part of a conservation area near the entrance bridge of the village. This "developer-frightening" site was purchased by Peter Blundell Jones and his family at an auction in the summer of 1994. The mill was the subject of critical reinterpretation and the promotion of a new, place-sensitive architecture in an old structure, based on his many powerful criticisms of tabula rasa modernism.

Blundell Jones started by working with the givens and the limitations of the site. The as-found not only produced echoes of encounters and references for an experienced and humanistic architectural historian but also, first and foremost, inspired a

fig. 9
Reading the territory of Padley Mill via an axonometric sketch. Drawing: Peter Blundell Jones. Source: Peter Blundell Jones Archive, University of Sheffield, 2023.

[20] Blundell Jones, *Hans Scharoun* (1995).

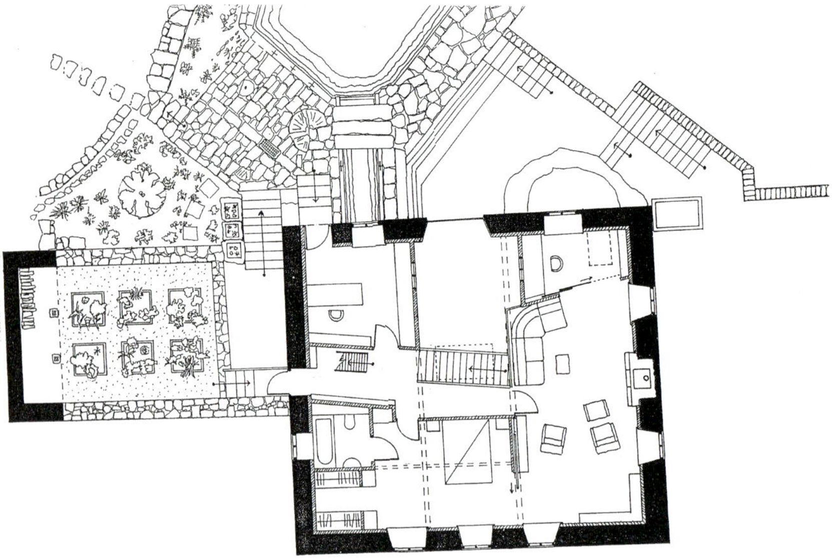

creative interpretation by an architectural critic. The walls of local stone with a thickness of five hundred millimeters and the double-pitched slate roof tiles were two retained elements. The restrained, modest configuration of the mill with its plain street frontage conceals a complex and unpredictable interior. The layout is determined by a cross axis, with the long one linking the front door, the main stair, and the garden door, as well as the stove in the old fireplace and the woodstore outside[21] ***(fig. 10)***. A new main beam of steel with a ten-meter span together with an aligned stair both disrupt and surprise visitors: they are set at an angle of six degrees to the old walls ***(fig. 11)***. This gesture accompanies domestic routines, with the living and dining spaces as the center of family life, directing the view towards the "big room"—a double-height void—and north towards the garden and pond, while protecting the visual exposure of the "small rooms" as a street spine navigating a vernacular settlement. The overall spatial trajectory enhanced from this gesture does not follow one defined view or coherent route but rather a series of spatial thresholds that articulates and holds together the fragmentary spaces of arrival, gathering, and circulation, full of intimate and individual incidents and their associated joys and surprises ***(fig. 12)***. As is common for a product made before the machine age, almost nothing in the original mill was straight or square, a quality that was respected and to which the response was organic: every millimeter's specificity deserved an individual evaluation and design decision, instead of applying a one-size-fits-all solution of the contemporary age of standardization. For example, the unexpected nonalignment in floor levels inspired both the cantilevered built-in sofa—an element seen frequently in Hans Scharoun's mid-period houses—and the eighty-two-degree skew in the study partition wall and sliding door, without disturbing the existing window relationships ***(fig. 13)***.

fig. 10
Ground-floor plan of Padley Mill. Drawing: Peter Blundell Jones. Source: Peter Blundell Jones Archive, University of Sheffield, 2023.
fig. 11
Padley Mill in adaptive reuse, with the new steel beam installed. Photo: Peter Blundell Jones. Source: Peter Blundell Jones Archive, University of Sheffield, 2023.

[21] Peter Blundell Jones, "Padley Mill: A Question of Interpretation," *Cuaderno De Notas* 17 (2016): 160–70; Peter Blundell Jones, translation and postscript by Xiang Ren, "Padley Mill: A Question of Interpretation," *Heritage Architecture* 1, no. 9 (2018): 71–82.

fig. 12
The skewed stair linking the ground-floor and the upper space. Photo: Peter Blundell Jones. Source: Peter Blundell Jones Archive, University of Sheffield, 2023.

fig. 13
The built-in sofa with the sliding walls overlooking the void. Photo: Peter Blundell Jones. Source: Peter Blundell Jones Archive, University of Sheffield, 2023.

It could be argued that Padley Mill represents an interior architecture that exhibits the fullest adherence to organic modernism. Its external appearance and aura speak of hundreds of years' presence, but its remodeled internal sequences and tectonics have become an organic, open-ended interpretation. The underground space of the building became Blundell Jones's archaeological site.[22] The built architectural criticism transcended the physical building through a series of gatherings of the University of Sheffield's architectural humanities researchers and the East-West Group, as well as academic publications in English,[23] Spanish,[24] and Chinese.[25] Padley Mill contributes to the discussions on retrofitting, the idea of the *plan libre* in contemporary architecture, the principles of adaptive reuse, and reinvestigating the roles of rooms, doors, and corridors in pre-modern architecture that were once studied as fragments along disciplinary lines.

[22] According to the author's interview with Peter Blundell Jones in March 2016.
[23] Davey, "Home Ground," 61–63.
[24] Blundell Jones, "Padley Mill," 160–70.
[25] Blundell Jones, translation and postscript by Xiang Ren, "Padley Mill," 71–82.

The Built Heritage of Peter Blundell Jones's Built Criticism

At first sight, there are no obvious similarities between the radial elements of the Round House on a generous site and the axial layout in a restrained existing structure of Padley Mill on a compact site. The irregular configuration of the Round House reflects a decentralizing tendency connected with the expression of human gathering rituals, moving away from a universal technique of axial and modular planning that was firmly developed by the Beaux-Arts and passed on to orthodox modernism. Distinct from this, the symmetric stability of Padley Mill is derived from a respect for the as-found. The mill's irregular formality is much more subtle and less explicit in its built form but rather expressive in detailed fragments, such as the angled stair, the plugged-in

northern glazing wall, the off-grid built-in sofa, and all the carefully preserved corners and turns of windows and doorways, that together constitute the silent backdrop to both the routine and the theatrical aspects of everyday life: reaching for a chair, putting a tea cup next to a window, opening the glazing to connect the living room to the garden on summer evenings ***(fig. 14)***, meeting guests on the corner sofa while overlooking another social gathering around the dining table, and so on. Both houses involve reading the site's territory—in the same way that Peter Blundell Jones's friend Giancarlo de Carlo would write[26]—and require creative design reinterpretations with the theatrical display of domestic rituals. Both presume the informality of the organic instead of the conventionality of the orthogonal. In both houses, the presence of human craftsmanship is the foundation of their architecture. However, spatial and visual similarities can be oversimplified; the presence of the spiritual and ethical at the

fig. 14
The newly added glazing wall opening to the garden. Photo: Peter Blundell Jones. Source: Peter Blundell Jones Archive, University of Sheffield, 2023.

[26] Peter Blundell Jones and Eamonn Canniffe, *Modern Architecture Through Case Studies* (London and New York: Routledge, 2007), 156.

human scale in both projects can be more significant than the visual and the haptic. That is the fundamental question of dwelling and how to dwell, and what it means in terms of design and use.[27]

For Peter Blundell Jones, the architect's range of expressions in built form and language is rich, extensive, and endless. Thus, it is possible for architectural critics to make a plea for their raison d'être and to create their own humble offerings to a world for which they hold an ethical responsibility to demonstrate how built culture might be readdressed, reintroduced, or repaired. Other British architects and architectural critics—Sir John Soane, John Ruskin, Reyner Banham, and Charles Jencks, to name a few—have used their own houses to demonstrate the fundamental human dimension of architecture. Jeff Malpas has unraveled the entanglements of "remembered place," "placed memory," "place-ness of the human," and the "humanness of place." In his sense, "the task of building, and of architectural design, becomes a task from which the ethical can never be excluded, and that is fundamentally tied to matters concerning the very formation of the human."[28] For Blundell Jones, the task of architectural criticism is to construct a view of the human in the formation of the world. As highlighted in his final book, *Architecture and Ritual*, "architecture provides a mirror that reflects our world, our knowledge about it and the way we interact with it."[29]

Peter Blundell Jones's architecture operates as an agent of change and exchange through an integrated practice of design and criticism in a single act of Built Criticism. Such an act is open to reinterpretations from multiple perspectives and authorships. Given this, architecture's quality as both a discipline and a profession lies in its capacity to reconcile the discursive and the built forms in a sustained and living tradition.

[27] Xiang Ren, "An Organic Connection with China: Architecture and Ritual by Peter Blundell Jones," *arq: Architectural Research Quarterly* 21, no. 3 (2017): 277–80.

[28] Jeff Malpas, *Rethinking Dwelling: Heidegger, Place, Architecture* (London: Bloomsbury, 2021), 119.

[29] Peter Blundell Jones, *Architecture and Ritual* (London: Bloomsbury Academic, 2016), 3; Xiang Ren, "Architecture and Ritual by Peter Blundell Jones," *Heritage Architecture* 2, no. 4 (2017): 112–13.

Biography

Xiang Ren (B Arch, MA, PhD) has taught and researched in architecture at The University of Sheffield School of Architecture since 2017. In 2016, he cofounded the RIBA chartered practice Studio Cloud. He is currently the School's director of architectural humanities research group, the founder of the Peter Blundell Jones Library, and the former director of the MA Architectural Design programme. His research has been shortlisted twice for the RIBA President's Research Awards in 2014 and 2016, and has continually attracted UK and international funding; the results have been published in leading architectural journals. From 2012 to 2016, Ren was taught by the late professor Peter Blundell Jones.

Architecture beyond Form

Naomi Mehta and Priyanka Salunkhe

fig. 1
The Kanchanjunga Apartments emerge as the modern spectacle amidst varying old and new vertical living typologies in the dense context of south Mumbai. Photo Courtesy: Harish Krishnamoorthy.

Conventionally, assessments of buildings are based on image narratives that prioritize form and aesthetics. This type of judgment lacks the critical engagement that is required to identify shortcomings in any particular design and leads to the reproduction of stylistic solutions as opposed to innovative strategies that seek to improve existing paradigms of design. Two "iconic" architectural projects are critically analyzed by comparing their spatial manifestations against their stated project intent, thereby engaging multiple scales of design through social, cultural, and economic lenses, alongside formal and spatial attributes. This approach constitutes a shift from perceiving architecture solely through its "iconicity and reputation" to celebrating instead the capacity of design to address binaries, establish equity through space, reimagine utilitarian templates, and serve both present and future needs. The critique of these two iconic modern projects, the Golconde by Antonin Raymond and the Kanchanjunga Apartments by Charles Correa, explores alternative designs in response – what could be called *Architecture as Critical Redesign.*

Introduction

Critical theory plays a crucial role in understanding the complexities and contradictions of architectural creation. In examining theory and practice beyond their original context, it offers practical insights and philosophical inquiries.[1] Like other professions, architecture relies on precedents, drawing inspiration from both past and present to shape the future and to navigate through the challenges of changing societal needs, values, and expectations. By reproducing precedents, the design failures that are concealed behind iconic imagery and lauded narratives are repeated. As Mark Wigley says: "Projects turn into projectiles and architectural quality is judged by the number of images that land around the world."

This "hyperconcentration of images" in today's world is a "distraction" overshadowing contemporary challenges that design needs to address.[2] The image-centric approach treats the architectural project like an object, focusing only on its *form* and ignoring the need for it to establish meaningful relationships with the physical and nonphysical context, that is, its *content*.[3] While form and aesthetics play a crucial role in creating architectural quality, they must also address the social, economic, and cultural dimensions of their context. Kevin Low argues that the allure of the image allows iconic reputation to overpower evaluation, preventing us from learning from a building's shortcomings, thereby perpetuating a cycle of stylistic solutions. Select contemporary buildings have been touted as symbols of perfection, ignoring their failings.[4]

Can such buildings be reimagined in alternate realities to transform them from being "objects of critique" to models of "critical redesign"?

Critical analyses of buildings incorporate broad parameters arising from spatial, programmatic, and sociocultural questions that are engaged across multiple scales of design. Thus, established notions of what constitutes "good quality design" could

keywords:

critical analysis, critical redesign, organizational strategies, design detailing

[1] Tonkao Panin, "Practice of Critical Theory in Architectural Schools: Twenty First Century Transformation," *Journal of Architectural/Planning Research and Studies* (JARS) 5, no. 3 (2018): 139-150. 10.56261/jars.v5i3.169103.

[2] Gianluca Croce, "Volume #2—Mark Wigley: Towards a History of Quantity," *Archis* (January 28, 2021), https://archis.org/volume/volume-2-mark-wigley-towards-a-history-of-quantity/.

[3] "Talk by Kevin Low | 31 Oct, 2020 | FA M20 Lecture Series," CEPT University, 2021, YouTube video, https://www.youtube.com/watch?v=6y0TSGqvWXs.

[4] "Talk by Kevin Low."

be challenged, allowing the prevailing discourse to be expanded to include considerations of culture, inclusivity, and sustainability. In this way, projects could be assessed beyond the architectural object.

To demonstrate this idea, two "iconic" projects are critically analyzed and evaluated across three scales of spatial response: first, at the scale of their interaction with the city; second, at the scale of their organization and planning; and third, at the scale of their materiality and design detailing. Following the critical analysis, the iconic projects are subject to critical redesign in the form of spatial reimaginations at the three scales through interventions within the existing projects. Critical redesign acts as a catalyst for positive change through the method of adaptive reuse, enabling these buildings to remain relevant, responding to multiple users and changed needs, breaking away from the utilitarian and formalist templates to arrive at innovative solutions.

The two iconic modern buildings to be evaluated in this essay introduced iconoclastic ideas of living to their respective contexts. The first case is the Golconde in Pondicherry (now Puducherry) (1937–45), a four-story dormitory designed by Antonin Raymond (1888–1976) for the disciples of Sri Aurobindo (1872–1950) that is known to be a material manifestation of the latter's philosophy. The second case is the Kanchanjunga Apartments ***(fig. 1)***, built from 1970 to 1974 in south Bombay (now Mumbai), a luxury condominium designed by Charles Correa (1930–2015). The former promotes the ascetic lifestyle of its users in the presence of lush green gardens, while the latter establishes a sumptuous living environment characterized by beautiful views and voluminous spaces. The following demonstrates how these two projects with varying intents, contexts, and design ideals can be scrutinized systematically through a set of philosophical, pragmatic, and spatial inquiries against the backdrop of their design objectives.

Towards a Critical Approach

The critical redesign methodology adopted here and outlined below draws from an academic exploration at CEPT University developed by the studio mentors Kevin Low and Shubhra Raje to provide versatile and project-specific criteria for intervention in given architectural projects.[5]

1. **The building as a part of the city**
   A building is not simply an object. As soon as it is placed in a larger context, it surpasses its form and spatial dimensions and becomes a part of the social, economic, cultural, and political phenomena of its surroundings. The profession's responsibility extends beyond the strict interpretation of the brief and the limitations of the site to include both its direct and indirect users.
2. **Organizational strategies and planning**
   A building's planar and sectional organization, when understood as a coherent whole, establishes the effective relationships between functions and interior and exterior realms. These design aspects have the potential to bring together users, light, air, movement, and program to create a holistic response that extends beyond utilitarian use.
3. **Materiality and design detailing**
   It is imperative to evaluate the consistency of the manifestation of the project's concept across scales, from its response to the city to its response to even a bathroom drain. A project's success can be defined by the sensitivity with which all types of human uses are reflected in the choice of materials and design detailing. Architectural details should reflect a combined effort towards aesthetic form, functionality, and the respectful engagement of the building with its users.

[5] Kevin Low and Shubhra Raje, "Towards a Critical Project and a Project of Critique," studio, CEPT University, spring 2022, Ahmedabad, India.

fig. 2
Golconde- a four-storeyed dormitory for the disciples of Sri Aurobindo

Golconde

Sri Aurobindo was an Indian philosopher whose preaching influenced a large segment of the population in and around the province of Pondicherry in the early 1900s, subsequently leading to the formation of the Sri Aurobindo Ashram in 1926. After his death, Mira Alfassa, famously known as the Mother, intended to crystallize his philosophy into the form of a built dormitory meant exclusively for the disciples to practice their *sadhana*, a practice of spiritual self-training and exercise to attain peace of mind.

In 1937, Golconde became the first modernist building in India ***(fig. 2)***, conceived by Tokyo-based Czech-American architect Antonin Raymond. It is a four-story dormitory in the now dense urban context of Puducherry. It was not until a couple of decades after its conception that architects around the world became aware of its existence, and soon Golconde gained iconic status by being lauded as an unsung masterpiece.

As stated by Raymond, it was clear that "the purpose of the dormitory was not primarily the housing of the disciples; it was the creating of an activity, the materialization of an idea, by which the disciples might learn, might experience, might develop, through contact with the erection of a fine building."[6]

[6] Pankaj Vir Gupta, Christine Mueller, and Cyrus Samii, *Golconde: The Introduction of Modernism in India* (Delhi: Urban Crayon Press, 2010), 29.

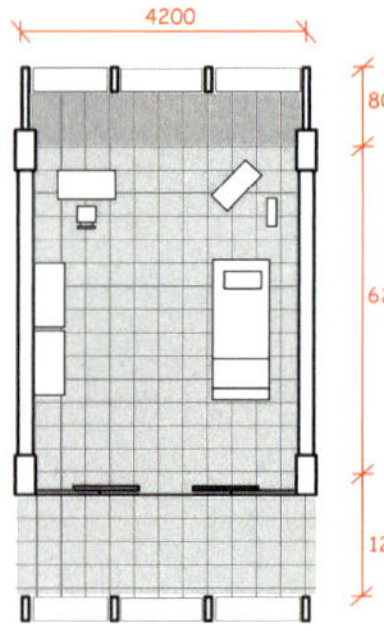

Single-room-unit plan

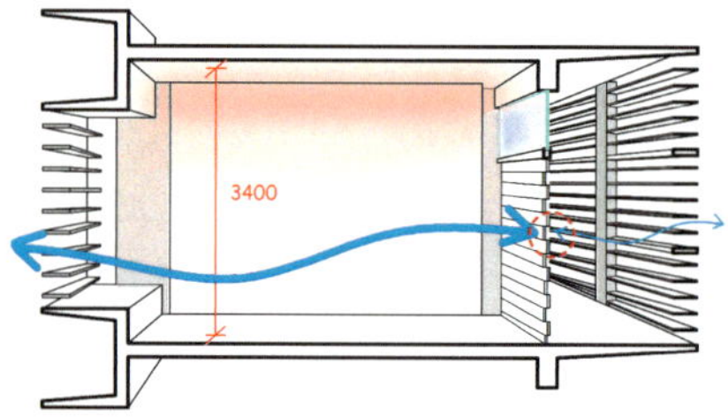

Single-room-unit section

Louvers

North corridor

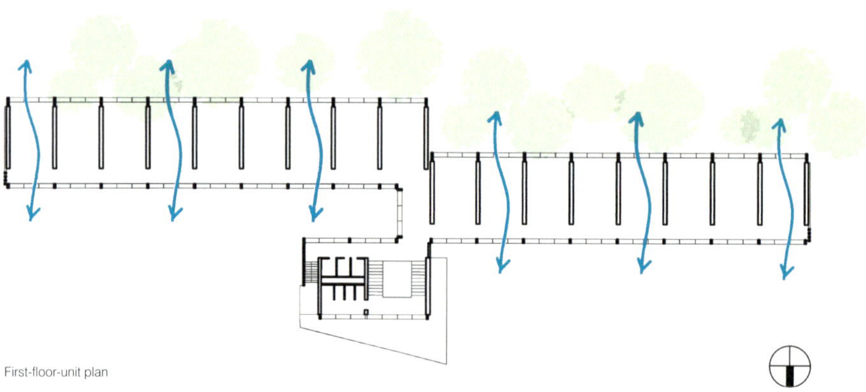

First-floor-unit plan

View of the north facade

fig. 3
Spacious and voluminous individual units are repeated along the two wings of the dormitory and connected by a staircase and toilet block. The corridors act as a buffer zone to protect the units from the harsh summer sun. Closely knit slats avoid compromising on the cross-ventilation of air.

This idea was twofold:

1. **Divine consciousness:** This encompasses a spiritual journey of reflection, meditation, and *asanas* (yoga postures), bringing the disciples to the realization that all details of external life are inconsequential to the larger scheme of things.
2. **Human unity:** Aurobindo believed that human unity is the deepest spiritual need, a future necessity.[7]

By practicing both these ideas in conjunction, Sri Aurobindo believed that a disciple would reach true transcendence. While the building is most celebrated for its technical finesse and extraordinary craftsmanship, a critical investigation becomes imperative to analyze how the abovementioned ideas are manifested in tandem with their spatial articulation in the building.

Critical Analysis

Single-Room Unit

The first idea of divine consciousness seems to have been expressed quite eloquently through the single-room units. The skin of the building consists of a hundred louvers that, when opened to the spacious individual rooms, make one feel like there is no building at all, only a suggestion of one. The finely crafted furniture pieces, too, feel like objects in space that only enable one's retreat. However, the closely knit slats of the wooden door compromise the ventilation across the louvered facades on either side of the building, and the glass panels prevent the expulsion of hot air from the room, resulting in an uncomfortable stay during the hot months in Puducherry ***(fig. 3)***.

[7] Sri Aurobindo preached true human unity "to pursue its upward evolution towards the finding of expression of the Divine . . . taking full advantage of the free development and gains of all individuals and nations and groupings of men, to work towards the day when mankind may be really and not ideally one family . . . it is evidently a part of Nature's eventual scheme and must come about." Human unity is hence understood as transcendence being achieved through engaging and uplifting fellow human beings in need so everyone can reach a level of divine consciousness. See Aravinda Ghose, *The Ideal of Human Unity* (Puducherry: Sri Aurobindo Ashram, 1950), 63–64.

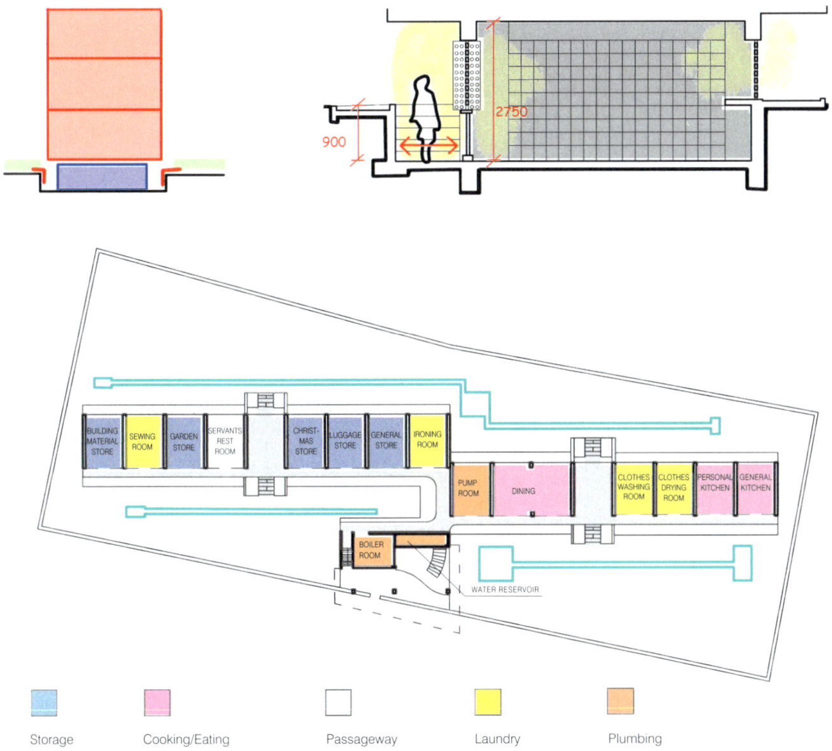

Basement–garden relationship

fig. 4
The top three floors accommodate the individual units, while the communal realm is located on the ground floor. The apologetic relationship between the ground floor and the gardens compromises the quality of light in the communal rooms. Because of the haphazard organization, the relationships between the storage facilities, cooking and eating activities, and laundry are not adequately addressed.

The Ground Floor Communal Space

The latter idea of human unity emerges when one further investigates the building in sectional terms. While the top three floors house the disciples' retreat, the ground floor means to engage them in communal activities.

However, the abrupt sectional separation of the gardens and ponds—which are treated as pristine entities—from the ground floor that hosts communal activities establishes a strident relationship between the two and causes the internal rooms to be overly dark. The south facade, with its fixed perforated windows, and the north facade, with a 900 mm wide corridor sandwiched between the outer wall of the inner corridor and the garden retaining wall, do not admit adequate daylight. Activities spill over into the exterior corridor, making it evident that residents long for daylight in order to carry on with their pursuits ***(fig. 4)***.

Furthermore, the different communal functions assigned to individual rooms also suffer from a lack of articulation as a result of haphazard distribution. Storage facilities, cooking and dining activities, and the laundry are not organized in proximity to other related activities, nor is the separate nature of public and private activities addressed ***(fig. 4).*** The series of rooms is simply a repetition of the structural modules devised for the top floors. Here, the rituals that foster communal life are neither valued nor expressed through the built form.

fig. 5
Golconde in the urban context of Puducherry.

Interface with the City

The idea of human unity is not only meant to foster communal relationships amongst the disciples but also was preached to engage the marginalized, as an act of service, so that everyone could reach a higher level of consciousness.

Golconde is located within the historic precinct of the French colony in Puducherry ***(fig. 5)***. A straight road with a canal running alongside racially separated the French Town from the Tamil Town (often the former was referred to as the *White* Town and the latter as the *Black* Town). A similar colonial mindset persists today towards the vendor community, the city's true residents, who are left unaddressed even though they constitute 50 percent of the city's population.

Golconde is surrounded by a 3.3 m high boundary wall, with the only breaks being for a main entry door and a service door, separating its grounds completely from the urban fabric of the city. If indeed transcendence is paramount—Sri Aurobindo speaks of the need to engage with fellow human beings and not to isolate oneself—how is it that this wall negates such a crucial aspect of the programmatic philosophy with its divisive character?

Architecture as Critical Redesign

The following design interventions respond to the critique raised by using the same framework proposed earlier in the essay.

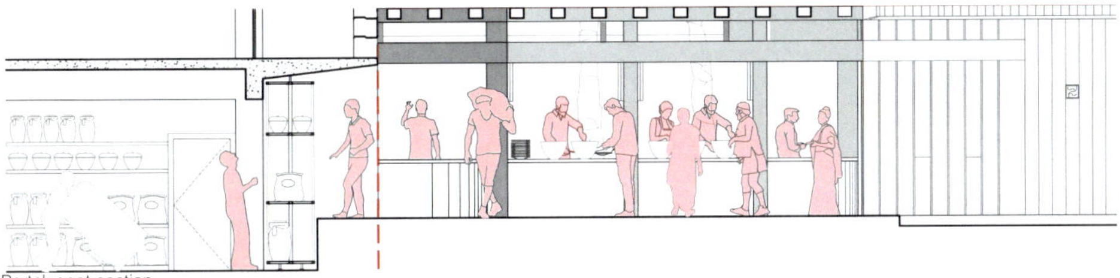

Portal: spot section

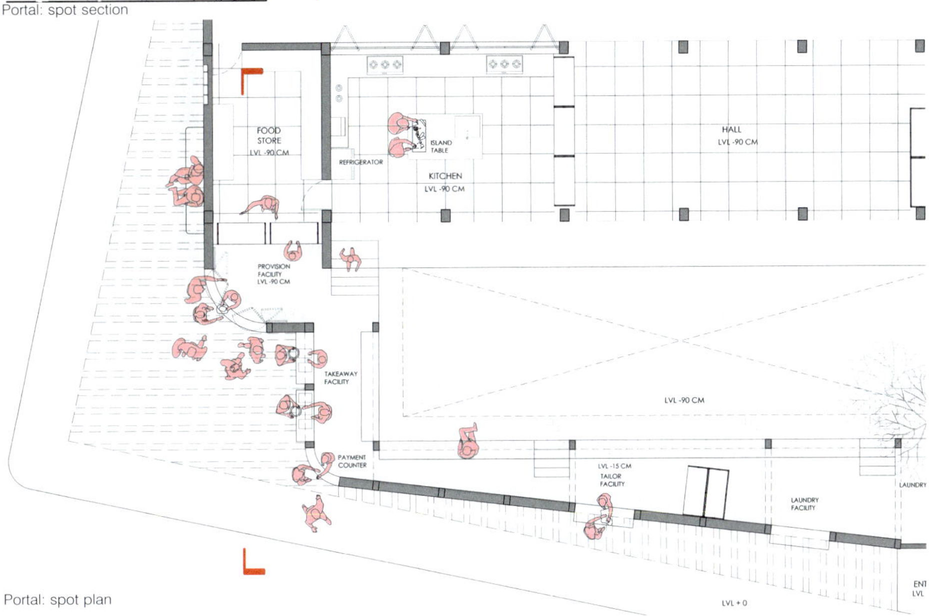

Portal: spot plan

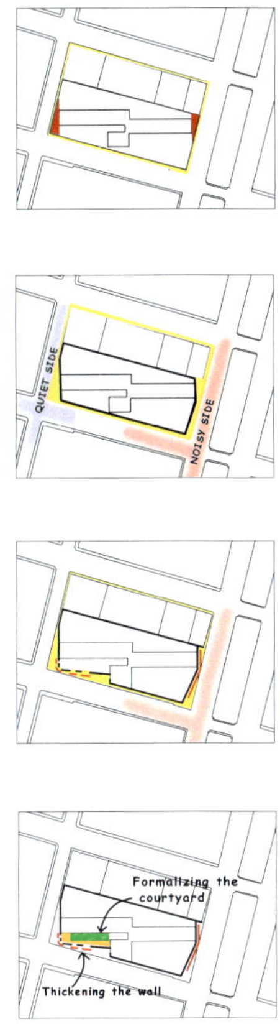

fig. 6
Proposed intervention: Portals along the boundary wall extend the services of subsidized cooking and laundry facilities to the ones in need.

The Building as a Part of the City

The boundary wall, a rather unexplored architectural element, is a building's first interaction with the city. Rather than being completely cut off from the neighborhood, this proposed intervention reimagines the northwestern edge of Golconde as one that provides *service*. Services representing the oeuvre of the ashram, such as cooking and laundry, are extended to the larger vendor and blue-collar community of Puducherry by thickening the boundary wall and inserting *portals* ***(fig. 6)***. These portals open once or twice a day and the cooking activities are extended as a provisions store as well as a takeaway facility. The laundry accepts clothes in the morning and returns them in the evening. The internal courtyard is reconfigured as one that allows for the delivery of services while also acting as a threshold between the private communal spaces and the public portals. The new proposal allows for the true essence of human unity to be realized, through the act of service.

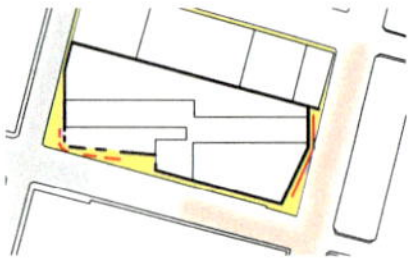

The Golconde interface

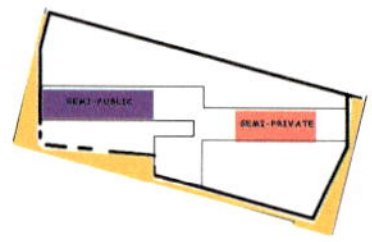

Separation of realms: activity and storage

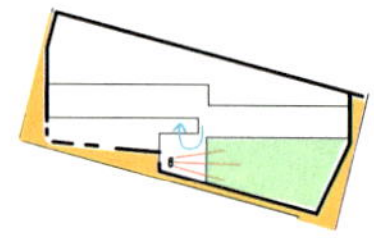

Curating a scenic entrance

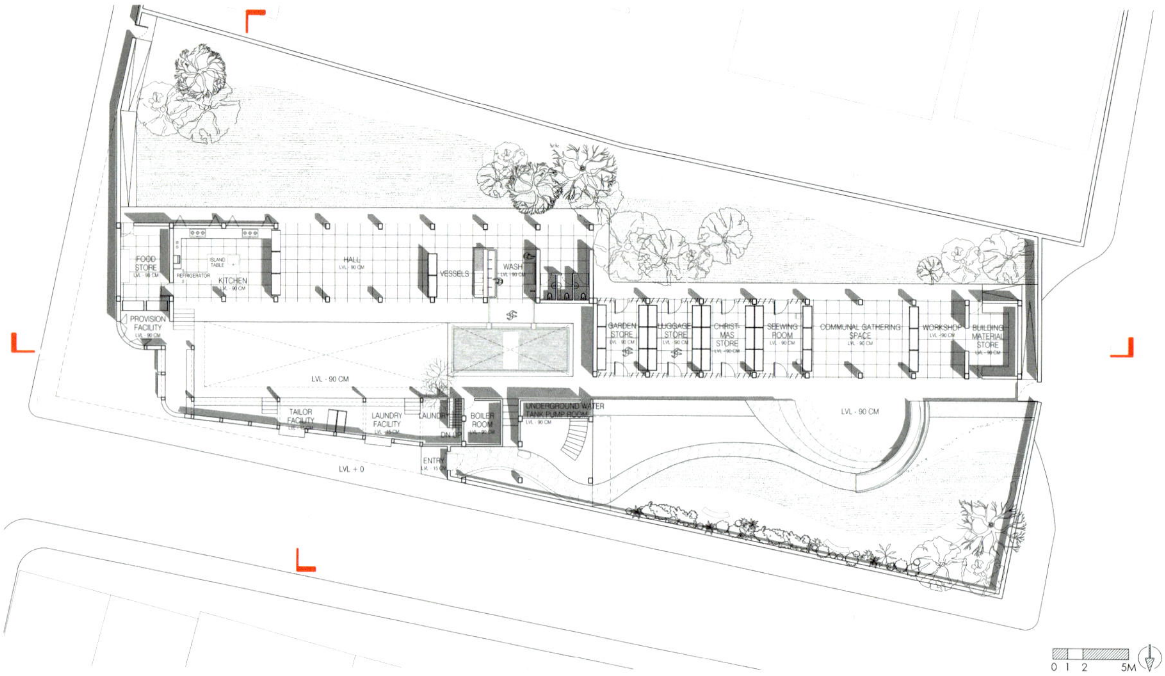

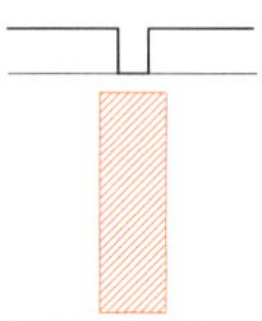

Hovering storage-serves the activity.

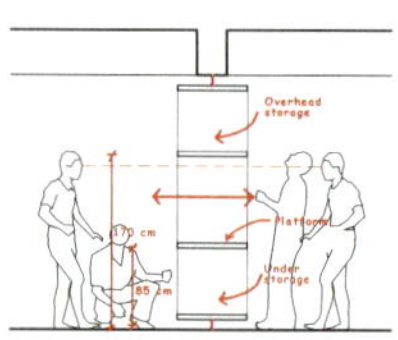

Modulating the unit in the above illustrated way makes it multi-functional.

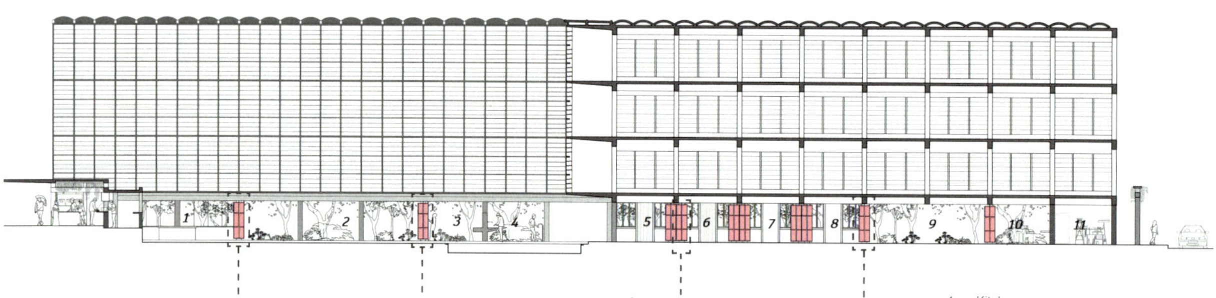

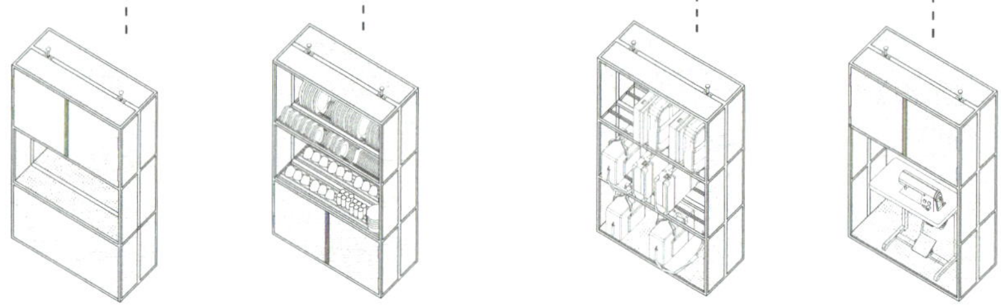

1. Kitchen
2. Dining Hall
3. Vessel washing
4. Hand washing
5. Garden store
6. Luggage store
7. Christmas store
8. Sewing room
9. Semipublic communal gathering space
10. Workshop
11. Building material store

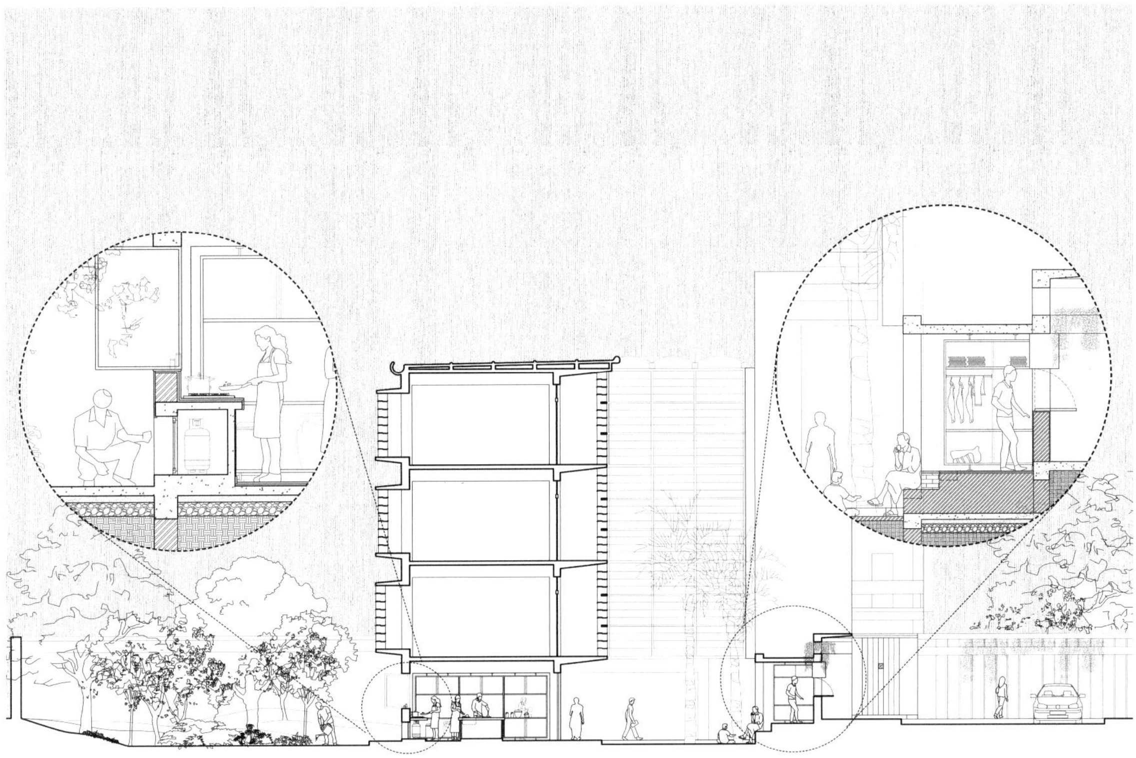

Organizational Strategies and Planning

The haphazard organization of the existing plan, which does not respect the daily activities as rituals but reduces them to mere functions, is addressed by a proposed reconfiguration of the plan that aims to free up the entire ground floor so it can be perceived as a veranda with the potential to accommodate various kinds of activities, with the storage units used as thresholds to indicate their separation from one another. The semiprivate realm containing intimate communal activities like cooking and the washing of vessels is separated from the semipublic realm. Dedicated storage facilities and meeting spaces, where smaller, more intimate gatherings can take place, are assigned to the west wing without disturbing the daily activities in the east wing. The newly formed entrance opens to a picturesque view ***(fig. 7)***.

Materiality and Design Detailing

To strengthen the idea of unity within the communal realm at a detailed level, storage is interpreted as a suspended volume, with the connections articulated in such a way that it appears to be an object belonging to a larger area while simultaneously subdividing the space and creating thresholds to either side ***(fig. 8)***.

The redesigned section across the kitchen encapsulates the new spirit of Golconde ***(fig. 9)***. Cooking and eating are now aided by cross-ventilation and carried out while looking over the lush green garden to the south, with kitchens and food service opening to the north in proximity to the remodeled boundary wall serving the marginalized urban community. The spatial ideas are reinforced at the scale of materiality and design detailing.

fig. 7
Proposed intervention: Reorganizing the ground floor to celebrate communal activities as daily rituals (semiprivate realm) rather than specific functions and to provide a formalized gathering space (semipublic realm).

fig. 8
Proposed storage units serve activities hosted on the ground floor and act as thresholds to separate the different spaces.

fig. 9
Reorganization of the ground floor is reinforced by design detailing, carrying forward the intent across all scales of design

The building is located in the dense, upper-echelon neighborhood of Mumbai.

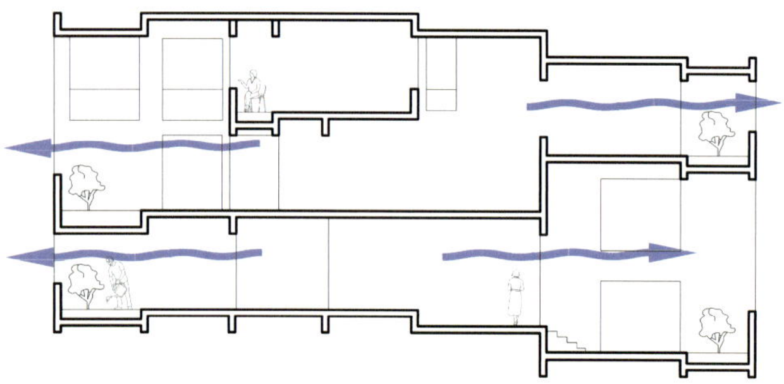

The iconic split-level section with interlocked apartments promises maximized ventilation, Original Design Concept.

Kanchanjunga Apartments

Vertical apartments were built during the second half of the twentieth century in response to the acute shortage of housing across the globe. Each of these projects reimagined the idea of vertical living in their differing contexts. In India, particularly in the dense city of Bombay, vertical housing projects were responding to the rapid increase in population by creating compact, modular apartments that could house a multitude of people.[8]

Deviating from the dominant paradigm of "matchbox living" that permeated the housing market, apartments for the urban affluent were designed to be relatively spacious and diverse. The Kanchanjunga Apartments conceived by Charles Correa in 1983 are an example of vertical luxury living of their time. Located in a dense upper-class neighborhood of Bombay, the apartments were considered a breakthrough in vertical luxury housing.[9] The novelty of the scheme was multifold ***(fig. 10)***:

1. Split-level apartments stretching facade to facade. The apartments were vertically interlocked with each other through combinations of three-, four-, and five-bedroom units. This was similar to the sectional relationship observed in Unité d'Habitation.
2. In accordance with the modernist architecture of that time, the bare, symmetrical elevations of Kanchanjunga stood out in the dense city context.
3. Unlike other apartments in Bombay, the promise of a large, cantilevered, double-volume terrace garden overlooking the cityscape was an enticing amenity for users.
4. All of these ideas were combined to deliver the promise of "a bungalow in the air," providing a sense of luxurious living. The iconic sectional drawing depicted the "maximized cross-ventilation" the apartments would provide and rooted them as a response to the local climate.

fig. 10
The iconic conceptual section and photographs emphasizing the panoramic views, large volumes, and modernist facade of the Kanchanjunga Apartments.
Existing Project photographs: Top: Photo by Rohinton Irani, copyright, Charles Correa Associates, courtesy Charles Correa Foundation. (Middle + Bottom): Photo by Charles Correa, courtesy Charles Correa Foundation.

8 Hasan-Uddin Khan, Sherban Cantacuzino, and Charles Correa, *Charles Correa: Architect in India*, rev. ed., (London: Butterworth Architecture, 1987).

9 Khan, Cantacuzino, and Correa, *Charles Correa*.

fig. 11
The existing ground-floor plan of the Kanchanjunga Apartments lacks distinct zones of circulation, parking, vehicular and pedestrian mobility, and well-articulated staff spaces. The photographs document the unarticulated and neglected conditions along the street edge, the dingy parking area, and the ill-considered staff spaces in the building.

The Kanchanjunga Apartments were a celebrated project; the design contributed to the architectural discourse with its new approaches to housing. After admiring its beautiful elevation from a distance, how does a critical analysis view this building beyond the iconic drawings, photographs, and narratives? How is the building experienced at the ground level? How does the bare facade respond to the heavy monsoons and the heat of present-day Mumbai? Do the spatial articulations of the apartment unit facilitate or inhibit cross-ventilation? These are some initial questions that arise before delving deeper into the macro- and microlevel.

Critical Analysis

The Ground Floor: An Interface with the City

Approaching from Peddar Road in Mumbai, the Kanchanjunga Apartments boast a sleek silhouette ***(fig. 10)***. At this scale, it appears like an object in the city. Inching closer, it reveals itself to be on a raised podium comprising shops and lobbies. Apart from the two entrance gates from the main road, the perimeter remains an under-articulated threshold between the street and the building, lined with car parking, scattered vegetation, improperly-disposed-of waste, and a bus stop. Set back from this perimeter is an array of shops with glass facades providing a visual relationship to the street but offering no access within. The public realm of the street, the semipublic realm of the shops, and the private realm of the building share no interfaces.

The building has accommodated multiple shops and residences since its inception ***(fig. 11)***. Today, it also houses consular offices on its lower floors. The multiple programs and users share a single arrival plaza at ground level, creating an intense overlap between pedestrian and vehicular movements. While one side of the ground floor is overburdened by an excess of movement, the other part is misused as a waste dump. An analysis of all these zones reveals the chaotic circulation at ground level. Programs with varying demands for privacy and security require spatial articulations with multiple thresholds that are currently absent. The result is a lack of a sense of arrival and transition from the bustling city into the precinct of the tower.

In the original design, the ground floor was not laid out to accommodate the needs of its dominant user group, the staff and security personnel. They have no shade and or designated areas of respite. As a result, they inhabit the crevices of the building, the entrance gates, the exposed arrival foyers, and the dark underground parking, which all lack light and ventilation.

The perfunctory ground level shows a rudimentary relationship between the tower and the immediate urban context. While the iconic section is intended to maximize cross-ventilation, its conceptual ingenuity is not extended to the design concerns at ground level. A project should also be judged on the way it situates itself vis-à-vis its surroundings.

fig. 12
The unit plan can be compared next to photographs of the apartment showing insufficient light and ventilation in parts of the kitchen, staff quarters, and living room.

fig. 13
The iconic section is redrawn to visualize the prevalent glass fenestrations and the unventilated ground floor. The diagrams highlight the climatic shortcomings arising from the building's formal aspirations of symmetry.

The Apartment Units

The building fulfilled its aspiration to offer cantilevered, double-volume balconies for each apartment by means of a shear-wall structural system. A central core containing elevators, staircases, and entrance foyers is surrounded by the apartment units, two at each level, mirrored along the northwest–southeast axis. Within each apartment, the balconies, the washrooms, and the staff quarters were placed on the periphery to act as "buffers" between the bedrooms, kitchen, and living room and the exterior. As a result of this plan organization, the central core has neither daylight nor fresh air. The entrance doors of the symmetrically facing apartments are opposite each other, limiting the grace and sensitivity of arrival into a residence and raising privacy concerns. Inside each apartment, the entrance door opens to the landing of the stairwell, creating an inconvenient junction at the entrance ***(fig. 12)***.

The small staff quarters are placed between two short shear walls, a blank wall, and a small fixed-glass window. The room can only be ventilated by opening its door. The kitchen (a key facility subject to continuous use in the Indian context), despite requiring maximum light and ventilation, was designed with a similar restrictive attitude.

Fixed-glass windows and glass doors are also used in the bedrooms. Cross-ventilation in the apartments is hampered by the lack of attention to design details that could allow the concept to work. Thus, despite the intention to facilitate maximized natural ventilation and function without air-conditioning, the compartmental composition and detailing of the apartment results in active strategies of thermal comfort still being required. There is also a sense of disregard for human privacy and comfort.

The intermediate levels create physical discontinuities across the iconic section. They separate the living spaces and terraces from one another into designer-defined zones that lack the possibility for transformation or expansion by the users. While the architects portrayed the idea of choice and customization thanks to a variety of unit types, the apartments' actual arrangement denies the users any flexibility in rearranging the unit. The use of a shear-wall structure restricts the inhabitants' dynamic needs by preventing post-construction changes.

The symmetrical organization of the units creates an elevational symmetry of openings and contributes to the building's unique formal expression. However, the identical mirroring of apartments along the northwest–southeast axis exposes the units facing southwest to constant harsh heat and heavy rains compared with those facing the northeast direction. Despite the different conditions depending on elevational

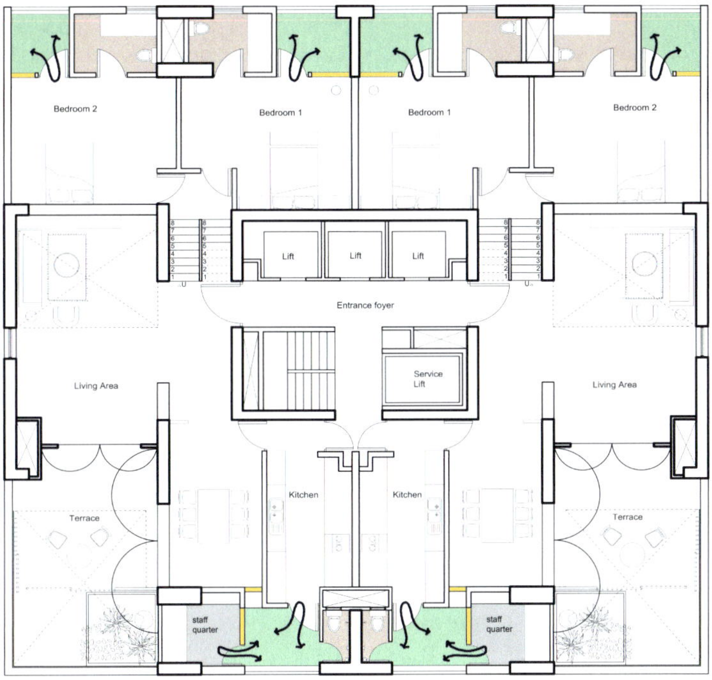

The articulation of details in the kitchen, bedroom, and staff quarters allows he passage of light but does not allow for suficent ventilation in the unit.

Top to bottom
Existing kitchen, bedroom, and living room are ventilated through open doors as the windows are designed with fixed glass.

The symmetrical plan is not designed to respond to the variations of heat and rain as experienced on the different building faces. The lack of overhangs on the bare facade exposes the building to the harsh monsoon climate of the city.

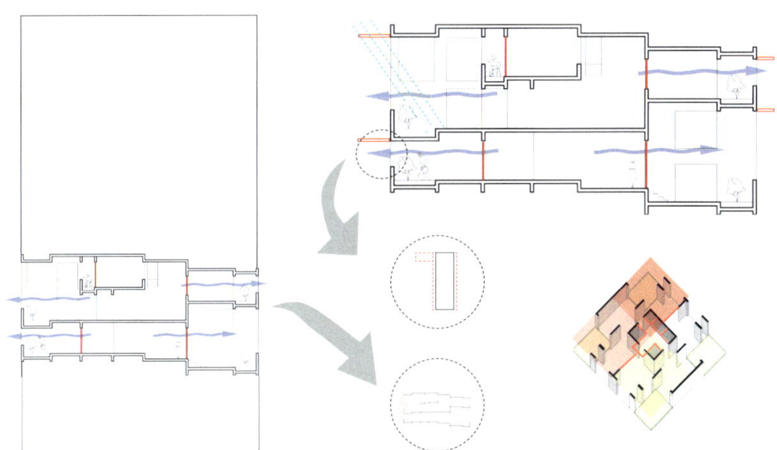

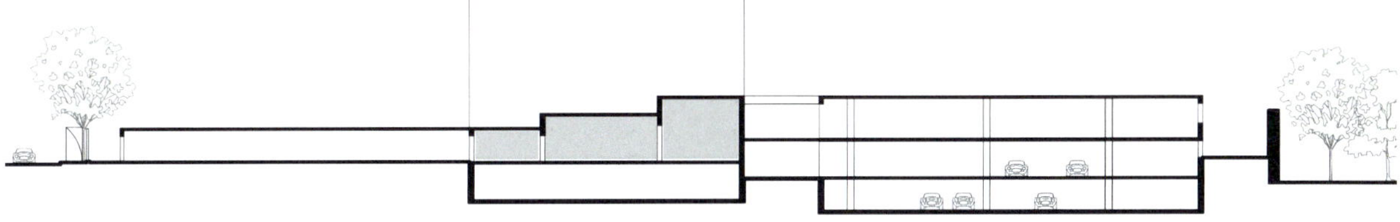

fig. 14
The reorganization of the ground floor creates green interfaces between various functions, enabling cross-ventilation of the ground-level section. The screens on the perimeter of the cantilevered terraces can be used to turn them into "outdoor rooms" at times of harsh heat or rain, or to retain their seamless relationship with the outside at other times.

orientation, there is no design response to tackle these issues. The lack of overhangs exposes the facade to constant weathering and heat gain ***(fig. 13)***.

These findings pose the questions: Is vertical luxury living in the Kanchanjunga Apartments limited by size, views, and form? Can these alone be used to define its architectural quality? How do we accommodate ideas responding to the context and to the multiple users and uses, as well as ideas of transformability, alongside aesthetic choices?

Architecture as Critical Redesign

The critical evaluation of buildings is the basis for their preservation and care. The following design interventions are a critical redesign as raised through the framework outlined earlier in the essay.

The Building as a Part of the City

Amid the dense city fabric, the ground plane of the apartment building is reimagined nestling between sunken courtyards ***(fig. 14)***. A series of shopfronts redefine the threshold of the project with the city, contributing to the public life of the street and offering glimpses of the serene courtyards beyond it. The green courts not only provide a climatic respite but also become interfaces between the varied private and public realms of the building, which have been reorganized to address the previous chaotic overlap of retail, residential, and consular traffic. Having a distinct entrance facade for each of these programs engages every face of the building, dissolving the idea of a "front" and "back." The reorganized ground floor allows multiple programs to coexist and facilitates a sense of arrival and transition from the city. The courtyards at the ground level are extended as light wells for the basement level, ventilating the often ignored abyss of

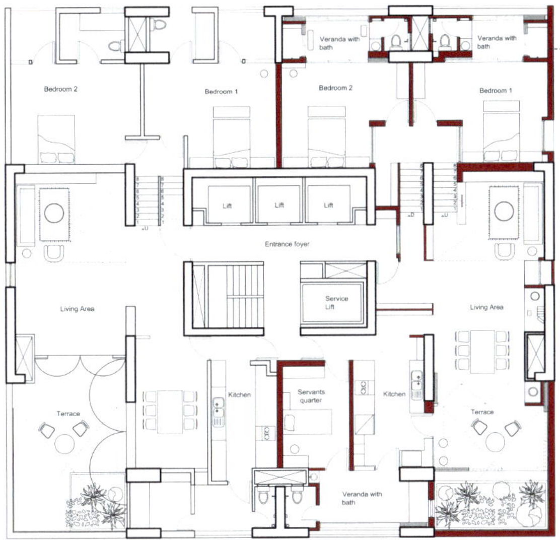

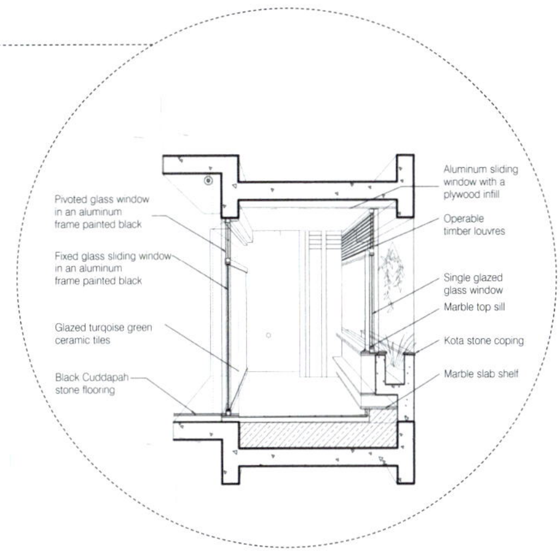

The new section reimagines the relationship of the bath and the veranda as expandable spaces with fenestrations that enable spatial transformation according to the user's organizational and climatic needs.

fig. 15
Comparison of existing and proposed apartment units; the latter are reorganized to resolve identified points of critique through interventions at different scales.

car parking. The new ground level also introduces areas of respite for the staff and security personnel, designed with the same human-focused sensibilities as the other parts of the project. The design strategies articulate the aspirations of Correa's iconic section, extending the implementation of the idea of cross-ventilation at ground level and, equally, to the other parts of the project.

Organizational Strategies and Planning

Catering to the dynamic needs of users and the prevalent sociocultural environment is essential in the design of domestic spaces ***(fig. 15)***. The building's structural frame constrains the intervention at the unit level. In reorganizing the unit plan, the living and dining areas, the kitchen, and the terrace gardens are redesigned to complement each others' functionalities, expanding into one another and allowing flexible use. The staff quarters are set back from the outer face of the building, shielding them from heat and rain and allowing for a better distribution of space, light, air, and privacy. The main entrance to the apartment is realigned to create a threshold with greater privacy and a sense of pause between the lobby and the home.

Materiality and Design Detailing

Detailing is vital in bringing the iconic section alive ***(fig. 16)***. The thresholds between different functions of the apartment are redesigned with varying degrees of permeability. Collapsible openings between the bath and the veranda enable the latter to transform into a large balcony at times or the two areas to be separated when in use. The screens on the perimeter of the cantilevered terraces can be used to turn them into "outdoor rooms" at times of harsh heat or rain, or to retain their seamless relationship with the outside at other times. The fixed-glass openings in the original design are replaced with transformable openings that allow the passage of light and air. These interventions ensure that responses to changing climatic conditions can coexist with the dynamic spatial experiences.

Together, the three scales of redesign work in unison to provide a holistic intervention, bringing the aspirations of the iconic section alive, from the ground level to the sky, and preparing it to serve the needs of today and tomorrow.

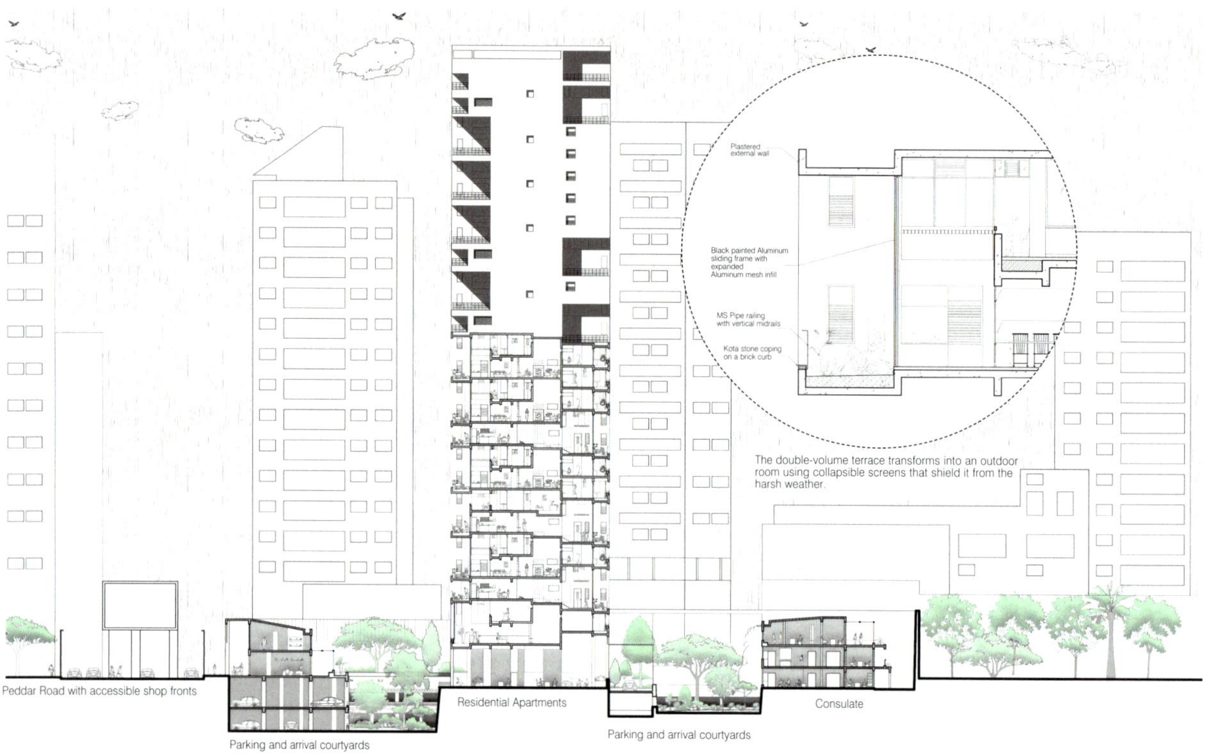

fig. 16
The redesigned section from the ground to the sky, realizing cross-ventilation at the three scales of the building.

Conclusion

The critical analyses of the selected iconic projects have guided a set of design interventions at various scales to complement the projects' original design intentions with sensitivity so the buildings are better able to meet contemporary needs and changing contextualities. This approach suggests that critical redesign can be seen as part of the ever-evolving adaptation process of a built fabric to enable it to respond to the respective changes in the context's social, cultural, and economic needs.

In both cases, the spatial experience and the quality of the buildings were explored in relation to the sociocultural responses to their contexts, given that architecture has the potential to create an impact that transcends its physical bounds. Thus, reimagining Golconde's boundary wall could transform how people interact with the rather secluded ashram and enable a new social pattern to emerge in the neighborhood, making the facility inclusive. Redefining Kanchanjunga's ground floor with lush courtyards and its apartment units with transformational elements could create a renewed living experience for its residents in an otherwise abandoned building and could generally encourage housing projects to reassess their approach towards the accommodation of staff. To paraphrase Samuel Mockbee, an architecture that celebrates goodness over greatness and compassion over passion outlines true quality.[10]

While the relationships and responsibilities of buildings towards their users and their social, cultural, and economic contexts are dynamic, the purpose of design to elevate and serve the human experience remains constant. Therefore, responses to climate change, thermal comfort, and dynamic user needs and experiences are indispensable in determining architectural quality. Beyond these responsibilities of buildings to serve their defined programs, clients and architects should recognize the potential they hold

[10] "Philosophy," The Official Website of Samuel Mockbee, 2015, https://samuelmockbee.net/philosophy/.

in shaping the city and era of which they are a part. Both the Kanchanjunga Apartments and Golconde, seen in the context of their time, made some pathbreaking deviations from the existing paradigms through their formal, spatial, and material strategies. While acknowledging their contributions to the architectural discourse, it is clear that parts of the critique hold true across time while some ideas arising from sociocultural concerns are more relevant to the present age.

For instance, Golconde was conceived as one of many buildings for the Sri Aurobindo Ashram organization. In fact, there are other operational dining rooms across the neighborhood providing subsidized food to people in need. The proposed intervention allowing food services through openings in the boundary wall may be easily conceived in the densely urbanized twenty-first century but may not have been possible in the 1930s, when residential land was restricted to private use. However, the criticism of the poor organization of the communal ground floor is one that is valid even for the time it was conceived.

In the case of Kanchanjunga Apartments, the inclusion of staff quarters within the apartment was a social and cultural advancement in 1983. However, the lack of light and ventilation should have been a valid concern then too. While the formal effect of an elevation devoid of overhangs and large cantilevered balconies is aesthetically memorable, the question of its suitability for the hot and humid climate of Bombay is a concern that could have been raised even in the 1980s. Lastly, while the aspiration of the iconic section was brilliant, it fell short in its detailed articulation across all scales of the design.

Developed from a critique of the dominant practice of demolition and tabula rasa, the method of critical redesign is one that is based on a thorough understanding of both the original design intentions and a building's shortcomings, leading to interventions that can conserve and improve existing buildings. This method of revitalization and adaptive reuse is a more viable and sustainable method of building fabric maintenance and development. A building that can be renewed to remain relevant over time embodies the idea of critical redesign that defines a new form of architectural transformation beyond conventional notions of design and inquiry, and is one that recognizes and responds to the needs of *all* its users without disparity.

Biographies

Naomi Mehta is an architect originally from Mumbai, India. She completed her undergraduate architecture degree at CEPT University, Ahmedabad, India. She is currently pursuing her graduate studies in Urban Design at the Graduate School of Design, Harvard University. Her research interests range across the architectural and urban realm and are currently focused on infrastructures and climate change in India, investigating ideas of power and social inequity translated into space. She is passionate about exploring ways to integrate data and spatial-analysis-driven research into the architectural and urban realm through design and policy.

Priyanka Salunkhe hails from Chennai, India, and is a recent graduate in architecture from CEPT University, Ahmedabad, India. She has been an exchange scholar at the Politecnico di Milano, Italy. She is currently an urban fellow at the Indian Institute for Human Settlements. Her current research includes formulating strategies to advocate for public infrastructure revitalization to promote climate resilience in urban India. She is interested in questions of architectural pedagogy and spatial justice, and is passionate about exploring ways in which civic participation in spatial planning can address and mitigate the challenges faced in the Global South.

The Embassy of Estonia in Vilnius as a Sign of Change in Architectural Ideals and the Development of Criticism in Lithuania

Algimantas Grigas

fig. 1
Embassy of the Republic of Estonia, in Vilnius. Designed by 3+1 arhitektid / Kolm Pluss Üks OÜ (Markus Kaasik, Andres Ojari, Inga Raukas, Ilmar Valdur). Street view of the finished building. Photo: unknown photographer, 1998. Courtesy of Estonian Museum of Architecture, Tallinn, Estonia.

The construction of the Embassy of the Republic of Estonia in Vilnius (1998, Lithuania) illustrates how architecture transcends its functional role to become a critical medium of cultural and political expression. This text further underscores embassies as a typology that can develop a critique of past regimes and envision future possibilities, serving as a link between nations while also reflecting internal cultural and political shifts. Through a comprehensive narrative covering 1995 to 2005, the essay explores two viewpoints on the Estonian Embassy: firstly, as a deliberate diplomatic project by Estonia; and secondly, as a catalyst for a critique of post-Soviet Baltic architectural practice.

Introduction

In Estonia's diplomatic history, the first purpose-built embassy was opened in Helsinki, Finland, in 1933.[1] It remained the only diplomatic residence built and owned by Estonia until 1998, when only the second Embassy of Estonia ever to be built was opened in Vilnius, Lithuania *(fig. 1)*. At the opening ceremony, the Estonian ambassador to Lithuania, H. E. Alar Olljum, asserted: "The embassy is more than a building of stone and glass, it is the crystallized spirit of the nation, a live bridge between two countries."[2] In order to appraise the impact of the Estonian Embassy, the period from 1995 to 2005 needs to be reviewed. This will both open the discussion and develop research on embassy typologies as acts of national semiosis to provide a general vector for the future.[3]

On the subject of the determination of national monuments, the vicissitudes of the plans to commemorate Vytautas, The Grand Duke of Lithuania, in Kaunas in the 1930s show the power of discourse. The original plans to erect a sculptural composition of Vytautas on horseback were reversed when the budget was redirected to build the monument in the form of a museum. Today it is known as Vytautas the Great War Museum. Political forces had the means to change the form of representation from a sculpture to a building. Similarly, the Estonian Embassy might be appreciated as a sculpture in a "Vilnius park"—conveying the same message of an object permeated with the national character of Estonia.[4] In this essay, criticism as built architecture is understood in Wayne Attoe's terms: ". . . as behavior, not as judgment."[5] However, in the case of a building, the edifice becomes the transmitter of a multitude of messages, and in this case the Estonian Embassy in Vilnius expresses Built Criticism owing to its specific physical context and the political times in which it was realized.

keywords:
3+1 architects, Estonia, embassy, national architecture, Built Criticism, postmodernism, Vilnius

[1] Architect Konstantin Bölau designed a functionalist-style villa with pavements incorporating Estonian dolomite.
[2] Jonas A. Patriubavičius, "Sveikinimai ir tostai Estijai ir estams" [Congratulations and toasts to Estonia and Estonians], *Lietuvos Aidas*, February 23, 1998, 3.
[3] Wayne Attoe, *Architecture and Critical Imagination*, (New York: John Wiley & Sons, 1978), 163.
[4] In German, *Botschaft* means both "embassy" and "message."
[5] Attoe, *Architecture*, 2.

An Architectural Fairy Tale

The realization of the Estonian Embassy in Vilnius is the result of the convergence of at least two narratives. The first one has its origins in Estonia and reads like an architectural fairy tale, in which a group of young architects, graduating from the Estonian Academy of Arts, opened an architectural office with the name 3+1 in 1994. A year later, the office entered an international competition for the Estonian Embassy in Vilnius. Markus Kaasik, Andres Ojari, Ilmar Valdur, and Inga Raukas, aged between twenty-five and twenty-six, were the winners from a pool of thirty-four other

fig. 2
Embassy of the Republic of Estonia, in Vilnius. Street perspective. Photo: Norbert Tukaj, 2016. Courtesy of Open House Vilnius, Architektūros fondas. © Norbert Tukaj.

fig. 3
Embassy of the Republic of Estonia, in Vilnius. A characteristic view from the courtyard showcasing the site planning. Photo: Kaido Haagen, 2000. © Kaido Haagen.

submissions.[6] The jury's vote was six against five, including a pair of established Lithuanian modernist architects. It is known that the government also preferred a young, recently founded architectural office that was asking for a relatively small fee.

In the second narrative, the central figure is Valvi Strikaitienė. She was Estonia's first ambassador to Lithuania (1992–96) following independence and could be considered as the godmother of the building.[7] Following the competition in 1995, the architects were required to present the design to the Vilnius Urban Planning Committee in Lithuania. Discussions centered around the height and size of the embassy volume amid the green, historical, elite neighborhood of Žvėrynas. In an informal account of the committee meeting, the critical voices were harsh and ruthless until a professor of architecture from Vilnius Academy of Arts stood up and interrupted loudly: "So tell me, do you want an Estonian embassy by the Estonian architects in Vilnius, or not?" It was enough to cut short the quibbles. Construction started with the laying of the cornerstone in August 1997 on the plot of land leased by the State of Estonia for one hundred years, and the new building was consecrated on February 23, 1998, one day before the celebration of the centenary of Estonian independence. Estonia's national image was enhanced by the fact that the embassy was constructed by the established Estonian contractor Merko.

A Prerequisite for Architectural Appreciation: Direct Engagement

The Estonian Embassy in Vilnius is a hybrid of an architectural ambition[8] and the State of Estonia's Lutheran cost-saving mentality. The latter part is essential, as affection for national identity can bear no price tag.[9] These ingredients alone do not lead to a building that is an act of architectural criticism. However, when the physical location or, more precisely, the architectural context is considered and when the historic moment is reconstructed and described, it is then possible to assign the building with the status of a Built Criticism.

The Estonian Embassy has a solid, stone-clad facade with rectangular openings, with the left-hand end of the building offset vertically by half a floor from the

[6] In Estonian the office name is "Kolm Pluss Üks." Inga Raukas left the office in 1998, just after the completion of the Estonian Embassy, to pursue an independent career and opened her own architectural design studio. From then on, the "+1" in the studio title would be taken to mean "society."

[7] Many facts for this research were drawn from a two-page letter by Valvi Strikaitienė that recounts the founding of the Estonian Embassy, written to the author on the occasion of the Open House Vilnius Festival 2015 and in preparation for the guided tour around the building.

[8] The architects admitted that their inspiration came from the group Tallinn Ten (who viewed architecture as art, and challenged and rebelled against the rigid, typified socialist modernism of their time) and from Swiss minimalism (Inga Raukas studied at ETH Zurich) with regard to the treatment of materials or programming—another influence being the Kunsthalle in Rotterdam (OMA, 1992). Andres Ojari, interview conducted by Algimantas Grigas, March 24, 2016, in Tallinn, Estonia.

[9] A considerable amount of unpaid effort was put into the project not only by the ambassador, Valvi Strikaitienė (taking extra steps to lobby for the embassy building), who was largely responsible

right-hand end ***(fig. 2)***. The architects admitted that the choice of limestone from the Ungru region was predetermined, owing to it being directly representative of the Estonian state; however, for weather protection, the architects also specified a light blue impregnation.[10] On the rear side, there is a completely transparent glass facade that, in some places, reveals utilitarian brick walls just behind the glass panels[11] ***(fig. 3)***. The ingenuity and inventiveness of the 3+1 architects had not been fully appreciated until 2015, when the Open House Vilnius Festival took place. During the series of guided tours, "[a] visitor, upon entering the building, is greeted with the play of ideas, allusions, resemblances and contrasts, that cannot be observed through the simple-looking *shell*. Interior spaces consist of a system of varying levels or floors that each have a distinct function and no corridors."[12] It was appraised internationally: ". . . inherently disciplined approach to architecture, one that prefers system to spectacle . . .,"[13] but for Lithuanian architects, the embassy was difficult to accept, as it unapologetically demonstrated a high level of craftsmanship in creating laconic, minimalist architecture ***(fig. 4)***. Lithuanian architects and clients were more accustomed to visually elaborate constructions with windowsills, plinths, and door casings. The exposed structure of the elevator, the bare ventilation shafts passing directly through holes in the glass panels, the use of industrial parquet, and a double-sided fireplace are just a handful of compelling innovations by the Estonian architects in constructing this Built Criticism. The first frameless glass facade in the Baltic states was seen as nothing less than a daring game by the young architects. Professional journals described the fascinating experience of encountering it: "[o]ne may not sense modernity from the street, given the green-blue wall [of the main elevation]. But once one steps inside, it feels like having gone outside: the courtyard is visible through the glass wall . . ."[14] ***(fig. 5)***. Another daily periodical quoted the words of critic Rasa Ambrasienė: ". . . bold and sterile. The building is fundamentally different from those that have been built in Lithuania so far."[15] It is appropriate to evaluate the impact of the Estonian Embassy from a long-term and wide perspective to fully grasp the changes that it brought, especially as it was the first purpose-built embassy building in Vilnius.

fig. 4
Entrance gate to the yard of the Embassy of the Republic of Estonia. Photo: Kaido Haagen, 2000. Courtesy of Estonian Museum of Architecture, Tallinn, Estonia. © Kaido Haagen.

fig. 5
Night view of the courtyard with the first frameless glass facade in the Baltic states. Photo: Kaido Haagen, 2000. Courtesy of Estonian Museum of Architecture, Tallinn, Estonia. © Kaido Haagen.

for compiling the building program, but also by the architects. They agreed to do extra hours of work (site visits would take seventy-two hours, with an eight-hour drive in one direction), employing their family members to implement unique design decisions—driven by idealism and affection for their national identity.

10 "Limestone was a conscious choice for the facade, because in 1992 it was declared an Estonian national stone" (Andres Kurg, "3+1 Architects," *Architectural Design*, July 2007, 111).

11 This kind of meta-modernist trick can be seen in Ghent, where it was used ten years later for Les Ballets C de la B and LOD by Architecten De Vylder Vinck Taillieu (2008).

12 Marija Drėmaitė, Rūta Leitanaitė, and Julija Reklaitė, *Vilnius 1900-2016: Architektūros gidas*, in collaboration with Architektūros fondas (Vilnius: LAPAS, 2016), 256.

13 Kurg, "3+1 Architects," 111.

14 Patriubavičius, "Sveikinimai ir tostai Estijai ir estams," 1.

15 In the *Būstas* supplement of *Lietuvos Rytas*, February 23, 1998, 1. Rasa Ambrasienė is an architect who worked at the time as *Arkitektas* magazine's editorial assistant.

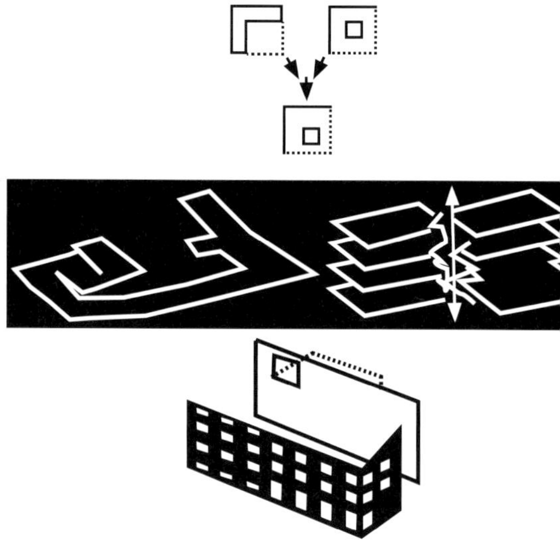

fig. 6
The first-ever purpose-built diplomatic building in Lithuania, constructed as the Vatican Diplomatic Residence (Nunciature) in Kaunas, Lithuania, in 1930. Photo: Stanislovas Lukošius, 1957. Courtesy of Architecture and Urbanism Research Center (AUTC), Kaunas, Lithuania.

fig. 7
Conceptual diagram from the 1996 competition for the Embassy of the Republic of Estonia. Hand drawing explaining the urban scale considerations and internal layout of the proposed building, 1996. Courtesy of 3+1 arhitektid / Kolm Pluss Üks OÜ. © 3+1 architects.

Image of the Nation

At the opening ceremony of the Estonian Embassy, the Prime Minister of Lithuania, Vytautas Landsbergis, stated: "the Embassy [is] more than a building," and continued to describe the embassy thusly: ". . . in its scale, appearance and successful construction, this embassy reflects the best qualities of Estonians today: vitality, ambition and dynamism."[16] Architectural compliments of this kind can be appreciated better knowing that the prime minister's father was the well-respected interwar-period architect Vytautas Landsbergis-Žemkalnis. He designed the first purpose-built diplomatic building on the territory of independent Lithuania ***(fig. 6)***: a modern, freestanding villa designed as a nunciature—a diplomatic mission for the Holy See—that was completed in Kaunas in 1930. While its exterior expresses a classical Palladian spirit, its asymmetrical plan with movable interior partitions was rather innovative for its time.[17] Embassies as built objects can also be emblems of power for the nation in which they reside. For example, the authoritarian President of Lithuania at the time, Antanas Smetona, denied the Vatican's diplomatic mission entry to the new building due to the Pope's activity in the then occupied region of Vilnius.

The fact that Estonians were the *first* to build an embassy in Lithuania, and not the other way around, automatically put Estonia in the position of power. In his praises for Estonian identity, Vytautas Landsbergis indirectly implied what Lithuanians lacked at the end of twentieth century. Just two days after the opening ceremony of the Estonian Embassy, a major shift of political power took place in Lithuania. Algirdas Brazauskas, who held both a leading position in the Lithuanian Communist Party during the last period of Soviet occupation of Lithuania and the presidency of independent Lithuania from 1992 to 1998, passed the presidential regalia to Valdas Adamkus, a modern Lithuanian from an expat family based in the United States.

Cultural divides between Estonia and Lithuania are not apparent at first sight. On the one hand, these two nations, together with Latvia, make up the Baltic states, sharing so much common history, such as the Baltic Way and exiting from the Soviet Union at the same time.[18] On the other hand, there are certain differences, such as in

[16] Patriubavičius, "Sveikinimai ir tostai Estijai ir estams," 3.

[17] Architecture and Urbanism Research Center, AUTC, accessed February 5, 2024, autc.lt/architekturos-objektas/?id=555.

[18] The Baltic Way took place on August 23, 1989. It was a peaceful protest against the repressive Soviet Union—two million people held hands to make a 690-kilometer human chain connecting the three capitals of the Baltic states.

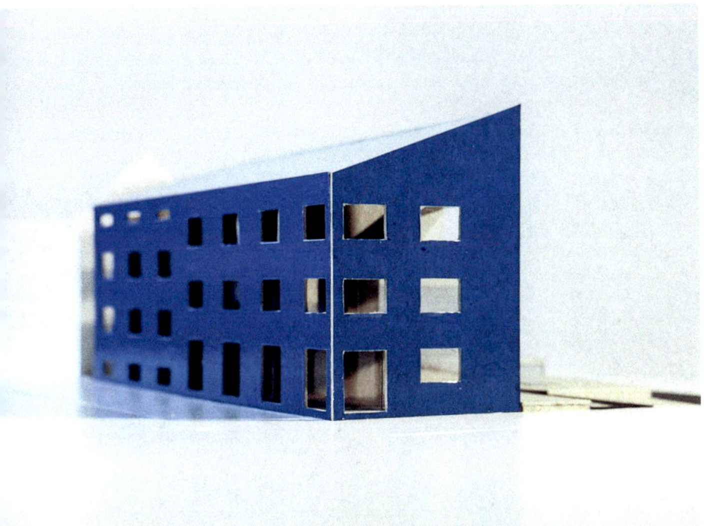

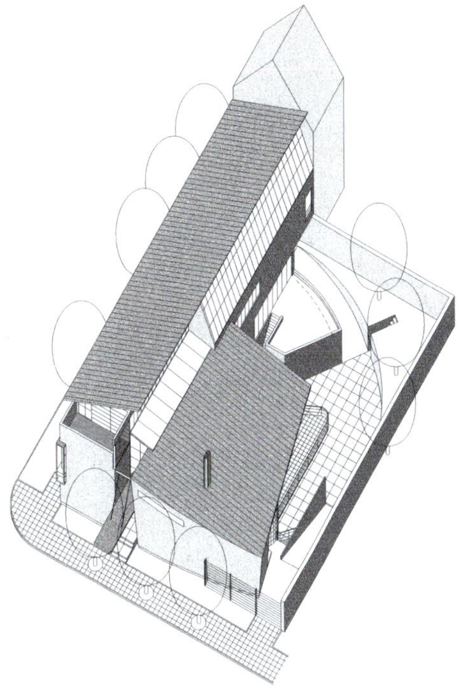

fig. 8
Scale model constructed from cardboard, 1996. Courtesy of Estonian Museum of Architecture, Tallinn, Estonia. © 3+1 arhitektid / Kolm Pluss Üks OÜ.

fig. 9
Second-place winner in the competition for the Embassy of the Republic of Estonia, 1996. Axonometric drawing displaying the use of Estonian materials for elevations: corner finished in tiles of limestone and the slightly curved volume covered in horizontal wood planks. Courtesy of OÜ Arhitektuuribüroo J. Okas & M. Lõoke. © Jüri Okas and Marika Lõoke.

their national characters, the origin of their languages (between Lithuania and Latvia on the one hand and Estonia on the other), and their religion.[19] Furthermore, despite its size Estonia is more nimble in regard to economic innovation and—as perceived in the critical self-reflection of Lithuanians—always one step ahead of its Baltic neighbors. For example, Estonia was the first of the Baltic states to join NATO in 2002 and in 2023 became the first of the fifteen former members of the Soviet Union to legalize same-sex marriage. When all this is taken together, the Estonian Embassy in Vilnius is a physical manifestation of imagined power and a vector in the relationship between the nations.

What Were the Alternatives in the Competition?

Comparison with some of the other competition entries for the Estonian Embassy in Vilnius sheds light on the radicalism of the winning proposal. Despite criticism in the popular Lithuanian press of the winning entry being indifferent to the Žvėrynas neighborhood, the proposal by 3+1 was based on a conscious analysis of the context ***(fig. 7)***. The volume respects the building line along the street; its visual impact on the corner of the plot is decreased by having the events hall located inside the courtyard, leaving the building to reveal quite a thin and elegant slab when viewed end on ***(fig. 8)***. The second-placed competition entry took a similar approach by being aligned with the existing pitched roof of the neighboring building and by splitting the proposed L-shaped volume in two with the insertion of a glass entrance, thus creating a visually smaller volume from the street ***(fig. 9)***. As architects of the second-placed entry Marika Lõoke and Jüri Okas explained in a conversation, during the competition there were no thoughts about Estonian identity, but simply considerations to use ". . . Estonian building materials such as wood and stone."[20] The architects also acknowledged that the main idea was not influenced by any architectural trends, but was simply the result of the analysis of ". . . the local environment and initial conditions." Actually, all of the awarded proposals distinguished themselves from the other participants by their consideration of materiality.[21] The remaining competition entries either chose

[19] Estonia is often associated with Scandinavian countries, where Lutheranism has traditionally dominated. In contrast, Lithuania has had closer ties with Poland and Belarus, sharing a historical tradition of Catholicism.

[20] Email exchange with Marika Lõoke, February 2, 2024.

[21] The third-placed scheme by Cerly-Marko Järvela and Peeter Varrak provided a three-dimensional visualization as the main image of the proposed embassy. It showed a volume with a single pitched roof. The main elevation was to be covered in thin, elongated slabs of stone and featured a rounded corner. Overall, irregularly shaped small openings and stone express stability and create the effect of a northern Germanic fortified tower.

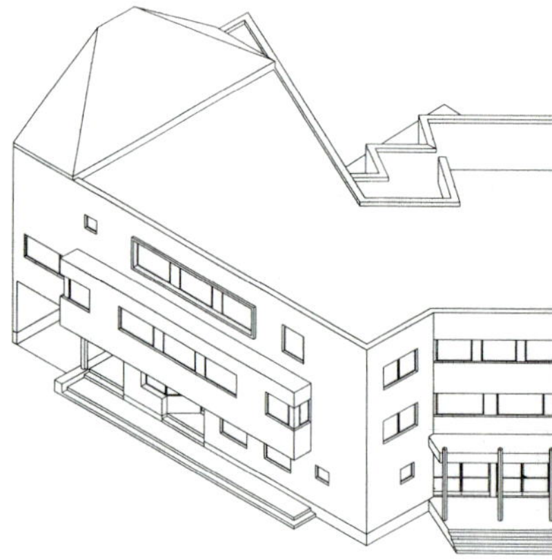

irregularly shaped volumes or had a jagged silhouette that complicated their relationship with the respected historical urban context. For example, the unawarded proposal by Kristel Ausing and Andres Siim created a "jarring note" in the "melody" of the street elevation ***(fig. 10)***.

While embassies are often located inside existing historical buildings, when the intention is to house them in a new building they often have to contend with double standards to obtain the construction permit. Embassies are required to adapt to their context, as a "lack of manners" might result in a bad reputation not only for the architects but also for the respective state itself. Seen from this point of view, it is understandable if there is a preference to build an embassy on a vacant piece of land or, even better, on a greenfield site, as was done in the case of the Embassy of the Czech Republic in Vilnius.[22]

Voldemar Herkel's excluded competition entry treats the building as an autonomous object. It resembles a composition of three irregular, slanted pieces of cake that pretentiously complicate the arrangement of functions. The axonometric view displays spatial decisions that are typical for postmodern architecture: the protruding volume of the second floor, and the variety and subdivision of its windows ***(fig. 11)***. Turning our eyes back on the 3+1 proposal, it is appropriate to cite Mart Kalm's appraisal: ". . . using pure and sensible materials and comprehensively composed by an architectural creative idea, the authors have developed the design of the building to the last detail with their sure vision."[23] The result is an inimitable act of building for a specific place and time with a cultural–political stance that constitutes it as a Built Criticism.

[22] Opened in Vilnius, Lithuania, in 2004, it was designed by Lennox architekti from Prague, Czech Republic.

[23] Mart Kalm in Andres Kurg, 3+1 architects portfolio, 2015. 3+1 architects have received the State Award of the Estonian Cultural Endowment.

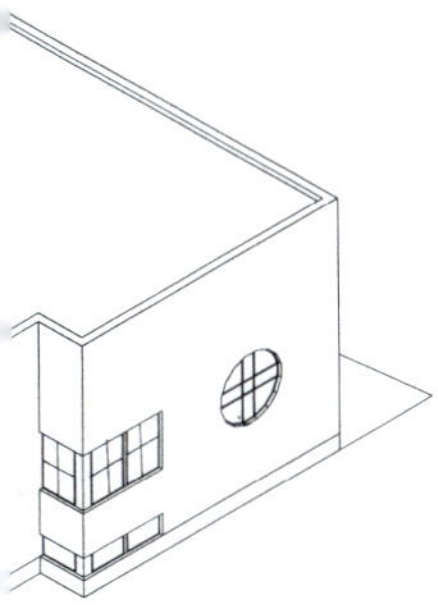

fig. 10
Unawarded entry in the competition for the Embassy of the Republic of Estonia, 1996. Produced by Andres Siim and Hanno Kreis, together with Kristel Ausing. Courtesy of Estonian Museum of Architecture, Tallinn, Estonia. © Siim & Kreis Architecture Studio.

fig. 11
Unawarded entry in the competition for the Embassy of the Republic of Estonia, 1996. Axonometric drawing of the building displaying the corner entrance in the proposal, produced by Voldemar Herkel. Courtesy of Estonian Museum of Architecture, Tallinn, Estonia. © Voldemar Herkel.

fig. 12
First-place winner in the competition for the Embassy of the Republic of Lithuania, in Berlin, 1999. Scale model constructed from cardboard displays a combination of functions: administration of the embassy, cultural center, and residences for the employees and guests of the embassy. Courtesy of the lead architect, Tauras Paulauskas. © Architectural bureau Unitectus.

fig. 13
The Lithuanian Embassy in Minsk, completed in 2000. A conversion of a typical 1970s two-block nursery into the reflection of a new, democratic state. Courtesy of Forma architectural office, authors: Leonardas Vaitys, Saulius Mikštas, and Romualdas Kučinskas. Photo: unknown photographer.

The Estonian Embassy as a Trigger for the Expansion of Lithuanian Diplomatic Missions Abroad

The process of building the Estonian Embassy in Vilnius made an impression on the Lithuanian Ministry of Foreign Affairs, as at the same time it initiated the construction of the Lithuanian Embassies in Germany and Belarus. The classicist embassy building that Lithuania owned in Berlin was destroyed during World War II. After the restitution of the site following the fall of the Soviet Union, the first architectural competition for the Lithuanian Embassy in Berlin was announced as early as 1995, with a second one taking place in 1999. The latter received only four entries.[24] The winning proposal came from the architectural office JAD under the leadership of Tauras Paulauskas. The architects continued with the development of the detailed design and even received the building permit in 2000. However, the building was never realized, and for a variety of reasons the site was eventually sold, with the limited economic capacities of a former Soviet Bloc country playing a major role. Based on various interviews, it appears that there was a conflict between East (the architects being used to working in centralized planning institutes) and West (applying economic, capitalist parameters to evaluate the architectural design). JAD's scale model shows that the program for the Lithuanian Embassy in Berlin was much larger than the other analyzed embassies in this essay ***(fig. 12)***. JAD's main configurational composition consisted of two large rectangular volumes intersecting at right angles, each treated in different materials. The upper green block was to be dedicated to the embassy employees' residences.[25] Entrance zones accentuated with glazed infill panels and occasional applications of wood cladding to the facades were to express the building's public character. Theoretically, were this design for the Lithuanian Embassy in Germany to be analyzed as a form of national expression, it might be read as using wood accents and the color green as signifiers of Lithuanian identity. However, in an interview with lead architect Tauras Paulauskas, he claimed neither the competition brief nor the jury expressed specific requirements for the expression of national identity in the building.

[24] The competition winners were JAD (Joint Workshop of Architects; groups 21 and 25, head architect: Tauras Paulauskas, other team members: T. Mazūras, S. Pamerneckis, G. Grakauskas). According to an interview conducted with Tauras Paulauskas, the competition was organized and conducted by a firm from Berlin. This had a lasting influence on the way architectural competitions were conducted in Lithuania thereafter. Essentially, the German competition model and principles were imported to Lithuania and became the standard.

[25] In reality, the employees of the Ministry of Foreign Affairs of Lithuania were not in favor of the idea of living and working in the same building. Similarly, Lithuanian ambassador Vaidievutis Gerulavičius was not interested in adding to his workload by having to supervise the construction of the new embassy when a preexisting building or apartment could just as easily be bought for the same function. It became one of the factors that led to the abandonment of the project in general.

The main task for the architects was to resolve the urban design challenges in an otherwise peripheral location.

The context was different in Belarus, where in 1998 the Lithuanian state acquired a site in a residential neighborhood of Minsk on which stood a typical Soviet-era nursery school building. To reduce costs, the idea was to remodel this existing building and use it for the Lithuanian Embassy. There are no records of an architectural competition; instead, the architectural office Forma, led by architect Leonardas Vaitys, designed and supervised the conversion. It was officially opened in 2000.[26] As the founder of the architectural journal *Archiforma*, Vaitys had a platform to publicize the completed work: he self-praised the result as providing a "gust of Western architectural trends" coming from Lithuania and influencing the "East," and he used adjectives such as "high-tech" and "contemporary architecture" ***(fig. 13)***. The project for the Lithuanian Embassy in Belarus also provided a novelty with the first use of suspended facade systems, in much the same way as the Estonian Embassy in Vilnius did with its frameless glass facade on its garden side. When questioned about the nature of any embedded Lithuanian national character in the Lithuanian Embassy in Belarus, Vaitys admitted an egocentric viewpoint: in the context of Western architecture transcending national borders, it should not be seen as a representation of national architecture. Instead, "[t]his architecture is as Lithuanian as its authors are shaped, inspired, and enriched by the Lithuanian culture."[27] Furthermore, the Estonian 3+1 architects and Lithuanian Forma belonged to different architectural generations, thereby leading them to assume different positions towards the contractors of the buildings. The Estonian architects, who graduated from architectural schools in the independent Estonia, closely collaborated with Estonian contractors, working as a unified team in resolving possible obstacles, an essential basis that allowed for the delivery of an innovative and striking building design. In contrast, the Lithuanian architect Vaitys admitted in an interview that they were not at all interested in the question of who would build the embassy. More interesting was his statement that ". . . there is no fundamental difference between the socialist period and the current era of provincial capitalism in the sphere of our interest. The relationship between designers and builders has returned to a logical state: the builders no longer oppose the designers by making all sorts of claims, but instead carry them out."[28] In other words, the architects of the Lithuanian Embassy in Belarus attempted to proceed using the conventional model from the socialist past that was based on overarching architectural authority, whereas the Estonian architects represented innovative values such as adaptability, collaboration, and willingness to discuss the financial aspects of architectural projects.

Postmodernism in the East and the West Differ

With the market economy prevailing in the early years of Lithuanian independence, few challenged the general indulgence of consumption—neither did the architects. It felt as if independent Lithuania wanted to construct its new identity from a collection of external influences and by shedding Soviet memories, sporadically employing signs of place-form in an exaggerated, almost comical way.[29] Grand open staircases, classical balustrades on open terraces or balconies, and arched entrances and windows reminiscent of grand churches were tools for the rejection of socialist abstinence, giving birth to the specific term "Kolkhoz Baroque."[30] At the end of the twentieth century, the architectural culture of Lithuania was riddled with an abundance of details in building elevations, skewed walls in building plans, and other features of postmodern architecture.

[26] The authors of the Lithuanian Embassy in Minsk are Leonardas Vaitys, Saulius Mikštas, and Romualdas Kučinskas.

[27] Original interview with Leonardas Vaitys, conducted by Dmitrijus Žukovas for *Archiforma*. The Lithuanian Embassy was constructed by a well-known, established Lithuanian contractor called Eika. The quote is taken from Leonardas Vaitys, *Architektūra* (Vilnius: Artseria, 2003), 130.

[28] Vaitys, *Architektūra*, 129.

[29] Kenneth Frampton, "Towards a Critical Regionalism," *Autoportret. A Quarterly on Good Space* 57, no. 2 (2017): 16.

[30] This unique term to describe an Eastern European specificity of postmodernism was first applied by the architectural historian Paulius Tautvydas Laurinaitis. It is mocking a lack of taste in private constructions.

[31] The residential building at 2 Mickevičius Street, Vilnius, was designed by Giedrė Eleonora Miknevičienė and Tautvydas Miknevičius, a pair of architects born in 1943 and representing the New Generation of Architects in Soviet Lithuania. They were at the peak of their careers at a time when there was a turning point in architectural ideology and aesthetics in the 1990s. Algimantas Mačiulis, ed., *Lietuvos architektai* [Lithuanian architects] (Vilnius: VDA, Union of Lithuanian Architects, 2002), 71, 426.

fig. 14
Residential building on the plot neighboring the Embassy of the Republic of Estonia, in Vilnius. The building was finished in 1997. Photo: Algimantas Grigas, 2023.

A comparison of the Estonian Embassy with contemporaneous buildings in the area reveals a stark stylistic contrast.[31] The adjacent corner building, built in 1997, is replete with historical references that were prevalent during the postmodernist period ***(fig. 14)***. Other cases include an apartment block that imitates an ocean liner through its composition of volumes, employing exposed brick with partially plastered patches in the elevations.[32] Another private residence, designed around a triangular site—considered a positive energy zone by physicists—also fulfills the clients' desire for a tower.[33] This house, with its oblique walls and covering of metal panels, is also reminiscent of a sailboat. In this physical context, the Estonian Embassy, given the specific conditions and political circumstances of its time, is a critique of the architecture prevalent in Lithuania at that point. Through the memoirs of the ambassador Valvi Strikaitienė and an interview with one of the 3+1 architects, the substantial backlash the Estonian Embassy project received at its public presentation in Vilnius can be recounted. While 3+1 architects respected the urban parameters and explored the appropriate courtyard typology for the Žvėrynas neighborhood, the Estonian Embassy still caused heated debate. The main arguments appear to have stemmed from a contrasting understanding of how architecture should be designed and crafted, a contrast originating from generational divides or simply due to conservative attachments to postmodern ideas.

On the Difficulty in Handling Built Criticism

Of the two major Lithuanian architectural journals, only one reviewed the Estonian Embassy.[34] *Statybų Pilotas* did not publish an authoritative, personal critique, but instead gathered a collection of comments from other architects and nonarchitects. The cover of *Statybų Pilotas*'s second volume of 1998 bore a caricature as a reaction to the recently completed embassy ***(fig. 15)***. Later, the sketch appeared with other captions, implying shifting emphases in the Baltic countries' architectural criticism.[35] Thus, there is a disparity in the reception of the Estonian Embassy in the two countries.

32 This building with thirty-two apartments is in Žvėrynas at 20 Paribio Street, architect Tauras Paulauskas, in *Archiforma*, 2 (1998): 18.

33 Review text about a house by architects Gintautas Blažiūnas and Darius Linartas. Edita Riaubienė, "Namas Latvių g. 1A, Vilnius" [A House at Latvių Street 1A, Vilnius], *Archiforma*, 2 (1998): 21–23.

34 In the quarterly journal *Archiforma*, there was no coverage of the Estonian Embassy in the 1998 or 1999 issues. The rival quarterly, *Arkitektas*, was founded in 1996 by Audrys Karalius and became the bi-monthly newspaper *Statybų Pilotas* in 1998. It dedicated its cover page to the Estonian Embassy. Audrys Karalius, "Didžioji Estų Mįslė: Ambasada Vilniuje—Šedevras ar Šaldytuvas?" [The grand riddle by Estonians: Embassy in Vilnius—a masterpiece or a fridge?], *Statybų Pilotas*, April 23, 1998. The annotation below the sketch translates as "The Elevation of the Baltic States."

35 Audrys Karalius, "25 Sizifiški Metai: Architektūrinės Žiniasklaidos Pradžia Lietuvoje" [25 years of Sisyphus: The beginning of the architectural press in Lithuania], *Statybų Pilotas*, February 9, 2021, accessed February 5, 2023, https://pilotas.lt/2021/02/09/varpine/25-sizifiski-metai-architekturines-ziniasklaidos-pradzia-lietuvoje/.

fig. 15
Caricature marking the opening of the Embassy of the Republic of Estonia in Vilnius, Lithuania. The sketch was published on the cover of the architectural periodical *Statybų Pilotas*, Vilnius, April 23, 1998, no. 2 (02). Courtesy of Audrys Karalius, editor of *Statybų Pilotas*.

In Estonia, the building coincided with the implementation of political reforms and launched the careers of 3+1 architects. In Lithuania, the reception was rather muted, stirring only the professional circles. Flat gray-blue stone seemingly assembled in an industrial process with small openings in the main street facade inspired the local inhabitants of Žvėrynas to call the building a "fridge" or "prison," thereby contributing to the disparaging headlines in the newspapers.[36] Among *Statybų Pilotas's* collected opinions, one person compared the Estonian Embassy to prefabricated mass housing.

Given the restricted access to the Estonian Embassy and thus the limited opportunities for its appreciation, the building was easily condemned. This explains in part why many architects in the conservative architectural context of Lithuania rejected the embassy. However, with the passage of time an improved understanding of the building had a butterfly effect on how architects in Lithuania wanted to build from then on ***(fig. 16)***. The Estonian Embassy became an influential Built Criticism for Lithuanian architects—it shook the authority of the well-established older generation of practitioners and paved the way for dynamic experimentation in materiality and functional planning. However, the process of change in Lithuania was slow, and subsequent change-making architects like Valdas Ozarinskas,[37] Kęstutis Lupeikis,[38] or Eugenijus Miliūnas[39] found it hard to convince authorities with their work in the following decade and after the economic crisis of 2008.

Conclusions

The lesson from the Estonian Embassy is that architecture can convey an impactful criticism if it makes an appropriate contribution to its location, time, and cultural context. Furthermore, such an act of building needs to be sufficiently reflected in critical texts and be accessible to interested people. In the eyes of Estonians, the embassy is criticizing the gray, mass-produced architecture of the socialist regime and celebrates the freedom gained by the newly independent Estonian state through the artistic treatment of its national identity. This act of criticism was pre-programmed by state politicians to communicate a diplomatic message to others. From the Lithuanian perspective, the building is a valiant criticism of the period's postmodernism and excesses of self-built projects without architects. The Estonian Embassy is critical not only from an aesthetic point of view in the treatment of the exterior or in the reduction of classical ornament but also in the functional programming of the building with

36 "Žvėryną niokoja dvikojai žvėrys" [Žvėrynas being destroyed by beasts on two legs], *Verslo žinios*, January 16, 2008, 7.

37 Valdas Ozarinskas was one of the designers of the Lithuania Pavilion at Expo 2000 in Hanover, Germany. He criticized the existing state of architectural practice and was consequently isolated from it, going on to work as an exhibition designer at the Contemporary Arts Center in Vilnius.

38 Kęstutis Lupeikis was a minimalist architect, from an earlier generation, who was most well known for the Prosecutors Headquarters in Vilnius (2008), which took the form of a black cube with slanted windows.

39 Eugenijus Miliūnas was an architect of an earlier generation who became famous for M. Žilinskas Art Gallery in Kaunas (1988)—a true icon of Lithuanian postmodernism. However, by 1998, the studio adapted functionality and pragmatism by winning a competition for the design of Kaunas Žalgiris Arena (competition 1999, realized 2011).

fig. 16
A night view of the Embassy of the Republic of Estonia, Vilnius. Photo: Algimantas Grigas, 2015.

how it prioritizes the needs of users by providing more daylight and proposing novel uses of space. Journalists and politicians who were present at the inauguration of the Estonian Embassy ascribed the building's distinctly contemporary features to the relative youthfulness of its architects. The petty criticism that appeared in the Lithuanian professional journals hid the fact that the embassy actually mocked the dilettante, stylistic, sculptural, or formalistic approaches to the design of buildings in Lithuania. An embassy built by one country in another country by definition communicates its national identity. It can be a critique of the established notion of physical space production and use by improving functional dispositions, by advancing construction technology, and by introducing new ways of representation.

Biography
Algimantas Grigas is a PhD candidate in History of Arts at the Institute of Architecture and Construction, Kaunas University of Technology, Lithuania. His dissertation focuses on the phenomena of architectural criticism in the then occupied Soviet Lithuania from 1945 to 1990. An architect with an individual artistic and design practice, he graduated from Vilnius TECH in 2010 and gained a Diploma in Architecture from the Mackintosh School of Architecture, Glasgow School of Art, in 2014. He is also a professional tour guide based in Kaunas, and cofounded EKSKURSAS—an informal initiative to promote Kaunas's modernist architecture from 1920 to 1940.

The First and Last Tower: Raimund Abraham's Austrian Cultural Forum New York

Eliyahu Keller

fig. 1
Raimund Abraham, The New Austrian Cultural Institute, New York City. Exterior perspective, 1993. Museum of Modern Art, New York. © 2024 Raimund Abraham.

From the announcement of the competition result in 1992, through its decade-long construction, and continuing well after its completion in 2002, the Austrian Cultural Forum in New York, designed by the enigmatic Austrian architect Raimund Abraham, has generated passionate reactions and a multiplicity of interpretations from admirers and critics alike. Abraham's proposal for the Cultural Forum is analyzed as a work of Built Criticism by exploring its history, its contemporaneous reception, and the meaning it has acquired in the years since its inauguration. Through this consideration, Abraham's slender tower emerges as a unique work of architecture, representing the history that led to its construction, criticizing the contemporary discourse that surrounded its design, and shedding new light on the future that has unfolded around it since.

keywords:

architecture, skyscrapers, Austria, Cold War, culture, representation

Introduction

In a short essay published after the competition for the new Austrian Cultural Forum concluded, the architect and historian Eduard F. Sekler offered a reflection on the chosen proposal. "To put Raimund Abraham's design for the new Austrian Cultural Institute in its historic context," Sekler observed, "will be an interesting task for a future architectural historian . . .." Acknowledging the restricted nature of his view, Sekler suggested that in their examination, future scholars should consider "the events that led to its genesis" and "the broader panorama of the multifarious interaction of Europe and the USA in the late 20th Century."[1] In his text, Sekler placed Abraham within a long lineage of Austrian compatriots who traveled to the United States either to seek professional and pedagogical opportunities or to flee possible Nazi persecution, thus leaving the Austrian cultural scene neglected for years to come.[2] Abraham belonged to the former group, having arrived in the United States in 1964 after an invitation from his countryman Friedrich St. Florian, who by then held a position in the Rhode Island Institute of Design.

Equally important in Sekler's account were the meaningful encounters that architects had with New York City. From Le Corbusier's admiration of its towering skyline to Rem Koolhaas's retrospective manifesto concerning Manhattan's subconscious, New York always demanded "strong architectural gestures" and "statements that contribute to renew its spirit."[3] For Sekler, Abraham was part of a generation of contemporaneous Austrians that were trying "to break through to a new, more dynamic and symbolically evocative architecture."[4] It was only fitting that the young architect would end up in the towering metropolis of Manhattan, where he would be able to further develop and ultimately test his ideas.

Thirty years later, Sekler's observation is still instructive, albeit for reasons somewhat different than those articulated in his text. The distance afforded by the three decades since the forum's inception allows more than the kind of historical placement that Sekler sought. Indeed, the tower housing the Austrian Cultural Forum packs into its form not only a complex history of national and global politics that led to its construction but also a critique of discourses regarding architectural contextualism and historicism, as well as of the role played by financial interests and the limitations of

1 Eduard Sekler, "An Austrian Architectural Statement in Manhattan," in *Austrian Cultural Institute, New York: An Architectural Competition*, ed. Ernst Bliem (Innsbruck: Haymon-Verlag, 1993), 12.
2 Sekler, "An Austrian Architectural Statement," 12.
3 Sekler, 17.
4 Sekler, 13.

unique architectural works. With that, it offers an opportunity to observe the relationship that symbolically rich architecture enters into not only with the past from which it emerges but also with the present of its making, and with the future that has occurred around it since its completion.

Past/Competition

The story of the Austrian Cultural Forum begins, in some respects, with Sekler himself. Like several of the architects of whom he wrote, Sekler too came to the United States by invitation, in his case that of the dean of Harvard's Graduate School of Design, Josep Lluís Sert, in 1960. Shortly after, it was Sekler who together with another Austrian architect, Carl Auböck, drafted the plans for the renovation of a small 1905 Manhattan townhouse on East Fifty-Second Street, which the Austrian government purchased in the early 1960s to serve as what was then called the Austrian Cultural Institute.

From its opening in 1963, the institute carried a political burden. As its director at the time of the 1992 competition, Wolfgang Waldner, noted, the institute's mission at its conception was "to deepen cultural relations between Austria and the United States and to establish and rekindle contacts with artists and intellectuals who had been forced into exile by the National Socialist regime."[5] This, Waldner explained, made the institute a meeting point for emigrants; a place to be Austrian outside the borders of the nation. In the mid-1980s, and as the functional needs of the institute grew, the Austrian government decided to demolish the existing townhouse and to erect a new building, one whose architecture would serve as a contemporary representation of the nation in the cultural capital of the United States.[6]

If the old Austrian Cultural Institute can be said to have stemmed from Austria's postwar history, the new forum was situated against the last years of the Cold War and the long decade that brought the twentieth century to an end. In part, the need to replace the old building was the result of intensified relations between Austria and the United States, which paralleled the slow decline of the Soviet Bloc and the fall of the Iron Curtain.[7] The competition's conception and the construction process that followed spanned across a decade that in some respects began in 1989 with the fall of the Berlin Wall and the proclamations of the end of history,[8] and which prompted discussion in Abraham's professional circles of the end of architecture as a utopian or social-engaged discipline.[9] The forum's opening, conversely, was marred by two seemingly unrelated events, which once again reflected the connection between history, nationality, and global politics. One was the formation of Jörg Haider's far-right nationalist coalition, which resonated for many Austrians with the past they sought to depart from, and which prompted Abraham to publicly renounce his Austrian citizenship. The other was September 11, 2001, the wounds of which were still fresh in the minds of New Yorkers. These wounds and the events which caused them, some noted, symbolized history's return.[10]

The competition itself was a deliberate attempt to address Austria's complicated postwar history. After reestablishing its independence in 1955 under the condition of an imposed neutrality, by the late 1980s the nation was ready to move closer to the West. For the Austrian government, the competition was an "Olympian event" meant to produce a building that would become the nation's "calling card."[11] As Alois Mock, the Austrian Federal Minister of Cultural Affairs at the time of the forum's construction, noted, on the one hand the organizers sought to "set a deliberate democratic signal in an issue of such importance for our country's self-presentation." On the other, by limiting the competition to Austrian nationals, their desire was to "demonstrate the creativity of Austrian architecture" to the world.[12]

5 Wolfgang Waldner, "A Meeting Place for Austrian Emigrants Turns into a Cultural Machine for the 21st Century," in *MANHATTAN AUSTRIA: The Architecture of the Austrian Cultural Institute*, ed. Gudrun Hausseger (Vienna: Architekturzentrum Wien; Salzburg: Verlag Anton Pustet, 1999), 11.

6 Waldner notes that there were several options to deal with the issue of expansion: renovating and extending the existing building, selling the building and purchasing a new one elsewhere, and demolishing the existing building and constructing a new one, which he recommended. Waldner, "A Meeting Place for Austrian Emigrants," 12–13.

7 Andreas Stadler specifically points to fall of the Iron Curtain and the events of 9/11 in his framing of the forum. See Andreas Stadler, "The Austrian Cultural Forum New York: Lighthouse and Carrier Rocket," in *Raimund Abraham & The Austrian Cultural Forum New York*, ed. Andres Lepik and Andreas Stadler (Ostfildern: Hatje Cantz, 2011), 30, 34.

8 Francis Fukuyama, "The End of History?," *The National Interest*, no. 16 (1989): 3–18.

9 Several of Abraham's colleagues gathered in Vienna in 1997 for a series of discussions under the topic "The End of Architecture?" See Peter Noever, ed., *The End of Architecture?: Documents and Manifestos* (Munich: Prestel, 1997).

10 For instance: Fareed Zakaria, "The Return of History: What September 11 Hath Wrought," in *How Did This Happen? Terrorism and the New War*, ed. James F. Hoge Jr. and Gideon Rose (Oxford: Public Affairs, 2001), 307–17, or Binoy Kampmark, "Fukuyama Down Under: Revising the End of the History after 9-11," *AQ: Australian Quarterly* 74, no. 6 (2002): 33–40.

11 Dietmar Steiner, "The Great and the Small," in Bliem, *An Architectural Competition*, 189.

12 Alois Mock, "Preface," in Bliem, *An Architectural Competition*, 7.

The selection of the competition's jury was reflective of these aspirations as well. The "felicitous" team was chaired by the noted architectural historian Kenneth Frampton, who reportedly persuaded two of his collaborators from their New York Five days, the American architects Richard Meier and Charles Gwathmey, to participate in the jury.[13] The three were joined by the Austrian architects Hermann Czech, Bernard Hafner, and Eberhard Graf, who were chosen by the Austrian government, as well as by several Austrian nonarchitects, including film director Axel Corti and the Foreign Affairs Ministry's representatives Peter Marboe and Peter Niesner, thus composing a team of local experts and renowned international authorities "to which even the luminaries of the Vienna architectural scene could not really object."[14]

After deliberating for approximately two straight days, the jury unanimously chose Abraham's proposal from 226 submissions ***(fig. 1)***. In their short appraisal, they noted the design to "possess a strong formal resolution and to convey at the same time a powerful sense of institutional form."[15] Of significance was Abraham's decision to place the mandatory emergency scissor staircase at the building's rear; a simple maneuver which no other architect in the competition employed, and which allowed Abraham's proposal to use the lot's full width ***(figs. 2-3)***. On December 16, 1992, the jury

fig. 2
Raimund Abraham, The New Austrian Cultural Institute, New York City, 1992–2002 (model). © Architekturzentrum Wien Collection. Photo: Elmar Bertsch.

fig. 3
Raimund Abraham, The New Austrian Cultural Institute, New York City. Sectional elevation, west, 1993. © Architekturzentrum Wien Collection.

[13] Bliem, *An Architectural Competition*, 23.
[14] Bliem, 25.
[15] Competition jury, quoted in Bliem, 57.

announced their decision to the public, signaling the beginning of an almost decade-long process until the new Austrian Cultural Forum would open its doors.

An examination of the runner-up proposals suggests that Abraham's placement of the staircase, though meaningful and distinct, was not the only reason for the jury's choice. The limitations imposed by the spatial, programmatic, and zoning regulations resulted in many formally expressive solutions, while the building's program and its relationship to its context were addressed to varying degrees. Hans Hollein, for instance, who was awarded the second prize, offered a denser articulation of the program, especially in its lower levels. Though in its higher floors his design allowed natural lighting from the back of the lot, the spaces left in the building's rear were especially small. Formally, it offered a dialectical gesture by creating a single building composed of two visually discrete parts. The bulk of the building was formed behind an elegant and sweeping glass wave that aligned itself almost perfectly with the neighboring structures, while at its bottom the building's first seven floors consisted of a smaller structure, designed to "reflect the purpose of the building and its cultural activities." This lower structure, meant to be visible from the adjacent Fifth Avenue, sought to express a certain "individuality and independence in contrast to the usual anonymity of office buildings"[16] ***(fig. 4)***.

fig. 4
Hans Hollein, Austrian Cultural Forum New York. Competition, second prize, 1992. Courtesy of © Private Archive Hollein.

Architects Georg Pendl and Elisabeth Senn, whose competition entry was awarded the third prize, suggested an opposite strategy. Their proposal, a clean and minimalist tower, was meant to be a "sober hall for multifunctional use."[17] The structure itself, a leaning glass monolith, offered what the jurors called an "audacious" gesture on the street level in the form of an extremely large, open-air lobby in place of the building's first few floors.[18] Despite its presence, this lobby, the jurors noted, created serious problems with both the building's circulation and its programmatic demands.[19] Flanked on its western side by a seven-story-high floating wall, the formally powerful statement stood in strange proportion to the rest of the tower's mass, while the signal it offered to Fifth Avenue was, somewhat oddly, a blank and opaque wall.

In this regard, Abraham's proposal offered a reconciliation not only between a difficult site and a difficult program but also between the architecture's form and the representational meaning that this form conveyed. The complex program—exhibition spaces, a library, an auditorium, offices, and the director's residence—is stretched to a height of 85 meters and spread across 24 floors, the largest of which is a mere 180 square meters. Responding to the site's "lateral compression," Abraham conceived the project as three separate and compressed towers: the distinct and anthropomorphic

[16] Competition jury, quoted in Bliem, 61.
[17] Georg Pendl and Elisabeth Senn proposal (third prize), quoted in Bliem, 66.
[18] Competition jury, quoted in Bliem, 65.
[19] Competition jury, in Bliem, 65.

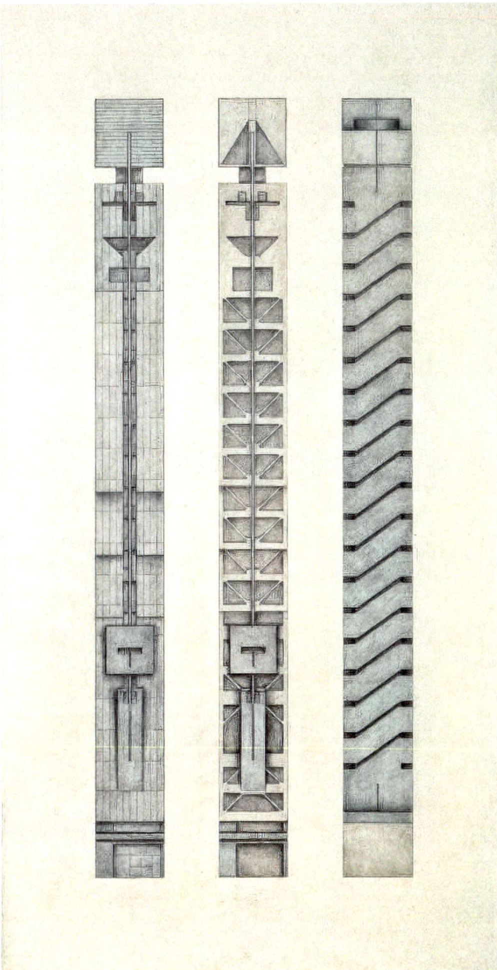

fig. 5
Raimund Abraham, The New Austrian Cultural Institute, New York City. Elevations, 1993. © Architekturzentrum Wien Collection.

street-facing facade, referred to by Abraham as "The Mask" or "Glass Tower"; "The Core" or the "Structural Tower," containing the building's programmatic spaces; and finally, "The Vertebrae," that is the already mentioned "Stair Tower," which Abraham noted as a reference to the invention of scissor staircases in New York City, and which he placed in the building's rear[20] ***(fig. 5)***.

Completing the perimeter block, the design fits almost precisely into its zoning envelope, allowing it to assimilate into its context while making its presence felt. Stepping forward while leaning back, its slanted face is symmetrically divided with a central axis. Evoking both the institutional power of the state and the symmetry of the human body, as Abraham's longtime friend Lebbeus Woods noted,[21] the facade emphasizes the tower's soaring dynamic while giving the impression that the glass is cascading down. While its horizontal divisions appear to be in line with the neighboring office building, its materiality and detailing suggest not a light, transparent curtain. Rather, as *New York Times* critic Herbert Muschamp remarked upon its inauguration, the glass becomes "more akin to masonry,"[22] appearing perhaps like a defensive armor or a reinforced barricade and signaling that the culture housed within is not simply peaceful, but is, in fact, a powerful force ***(figs. 6–8)***.

These seeming contradictions reflect the historical complexities that came to shape Austrian national identity in the second half of the twentieth century, a kind of paradoxical formation that, as historian Oliver Rathkolb noted, stemmed from the nation's difficult relationship with its dual role as victim and perpetrator under Nazi occupation and rule.[23] This difficult relationship of Austrians with their past manifested itself in a postwar culture of an ambiguous and at times contradictory character, fluctuating between a heightened sense of national pride on the one hand, and a desire to be accepted by both Western European democracies and the United States on the other. In more ways than one, Abraham's forum captured this singular paradox of a country in which, as historian Patricia Gronzka noted, "an avant-garde gallery has been funded by the Catholic church."[24] It offered a monument whose architecture was as ambiguous as the nation's relationship to its history, and as paradoxical as the culture it produced.

20 "Raimund Abraham in an Interview with Kenneth Frampton," in Hausseger, *MANHATTAN-AUSTRIA*, 37.
21 Lebbeus Woods, "A Challenging Legacy," in Lepik and Stadler, *Austrian Cultural Forum*, 100–101.
22 Herbert Muschamp, "ARCHITECTURE REVIEW: A Gift of Vienna That Skips the Schlag," *New York Times*, April 19, 2002.
23 Oliver Rathkolb, *The Paradoxical Republic: Austria 1945–2020*, 2nd ed. (New York and Oxford: Berghahn Books, 2021).
24 Patricia Gronzka, "Better Bodies," *Frieze*, no. 43 (November 11, 1998).

Present/Reception

In the weeks and months that followed the announcement of Abraham's triumph, the proposed design largely drew praise. Herbert Muschamp, for instance, remarked that "There hasn't been a building like this in Manhattan for more than 25 years," since Mies van der Rohe's Seagram Tower or Frank Lloyd Wright's Guggenheim.[25] Terrence Riley, the curator for architecture and design at the Museum of Modern Art, complemented Muschamp's praise by noting that the forum made manifest in built form the kind of critique that had characterized the work of various "theoretical" architects and designers from Austria and elsewhere, and that, until then, had mostly been limited to the space of the drawing.[26] Later, however, when addressing what *The Washington Post*'s critic Benjamin Forgey called "Manhattan's depressed architectural market," Riley suggested that the forum could be not only "one of the first skyscrapers in New York in the '90s" but also "one of the last."[27]

A year after the competition concluded, *Oculus*, the journal of the American Institute of Architects in New York, decorated its cover with the forum's twenty floorplans and dedicated a section to a debate on the design's merits, faults, and historical significance. To confront Muschamp's unequivocal endorsement and slight offense to everything built in Manhattan over the preceding quarter of a century, the editors solicited responses from several renowned architects, all of whom had intervened in Manhattan's fabric during these supposedly impoverished years. Contributing to and concluding the discussion was the journal's editor, Suzanne Stephens, who praised Abraham's intervention as demonstrative of the need of architecture to relate to both its physical context and its time. Pointing to the response of the building's tiny footprint—7.5 meters wide and 24.5 meters deep—to the zoning limitations, she noted the building's "cockamamy" plans and the "astonishingly small amount of office space"

fig. 6
Raimund Abraham, Austrian Cultural Forum. Photo: David Plakke, 2002. Courtesy of the Austrian Cultural Forum New York.

fig. 7
Raimund Abraham, Austrian Cultural Forum. Photo: Michael Moran, 2002. © Michael Moran/OTTO.

[25] Herbert Muschamp, "Architecture View; A Nervous Prism of a Building for Manhattan," *New York Times*, September 26, 1993.

[26] Terrence Riley, "Raimund Abraham, Architect," in Bliem, *An Architectural Competition*, 58.

[27] Terrence Riley interviewed by Benjamin Forgey, "A Towering Pipsqueak," *Washington Post*, January 4, 2024.

fig. 8
Raimund Abraham, Austrian Cultural Forum. Photo: Michael Moran, 2002. © Michael Moran/OTTO.

offered to its inhabitants.[28] Yet it was precisely the building's unusual program—not a residential or typical office tower—that partly relieved, as Stephens noted, the Austrian government from the financial burden that is an essential part of architectural production in New York City's most densely populated borough.

The uniqueness of Abraham's design lent itself to many figurative interpretations by admirers, critics, and colleagues. These, collected by Wolfgang Waldner, included:

> **. . . residential and cultural machine, metronome, glass needle, guillotine, vertical stapler, architectural waterfall, living elevator, thermometer, totem pole, glass-knight, thunder bolt, exclamation mark, computer chip, space needle, apocalyptic vision of a culture in crisis, long pole, pump, ski binding, ball machine, Austrian pyramid, half-baked skyscraper, Aztec figure, personal skyscraper, rocket, culture-castle, space strudel.**[29]

The words of Archigram's Michael Webb, a friend and colleague of Abraham, can be added to the list. In a *Domus* article, he referred to it as a "knife slicing through the blocks of dough that flank it." This analogy, importantly, was not only figurative. For Webb, the forum stood in contrast to the corporate towers in its vicinity, being a kind of "slap in the face of reaction, political and aesthetic" and a catalyst for the future of avant-garde architecture in New York.[30]

[28] Suzanne Stephens, "A Debate: Raimund Abraham's Design for the Austrian Cultural Institute," *Oculus* 56, no. 5 (January 1994): 7.
[29] Waldner, "A Meeting Place," 15.
[30] Michael Webb, "Austria in New York," *Domus*, July 29, 2002.

fig. 9
Christian de Portzamparc, LVMH Tower. Photo: Nicolas Borel, 2018. © Nicolas Borel.

For Waldner, this array of interpretations was an indication of "the emotions evoked by high-quality architecture."[31] One could argue, however, that it reflected precisely the kind of difficulty anticipated by Sekler in qualifying the building. Indeed, the difficulty here was not only in articulating the historical narrative leading to the forum's design. Rather, it also related to our understanding of the building not as an autonomous object but as a particular work of architecture, in a specific context, both physically and historically. In this regard, the architecture of the Austrian Cultural Forum can be seen both as a reflection of certain currents in architectural discourse in the years leading to the competition and as a reaction against them; namely, the contemporaneous debates that revolved around a reconsideration of architecture's relationship with both history and context, its semiotic meaning, its embrace of financial and corporate interests, and its withdrawal from all matters sociopolitical in the decades after the war.[32]

Unlike the historicism promoted by the figureheads of postmodernism, Abraham's tower does not refer to a past discarded by modernism; its architecture offers a resurrection neither of classical styles nor of the utopian promises that collapsed with the horrors of World War II. Its anthropomorphic mask presents the kind of archaic and archetypal imagery that has been noted to be a common characteristic of various postwar Austrian artists.[33] Moreover, it is clearly reminiscent of the corporeal motifs within the work of Abraham's early collaborator, the artist and architect Walter Pichler, and arguably of earlier works by Hans Hollein as well. Regardless of what the association may be,

[31] Waldner, "A Meeting Place," 15.
[32] Mary McLeod, "Architecture and Politics in the Reagan Era: From Postmodernism to Deconstructivism," *Assemblage*, no. 8 (1989): 23–59, https://doi.org/10.2307/3171013.
[33] Alessandro Melis, Michael John Davis, and Allan Balaara, "The History and Invocation of the Arche in Austrian Radical Architecture Thinking," ed. Silvio Caputo, *Cogent Social Sciences* 3, no. 1 (January 1, 2017), https://doi.org/10.1080/23311886.2017.1368366.

fig. 10
Tod Williams Billie Tsien Architects, American Folk Art Museum. Photo: Michael Moran, 2002. © Michael Moran/OTTO.

the tower itself is a seamless amalgam of references and histories. Neither modern, postmodern, nor pre-modern, it probes the ways in which history infringes on the present, while presenting an image of a future relic from a culture always already lost.

Future/Anticipation

In expectation of the building's completion, the Austrian author Gudrun Hausegger wondered not about the Cultural Forum's place in architectural history but about the future of the metropolis in which it was placed, and speculated whether the building's "singularity will have an impact or whether it will remain a forlorn signal in the jungle of cloned skyscrapers." This, Hausegger remarked, was in part a financial question. Abraham's tower could potentially "act as a catalyst, motivating other developers and institutions to act as courageously to leave the beaten track,"[34] or it might become one of New York's last towers, as Terrence Riley already predicted in 1995.

In her text, Hausegger pointed to another unique skyscraper, the Louis Vuitton (LVMH) Tower, designed by the French architect Christian de Portzamparc ***(fig. 9)***. Located just a few blocks away from Abraham's forum, the LVMH opened three years earlier in December 1999. Hausegger was not the only one to pair the two. Abraham's *New York Times* proponent Muschamp also linked the towers by noting that both "rise from the level of real estate to the plane of architecture."[35] Writing for *The Wall Street Journal*, Ada Louise Huxtable also referenced both buildings while adding a third member—the American Folk Art Museum, designed by Billie Tsien and Tod Williams—to the list of "New York's best new buildings, all of which seem to come in small packages"[36] ***(fig. 10)***. Several years later, architectural writer Karrie Jacobs also connected the three "thin" buildings, labeling them "skinny midblock masterpieces" and grouping them together "as barriers against encroaching homogeneity."[37]

The comparisons between the Cultural Forum, the LVMH, and the American Folk Art Museum are instructive for reasons not necessarily intended by the authors. While all three buildings were lauded for their uniqueness within the repetitive skyscraper landscape, their intertwined history points to the growing power of capital in shaping the city's form and skyline, and the role that architecture has played in constructing what architectural historian Reinhold Martin has referred to as "financial imaginaries."[38]

[34] Gudrun Hausegger, "Counterforces of Gravity: The Long Road from Competition to Completion," in *MANHATTAN AUSTRIA*, 32.

[35] Herbert Muschamp, "ART/ARCHITECTURE: The Spirit of Deco Rises from the Dead," *New York Times*, June 27, 1999, sec. Arts.

[36] Ada Louise Huxtable, "Merging Culture and Commerce in Architecture," *Wall Street Journal*, May 16, 2002, At Leisure.

[37] Karrie Jacobs, "Against Homogeneity," accessed February 14, 2024, https://karriejacobs.com/2013/04/667/.

[38] Martin suggests that at the dawn of the twenty-first century, architecture is no longer merely funded or directed by capital but has become an essential component through which capital, as a cultural construction, is circulated. See Reinhold Martin, "Financial Imaginaries: Toward a Philosophy of the City," *Grey Room*, no. 42 (January 1, 2011): 60–79.

fig. 11
Billionaires' Row. View from the southeast. Source: Wikicommons, CC-BY-SA-4.0.

Indeed, it was Portzamparc who only a few years after completing the LVMH designed ONE57, the first of what would soon become a staple of twenty-first-century real estate development in Manhattan: the so-called "ultra-thin" or "super-slender" luxury residential tower. After fifteen years of assembling property rights for its construction, Portzamparc's tower broke ground in 2009. Completed five years later, it paved the way to several others, producing the conspicuously titled "Billionaires' Row" along and around Fifty-Seventh Street, south of Central Park ***(fig. 11)***. A short ten-minute walk away stood Tsien and Williams's Folk Art Museum, which was completed in 2001. The lot on which it stood was purchased by the Museum of Modern Art (MoMA), which absorbed it as part of its expansion plan. To fund this scheme in part, the slender residential goliath 53 West 53 tower was developed and designed, this time by the French architect Jean Nouvel. In 2014, only thirteen years after it opened its doors, the Folk Art Museum was demolished, its sculptural and expressive copper and bronze facade panels disassembled, dismantled, and put by MoMA into storage, where they patiently await a future unknown.

What allowed the design and construction of these impossibly thin, capital-producing machines was a transformation in zoning codes that had taken place more than half a century earlier. With the 1961 introduction of floor-to-air-ratios (FARs) and transferable development rights (TDRs) or "air rights," developers were able to assemble portions of different lots, to move air rights from one plot to its adjacent ones, and to construct unimaginably tall structures on lots that traditionally would have been considered too small to accommodate such heights.[39]

Abraham's tower was not part of these developments. This is not to say that financial considerations did not influence its construction. But its cultural function relieved it, at least partly, from the kind of efficacy demanded by real estate development in New York City and its design took full advantage of its zoning limitations, leaving no development rights to be transferred, while the lot's ownership by the Austrian government may have protected it from the kind of private interests that put weaker cultural institutions like the American Folk Art Museum—however celebrated and unique their architecture may be—under the threat of real estate developers and institutional giants. Still, and with ample reservations notwithstanding, the pairing of the forum's form and history with that of the ultra-thins suggests a connection between what might seem to be two disparate histories. Indeed, the passing of years since the forum's design and construction and the continuous increase in the number of slender towers recall the words of art historian Thomas Crow, who cautioned against the use of the avant-garde as "a kind of research and development arm of the culture industry."[40]

It is against these histories of creation, reception, and evolution that the Austrian Cultural Forum affords a critique which exceeds the one it originally performed, and that can be said to revolve around the various anticipations surrounding its design. This critique begins with the desire of those who had commissioned and conceived the forum that it should serve as a kind of lighthouse for contemporary Austrian culture and democracy in the United States. It continues with the expectations of architectural critics, who saw in the forum the kind of power they imagined great works of architecture could hold, and who had hoped, however naively, that this single building would help transform an entire city ruled by financial interests; that through it, perhaps, the meaning, purpose, and power of architecture at the turn of the twentieth century might be reclaimed. And it ends with a kind of inadvertent revelation that the Austrian Cultural Forum offers after the fact. Namely, that architecture's power of critique is not limited to its past or present. Rather, certain architectures hold the capacity to gain additional layers of meaning as the present continues, and as history unfolds.

[39] Oliver Wainwright, "Super-Tall, Super-Skinny, Super-Expensive: The 'Pencil Towers' of New York's Super-Rich," *Guardian*, February 5, 2019, Cities, https://www.theguardian.com/cities/2019/feb/05/super-tall-super-skinny-super-expensive-the-pencil-towers-of-new-yorks-super-rich.

[40] Thomas Crow, *Modern Art in the Common Culture* (New Haven, CT: Yale University Press, 1996), 35.

Biography

Dr. Eliyahu Keller is an architectural historian, researcher, and educator, currently serving as an assistant professor at the Technion Faculty of Architecture and Town Planning in Israel. He holds a Bachelor of Architecture from Ariel University, an MDes from the Harvard GSD, and a PhD in History, Theory and Criticism of Architecture from MIT. In his research, Keller explores the intersection of architectural representation, technological advancement, geopolitics, and critical thinking. He is currently developing his dissertation into a book project, titled *Drawing Apocalypse*, in which he investigates the relationship between the advent of nuclear weapons, apocalyptic thinking, and speculative architectural visions in the Cold War United States.

Going the Opposite Way: Giorgio Grassi and the Anxiety of Influence

Ricardo Leitão

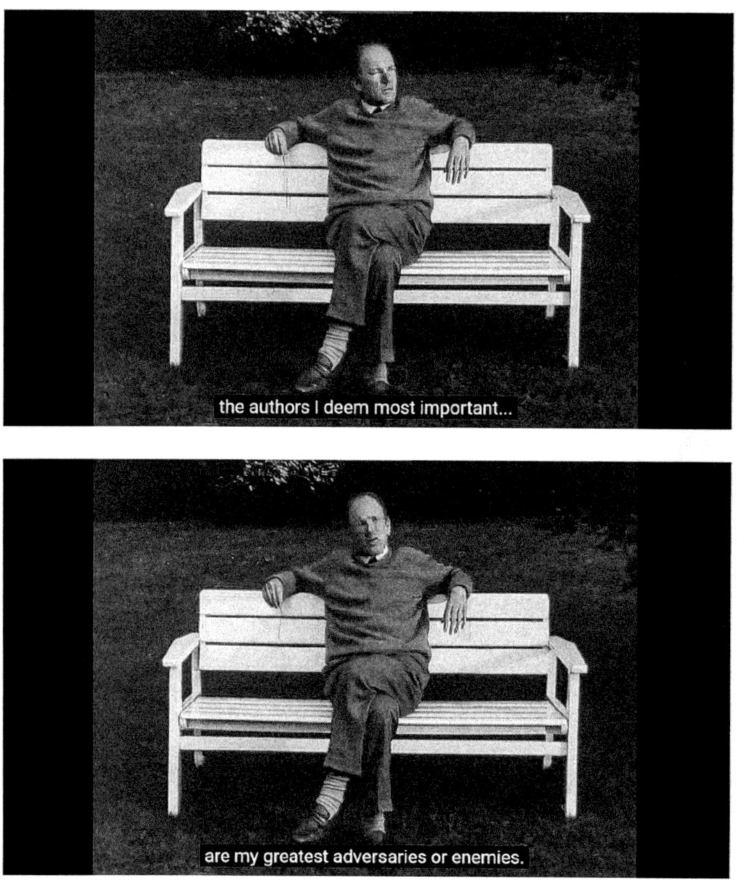

fig. 1
Double frame of Thomas Bernhard's monologue in the film *Drei Tage*.
© Ferry Radax, 1970.

Giorgio Grassi belongs to a select group of architects who write and draw with equal determination, displaying rigorous consistency in developing theoretical discourse. His critical engagement implies a doubled effort to interpret the vicissitudes of his time—a period which he does not recognize himself as belonging to—prompting him to boldly take positions to their extremes and, often in a hyperbolic way, firmly pointing in *the opposite direction.*

"Going the Opposite Way" not only tries to clarify Grassi's critique of his contemporaries but also delves into the crucial influence of his "Alte Meister" in shaping his critical perspective.

keywords:
Giorgio Grassi, Cassa di Risparmio di Firenze, "Alte Meister," Harold Bloom, influence, tradition

On the Idea of Criticism

> "A critical spirit is the great achievement of the modern age. Our civilization was founded on the idea of criticism: nothing is sacred or untouchable, except the freedom to think. Thinking that rejects criticism, especially self-criticism, is not thinking. Without criticism, that is without rigor or experimentation, there is no science; without it there is no art or literature. I would even say that without it there is no healthy society. Today, creation and criticism are one and the same thing. The history of modern literature, from Cervantes to Joyce, is the history of criticism converted into creation. Criticism of society and of language, criticism of values and of gods, criticism of power and of ideas. A writer is not the servant of the church, the state, the party, the homeland, the people or social morality, as he or she is a servant of language. But writers only really serve it when they raise suspicions about it: modern literature is above all criticism of language. . . . Criticism of language and criticism of reality are part of the same search."
> —Octavio Paz, *Pasión crítica*

In the words of Alfonso Berardinelli, *criticism* is like the endocrine system: "it's not every visible, but when it isn't working properly, all the other systems suffer; they become deformed, put on weight, shrink, lose balance . . ."[1] And we would even argue that the end of criticism is a deadly condition for the body of any discipline. Berardinelli points out that "in the past criticism was usually born out of a theory, and that theory was Marxism,"[2] although in general terms criticism of ideology descends from satire, which in a way announced it historically after the Enlightenment.

1 Alfonso Berardinelli, "The Problem with Today's Culture is that it Doesn't Tolerate the Existence of Criticism," interview by António Guerreiro, *Electra*, no. 20 (2023), 19.
2 Alfonso Berardinelli, "Problem with Today's Culture," 22.

Regarding Giorgio Grassi's architecture, Kenneth Frampton situates it within the boundaries of a possible dichotomy between two equally established neo-Marxist critical positions: on the one hand, Theodor Adorno's negative dialectic, "in which the autonomy of committed art is such that there cannot be any kind of reconciliation between the logical discipline of the architecture and the emotive propensities of the general public,"[3] and, on the other hand, the anti-vanguardist social accessibility of traditional culture, as initially formulated by György Lukács concerning literary *realism*, which is of particular relevance in the following analysis. This is an essential clue for considering and understanding a hypothetical side that Grassi would probably take in the notorious "Debate on Expressionism"[4] between 1935 and 1940.

In fact, in the text entitled "It Is All about Realism!,"[5] György Lukács frames an idea of progress in literature precisely against the superficial immediacy that he detects in avant-garde movements. Drawing on Hegel's thought, Lukács even suggests a possible correspondence between *immediacy* and *abstraction*, warning that through immediacy, only abstract thought can emerge. This sentence could also be part of the text "Questions about Architecture and Realism,"[6] in which Grassi characterizes the architecture of expressionism as a marginal and pictorial experience that does not distinguish between the *nostalgic* gaze and the *evocative* one. For him, unlike the uncritical immediacy of the nostalgic eye, the evocative gaze has the advantage of observing historical experience as a *shareable corpus*, recognizing its repetitive moments and looking to it to confirm his own solutions.

Throughout his extensive writing, Grassi often uses Lukács's evocation of architectural "adequacy"[7] to pursue his obsession with the need for architecture to confront itself and avoid becoming something increasingly removed from life—a *dead language*.

Thus, Grassi can be seen as an architect who struggled all his life against a distorted idea of expression promulgated by the masquerade and the misuse of language. This fight is perhaps the point that binds him to Thomas Bernhard ***(fig. 1)***, an Austrian writer Grassi confesses to admiring and whose excessive, honest, and disarming criticism he admits genuinely encourages his work. Bernhard is an essential member of the spiritual family Grassi chose early on, a brilliant point of orientation in a larger constellation that would include, outside the architectural spectrum, figures such as Bertolt Brecht, Samuel Beckett, Robert Bresson, and Arturo Martini.

Grassi and Bernhard both hold an unshakeable belief in an almost extinct language that is losing meaning in a world speeding towards the abyss. Furthermore, this accelerated and indulgent pace of decline is one of the significant objects of their critical engagement, which implies a doubled effort to interpret the vicissitudes of their time—a period which they do not recognize themselves as belonging to—prompting them to take positions to their extremes and, often in a hyperbolic way, firmly pointing in the *opposite direction*. Somewhat like Bertolt Brecht's economy of means and attachment to elementary questions, both Bernhard and Grassi could never be recruited for any humanist rhetoric since they are closely united by their feelings of repulsion towards a generalized mediocrity and are capable of refusing, most of the time cynically and brutally, the superfluous and the condescending. Their attitude is analogous to Brechtian theater,[8] and follows a principle of lapidary radicalism, which can exclude any passive spectator they never intended to please.

3 Kenneth Frampton, "Giorgio Grassi a Firenze," in *La Nuova Sede della Cassa di Risparmio di Firenze di Giorgio Grassi* (Florence: Scala Group, 2009), 29.

4 Regarding this polemic, in *Realismo Materialismo Utopia—Uma polémica 1935–1940*, João Barrento clarifies that it was not just a closed and sterile academic discussion. *German expressionism* arose from the historical conditions created by the growing threat of fascism. It clarified positions that had been clashing in the process of consolidating Marxist aesthetic theory, particularly regarding the formulation of a theory of realism and the social and political function of literature and art.

5 This essay by Lukács was originally published in *Das Wort* (Moscow) 3, no. 6 (1938), under the title "Es geht um den Realismus."

6 This text was originally published under the title "Architekturprobleme und Realismus" in the "Realismus in der Architektur" issue of *Architese* in 1976. Our reading was based on the Portuguese version in the anthology *Escritos Escolhidos, 1965–2015*, translation, notes, and introduction by José Miguel Rodrigues (Porto: Edições Afrontamento and Fundação Instituto Arquitecto José Marques da Silva, 2018).

7 In several of his writings, Grassi often returns to an aphorism from Lukács's *Aesthetics*: "Architecture creates a real and adequate space, intended to evoke adequacy visually."

8 Brechtian theater adopts the attitude of questioning everything until no certainties are left standing, with the clear ambition of bringing to the surface everything that is most difficult and *uncomfortable*. Bertolt Brecht realized that the best way to be *inconvenient* in a decadent society is to be lapidary to the point of radicalism. The radical experience of his plays becomes didactic, posing elementary questions in the most unpredictable ways, plundering tradition to the extent of plagiarism to create original works.

Alte Meister or the Anxiety of Influence

> "The masters of the modern movement reached implicitly for the values of tradition. Thanks to them, later generations could learn more explicitly the concept of "Continuità," either because they recognized them as fathers (and starting from their work, they are developing unexplored themes) or because by investigating the genealogy of these "fathers" they could understand multiple family relationships along the winding and dramatic process that is history."
> —Ernesto N. Rogers, *Esperienza dell'architettura*

In *The Anxiety of Influence: A Theory of Poetry*,[9] Harold Bloom argues that "poetic history is held to be indistinguishable from poetic influence."[10] In the sequel, *A Map of Misreading*,[11] the literary critic combines the ideas of "influence and criticism," emphasizing that "all poetry necessarily becomes verse-criticism, just as all criticism becomes prose-poetry."[12] Bloom suggests that one of the functions of criticism is to make the work of a good poet more challenging to accomplish, as only the overcoming of genuine difficulties can result in poems entirely suited to a time as consciously belated as ours.

T. S. Eliot's aphorism "Immature poets imitate; mature poets steal" underscores the intrinsic indebtedness of creative acts to precursors. Bloom's proposition involves crafting a narrative for extraordinary "thefts," offering a unique approach to critical reading. The potential in what he terms "misprision" reveals diverse facets of any author's thinking, enabling readers to gather dispersed fragments and rearrange them, akin to a Warburgian atlas, according to new creative logic.

The same can be applied as a critical tool and serve as a valuable analytical instrument within architectural discourse. The act of appropriation, frequently observed in creative processes, does not merely involve replicating the work of predecessors. Instead, it can involve fighting against some of their ideas to suit our context and experiences. As architects engage in this ongoing dialogue (or discussion) with the past, it is crucial to recognize that architectural history can represent a gradual accumulation and intermingling of solutions—an enduring cycle of revisiting and renewing responses to lasting challenges spanning generations. In this regard, a broader *image of thought* can be circumscribed that also allows thinking in *constellations*: history transformed into an infinite repository of solutions; a tool for the persistent renewal of answers to perennial problems. In essence, history becomes a container of ideas available for cyclical movements of reappropriation, thereby paraphrasing and re-signifying Bloom's notion that the history of architecture is *also* indistinguishable from the influence between architects.

In the theory imagined by Bloom, there is a particular interest in the strength implicit in concepts such as *misreading* and *swerving* as ideas capable of establishing a critical modus operandi in the face of any influence.

One of the six revisionary ratios explored in his poetic theory is called *kenosis*, and it focuses on the possibility of operating critically in *opposition* to a preceding influence: the subversion or emptying of a precursor can greatly reinforce *the new poem*. Bloom presents this revisionary ratio as a critical act in which a strong poet empties and attempts to dissolve a precursor, highlighting this action as a defense mechanism. Bloom goes on to explain that according to Freud, "the purpose of any defense mechanism is to prevent danger."[13]

9 Harold Bloom, *The Anxiety of Influence: A Theory of Poetry* (New York: Oxford University Press, 1973).

10 Bloom, *Anxiety of Influence*, 5.

11 Harold Bloom, *A Map of Misreading* (New York: Oxford University Press, 1975).

12 From Harold Bloom's perspective, the critic has to push the fatal encouragement that prevents any poet from forgetting the weight of their inheritance. As Bloom conceives it, influence means that "there are no texts, but only relationships between texts. These relationships depend upon a critical act, a misreading or misprision, that one poet performs upon another, and that does not differ in kind from the necessary critical acts performed by every strong reader upon every text he encounters. The influence-relation governs reading as it governs writing, and reading is therefore a miswriting just as writing is a misreading" (Bloom, *Map of Misreading*, 3).

13 Bloom, *Anxiety of Influence*, 89. As we will see later in this essay, the idea of creating under a potential threat or danger makes particular sense in Grassi's case.

Some architects work from multiple, unrelated *references* that appear more or less randomly on their desks. Giorgio Grassi is not one of those architects. We can read his work in the light of an idea of *influence* that we would like to stress, above all because Grassi is an architect who does not hide his influences in the same way that he does not hide the problems that these influences place in his path and with which he necessarily has to deal.

In "Alte Meister,"[14] the Italian architect sets out to write about some individuals whom he has consistently observed with "admiration and instinctive sympathy, albeit always from a distance, as if they belonged to another world."[15] This provides a crucial insight into how influence operates in his work. As he indicates, this "other world" sharply distinguishes between the influence of two types of masters he identifies: the new ones (whom we choose) and the old ones (who impose themselves on us). Grassi cautions that his text will not primarily focus on the works of Karl Friedrich Schinkel, Heinrich Tessenow, or Ludwig Hilberseimer—masters he personally selected. Instead, he directs attention towards voices from an ancient and distant world, to masters who were not chosen by us yet stand before us inevitably and with a profound impact, much like their buildings, imposing their presence and serving as exemplary models.

Initially, Grassi suggests that, in a broader sense, all his work entails a continual *confrontation* with those works that he believes offer comprehensive solutions to the problems he frequently encounters in his projects. His approach to architectures and architects, whom he collectively calls "Old Masters," indicates that if a similar question was addressed and resolved definitively in the past, we must carefully examine and scrutinize those models, recognizing that nothing can be replicated exactly in the same manner. The new conditions inherent in each case strongly affirm Bloom's perspective on influence. He argues that reading the past, even when subjected to misinterpretation, becomes a crucial tool for poets striving for imaginative freedom and liberation from historical lateness.

It is not certain that Grassi would fully agree with Bloom on this point, especially because he declares that he does not see his architecture as art, at least not the *ars poetica* on which Bloom is focused. However, Grassi ought to be seen as one point in a larger constellation of architects who are associated with the idea of architecture anchored in the notion of *Baukunst*[16]—despite its "*Costruzione Logica*"[17]—since one of his primary influences is the author of the famous *De Re Aedificatoria* (*On the Art of Building in Ten Books*).[18]

The permanent confrontation with Leon Battista Alberti—whom Grassi considers one of the most challenging masters, if not the most—coincides with the apparent conflict he has with himself. When Grassi states that Alberti's treatise is nothing more than a coherent way to put his entire life as an architect into perspective, it reflects his earnest desire. Grassi confesses that he cannot discuss his master's work without intertwining his own experiences and the ideals he has consistently pursued for himself and his work. This acknowledgment underscores his genuine aspiration to comprehend Alberti's legacy through a lens shaped by his own professional and personal journey.

The pact with the Old Masters—a loyal, stable, and lasting pact—that Grassi defends is nothing more than the character of *generality* that establishes the common thread between his architecture and Alberti's, and between Alberti's and the figure of the Roman architect who appears to be their main point of reference.

The intense bond between theory and practice, that is, between what they write and what they build, is absolutely crucial in the elaboration in which they both engage, reappropriating a certain historical experience from which a system had developed

14 Giorgio Grassi, *Escritos Escolhidos, 1965-2015*, translation, notes, and introduction by José Miguel Rodrigues (Porto: Edições Afrontamento and Fundação Instituto Arquitecto José Marques da Silva, 2018).

15 Grassi, *Escritos Escolidos*, 473 (translation by the author).

16 Kenneth Frampton places Grassi in the sphere of *Baukunst*, within a genealogy of architects such as Heinrich Tessenow and Adolf Loos, precisely on the threshold between two poles: on the one hand, European vernacular architecture without author and time, the so-called analogue architecture, and, on the other, the romantically classical paradigms of the German Enlightenment. An important nuance should be added to the term, particularly dear to Giorgio Grassi—*Stadtbaukunst* or "the architecture of the city."

17 *La Costruzione Logica dell'Architettura* was published in 1967 by Giorgio Grassi with the intention of establishing a rational framework based on the requirement of generality that would address a theory of design in architecture. One of its aims was to establish a genealogy of rationalism, clarifying the methodical significance and theoretical value of some of its architectural examples.

18 Leon Battista Alberti, *On the Art of Building in Ten Books*, trans. Joseph Rykwert, Neil Leach, and Robert Tavernor (Cambridge, MA: MIT Press, 1991).

that was both *constructive* and *compositive* and extending it through successive improvements.

In the example of Alberti, Grassi sees what he considers to be an audacious architect capable of assuming the risk and responsibility of taking architecture backwards, then returning to the point where he believes it had achieved its greatest results, thus recovering the common thread where those results had been lost.

The presumed difficult relationship between Alberti and his contemporaries can be seen here from Grassi's reading.[19] The naive and sometimes rudimentary appropriation of the forms of Roman architecture by certain of Alberti's contemporaries—the so-called archaeologism—is seen as a target of his treatise, which includes direct advice to the architect unable to avoid "frivolity, obstinacy, ostentation, or presumption,"[20] as if the claimed superficiality of some of his colleagues were here serving as an example not to be followed.

In *De Re Aedificatoria*, Giorgio Grassi finds "a handbook for good construction—an extraordinarily up-to-date manual (or outdated, depending on your point of view), that is, despite its age, an incredibly modern manual if you think that it is also the only one that could still be proposed today in the face of the embarrassing spectacle that is being inflicted on contemporary architecture."[21]

His project for the New Headquarters of the Cassa di Risparmio di Firenze is an outstanding example of Grassi's ambition to confront both Alberti and the Roman architecture that the author of *De Re Aedificatoria* had tried to revive, particularly in terms of construction methods and its way of organizing the complex system that we call *city*, thereby putting the Albertian lessons to the test and simultaneously weaving a subliminal critique of the architecture of his own time.

Architecture and Opposition

The project of Cassa di Risparmio in Florence

It is curious that one of the most notable works of Grassi—who was presumed to be ideologically linked to the left—is the headquarters of one of Italy's oldest and most important banking institutions. Criticism indeed might begin exactly from this point, possibly echoing extreme Bernhardian irony and gradually developing from within.

The project for the New Headquarters of the Cassa di Risparmio di Firenze ***(fig. 2)***, the competition for which Grassi won in 2004, is based—albeit not solely—on his absolute necessity to settle scores with both Leon Krier's 1994 master plan ***(fig. 3)*** for that area of Florence and "the unpredictable object suffering from irresistible gigantism"[22] of Leonardo Ricci's Palace of Justice. The Florentine project highlights the way Grassi's buildings are inscribed in *an opposite idea of the city*—and, by extension, *society*—entering itself in a second phase[23] of his work that seems to us to corroborate Carlos Martí Arís's interpretation when he argues that "the projects, by assuming the primordial role in the cognitive process, start to then feed the critical reflection that, in turn, reaffirms the project work itself."[24] Thus, it can also be seen as a project he envisioned as an opportunity to make a direct critique of his time, aligning himself closely with the masters who all, at one point or another, undertook similar endeavors, persistently defending the integrity of their buildings. The Shell Building by J. J. P. Oud ***(fig. 4)*** is the critical reference followed by Grassi, who openly declared that his Florentine project is, at least for him, the equivalent of Oud's controversial ***palazzo***.[25] Both buildings are associated with capital-related companies, adopting a language that is, at least in their eyes, misunderstood by critics, mixing traces of classicism and modernism, and evoking a sense of lost monumentality. In addition, both are the consequence of the need to express a state of intolerance through a gesture of freedom. By commending

[19] Regarding Alberti and his contemporaries, Grassi establishes a fundamental difference between the approaches to Roman ruins. On the one hand, Alberti designs by putting some already consolidated typologies to the test, critically reflecting on ways of building, whenever possible, and avoiding the attraction of the archaeological approach; on the other, there is the vision of some artists who, having been amazed by the extraordinary Roman ruins, returned to their studios excited by the idea of simply copying them, imagining fanciful ways of completing them without worrying too much about why.

[20] Alberti, *Art of Building*, 315.

[21] "Projectar racionalmente (o sapateiro e o arquitecto)," in Giorgio Grassi, *Leon Battista Alberti e a Arquitectura Romana*, translation, notes, and introduction by José Miguel Rodrigues (Porto: Edições Afrontamento and Fundação Instituto Arquitecto José Marques da Silva, 2015), 121 (translation by the author).

[22] "Uma ideia de arquitectura, um modo de trabalhar e o seu porquê" (2012), in Grassi, *Escritos Escolhidos,* 598 (translation by the author).

[23] In Giorgio Grassi's work, Carlos Martí Arís identifies two distinct phases in the relationship between writings and projects. The first phase spans approximately from 1960 to 1980, during which the projects served as experimental validations of theories established and affirmed in his writings. Subsequently, a second phase emerges wherein the projects become sources that feed theoretical reflections.

[24] Carlos Martí Arís, "Los maestros difíciles," in *Arquitectura, lengua muerta y otros escritos*, ed. Giorgio Grassi (Barcelona: Ediciones del Serbal, 2003), 9 (translation by the author).

[25] On this controversy, see the lecture presented by Grassi on May 19, 1970, at the Facoltà di Architettura del Politecnico di Milano, fully transcribed under the title "Arquitectura e Racionalismo," in Grassi, *Escritos Escolhidos*, 59.

fig. 2
"Neighborhood relations" between the Cassa di Risparmio by Grassi and the Palace of Justice by Ricci. © Luca Bosco.

fig. 3
Grassi's site plan of the Cassa di Risparmio di Firenze. Giorgio Grassi, 2004–8. © Fondo Giorgio Grassi – Fondazione MAXXI, Roma.

fig. 4
View of the principal facade of the Shell Building, The Hague, Netherlands. J. J. P. Oud, c.1946. © Collection CCA – Canadian Centre for Architecture, Montreal.

fig. 5
View of the Palazzo Rucellai from Via del Purgatorio, Florence. Leon Battista Alberti, c.1446–51. © Luca Bosco.

Oud's bravery and conviction, Grassi appears to formulate his own critique based on a simple, almost ethical question: What truly defines the character of a building?

He provides the answer himself, clarifying that "the character of a building is not determined by a form liberated from any connection or precedent but precisely the opposite."[26]

The final form emerges from what is termed the character of a building, integral to its complete expression as an architectural object serving a collective urban ideal. In this context, the enduring subliminal influence of Leon Battista Alberti is undeniable, particularly from the example of the Palazzo Rucellai ***(fig. 5)***. It should be noted that the Palazzo Rucellai corresponds to a new prototype of a city palace and, along with the Sant'Andrea in Mantua, is considered by Grassi to be the most interesting of all Alberti's projects since it is one of the most detailed. However, this architectural experiment is not entirely successful for two reasons: firstly, contrary to what would be expected for a prototype model, the project's context is highly complex, full of constraints in the configuration of the urban plot where it is located; secondly, because it tries to solve this intricate equation by making it dependent on the design of its facade, which has the unbridled ambition of freeing the model of the Florentine palace from a series of formal restrictions. Even so, the starting point of Grassi's building goes back to an idea of Florentine tradition refined by Alberti's *palazzo*, as both buildings are committed to redesigning their respective urban surroundings and aim to express a construction principle ***(figs. 6–7)***. Without any reverential awe, Grassi points towards the old Florence, literally in the opposite sense to the new buildings in that sprawling and, at least for him, unrecognizable part of the city known as Novoli.

The project of the New Headquarters of the Cassa di Risparmio is founded on principles that could only have been approached by precisely departing from the constraints of the city imposed by Krier's plan, which Grassi openly criticized—"a building open to the public and obliged to be divided into several buildings to satisfy an equally extravagant idea of a garden city."[27] However, Grassi ultimately followed the "Spinelli Variant" associated with Krier, but poetically subverted it. He exposed and

[26] "O carácter dos edifícios" (lecture given upon the inauguration of the 2003/4 academic year at the Facoltà d'Architettura Civile del Politecnico di Milano, December 4, 2003), published in *Casabella* 722 (May 2004), in Grassi, *Escritos Escolhidos*, 511 (translation by the author).

[27] "Uma ideia de arquitectura, um modo de trabalhar e o seu porquê," 591 (translation by the author).

emphasized what he considered to be its incongruities, viewing them precisely as the primary expressive theme of the large brick building surrounding a green courtyard ***(fig. 8)***. An example of this is the obliquely cut facades and the violent interruption of moldings and cornices in the volumes' breaks that have enriched the relationships established within the composition and which, like some examples of Roman ruins pointed out by Grassi, are gutted to the point of revealing the secrets of their constructive apparatus ***(fig. 9)***.

The critique gains further clarity when confronted with opponents such as Ricci's building—the complete antithesis of Grassi's proposal. It is crucial to emphasize that Grassi's building exerts an even greater impact when situated next to this "nuisance neighbor." Their stark contrast underscores the significance of Grassi's project, as their discordance is so evident that both structures verge on caricatures of themselves: a paradox as the best way to combat another paradox, perhaps.

Grassi is perfectly aware of this. He is aware of it from the moment he realizes that he has to measure his extremely banal cardboard scale mock-up against the super-sophisticated models of the other participants in this competition.[28] It is with particular enthusiasm that he quotes the passage by Alberti criticizing impeccably finished, elegant, and shiny representational models,[29] placing himself in favor of Alberti's predilection for models without frills and without the possibility of misleading.

When Grassi writes that "the model of a city does not always prescribe but adapts until it sometimes becomes a parody of itself,"[30] he is fully conscious of what his own expressive choices can mean. The result is an architectural artifact comprising a tripartite continuous body with distinct internal and external faces extending along the entire perimeter of the area: a sort of miniature city aspiring to align with the Florentine architectural tradition. The building's two faces—one clad in brick and the other in sandstone ***(figs. 10-11)***—contribute to the idea of a logical and hierarchical construction that creates a genuine Albertian civil facade. In the case of Palazzo Rucellai, Alberti abruptly interrupts the cladding of its facade, aiming to show the

fig. 6
Detail of the public seat designed by Alberti for the facade of the Palazzo Rucellai. © Luca Bosco.

fig. 7
View of the public loggia of the Cassa di Risparmio di Firenze. © Luca Bosco.

[28] The list of architects participating in this competition included names such as Mario Bellini, Foster & Partners, Steven Holl, Kohn Pederson Fox, Fabrizio Rossi Prodi, and Paolo Zermani. The mock-up presented by Grassi was a simple cardboard model with the elevations printed and glued on—a sort of study mock-up, compared with some of his adversaries whose wooden mock-ups had sophisticated mechanisms that allowed lights to be switched on inside.

[29] Alberti, *Art of Building*, 34.

[30] "Arquitectura e racionalismo" (1970), in Grassi, *Escritos Escolhidos*, 67 (translation by the author).

incompleteness of his prototype *(figs. 12-13)*. Likewise, by openly exposing the fractures of his unitary building, Grassi underlines what he believes to be the formalist nature of the constraints imposed on him, hyperbolizing his critique to the point of revealing constructive sections in the side facades with the ambition of being didactic *(fig. 14)*.

fig. 8
View of the central green courtyard of the Cassa di Risparmio di Firenze. © Luca Bosco.

fig. 9
View of one of the public facades of the Cassa di Risparmio, interrupted according to the guidelines of Krier's plan. © Luca Bosco.

> **This is how an apparently complete stone façade, i.e., apparently complete in all its parts, from any point of view other than the perfectly orthogonal one, reveals that the building is, in reality, a scenarium. In other words, it is the expression of a profound contradiction, unsurpassed from a constructive point of view, and it shows at every point where that continuous building is left over or interrupted, revealing the curtain of brick that lies behind it and that covers all the internal fronts and façades, finally making it apparent at the four vertices of the large quadrilateral, where the stone from one side adjoins that from the other without ever touching, thus leaving the brick behind it exposed[31] *(fig. 15)*.**

The incorporation of the classical cornice *(fig. 16)*—one of the peculiarities of this building—can perhaps be understood as a rare act of audacity since, when compared with the work of J. J. P. Oud, it could be read in the light of what Grassi himself considers to be the absolute necessity of tackling the problem of ornament in architecture.[32] This detail is clearly an allusion to the fact that sometimes it is necessary to take one step backwards to take two steps forwards. And it is precisely here that Grassi comes closer to Oud.

The premises evoked by the Dutch architect in defense of his own building, from which he fiercely criticizes the official line of the modern movement embodied by Walter Gropius, are very clear in the sense that he combines forces and arguments "to once more bestow upon building the halo that stamps it as architecture."[33] Oud further demonstrates this when he writes the following:

[31] Grassi, *Leon Battista Alberti e a Arquitectura Romana*, 50 (translation by the author).

[32] For both Oud and Grassi, the problem of ornament in architecture was a critical and decisive factor in defining the language of architecture. The figure of Oud, who had achieved truly incontestable results in the past, and his courage in putting everything on the line again by literally compromising his career from that moment on, represent for Grassi the ultimate example of how this issue should be read again and not ignored in the light of contemporaneity.

[33] Ed Taverne and Dolf Broekhuizen, *J. J. P. Oud's Shell Building: Design and Reception* (Rotterdam: Nai Uitgevers Publishers, 1995), 8.

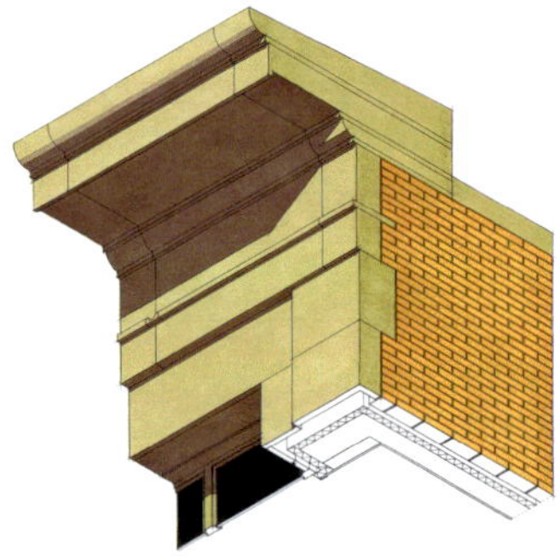

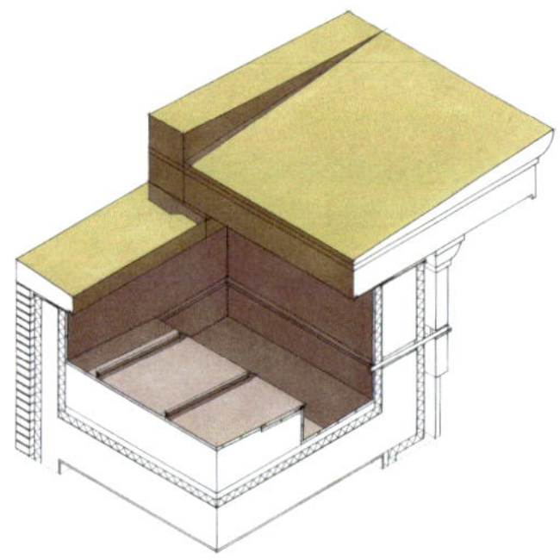

figs. 10–11
Grassi's details of the internal and external facades of the building. © Fondo Giorgio Grassi – Fondazione MAXXI, Roma.

figs. 12–13
Details of the dissolution of the facade cladding in the Palazzo Rucellai. © Luca Bosco.

fig. 14
View of one of the didactic construction sections of the Cassa di Risparmio. © Luca Bosco.

fig. 15
View of the open corner detail of the Cassa di Risparmio. © Luca Bosco.

fig. 16
Grassi's details of the building's classical cornice. © Fondo Giorgio Grassi – Fondazione MAXXI, Roma.

> **The building could perfectly well do without [ornament], but its function is to underline the building's significance. The decorative elements—for example, the balusters of the staircase—do not deform the material or the construction method; on the contrary, they have been modelled on the nature of the material and the construction method. The roof ornament is not just another ornament: it allows light to filter through the gaps. It is designed for that same light, not for the shadow of its frames. The same can be said of the decorative element above the entrance: light and life come into play through the ornament.[34]**

Like Oud's building, Grassi's cornice pursues the idea of ornament for architectural and not merely sculptural purposes and clearly aims to accentuate the unitary and monumental character of the building. Without it, the criticism subjacent to his proposal would not deliver such a violent blow. Still, Grassi admits that he may have given in to overenthusiasm in Cassa di Risparmio by using such an unlikely and—for some—needless element. Nevertheless, it seems logical, as it is ironically sincere, that his expressive choices in this project come close to what he himself considered a potential act of exaggeration regarding the theme of decoration in some of Alberti's Florentine projects, such as Santa Maria Novella or the Rucellai Chapel: Were they a "gesture of impatience"? Or were they "the final unmasking"?[35]

In fact, and once again ironically, Grassi could not be closer to the Renaissance master when he states that, faced with Florentine decorativism, "Alberti has no other response than negation (the old, practical, always useful and effective rejection),"[36] a response that is, above all, a self-exclusion: negation as an opportunity for a confrontation; a form of *Built Criticism* that Alberti (and of course Grassi) consistently applied to his projects.

Biography
Ricardo Leitão (Porto, 1991) is an architect who graduated from Faculty of Architecture of the University of Porto (FAUP) in 2015 with time spent at ENSA Paris-Belleville as part of the Erasmus Programme. In 2020, he received a literary grant in poetry from DGLAB (Portuguese Ministry of Culture). Joining FAUP's Architecture PhD program in 2021 with a scholarship from FCT, he explored the potential application of Harold Bloom's literary theory in the field of architecture. Currently, he is a visiting professor at FAUP, teaching History of Modern Architecture, and an integrated researcher at CEAU-FAUP, contributing to the T2P research group. In 2023, along with Rita Furtado, he was the winner of the first edition of the Manuel Graça Dias Award, dst-Ordem dos Arquitectos for his first built work, House in Freamunde.

[34] Oud quoted by Grassi in the text "Arquitectura e racionalismo," 79 (translation by the author).
[35] Grassi, *Leon Battista Alberti e a Arquitectura Romana*, 91 (translation by the author).
[36] Grassi, 171 (translation by the author).

Contemporary Paradigms

Building Breaches in Medellín

Luiz Recamán and Mariana Wilderom

Architecture has the potential to transform urban space and, consequently, aspects of social reality, even if contemporary reality is largely dominated by the dynamics of necessity or economic logic. The analysis of the Antonio Derka School project in Medellín, Colombia, designed by Obranegra Arquitectos, shows how architecture is able to create possible urbanities in given social and historical contexts through its specific disciplinary means, thereby addressing urgent challenges faced by socially vulnerable communities and urban environments.

The Antonio Derka School (2008) emerged in a politically complex and socially vulnerable context in Medellín, Colombia. It was part of the Northeast Integrated Urban Project (PUI), which included urban improvements and the construction of public facilities and housing along the K Metrocable line. The school's design responded to the challenges arising from this situation, using the imperative of Medellín's topography as leverage against the narrow range of possibilities afforded by the circumstances. At the same time, the school seamlessly integrates with the landscape. The relationship between different urban scales, from the noteworthy overall topography to the spatialities resulting from the hillside settlements forming the communities, is emphasized.

The project's strategy prioritized spatial continuity and openness while preserving the functionality of the school's volume and enhancing its collective significance. The analysis highlights the project's ability to interact with the existing urban fabric and the city's geography, ultimately presenting itself as an architectural statement of hope on the collective horizon.

The Antonio Derka School constitutes itself as a critical exercise in exploring the possibilities of transforming into the architectural realm—that is, mediated by architecture, and therefore with some degree of *concrete utopia*—the results of everyday efforts to transcend their own limitations. It challenges traditional disciplinary boundaries, creating a rare material and relational continuity within its context. This analysis underscores the importance of critically examining the role of architecture in contemporary urban and social contexts, challenging established categories and celebrating the autonomy of the architectural moment in the transformation process.

keywords:

Obranegra Arquitectos, Antonio Derka School Medellín, Integrated Urban Project, Concrete Utopia

Introduction

Octavio Paz described poetry as a form of knowledge capable of unveiling this world and, in addition, creating another world through revolutionary, liberating, and spiritual means encapsulated in the power of language.[1] Henri Lefebvre, a thinker who never separated poetry from praxis, wondered if it were possible to create something capable of revealing and transcending the abstract economic order within a contradictory, hierarchized, and rationalized world, shaped by modern thought.[2] By accepting the phenomenon of capital's direct management of land,[3] Manfredo Tafuri outlined a disillusioned political task for an architectural culture that can operate within reality's breaches. According to these three authors' various perspectives, transforming the world depends on a unique ability to understand it. Based on these reflections, one can consider that the critical significance of an architectural work lies in its potential to access, even if contradictorily, the totality of its reality through a disciplinary lens, creating a new reality whose integrating expression between object and context may have the power to produce an "other" urbanity. This is not a task solely achievable through the acuity or descriptive and analytical comprehensiveness of the intervention's technical or programmatic context, nor is it solely attainable through sensitivity to socio-spatial phenomena, although this pathway may facilitate it. There is a demand for a different type of knowledge that transforms reality, and perhaps this was the goal of Henri Lefebvre's intellectual life when he sought to capture the key to transform the world in an emancipatory sense, both in the dialectical thought movement and in the act of "inventorying acquired experience . . ., [to] help bring forth the possible."[4]

The Antonio Derka School in Medellín, Colombia, could be part of a Lefebvrian inventory with its creative–revealing power over reality's contingent and fertile aspects. It critically accepts life's circumstances and the everyday spaces that shape it as structuring elements of the possibilities created by its spatiality, giving rise to a social and urban potentiality that transcends the school's typology.

1 Octavio Paz, "Introdução: poesia e poema," in *O Arco e a lira* (São Paulo: Cosac Naify, 2012), 19–34.
2 Henri Lefebvre, "Prefácio: a produção do espaço," *Estudos Avançados* 27, no. 79 (2013): 129.
3 Manfredo Tafuri, *Architecture and Utopia: Design and Capitalist Development* (Cambridge, MA: MIT Press, 1976), 170.
4 Henri Lefebvre, "Humanismo y urbanismo. Algunas proposiciones," in *De lo rural a lo urbano*, ed. Mario Gaviria and Javier Gonzalez-Pueyo (Barcelona: Ediciones península, 1971), 149.

The Project

The Antonio Derka School (2008), designed by Obranegra Arquitectos,[5] was built during Sergio Fajardo's time as mayor (2003 to 2007) in Medellín, Colombia, as part of a political agenda driven by tight deadlines and the social expectations arising from his election.[6] Moreover, it bore the specific conditions of a territory marked by high social vulnerability ***(fig. 1)***. The Santo Domingo Sávio community, located on the northeastern slope of Medellín, faced several of the common socio-spatial problems that were besetting a country whose historical dynamics of violence had been shaped by the crises triggered by the decades-long narcotics trade afflicting the wider region.

The school was part of the Integrated Urban Project (PUI; Proyecto Urbano Integral) for northeast Medellín that included urban improvements and the construction of sports and cultural facilities, public spaces, and housing along the K Metrocable line. It was part of a political strategy to ensure that new buildings physically opened to the surrounding environment, acting as spatial symbols for their communities, in contrast to previously isolated and aggressively introverted public facilities. Fajardo's motto, "*lo más bello para los más humildes*" (the most beautiful for the humblest),[7] was interpreted in different ways by architects responding to this demand. This analysis focuses on the architects' design strategies for the spatial realization and construction of the Antonio Derka School as an alternative way of constituting the relationship between architecture and the city, especially in contexts characterized by high social vulnerability. The project stands out in the Latin American context in that it tackles severe social circumstances—violence, segregation, and poverty—by emphasizing the school's urban environmental qualities.

The topographical imperative of Medellín's geography simultaneously intensifies the precariousness of spontaneous occupation and the landscape's uniqueness. A continual awareness of what is close and what is distant allows for an intricate spatial

5 Colegio Santo Domingo Sávio. Address: Carrera 28, n. 107–295, Barrio Santo Domingo Sávio, Medellín, Colombia. Authorship: Obranegra Arquitectos (lead architects: Carlos Pardo Botero, Mauricio Zuluaga Latorre, Nicolás Vélez Jaramillo; coordinating architect: Arq. Juan Camilo Llano C.; collaborating architects: Alejandro Ochoa, Carlos Andrés Holguín, Felipe Campuzano). Structural calculation: Wilmar Vélez (E.D.U.). Project start date: December 2005. Work carried out: February 2007 to March 2008. Built area: 7,500 m². Construction: A.I.A (Arquitectos e Ingenieros Asociados). Promoting company: E.D.U. Urban Development Company of Medellín. Client: Alcaldía de Medellín.

6 Mariana Wilderom, "Conversa com Carlos Pardo: arquitetura educacional como intervenção urbana" [Interview with Carlos Pardo: educational architecture as an urban intervention], *Entrevista* 14, no. 056.01 (October 2013), https://vitruvius.com.br/revistas/read/entrevista/14.056/4894.

7 This motto, often echoed in Sergio Fajardo's public speeches, underpins his "Medellín, la más educada" (Medellín, the Most Educated) policy and the "Colegios de Calidad" (Quality Schools) program. The initiative, which involved constructing ten new schools and renovating 128 existing ones, aimed to transform public schools into community hubs and quality educational centers through high architectural standards. Fajardo's team ensured this quality by selecting architects with proven experience and notable recognition in at least three of the last ten National Architecture Biennials.

fig. 1
Satellite image of the Santo Domingo Sávio neighborhood and the surroundings of Antonio Derka School between the two existing schools. © Google Earth.

fig. 2
Aerial view of Antonio Derka School, displaying the topographical integration strategy of the "L"-shaped building complex, with the access square as a continuation and widening of the winding street, the larger volume projecting as an observation point, and the cubic volume of the community room elevated on stilts. © Luis Adriano Ramírez.

fig. 3
View of the staircase ensemble providing access to the different levels of the school on its exterior. © Alfonso Posada.

fig. 4
View from the classroom floor showing the porous relationship between the building and the landscape. © Alejandro Arango.

cohesiveness that characterizes the city. The project's initial move captures this dimension of the place, reverberating across all its levels—program, volumes, and materials *(fig. 2)*. Thus, the project enhances the topography by creating a rare patch of flat ground, expanding its socio-spatial and landscape possibilities. The L-shaped volume is set below the level of the street, thereby widening the latter. Starting from the sidewalk, a staircase with multiple landings provides access to the school's different levels, taking advantage of the steep slope *(fig. 3)*.

The architectural program interplays with the context by organizing its spaces in a descending sequence. On the first two levels, located below street level and adjacent to it, laboratories and support areas are accommodated. Meanwhile, the arm extending towards the valley integrates the landscape through the strategic spacing of twenty-four classrooms across two levels divided into six segments, interspersed with extensive balconies, vertical brise-soleils, and openings that connect the two levels. As the porous floors expand horizontally, traditional corridors evolve into "public spaces" and vertical slits open up to "visual landmarks" *(fig. 4)*. The subsequent levels, reserved for the playroom and the shop, recede in height and area. This topographical adjustment gives rise to a triple-height monumental courtyard that gently sits above the dining area on the lowest level *(fig. 5)*.

The school's design strategy unfolds in the structural logic *(fig. 6)*. It builds spatiality through rare physical and perceptual continuity *(fig. 7)*. The threshold between the exterior and the interior extends from the street, continuing over the school's flat roof, which becomes a 3,900 m^2 plaza, an observatory, and an open space ready to embrace moments of the unexpected *(fig. 8)*. Unlike other modern traditions, such as the hegemonic paradigm in Brazilian architecture,[8] there is no attempt to create a counterpoint that emphasizes the introverted and deterritorializing autonomy of the architectural object. Here, the void is not the negative of the appealing volume; it

fig. 5
View of the built volume projecting from the hillside as an observation point that simultaneously serves as a continuation of the street level, perceived as a square by pedestrians passing through it. © Carlos Pardo.

fig. 6
Side view of the school revealing the complexity of topographical accommodation of the different levels of the building. © Carlos Pardo.

fig. 7
Rear view of the school, from a street in the vicinity, highlighting integration with the surroundings as a strategy to promote various perceptible forms of continuity in relation to its context. © Carlos Pardo.

fig. 8
View of the observation square: a place that allows for different forms and temporalities of appropriation. © Isaac Ramírez.

fig. 9
View of the architectural ensemble, where horizontal lines stand out as an expanded boundary between the school and the street. © Alejandro Arango.

manifests itself as the roof's vast relational open space or through an overall grained porosity. This does not define the school's volume, since the strategy in shaping the volume is primarily committed to enhancing its contextual functionality, thereby turning the school into a collective urban symbol.

Openness, fluidity, and continuity establish a radical reality that under conventional circumstances would require immediate nonarchitectural interventions such as fences, guardhouses, and barriers. The broad slab—the extended threshold—is a clear boundary between the street and the school. Thus, this horizontal material boundary takes on an opposite meaning to the anti-urbanity of its vertical counterpart (property walls). That is, it enhances what already exists with no didactic ruptures from the disciplinary tradition that separates form and everyday life. The school's spatial apprehension also breaks away from passive contemplation. From a distance—an inherent condition of the city's geography—it presents itself affirmatively, architecturally ***(fig. 9)***. The school's volumes and the steel-framed meeting room are clearly announced in the city's skyline. They challenge the topography with a degree of freedom, making their presence known.

When observing the architectural ensemble up close, we notice that temporality takes precedence over volumetric stability, allowing bodies to perceive the new space in a fluid and ambiguous manner. The meeting room volume sitting atop pilotis separates itself from the roof-ground, becoming a local marker of the new building ***(fig. 10)***. The volumetric unity is partially maintained as the building is approached, while the functionality diversifies into different meanings along the way. It reinforces a sense of community and noncommercial symbolism, delineating the nearby collectiveness while allowing independent use apart from the rhythms of spatiality and strictly school-based routine. Its form, in its prominence, affirms the daily rhythms of this particular social group.

In this way, the project elements—the meeting room, the school, the plaza, and the schoolyard—and the different temporalities to which they respond, are demarcated in continuity. This interplay between individual and collective perceptions is emphasized by a continuous circulation between the neighborhood and the archi-

[8] See Luiz Recamán and Mariana Wilderom, "The Meaning of Counter-Hegemony Possibilities in Architecture," *V!RUS* 24 (December 2022), http://www.nomads.usp.br/virus/papers/v24/734/734en.php; and Mariana Wilderom, "Arquitetura para cidades na América Latina contemporânea: distâncias e aproximações entre São Paulo e Medellín" (doctoral thesis, Faculdade de Arquitetura e Urbanismo, Universidade de São Paulo, 2019), https://teses.usp.br/teses/disponiveis/16/16133/tde-24102019-165125/pt-br.php.

tectural complex—the sidewalks only widen within the school area. The inherent movement follows the same scale and rhythm, from the descending access to the school via the staircase, reinforcing the close connection between interior and exterior without compromising its formal, functional, and social definition. Entering "downwards" aligns the project with the construction logic of housing; it subverts it by attributing a more liberated and "beautiful" character associated with the collective need. It elevates precariousness of direct access to the potential freedom provided by group action ***(fig. 11)***.

Highlighting these aspects of the project, among many other possible interpretations, the aim here is to understand it from a specific critical perspective, and to challenge it in its relation to reality; in other words, questioning the strength of critical categories and their validity in the somewhat blurry contemporary urban and social context.

fig. 10
Perceived as a local landmark from far away, the meeting room turns into a welcoming community space when approached through the plaza. © Alejandro Arango.

fig. 11
A panoramic view of the city from the school's observation point. © Mariana Wilderom.

Conclusions

The Antonio Derka School is created in a rare material and perceptual continuity, considering the formal polarity between reality—guided by necessity—and a possibility brought into reality—guided by a logic that inevitably gives autonomy to the architectural "moment" of its process.

This work was supported by the São Paulo Research Foundation (FAPESP) [Grant Number 2020/11816-5 and 16/22704-8]

Biographies

Luiz Recamán (1960–2024) obtained his master's and PhD degrees in aesthetics at the School of Philosophy and Human Sciences of the University of São Paulo. He was an associate professor in the Faculty of Architecture and Urbanism of the University of São Paulo (FAUUSP). His main work addressed the critique of architecture and aesthetics, and modern Brazilian and contemporary architecture. He was editor-in-chief of the journal *Revista ARA FAUUSP* and coauthored *Brazil's Modern Architecture* (Phaidon, 2004), *Vilanova Artigas—Habitação e Cidade na Modernização Brasileira* (Unicamp, 2014), and *The New Urban Condition: Criticism and Theory from Architecture and Urbanism* (Routledge, 2021), and was the founder and coordinator of the research group Critical Thinking and Contemporary City (PC3).

Mariana Wilderom is an architect, holds a master's and a PhD in architecture and urbanism, and carries out her postdoctoral research at the Faculty of Architecture and Urbanism of the University of São Paulo (FAUUSP). She is an associated researcher in the Critical Thinking and Contemporary City (PC3) research group at FAUUSP. She studies architecture theory and criticism, architecture and the contemporary city in Latin America, urban design, and educational architecture. She is the author of chapters in the books *Marcenaria Baraúna: Furniture as Architecture* (Olhares, 2017) and *Social Urbanism in Latin America* (Springer, 2019).

Inventing the Present: The Case of Tainan Spring between Criticism of the Recent Past and Environmental Urgencies

Patrizia Mello

fig. 1
MVRDV, Tainan Spring, Tainan, Taiwan, 2020. Photo: Daria Scagliola.

To think about the now implies first of all recovering the critical vision. Reflecting on the now does not imply relinquishing the future or forgetting the past: the present is the meeting place for the three directions of time.[1]

keywords:
MVDRV, Tainan Spring, urban regeneration, aesthetic realism

Octavio Paz's statement seems particularly suitable as a metaphorical introduction to MVRDV's "Tainan Spring" project (Tainan, Taiwan, 2020). It could be seen as a condenser of issues that have been discussed in metropolises since the turn of the millennium, critically reconsidering the abnormal growth of recent decades in favor of recovering places for the public to share their everyday lives in a leisure and landscape setting.

In the case of Tainan Spring, the creation of a real "urban lagoon" overlaps with the recent past of a building—the Chinatown Mall (completed in 1983)—which had fallen into disuse in the 1990s and was demolished in 2016, but whose memory continues to "animate" the new public space owing to the way the designers incorporated the existing structure of the underground parking into the project, leaving it exposed, thereby offering a direct comparison between the new building and Tainan's recent past. But what past is this?

Functional Interchanges between Past and Present

Tainan is the oldest city in Taiwan. Maritime traffic is its beating heart. The port is a base for fishers and a node for a dense network of canals. Water and lush natural habitats are its most authentic features and, for a long time, these characterized the city. The Chinatown Mall was created in 1983 on a dead arm of the port that had dried up in the 1960s. The mall was built for the annual markets that were traditionally held there, from the Spring Festival, or Chinese New Year, to the Lantern Festival. Prior to the mall's construction, these were open-air markets with much sought-after stalls for small-scale traders. The mall comprised a representative entrance facade, inspired by local architecture, and an anonymous eleven-story residential block at the rear; it occupied an area of 180 by 45 meters and, in addition to the various types of shopping, it also included an ice rink, a playground, and the Chinatown Theatre.

At the heart of the Chinatown Mall project was a desire to create a "modern" meeting place for cultural and commercial activities in a reassuring architecture that should inspire the local population even though it was not particularly appealing from an aesthetic point of view due to its hybrid nature.

In the early 1990s, the mall began to suffer from a gradual decline; its raison d'être as a bustling meeting place disappeared, especially at weekends. Commercial competition as a result of the rapid multiplication of new stores near the train station; the project for a new underground commercial road where Hai'an Road is now located, which later failed miserably; and the bankruptcy of the construction company that was supposed to build apartments at the back of the mall (subsequently sold to the highest bidder for nonresidential functions) all resulted in the mall's demolition. With its removal, it became possible to recover the hydrophilic character of the former port area (now called Chinatown Plaza) and to create a generous urban landscape along the T-axis from Huanhe Street in front to the canal bank to the west and Hai'an Road to the east.

[1] Octavio Paz, "What is Modernity?," *Casabella* 664 (1999): 51; the text documents the second part of the conference "In Search of the Present," which Paz held on December 8, 1990, on receiving the Nobel Prize for Literature: https://www.nobelprize.org/prizes/literature/1990/paz/lecture/ (accessed January 23, 2024). See also Patrizia Mello, *Twentieth Century Architecture and Modernity: Our Past, Our Present* (Los Angeles: Oro Editions, 2022), 176; in the book, Paz's concept is one of the fundamental theoretical references (together with one by philosopher Marshall Berman and another by architectural historian John Summerson) in the analysis of the concept of "modernity" in relation to the development of architecture from the first decades of the twentieth century until today.

The MVRDV Project: New Regenerative Lifeblood for Tainan

The project was selected from the five finalists of the 2015 International Landscape Competition for Tainan Axis Landscape Transformation, organized by the Urban Development Bureau of the Tainan city government. The competition was part of the Tainan Canal development plan initiated in 2002, which was connected to the Star Diamond Canal Development Plan and the Chinatown Planning and Redevelopment Master Plan. The starting point for all of these plans resides in the rich cultural heritage and landscape ecology of Tainan: their common aim is to achieve a sustainable low-carbon environment.

The MVRDV proposal is particularly effective for various reasons. Firstly, in preserving the 162 reinforced-concrete pillars of the former underground car park, the proposal encourages the local residents to directly compare past and present to effectively evaluate the change resulting from the replacement of the old mall by the new public space; the latter, being articulated with water features, microclimatic variations, hills, and numerous plants, is particularly suitable for children's play and adults' relaxation. The bed of the lagoon is formed of resin-bound fine pebbles, offering a good nonslip surface as well as enabling a straightforward cleaning regime.

Thanks to discreet lighting that enhances the gentle curvatures of the lagoon landscape, the space is also accessible at night and already used for various types of events, including an open-air cinema. Over time, the fragmented remnants will be used for new alternative functions, not just commercial purposes; a teahouse has already been set up and a small library is being planned. The history of the place is made visible by a glass floor that allows visitors to see the original foundations of the old Chinatown Mall. At the same time, the new ground level has become a landscaped promenade overlooking the lagoon.

fig. 2
Lǐ Zǔyuán, Chinatown Mall, Tainan, Taiwan, 1983. The entrance to the Mall. Credit: MVRDV Archive.

fig. 3
Lǐ Zǔyuán, Chinatown Mall, Tainan, Taiwan, 1983. The eleven-story residential block at the rear. Credit: MVRDV Archive.

fig. 4, 5
Lǐ Zǔyuán, Chinatown Mall, Tainan, Taiwan, 1983. Credit: MVRDV Archive.

The second reason the MVRDV proposal is effective is that, by reusing the former underground parking, it became possible to create a protected public park away from traffic. As an "enclosed" space, it also works well from an acoustic point of view, thus proving to be suitable for occasional outdoor concerts.[2] Furthermore, the old supporting structure of the Chinatown Mall now surrounds the lagoon, creating covered porticoes that protect visitors from the sun.

Thus, while the project began with a demolition, it progressively found its raison d'être as a public space during the process of being reunited with the previously mentioned essential elements of Tainan, namely the sea and the landscape, that have always provided the backdrop for the life of the inhabitants, even today when that idyllic world seems lost forever due to excessive construction. According to Winy Maas (founding partner/principal architect, urban planner, and landscape designer, leading MVRDV since 1993): "Inspired by the history of the city, both the original jungle and the water were important sources of inspiration. Tainan is a very grey city. With the reintroduction of the jungle to every place that was possible, the city is reintegrating into the surrounding landscape."[3] The aquatic landscape, the lush nature, and the desire to create a new comfort in everyday life for residents are the three elements that, combined together, inspired the project to reactivate the character of the place in a sequence of operations: first, "the ouverture" to restore the water-based function of the place; second, the creation of a lagoon plaza, a new public space for the city; third, the partial recovery of the existing structure of the Chinatown Mall with which to create a forum; fourth, the installation of a water-recycling system that also reduces temperatures in summer; fifth, the introduction of vegetation into the urban lagoon and along Hai'an Road, and the reuse of the numerous ventilation shafts.

[2] Similarly, Diller Scofidio + Renfro's "High Line" (2000–2019) in New York City is a transformation of a former elevated railway track from the 1930s into a public park that leaves traces of the tracks to "automatically" create a walkway that is separated from urban traffic: an agri-tecture strategy—says Scofidio—designed to combine artificial and organic materials in a blend of "vegetable and mineral." The result is a gain of new public space that offers users an unusual dialogue between past and present.

[3] Winy Maas, accessed January 21, 2024, https://www.mvrdv.com/projects/272/tainan-spring.

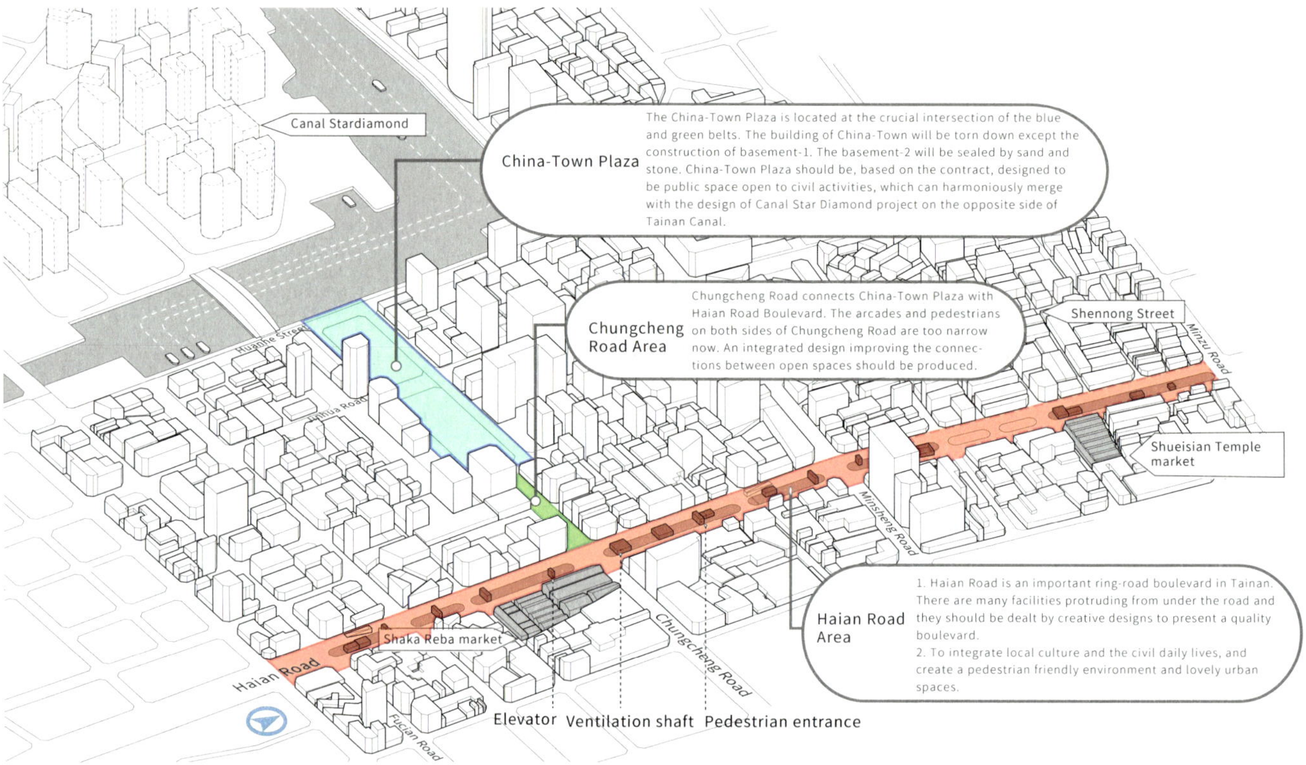

fig. 6
International Landscape Competition for Tainan Axis Landscape Transformation, 2015. The design requirements. © Urban Development Bureau of the Tainan City Government.

Thus, a new microclimatic zone has been introduced within the city via water in the lagoon, which can increase or decrease in volume depending on the seasons (water levels are adjusted with mains water when necessary, but generally during the monsoon season they will be higher, at seventy centimeters, and in the dry summer months will be lower, at thirty centimeters), and refreshing mist sprays. The successive planting of a large variety of local plants (*Palaquium formosanum*, *Terminalia catappa*, *Plumeria*) will gradually characterize the lagoon square and Hai'an Road as a green retreat. Previously one of the busiest roads in Tainan, Hai'an Road now has only one lane in each direction, resulting in a significant reduction in vehicular traffic.

In a certain sense, with this transformation, vegetation has regained the position that it lost with the construction of the Chinatown Mall, the memories of which are contained in the ruins that remain. This a theme that is associated with James Wines, whose investigations into the "critical questioning" of architecture (de-architecture, i.e., shifting the attention from formal and structural disquisitions on buildings to the possibility of weaving through the same dialogues but only in the mind)[4] have been aimed at emphasizing the dominance of nature over architecture, where "Built Criticism" urges the public to reflect on possible future developments of the contemporary "Built Criticism" city, thereby anticipating topics of relevance today. One example is the Forest Building for BEST (Richmond, Virginia, 1980), about which Wines states: "The building had a very strong message, which is acutely relevant today—why should landscape architecture always have these cute little trees and squiggles on a cutely manicured lawn? My point was—just let nature do its thing!"[5] At the same time, it is the very "nature" of shopping centers that Wines calls into question, as in the case of the facade for the BEST project in Houston, Texas (1974): "We used the

4 See James Wines, *De-Architecture* (New York: Rizzoli International Publications, 1987).

5 Vladimir Belogolovsky, "Architecture Needed to Be Liberated from Itself," interview with James Wines, *STIRworld*, August 30, 2022, accessed January 21, 2024, https://www.stirworld.com/think-columns-architecture-needed-to-be-liberated-from-itself-says-james-wines-of-site.

fig. 7
MVRDV, Tainan Spring, Tainan, Taiwan, 2020. Photo: Daria Scagliola.

fig. 8
MVRDV, Tainan Spring, Tainan, Taiwan, 2020. Photo: Daria Scagliola.

big box shop archetype that everyone would recognise, and the idea was to create architecture that would become its own critique."[6] In the case of Wines, these were clearly provocations that brought art closer to architecture; nonetheless, in just a few years they have taken on a "concrete" importance in the debate on contemporary urban development that is, on the one hand, besieged by the proliferation of shopping centers in historic cores and, on the other hand, lacking green spaces and pedestrian areas that would improve the quality of life of the inhabitants.

The green theme has become a leitmotif for architects, supposedly standing for "sustainability" (Wines was an early pioneer, successfully mixing literary provocation and visionary wisdom) but instead often trivializing the issue. While many architects' interventions are isolated objects in a concrete jungle offering comfort to a limited few, what should be encouraged are precisely transformations like Tainan Spring, where greenery is public and where the project's "sustainability" also lies in the recycling of 95 percent of demolition material and in the partial reuse of an existing structure. In this regard, Maas explained that removing the old structure was a sleight of hand, since the west end of the plaza was part of the canal's retaining wall, so there were collateral effects. In particular, with the first level of the mall car park, which now forms the new lagoon level, the removal of 80 percent of the building's original mass needed to be compensated for in what remained to ensure that the groundwater would not cause uplift in the retained slabs.

Less convincing, however, has been the reuse of the numerous large ventilation shafts from the underground car park on Hai'an Road, since, by entrusting them to local artists to supposedly improve their aesthetics, their volume has been paradoxically accentuated, often with rather awkward and banal results.

[6] Belogolovsky, "Architecture Needed to Be Liberated."

MVRDV's fellow competitors, for example the second-placed Weng Zumo Architects, took the theme of reuniting the site with the sea to even greater extremes by literally allowing the latter to invade Chinatown Plaza to reintroduce prosperity in this run-down area of the city. Local culture would be represented by a designed "edible landscape" on Hai'an Road from which restaurateurs could directly source typical Tainan produce for use in their kitchens . . . These design intentions, if implemented, would, however, be less effective than the verbal criticism, in particular with respect to the conception of the new square, where the idea of social aggregation would be translated into a series of panoramic terraces that would render people as passive spectators rather than protagonists within the landscape.

fig. 9
Weng Zumo Architects, International Landscape Competition for Tainan Axis Landscape Transformation, 2015. Second place. © Weng Zumo Architects.

fig. 10
MVRDV, Tainan Spring, Tainan, Taiwan, 2020. Photo: Daria Scagliola.

fig. 11
MVRDV, Tainan Spring, Tainan, Taiwan, 2020. Photo: Daria Scagliola.

Towards an "Aesthetic Realism"

MVRDV's new "urban landscape" of Tainan Spring creates the impression of being inside a contemporary Roman forum, as Winy Maas stated: "In Tainan Spring, people can bathe in the overgrown remains of a shopping mall. Children will soon be swimming in the ruins of the past—how fantastic is that?"[7] From my point of view, the project could be regarded as an instance of "aesthetic realism." Contemporary architects increasingly find themselves having to carve out spaces for interventions like this and to attribute new meaning to existing structures, since they find themselves operating in extremely congested metropolises, in which the buildings are of low quality, environmental pollution is a major problem, and there is an excessive proliferation of shopping malls—very numerous in Tainan—which not only invade our lives with often useless things but also are slowly compromising the authentic character of our historic centers by enabling the spread of global fashion brands and over-touristic vulgarization at the expense of literary cafés, traditional artisan shops, historic bookshops . . .

[7] See project press release by MVRDV https://www.mvrdv.com/projects/272/tainan-spring.

In general, shopping malls represent one of the best-known "drifts" of our time that the anthropologist Marc Augé (1935–2023) had identified among the main "non-places" of the contemporary era, those "contractual" places governed by anonymity and by the different forms of exchange, the only aspects that define an identity: "Alone, but one of many, the user of a non-place is in contractual relations with it (or with the powers that govern it). He is reminded, when necessary, that the contract exists . . . the ticket he has bought, the card he will have to show at the tollbooth, even the trolley he trundles round the supermarket, are all more or less clear signs of it."[8]

Certainly, the rapid multiplication of these non-places has diminished the identity and spontaneity of the collective, progressively narrowing people's horizons. According to Octavio Paz: "The topic of the market is intricately related to the deterioration of the environment. Pollution affects not only the air, the rivers and the forests but also our souls. A society possessed by the frantic need to produce more in order to consume more tends to reduce ideas, feelings, art, love, friendship, and people themselves to consumer products. Everything becomes a thing to be bought, used and then thrown in the rubbish dump. No other society has produced so much waste as ours has. Material and moral waste."[9]

At the same time, urban space is sold, clogged, and occupied at full capacity to make way for places of pure consumption. In light of the dramatic events related to Covid-19, the issue of how our contract with the urban space can be renewed has returned to the fore with a vengeance. The new scenarios that suddenly emerged under our astonished gazes have elicited a series of questions about what life in cities could be like following the period of forced distancing from the bustle of urban life.

One thing is certain: we will need more spaces for living and less excessive consumption. Consumerism has turned us into fragile entities, vulnerable objects at

[8] Marc Augé, *Non-Places: Introduction to an Anthropology of Supermodernity* (London and New York: Verso, 1995), 101.

[9] Paz, "What is Modernity?," cited in Mello, *Twentieth Century Architecture*, 172.

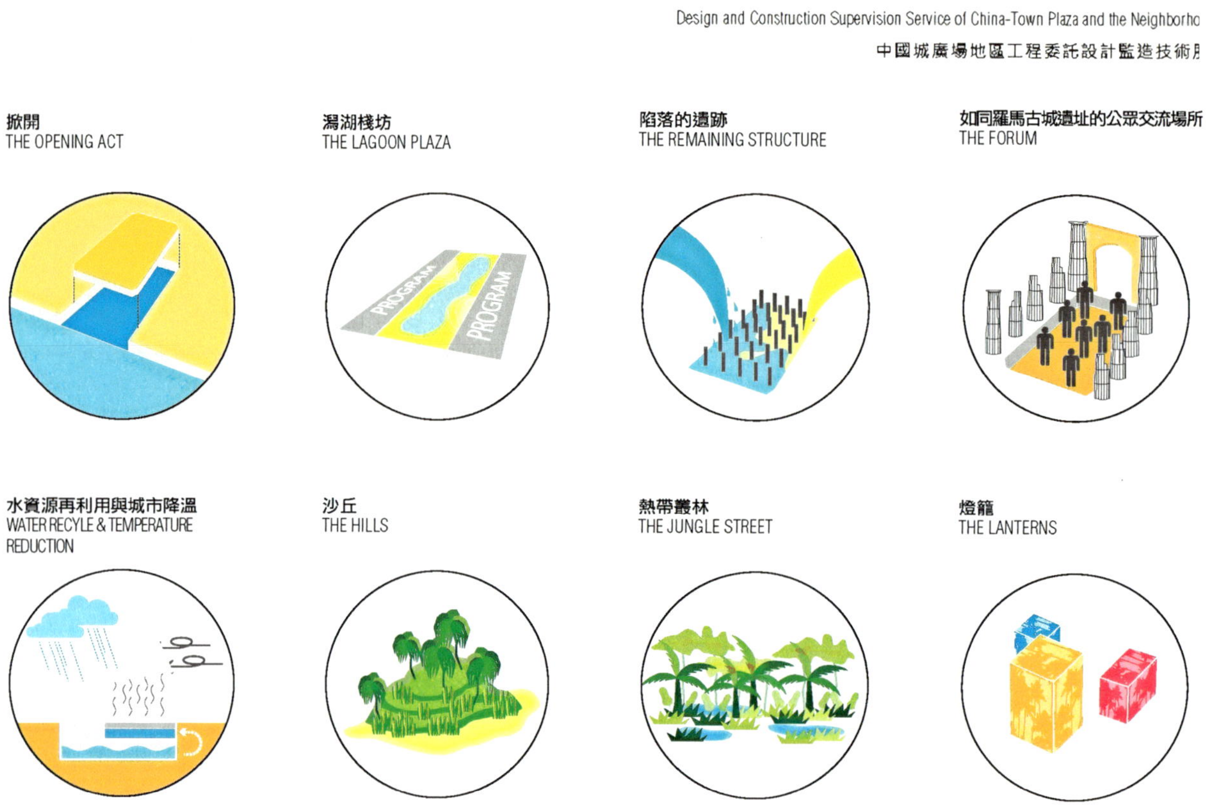

fig. 12
MVRDV, Tainan Spring, Tainan, Taiwan, 2020. Design and construction of Chinatown Plaza and the surrounding neighborhood. © MVRDV.

the mercy of possessive brands and victims of all kinds of devitalizing "abuse." Note the contrast between the narrow-mindedness of developers that has led to people being squeezed into cramped houses and the contemptuous pomp of consumption: shrinking existence on the one hand and an enlargement of its accessories on the other, from the toxic to the kitsch.

Ultimately, in the case of projects like Tainan Spring, it would be possible to talk about what I have defined as "an era of Rembrandt beauty,"[10] that is, an era in which beauty springs from the progress of life itself, just as it continually regenerates itself, based on its own driving forces and intertwined with destiny. It is in this sense that the era can produce either beauty or ugliness, by chance. "Rembrandt's figures are almost never beautiful," observes Georg Simmel (1858–1918). "For Rembrandt never sought any of his decisive values in beauty. . . . Anyone immersed in Rembrandt for a while sometimes finds beauty to be almost like an outward appendage to life's development from its own innermost sources."[11]

In this sense, the Tainan Spring project exemplifies the process of critical revision of contemporary urban development that is underway in some metropolises, revealing the desire to intervene by creating larger-scale views of the surrounding context, reestablishing characteristic flows of microclimate and people, and reviving ancient social and cultural traditions. In Tainan Spring, it is no longer the routine of purchases, the repetition of gestures that dominate, but creativity and improvisation, fun and adventure. The resulting degree of beauty is densely present, animated by personal and collective memories yet at the same time pregnant with the "hypermodern" desire for change that is within everyone's reach, at everyone's service,

[10] See Mello, *Twentieth Century Architecture*, 181–6.

[11] Mello, 182–3. The reference is to Georg Simmel, "Germanic and Classical Romantic Style" (1918), *Theory, Culture & Society* 24, no. 7/8 (2007): 49.

fig. 13
MVRDV, Tainan Spring, Tainan, Taiwan, 2020. Hai'an Road: aerial view. © MVRDV

fig. 14
MVRDV, Tainan Spring, Tainan, Taiwan, 2020. The reuse of one of the numerous large ventilation shafts on Hai'an Road.

capable of confusing even the minds most educated about the culture of fast food and cheap, vulgar fashion. It is as if modernity has collapsed on itself, rotated, and then re-emerged naked in a very successful merging of past and present, "close" but "distant," a little like the rules imposed by the pandemic . . . and with the burden of contradictions that the truest modern spirit carries with it, since, as stated by Marshall Berman (1940–2013), "to appropriate the modernities of yesterday can be at once a critique of the modernities of today and an act of faith in the modernities—and in the modern men and women—of tomorrow and the day after tomorrow."[12]

Returning to Paz, modernity is in fact not a doctrine but a "tradition," which would allow it to persist and change at the same time, guaranteeing its own diversity, precisely in relation to the critical gaze that is activated from time to time, since what is new is set over and against what is old, and it is this continual contrast that constitutes the endurance of tradition:

> **Modernity is not outside but within us. It is today and the most ancient antiquity; it is tomorrow and the beginning of the world; it is a thousand years old and yet newborn. It speaks in Nahuatl, draws Chinese ideograms from the 9th century, and appears on the television screen. This intact present, recently unearthed, shakes off the dust of centuries, smiles and suddenly starts to fly, disappearing through the window. A simultaneous plurality of time and presence: modernity breaks with the immediate past only to recover an age-old past and transform a tiny fertility figure from the Neolithic into our contemporary.**[13]

Ultimately, the idea of creating an "urban lagoon" is nothing less than bringing back an ancient past into the notion of the city; combining the idea of previous indiscriminate urban growth with the promise of new public spaces, of a comforting nature capable of establishing new forms of understanding between the ideal of a past rich in visions of fascinating landscapes and the "pressing" images of the present that characterize the city of Tainan today.

fig. 15
MVRDV, Tainan Spring, Tainan, Taiwan, 2020. Photo: Daria Scagliola.

fig. 16
MVRDV, Tainan Spring, Tainan, Taiwan, 2020. Photo: Daria Scagliola.

[12] Mello, 186. The reference is to Marshall Berman, *All That Is Solid Melts into Air: The Experience of Modernity* (London and New York: Penguin Books, [1982] 1988), 36.

[13] Mello, 89. The reference is to Paz, "What is Modernity?"

Biography

Patrizia Mello is interested in the theory, history, and criticism of contemporary design, subjects on which she carries out teaching and research activities. She currently teaches Architecture of Public Spaces at Ca' Foscari University of Venice.

Her publications include: *Twentieth Century Architecture and Modernity. Our Past, Our Present*, Los Angeles: ORO Editions, 2022; *Neoavanguardie e controcultura a Firenze. Il movimento Radical e i protagonisti di un cambiamento storico internazionale*, Florence: Angelo Pontecorboli, 2017; *Firenze e le avanguardie Radicali. Un seminario di ricerca*, Florence: DIDA press, 2017; *Design Contemporaneo. Mutazioni oggetti ambienti architetture*, Milan: Mondadori Electa, 2008; *Ito Digitale. Nuovi media, nuovo reale*, Rome: Edilstampa, 2008; *Metamorfosi dello spazio. Annotazioni sul divenire metropolitano*, Turin: Bollati Boringhieri, 2002; *L'ospedale ridefinito. Soluzioni e ipotesi a confronto*, Florence: Alinea Editrice, 2000; and *Progetti in movimento. Philippe Starck*, Florence: Festina Lente, 1997.

Discursive Ecology: The Inujima Seirensho Art Museum and the Means of Modernization

Trenton Sexton

fig. 1
View of the Inujima Seirensho Art Museum.
Photo: Daici Ano – courtesy of Fukutake Foundation.

Sustainable design is all too often relegated to the outskirts of critical discourse. Broad strokes of "effective" and "ineffective" may be applied, yet the complexity of culture, of perception and influence, is regularly conceived as a category separate from sustainability—especially its technological, quantitative elements. Such elements are frequently regarded as additive or supplementary, not integral to the conceptual essence of a building. The Inujima Seirensho Art Museum offers us an alternative to this compartmentalization, a critical environmentalism in which the qualitative and quantitative are simultaneously constitutive to one another and to a conceptual whole.

Introduction

Every instance of architecture proposes both a way of seeing the world and a way of living within it. Through this lens, every intentional work of architecture is inherently critical. To judge the quality of this criticism, we must first note that the power of criticism lies in its ability to render change in the world by describing and advocating for betterment. This change is rendered through an audience, without which criticism is powerless. Pivotal, then, for a building to act as criticism is its ability to speak as well as be heard, and this constitutes a way in which we might assess the quality of a building's critique: How well does it communicate this critique to its audience, the public?

Central to this analysis is the understanding that the language of Built Criticism is fundamentally different from that of textual criticism; it is a language of aesthetics rather than one solely of linguistics. Leaning on the work of Alexander Baumgarten and Walead Beshty, the concept of aesthetic understanding is rooted in the Greek *aisthētikos*, "relating to perception by the senses" rather than an understanding reductively limited to visual information.[1] Thus, aesthetic meaning arises through physical experience. If meaning is that which engenders particular outcomes, then aesthetics are a form of communication which manifest certain ways of acting and living. Both architecture and art are capable of staging discourse through aesthetics, and this case study is a rare example of architecture doing so in a way distinct from the capabilities of art while also in intimate concert with both artistic and environmental production.

Completed in 2008, the Inujima Seirensho Art Museum ***(fig. 1)***, designed by Hiroshi Sambuichi Architects, is sited on the remains of an abandoned copper refinery[2] on an island in Japan's Seto Inland Sea. This adaptive reuse project is a potent case of radical environmental design, positioned critically within both the ruins and the continuing legacy of industrial modernization in Japan. The museum—which provides all water, ventilation, heating, and energy for itself through on-site passive means, excepting emergency lighting—houses the work of artist Yukinori Yanagi as its sole exhibition. Yanagi's work, in concert with the architecture, provides a critical commentary on Japan's cultural trajectory and is in turn housed within the physical and intellectual lineage of Yukio Mishima, a writer whose incendiary critique of Japan's modernization led dramatically to his death in 1970.[3]

keywords:

critical sustainability, architectural communication, modernization, passive design, Hiroshi Sambuichi

1 Walead Beshty, "Notes for an Introductory Lecture," https://www.actionstakenunderthefictitiousname-waleadbeshtystudiosinc.com/lesson-notes-for-an-introductory-lecture.

2 One of thirty-three locations designated Industrial Modernization Heritage Sites by the government of Japan.

3 Mishima was concerned with the cultural cost of the postwar process of industrialization and modernization in Japan, that it was making the country "inorganic, empty, neutral, [and] drab," and he made these concerns quite public. Midori Yamamura, "Yukinori Yanagi," *Art in America*, December 19, 2016, https://www.artnews.com/art-in-america/aia-reviews/yukinori-yanagi-62291/.

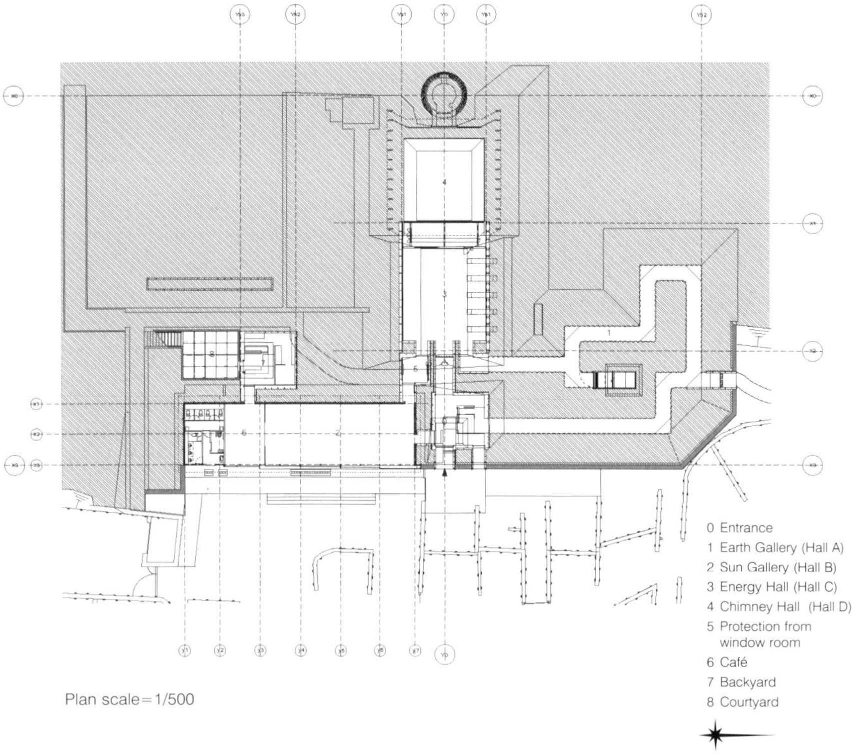

fig. 2
Plan of Inujima Seirensho Art Museum. Image: Hiroshi Sambuichi Architects.

fig. 3 a,b
Earth Gallery and *Icarus Cell*. Photos: Hiroshi Sambuichi Architects.

The prevailing canon of architectural thought—as well as the preponderance of architectural work in the past century—positions architecture and industrial modernization as allied forces in both their means and ends, a discourse championed by such influential voices as Le Corbusier. Rarely do modern architectural works interrogate the legitimacy or utility of this view; however, in the Inujima Seirensho Art Museum this complex discourse between art, architecture, and an engaged public is staged through architectural semiotics, transforming and recontextualizing symbols at the scales of both local and regional cultural icons as well as universal architectural icons, but it is also communicated by wielding sustainable architectural features as discursive ecological aesthetics, moving beyond solely technical functions and into the phenomenological, a deeply important critical position on which to found sustainable architecture.

The Inujima Seirensho Art Museum

Inujima is a small island located off the eastern coast of Japan in the Seto Inland Sea.[4] Historically, the island was used for granite quarrying, with one quarry on its western edge still in use today. On the eastern edge of the island lie the more-than-century-old remains of a copper refinery; enmeshed therein stands the Inujima Seirensho Art Museum.[5] Upon reaching the museum site, the remains of dark brick walls and floors extend outwards, mostly unchanged from their original layout. The black brick, found throughout the ruins as well as inside the museum, is in fact Karami brick, produced from the slag byproduct of the copper smelting process.[6] This brick, containing a large percentage of iron and glass, has special thermal qualities: it has an exceptionally high thermal capacity while also readily conducting heat from the air due to its metallic content.

After the procession among the ruins, the singular path through the museum is composed of the Earth Gallery, the Energy Hall, the Chimney Hall, and the Sun Gallery

[4] The island is small, approximately four kilometers in circumference, and hosts a similarly small population of aging residents.

[5] The refinery was built on Inujima in 1909 during the Meiji period—an era of rapid modernization and assimilation of Western ideas in Japan—being slated for the island after several inland refineries were labeled "problem facilities" due to their high output of damaging pollutants. The resulting industrialization of natural resources on Inujima, unsurprisingly, led to rapid contamination of the island and surrounding sea. After just ten years, the refinery was shut down and left to ruin, virtually untouched until it was selected as a museum site by the Benesse Corporation in 2001. Graeme Brooker and Sally Stone, *Re-readings 2: Interior Architecture and the Principles of Remodelling Existing Buildings* (London: RIBA Publishing, 2018), 233–34, https://books.google.com/books?id=SvWfDwAAQBAJ&printsec=frontcover#v=onepage&q&f=false.

[6] Hiroshi Sambuichi, *Hiroshi Sambuichi and the Inland Sea* (Tokyo: Toto, 2016), 126.

fig. 4
Steel sheet piles in practice. Photo: Wikimedia Commons, User: MBargo https://commons.wikimedia.org/wiki/File:V%C3%A4stl%C3%A4nken,_byggnation_2020_i_kanalen_i_Rosenlund_i_G%C3%B6teborg.jpg.

(fig. 2), leading visitors through Yukinori Yanagi's artwork *Hero Dry Cell*, composed in six parts.[7] The theme about which these works revolve is the issue of modernization and Japan's complex relationship with it. Intertwined within are artifacts of the controversial life and death of Yukio Mishima.[8]

The museum enters this narrative first through the Earth Gallery, which houses Yanagi's *Icarus Cell* ***(fig. 3)***. The Earth Gallery appears as a long hall leading towards a strange blue-white light. Recorded sounds permeate the space, calling to mind the howls of wind, the droning of machinery, or perhaps the roar of furnaces. At the beginning of the hall is a projection of the sun, casting a red glow on the Karami bricks forming the path. The walls are composed entirely of undulating Corten steel, resembling corrugated steel sheet piles, industrial prefabricated elements often used in or near water ***(fig. 4)***. The seemingly infinite extension is upended when one reaches a turn in the hall. What had once appeared endless and straight is in fact a series of ninety-degree turns framed by large mirrors. As this winding path reaches its terminus, one finds a mirror placed in the ground beneath a skylight. The light at the end of the hall is actually a reflection of the sky, the skylight angled just far enough north to avoid any glimpse of the sun throughout the year.

Visitors then pass into the Energy Hall ***(fig. 5)***, which opens from the Earth Gallery into a large, vaulted space. In the center lies Yanagi's *Solar Rock*, the disassembled remains of writer Yukio Mishima's study suspended over a forty-four-tonne slab of Inujima granite upon which a pool of water rests.[9] Behind the piece is a semicircular wooden construction resembling a house's facade in black with sunlight peeking over the edges. Passing through the facade reveals *Slag Note*,[10] with *Icarus Tower* located in the Chimney Hall beyond ***(fig. 6)***. The Chimney Hall is a glass structure set at the base of the chimney, directly connected to its air intake. *Icarus Tower* itself is composed of more disassembled pieces from Mishima's home: a staircase among urinals and sinks

7 Yukinori Yanagi, "Seirensho 'Hero Dry Cell' 2008," http://www.yanagistudio.net/exhibition/photo_seirensho_eng.html.

8 At the height of his protest, Mishima formed a private militia and attempted a coup of the Japanese government, traveling to the eastern headquarters of Japan's Self-Defense Forces in 1970 and taking the commandant hostage. He then attempted to rouse the soldiers on base to rebellion, delivering his final manifesto (*Geki*) from the commandant's balcony. In it, he decried modern Japan for becoming "infatuated with economic prosperity," resorting to "temporary solutions," and exuding "greed for power," all the while degrading Japan's history and culture, allowing the country to sink into an "emptiness of spirit." The attempt to rouse the soldiers failed, however, and in the following moments Mishima died by ritual suicide (*seppuku*). Alexander Lee, "Portrait of the Author as a Historian: Yukio Mishima," *History Today* 67, no. 4 (April 2017), https://www.historytoday.com/archive/portrait-author-historian-yukio-mishima; Andrew R. Smith, "Mishima's *Seppuku* Speech: A Critical-Cultural Analysis," *Text and Performance Quarterly* 10, no. 1 (June 2009), https://www.tandfonline.com/doi/abs/10.1080/10462939009365951.

9 Yanagi, "Seirensho 'Hero Dry Cell' 2008."

10 A small room containing light bulbs, outlets, and other electrical parts from the Western-style room of Mishima's home, with plated iron characters—sourced from various writings by Mishima and made from Inujima smelter slag—in a pile on the floor. Yanagi.

arranged in a faux Zen garden with a series of doors and windows hanging above the raked black gravel.[11]

In addition to the life of Yukio Mishima, the other primary narrative at work in *Hero Dry Cell* is the myth of Icarus. *Icarus Cell* plunges visitors underground in suspension between earth and sky, resembling the mythological labyrinth in which Icarus and Daedalus, an inventor, were imprisoned.[12] As in the story, in *Icarus Cell* the sun—accompanied by sounds resembling a smelting furnace—is what we are running from. What are we running—or falling—towards? The sky or a deadly blue sea? When we reach *Solar Rock* in the Energy Hall, we find that we have been running towards the shattered remains of Mishima's life. The echoes of the question Mishima poses in his poem "Icarus" are almost palpable: Am I a child of the earth or of the sky?[13]

The Chimney Hall is the terminus of this initial sequence. Upon reaching it, the visitor turns around and exits towards the Sun Gallery, first passing through a small room, *Mirror Note*. This room is a scale recreation of the six-tatami-mat room in Mishima's home.[14] Words, projected in red light, scrawl endlessly up and down the walls. These words are from Mishima's short story "Eirei no Koe" (The Voices of the Heroic Dead), in which the curse "Why would his majesty become an ordinary man?" is repeated.[15]

Beyond *Mirror Note* lies the Sun Gallery, where one is released from the dark subterranean into a glazed, sunlit hall of wood, steel, and brick. Here lies Yanagi's last piece in *Hero Dry Cell*, the *Solar Note*. Again, the latter is made from the remnants of Mishima's once-home, this time from his eight-tatami-mat room. In the center, among broken bricks, lies Mishima's travel bag; all around hang gold-plated iron characters—the final manifesto Mishima gave aloud just before his death.[16] One then exits

fig. 5
Energy Hall and *Solar Rock*. Photo: Hiroshi Sambuichi Architects.

fig. 6
Chimney Hall and *Icarus Tower*. Photo: Hiroshi Sambuichi Architects.

[11] This gravel is made of slag collected on site, the deep black in stark contrast to the light gravel more typical of Japanese rock gardens. Yanagi.

[12] As the story goes, Daedalus crafted wings for himself and Icarus to escape; however, when they made their flight, Icarus became overconfident and flew too close to the sun. His wings melted and he fell into the sea and drowned. It is worth noting, too, that the labyrinth in which they were imprisoned was built by Daedalus himself, both an architect and an inventor, at an earlier time, his own creation ensnaring him. Yukinori Yanagi, "Making Art and Environments in Regional Areas that Critique," Asia Hundreds, Innovative City Forum, Tokyo, 2016, https://jfac.jp/en/culture/features/f-ah-icf2016-yukinori-yanagi/.

[13] Yukio Mishima, *Sun and Steel* (San Francisco: Kodansha USA, 2003), 102–3.

[14] Yanagi, "Seirensho 'Hero Dry Cell' 2008."

[15] Just months after the atomic bombing of Hiroshima and Nagasaki and the subsequent Allied occupation of Japan, Emperor Hirohito renounced his claim to divinity (or the idea that it ever existed) to the Japanese people. The

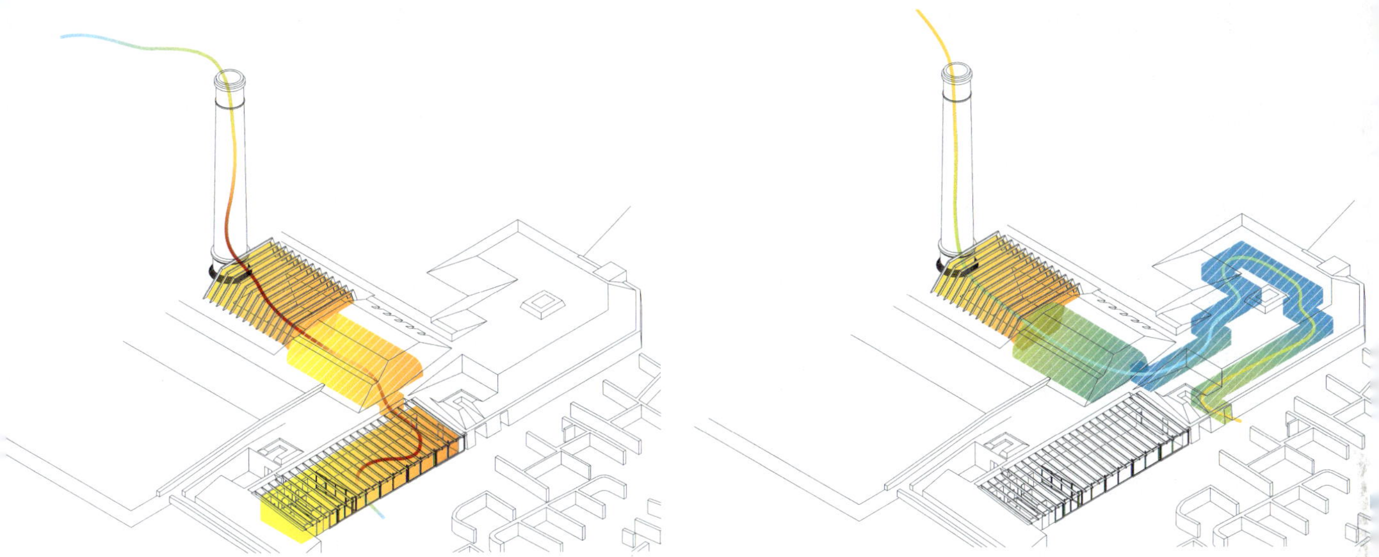

fig. 7 a,b
Passive air-heating system (left) and air-cooling system (right). Image: Hiroshi Sambuichi Architects.

the museum through a small court and is given the option either to process on top of the building for views of the sea or to explore the ruins of the copper refinery beyond.

So visitors are confronted with the story of Yukio Mishima and the myth of Icarus, both bringing into question the dangers of modernization and the allure of technology, the dismantled study of Mishima hovering precariously over a "sea" of water backgrounded by a semicircular black facade resembling a solar eclipse or black *Hinomaru*,[17] stairways and doors beyond this eclipse leading to nowhere in a perverse Zen garden littered with modern plumbing, the words of dead Japanese soldiers cursing the loss of their emperor as deity after World War II, and a room containing Mishima's final manifesto decrying Japan's postwar industrialization. Clearly, the sociocultural cost of modernization in Japan is a question Yanagi wants us to encounter.

The architecture of the museum is inseparable from the art, being incorporated intrinsically into each piece, and yet it also provides a critique that stands on its own. While Yanagi's work is more concerned with the sociocultural implications of modernization, the architectural semiotics—which include sensorial phenomena—offer a supplemental framework for contemplating the effects of modernization on our environment.

The whole of the Inujima Seirensho Art Museum is intimately tied to its natural circumstance. The museum procession itself is designed as a passive heating and cooling engine ***(fig. 7)***, tuned with extraordinary sensitivity to its site. This is accomplished first in terms of the building's orientation. The museum entrance opens to the east towards the sea, the direction of prevailing winds on site, creating a consistent air intake for the museum, moving from the sea into the entryway.[18] The movement of air is further driven by the Chimney Hall. The glass atrium at the base of the chimney heats the air,[19] reducing pressure and consequently pulling air from the Earth Gallery

invention and use of the atomic bomb, a major landmark of modern physics, led to the renunciation of a divinity for which many Japanese soldiers gave their lives. The meaning those deaths held for many was lost. "Imperial Rescript Denying His Divinity (Professing His Humanity)," Documents with Commentaries, National Diet Libraries, https://www.ndl.go.jp/constitution/e/shiryo/03/056shoshi.html.

16 Yanagi, "Seirensho 'Hero Dry Cell' 2008."

17 The crimson circle which defines the national flag of Japan. The full circle is completed through the semicircular facade's reflection in the water.

18 The relationship of sea to entry is emphasized by two pairs of granite posts among the ruins, one marking the path to entry, the other marking the path to the sea.

19 Aided by the high thermal capacity of the recycled black slag which simultaneously serves as the gravel for *Icarus Tower*'s "Zen garden."

towards it while also allowing hot air to rise and escape through the chimney, whose air intake is connected to the Chimney Hall. This driving force from either end of the air's path keeps it moving through the museum, creating ventilation and cooling as it travels the long, highly insulated Earth Gallery. The Karami bricks, with their high thermal storage capacity and conductivity, draw the heat out of the air as it passes through the long tunnel. The length of the tunnel, in fact, was chosen not only for efficacy of the art but also to allow ample surface area for drawing heat out of the air.[20]

In the winter, the doors to the Earth Gallery are closed, and the doors to the Sun Gallery are opened, creating a new flow of energy. Geothermal energy allows the Earth Gallery to retain some warmth, while the Sun Gallery lets in sunlight to heat the air inside. Because the Sun Gallery has no vertical exhaust, the hot air is circulated towards the low-pressure center in the Chimney Hall, providing heat throughout the building. Therefore, the museum's ventilation processes, entirely free from mechanical HVAC, are governed by the processes of the sun and Earth.

The lighting of the museum similarly relies solely on the sky and sun. The Sun Gallery and Chimney Hall are illuminated via their large, glazed portions, and the Earth Gallery, an eighty-meter-long underground tunnel, is lit entirely by a single skylight and nine mirrors.[21] Even small rooms such as *Mirror Note* and the egress court contain small skylights for illumination.

And, crucially, all these things communicate poetic content. The notion of moving towards the sky/sea, so central to the art, also acts as the ingenious device for lighting the entirety of the underground tunnel. The constant rise of air, heated by the sun, further echoes the narrative of Icarus while also functioning as passive ventilation. In fact, in the Energy Hall, where the volume opens for convection, the artworks become suspended, sensitive to movement in the air. Consequently, the doors and windows hanging in *Icarus Tower* spin slowly as air is drawn into the chimney, each

[20] *JA 81: Hiroshi Sambuichi* (Tokyo: Shinkenchiku-sha, 2011), 83.
[21] *JA 81*, 83.

one revolving at a different rate depending on its size. The movement of air is subtly but legibly made visceral in experience, all while being dexterously integrated with the art. The movement of air, the passage of the sun—these processes of the Earth are made explicit in the architecture, in conversation both with the art and with the Earth. Thus, most architectural moves function at multiple levels, both poetic and pragmatic.

This ecological associativity continues in multiple ways. First, trees are planted on the roof over the Earth Gallery to provide greater insulation and shade for thermal stability. More trees are planted on the south side of the site, beside the Energy Hall; however, in this case they are citrus trees, planted not only to supplement food in the museum's café but also for soil remediation on the once heavily toxified site.[22] Waste and water reuse also takes place on site. Water is visibly purified with help from special on-site vegetation before being conveyed to hydrate other plants, and waste is processed as fertilizer for the trees ***(fig. 8)***.[23]

One of the most explicit sustainable connections to circumstance, however, is the museum's status as historic reuse: it is literally formed on the ruins of Inujima's once thriving refinery.[24] All granite in the museum was sourced from Inujima's quarry, less than a kilometer away, as well. This not only gives the museum a conspicuous connection to its context and its history but also considerably mitigates the building's environmental impact.

The materials, additionally, provide substantive expressive content regarding the building's relationship with the earth. The Karami brick has a discernible relationship to the site's industrial history, a discernible nature as an industrial byproduct—the iridescent sheen from the slag is visible on most bricks—and a discernible thermal

fig. 8
On-site water remediation pool and citrus trees. Photo: Trenton Sexton.

fig. 9
Iridescent Karami bricks among the refinery ruins.
Photo: Trenton Sexton.

fig. 10
Quarrying marks on the museum's granite walls.
Photo: Trenton Sexton.

22 Geeta Mehta and Deanna MacDonald, *New Japan Architecture: Recent Works by the World's Leading Architects* (North Clarendon, VT: Tuttle Publishing, 2015), 197.

23 *JA 81*, 91.

24 Over seventeen thousand bricks—once part of the refinery but then dumped in the ocean and surroundings—were collected and reused as part of the museum. *JA 81*, 88.

fig. 11
Speckled patina on the Corten steel gate at the museum's entrance. Photo: Trenton Sexton.

fig. 12
(Top) Skylight angle detail. Photo: Trenton Sexton. (Bottom) Sun Gallery roof detail, viewed from the exterior. Photo: Trenton Sexton. (Right) Structure and ventilation registers are expressed in terms of the Karami brick metering system. Photo: Hiroshi Sambuichi Architects.

property—if touched, the high thermal content can be easily felt ***(fig. 9)***. The brick reminds one of the site's industrial past, of our past and present history of harmful production processes, all while functioning as a highly effective thermal regulator throughout the museum. Karami bricks line the Earth Gallery to draw heat out of the air and dissipate it in the ground, cooling the space, while they line the Sun Gallery to absorb and store the sun's heat. In the Earth Gallery, their iridescence reflects the reddish light from the projected sun and the blue-white light of the sky at either end of the passage, evoking images of a furnace. In the Sun Gallery, they glitter with the true sun. The material is used to its full potential to fulfill sustainable functions, to make them palpable, and to remind us of the nature of our relationship to the Earth.

The granite used throughout the building carries similar expressive content. The stone is taken from Inujima's once bustling quarry. The granite explicitly expresses the scars left on the stone from the quarrying process ***(fig. 10)***. The fact that this stone was taken from the earth, that it had to be torn from the ground with industrial tools, is made a part of its surface patterning.

The third principal material, Corten steel, is related to the context in a rather straightforward way: it weathers. This speaks to the particularity of Inujima as an island—the Corten has developed a rust patina in an especially potent speckled pattern due to the salty sea breeze ***(fig. 11)***—but it also speaks more specifically to the circumstances of the museum's passive processes. The fact that the steel inside the building has weathered is a subtle reminder: this building is open to the elements; the

fig. 13
The Sun Gallery with sliding glass walls opened, showing the trabeated structure of Japanese cypress and stainless steel. *Solar Note* can be seen in the center of the room. Photo: Hiroshi Sambuichi Architects.

fig.
14 Example of *tokyō* bracketing at the Hōryū-ji pagoda in Ikaruga, Japan. Photo: Wikimedia Commons, User: Reggaeman https://commons.wikimedia.org/wiki/File:Horyuji_Temple_04.JPG.

sea breeze that weathered the steel outside is also being drawn in here. Indeed, the Corten, as almost every other facet of the museum, carries a dual function to contribute to these passive processes. The sinuous walls of Corten along the Earth Gallery readily collect condensation and channel it to the crushed brick at their base, helping to regulate humidity inside the museum. The movement of wind and water through the building is traced onto its skin. Quantitative and qualitative aspects of sustainability are, again, addressed as one.

This conceptual content does not stop with the material choices themselves but extends to their nature of construction and detailing. Almost all the details speak to the relation that the building, and thus we, enjoys with the earth. The exterior of the steel on the Earth Gallery's skylight is angled on the north and south ends at the same angle as the interior, while the east and west sides remain plumb, subtly reinforcing the importance of the angle in avoiding any glimpses of the sun. The glass roof on the Sun Gallery slips over the edges of the walls, emphasizing its function of drawing in light and heat ***(fig. 12)***. Brick is used as a metering system for details such as ventilation registers, highlighting passive components while also highlighting the modular, industrial quality of the material. Every level of user experience contains cues underlining the way materials move.

One particularly interesting cue can be found in the structural detailing of the Sun Gallery ***(fig. 13)***. Upon entry to the Sun Gallery, there is a complete shift in structural logics. The solid, bearing structure of the subterranean portions is replaced by a light

fig. 15
(Left) Inujima Seirensho Art Museum entry, with steeper walls of granite on the lower level. Photo: Trenton Sexton. (Right) The walls of Osaka Castle's defensive mound, rising from the moat. Photo: Wikimedia Commons, User: Kakidai https://commons.wikimedia.org/wiki/File:2018_Osaka_Castle_03.jpg.

wooden-and-steel trabeated structure, a moment of embracing the sun and sky after being so long underground. Of particular note here are the steel connectors between the columns and beams. Their shape suggests, in the negative space, the ghosts of traditional *tokyō* bracketing at the column capital ***(fig. 14)***. The wood is robbed of its ability to bear on wood, instead requiring industrial mediation. This explicitly brings into question what is given and what is taken away by modernization, literally outlining the ghost of "what has been lost" while also emphasizing that much less material is now required for the connection. The "empty" connection from wood column to beam is also a stark contrast to the explicit heaviness and bearing of the stone structure, further emphasizing that this room is about openness to the sun and heat, while the mound is about cooling by way of closedness and massiveness. Steel rods, replacing wooden beams in the longitudinal axis, additionally contribute to this conversation, binding the structure together while blocking less sunlight from above.

Of primary significance is the construction of the granite walls: each piece of stone is custom cut to fit among its neighbors. Rather than a standardized, consistent module, each stone is unique; this is a decidedly pre-modern technique, one that was assuredly accompanied by a significant cost. This was not a decision the architect would make lightly, and it adds a potent ambiguity to the work: it is a modern building, but it is built using both modern and pre-modern techniques. Thus, the modern and pre-modern are each made characters in our story to compare and contrast, the brick and the stone representing each.

At the entrance of the museum the industrial and the pre-industrial meet, the strictly metered, modular construction of the brick coming into sharp relief against the individuality and particularity of the stone. The slag-infused, black iridescence of the brick is stark against the matte, white granite, forming a gaping hole, almost a wound, for entry. We have a wealth of complexity at this moment. The granite walls make a show of their pre-industrial, hand-cut quality while at the same time expressing their machinic marks from modern quarrying. The historic ruins of brick are industrialized

fig. 16
(Left) Secondary mound over the Energy Hall using primarily uncut granite. Photo: Trenton Sexton. (Right) Hachimanzuka Kofun at the Hodota Kofun Cluster, Takasaki, Japan. Photo: Wikimedia Commons, User: Saigen Jiro https://en.m.wikipedia.org/wiki/File:Hodota-kofungun_Hachimanzuka-kofun-1.JPG.

while the granite wall, the modern element, is primarily pre-industrial in expression. This constant play of modern and pre-modern technologies, and therefore ideologies, against one another underlines the fact that, while these things are deeply different, they also share commonalities. This provides a framework for critically contemplating the process of modernization rather than for a polemic.

The building's configuration also contributes to the conceptual framework. The entirety of the building, excluding the Sun Gallery, is shaped as a large mound with a second, more pronounced mound rising over the Energy Hall. The granite on the lower portion of this mound is built in the very same way that the defensive mounds of ancient Japanese castles were built—large cut stones pieced together at a steep slope. In fact, the granite from Inujima was used for the defensive walls of the Okayama and Osaka Castles ***(fig. 15)***.[25] However, rather than a castle on top of our mound, our expectations are undercut, and we simply get another, more shallowly sloped mound covered in nothing but grass. In this mound over Mishima's disassembled study, the stone is round and uncut, calling to mind the Japanese *fukiishi* (roofing stone) method of covering *kofun* (burial mounds), in which river stone was affixed to low-angle slopes and mortared together ***(fig. 16)***.[26] What was expected to be a castle—perhaps for the copper refinery; perhaps for Yukio Mishima—is instead a grave.

Throughout the museum, we are given palpable representations of the impacts of modernization while always having a background exhibiting the pre-modern, reminding us that there are other viable options for progress available to us. However, this is not a building about explicitly condemning or affirming modernization; rather, it prompts us to critically reassess modernization's role in our lives and how it has changed the way we relate to the Earth, to think about both what is given and what is taken away by it.

Interwoven with this narrative is the building's ecological aspect. The building is quantitatively sustainable—it relies entirely on passive ventilation and natural lighting, it reappropriates waste, and it reuses large amounts of abandoned and local

[25] Sambuichi, *Inland Sea*, 138.

[26] "Life and Death in a Changing Society" (Online Resource for Japanese Archaeology and Cultural Heritage, 2019), https://orjach.org/module/life-death-changing-society/.

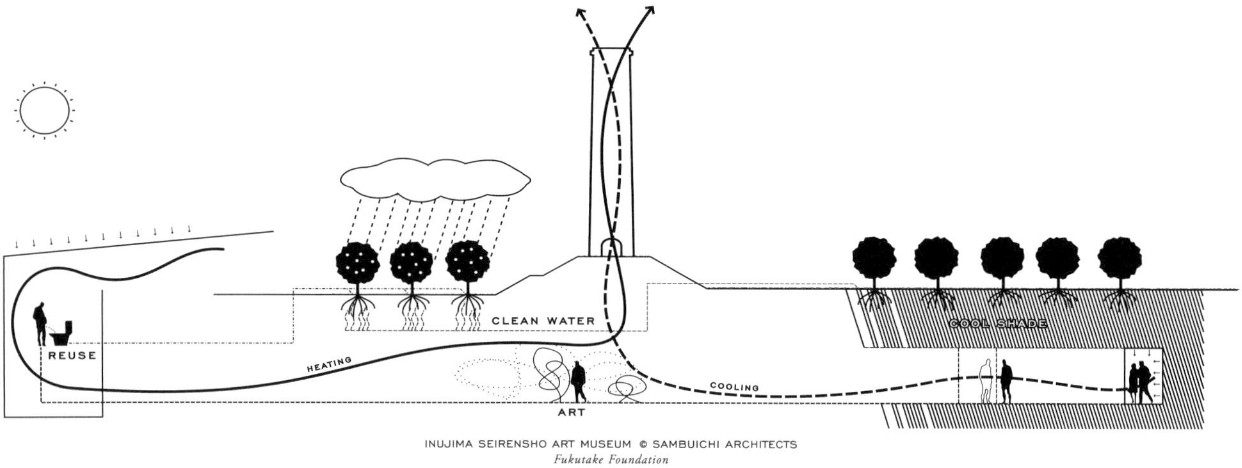

fig. 17
Material flow diagram. Image: Hiroshi Sambuichi Architects.

materials—yet it also makes this qualitatively clear—human procession and ventilation take the very same path, and details consistently indicate their relation to local material flow. Thus, the Inujima Seirensho Art Museum offers an alternative of what a modern building can be: one that utilizes both modern techniques and pre-industrial passive techniques with a critical eye, offering an alternative to the modernized conception of consumption and energy use.

Conclusion

One final point of interest is the restroom, accessible at the end of the museum's procession, where the role of people in the processes of the site is made didactic. Above all restroom utilities is the diagram showing the movement of materials (heat, air, water, waste), which demonstrates plainly how even one's activities in the restroom participate in the ever-unfolding flow of materials across the site ***(figs. 17-18)***. One might be inclined to criticize such forceful didacticism; yet if the quality of a building's critique can be measured by how well it communicates this critique to the public, perhaps such elements are to be praised.

Through this discourse, the architecture takes the narrative of the art and reframes it, shifting the conversation towards the nature of our relationship with the Earth. How does our process of quarrying affect the Earth? How does the use of glass affect the air around us? How can our waste be adapted for reuse? How then should we shape modern environmental interventions? By creating a building legibly shaped by natural processes, Hiroshi Sambuichi Architects have at once posed these questions and offered potential answers to them.

The museum is an exceptional example of wielding sustainable design not only as a means for reducing its own environmental impact but also as a means of changing the way users see the world. Through intentional articulation of the sensory experience concomitant with passive strategies, materials with expressive content regarding both natural and industrial processes, construction and detailing that reinforce this content, and a spatial arrangement designed to provoke reflection on

fig. 18
Material flow diagram in restroom. Photo: Trenton Sexton.

these things, Hiroshi Sambuichi Architects, in collaboration with Yukinori Yanagi, have created a building that is integral in every part: each component serves the purpose of describing our relationship to the world. The processes of the Earth and how we influence them are reiterated in different ways at every level. The line between the poetic and pragmatic dissolves, and these things become integrated in one conceptual essence.

In this way, the building provides a new critical framework on which to position sustainable design and carries it out successfully. It is ultimately about changing the way we see the world and our place within it, and it does so by marrying the mechanisms of sustainability with expressive content. If we better understand our relationship to the Earth's processes and the way we affect them, then the better prepared we are to constructively reshape that relationship. Thus, the museum is an exemplary attempt to utilize ecological elements discursively, to reframe the way in which one lives and the way in which one relates to the Earth, addressing sustainability as the richly complex cultural problem that it is, one that requires ecological practice in multivalence as both a technical and an emotional element, simultaneously a practical tool and one of abstraction, for an architecture of effective, perceptible environmental criticism.

Biography
Trenton Sexton is a designer and a member of the International Committee of Architectural Critics (CICA), where he serves as Associate Director of Awards. He received his Master of Architecture from the University of Texas at Austin (2022) and holds degrees in Applied Physics from Trevecca Nazarene University (2016) and Civil Engineering from Vanderbilt University (2017). He has worked in the United States at the firms of Kieran Timberlake and Clayton Korte, and his research interests include the function of ornament in both an economy of means and sustainable design.

The Brochstein Pavilion and the Pragmatics of Critique[1]

Yifei Zhang

fig. 1
Colonnade of Lovett Hall, a replica of that of the Doge's Palace in Venice. Photo: Yifei Zhang.

The essay advocates a pragmatic approach to architectural criticism, emphasizing buildings' power to critique and reshape society. Using the Brochstein Pavilion at Rice University as an example, the essay illustrates how architecture can effectively critique and transform its surroundings. Situated in the Central Quadrangle, the pavilion revitalized a neglected space, fostering a vibrant communal life on campus. Its design contrasts with the nearby Academic Quadrangle, critiquing its lack of comfort and practicality despite visual appeal. The pavilion's success lies in its ability to blur indoor–outdoor boundaries, offering transparency, accessibility, and comfort. While acknowledging the limitations of Built Criticism, the essay highlights the pavilion's role in inspiring change and critical reflection, influencing the university's decision to revamp its architectural landscape.

An Attempt at a Pragmatic Definition

Insofar as architectural theory has taken an interest in linguistics, it has concentrated on semantics and syntax; an alternative approach proposed here is that of pragmatics, the study of language and its users. "Architecture as criticism" understands architecture's outward manifestation of power towards its users in its contingent spatial and temporal context rather than requiring architectural literacy from its readers. To understand architecture's outward functioning is not to produce generalizable rules deployable for future designers—in other words, to resuscitate functionalism or to confuse architecture with building science. It is to acknowledge the limit of the author's reach—the improbability of a perfectly intact *communication* of the author's intention into the contingent morass of the real—and to observe the many unexpected, intermittent, polyphonic episodes that are products of an imperfect *translation.* This pragmatic study of building as criticism focuses on its power to reshape the life of a pluralistic public. Architecture *acts* as criticism—a building is critical only when it critiques, rendering its object of criticism lacking in comparison. The power of architecture as criticism could be tested by posing questions such as:

1. What qualities of life have been improved since the building came into being (a critique of history)?
2. Does the building reveal inadequacies of buildings of its sort (a critique of type, a parody, or an exemplar)?
3. Does the building render the exterior uninhabitable (a critique of climate and environment)?

The majority of buildings would qualify under the third question. Human volition for self-preservation and flourishment by creating insulated shelters and later well-tempered interiors—the raison d'être of architecture—is in itself such a critique.[2] This critique, however, is not presented by decoded symbolism but by the fact of humankind's behavior in continuing to build and transform the surface of the Earth.

keywords:
architecture theory, architecture criticism, Brochstein Pavilion, Rice University

[1] Special thanks to K. Michael Hays, without whose seminal work, lectures, seminars, and tens of hours of discussion in the past year this essay would not have been possible. I would also like to thank Robert McCarter and Wilfried Wang for their guidance on the development of this text; Hayley Eaves for reading draft versions of this essay and her generous critique; and friends, colleagues, and teachers at Rice University and Harvard GSD.

[2] Reyner Banham, *The Architecture of the Well-tempered Environment* (Chicago: The University of Chicago Press, 1984), 18–28. It is important to note that this formulation is like all the other origin stories of architecture, nothing but a myth. To raise the point here is only to highlight architecture's enduring role of creating enclosure. Architecture need not have a singular, causal genesis.

fig. 2
Hammond Beeby & Babka and Morris Architects, James A. Baker III Hall, Rice University, 1997. Photo: Yifei Zhang.

The pragmatic approach to such a critique focuses on the effect and affect of the built structure over the architect's intention. The seeming oxymoron of "Built Criticism" can be resolved following a new definition that no longer depends on textual forms. Studying this new definition of criticism requires moving away from reading or interpreting architecture's message to observing the motion and emotion it unleashes among its users.[3] Following this new definition, the Brochstein Pavilion at Rice University is selected as an example of an architecture that produced an effective criticism. The choice to write about the pavilion is, of course, influenced by the author's own familiarity with the object of study. This personal dimension allows the following words to serve at once as an analysis and a testimony to the critical power of architecture.

Brochstein Pavilion and Rice University

Rice University was founded in 1912 in Houston on the wealth of William Marsh Rice, who made his fortune by "providing supplies to plantation owners and selling cotton and sugar crops, produced in large part by enslaved labor."[4] The university's first structure, Lovett Hall (formerly the Administration Building), was produced out of an identity crisis ***(fig. 1)***. When the Boston-based Cram, Goodhue & Ferguson arrived in 1909, their signature Collegiate Gothic style was deemed out of place in the Texas heat. The local architectural landscape of Houston, a city founded only in 1836, was humdrum to the Beaux-Arts architects. The result was a climatic appropriation of the Mediterranean for the American South. Iconographies of the Mediterranean were deployed on the Texan prairie *ex nihilo*: Venetian colonnades, medieval turrets, Roman arches, Moorish corbels, and French gardens provide a kaleidoscopic feast for the trained eyes.

Architecture on the university's campus has been laden with invitations to read ever since. Lovett Hall uttered the first Mediterranean *parole*, to seek "continuity with the high cultural traditions of western Europe,"[5] while a mature architectural language

3 The metaphor of motion and sound for architecture's influence can be traced from Wittgenstein's aphorism that architecture is a gesture that makes one respond with a gesture. See Ludwig Wittgenstein, *Culture and Value*, ed. G. H. von Wright, trans. Peter Winch (Oxford: Blackwell, 1998), 49e, MS 126 15r: 28.10.1942. The metaphor of motion can also be found in Keller Easterling, who introduced the concept of "english," the unexpected spin of a billiard ball which she took as the agency of an object that eludes the subjective intention. See Keller Easterling, *Extrastatecraft: The Power of Infrastructure Space* (New York: Verson, 2014), 235–36.

4 "A Brief History of Rice University," Rice University, accessed September 8, 2023, https://www.rice.edu/about#block-aboutbriefhistory.

5 Stephen Fox, *Rice University: An Architectural Guide* (New York: Princeton Architectural Press, 2001), 9.

fig. 3
Fisher Dachs Associates, The Brockman Hall for Opera, Rice University, 2020. Photo: Yifei Zhang.

was steadily developed in the next hundred years. Spoken loudly or quietly, this language is recognized for its consistency in red St. Joe brick, stucco, and marble. Indeed, the campus was so eager to be read that a 1984 architecture guide is dedicated almost exclusively to decoding the occult symbols dwelling in the column capitals, sculptures, inscriptions, bas-reliefs, panels of stone, ceramic, and metal, from a lamassu bearing a cuneiform tablet to the DNA double helix, and everything in between.[6]

The birth of a language also begets myths and fictions. Time has little import on a campus where buildings from the 1910s, 1990s, and 2020s are stylistically indistinguishable. Although new constructions generally reinterpreted the Rice language in their contemporary conditions, anachronistic ruptures are noticeable. Thomas H. Beeby's 1993 Baker Hall has its four facades pristinely decorated with mosaics, marble pilasters, and *ablaq* patterns—a facade so detailed that it "might have come from the drafting boards of [the] Cram & Ferguson office in the 1930s"[7] ***(fig. 2)***. The incredibly rich surface and elegant architraves are only to be interrupted awkwardly by gutter pipes. Its plain, unanimated interior would immediately underwhelm and disillusion those seeking history's patina. The Brockman Hall for Opera completed in 2022 can barely allow one to dwell in the Mediterranean fantasy ***(fig. 3)***. Despite copying elements directly from Lovett Hall, the incongruity between the modern demand for natural light and transparency and the monumental solidity it seeks to emulate results in a cumbersome jumble common in suburban Texas. To be sure, this is not a stylistic debate of traditional versus modern. Rice's Humanities Building (2000), despite using the same flimsy language as Brockman Hall, provides the setting of one of the most exquisite sites on campus ***(fig. 4)***. Nestling along the library and Rayzor Hall, the Humanities Building sets out a series of exquisitely labyrinthian courtyards pleasantly shaded by mature oak trees. The flimsiness of its traditional facade becomes obscured in the intimacy it creates, engaging with its users in the tactile dimension.

6 See James C. Morehead Jr., *A Walking Tour of Rice University*, 2nd ed. (Houston, TX: Rice University Press, 1990).
7 Fox, *Rice University*, 124.

fig. 4
Humanities Building with a courtyard between Fondren Library to the right and an arcade towards Rayzor Hall. Photo: Yifei Zhang.

fig. 5
Brochstein Pavilion with Fondren Library on the left, looking down a pedestrian path towards the south. Photo: Yifei Zhang.

The preoccupation with reading dissolves. When reading is at best caught up in an anachronistic neurosis, and at worst pastiche signaling to fabricated pedigree, architecture's power to act and to produce is ushered to the fore.

Brochstein Pavilion has very little to offer for readers, nor does it require much explanation. It sits on the central east–west axis of the university, surrounded by a grove of mature elms and oaks. To its east is the monolithic brick facade of Fondren Library ***(fig. 4)***, and between the two buildings runs a major pedestrian path lined by trees and reflection pools. To its west, the landscape gently slopes downwards to a grass lawn, where the Jamail Plaza fountain and James Turrell's skyspace are distantly visible. As for the building itself, it "could not be simpler."[8] The 560-square-meter interior is square in plan and contains a small café ***(fig. 5)***. The exterior is capped by a trellis canopy supported by slender steel columns that form a widely spaced colonnade around the glass box ***(fig. 6)***. In fact, the simplicity in its architecture is often mirrored in the appraisals it receives: "The Brochstein Pavilion makes you feel happy. It's rare for any building to exert such power."[9] "People don't understand why they like it."[10] "[The pavilion is] unselfconscious and joyful."[11] "I really do like Brochstein—everything from the architecture to the way people gather there . . . [Brochstein] served that function [a space for people to come together] so well that everyone wanted to use it."[12] It seems the power of the pavilion simply defies explanation, or the sophistication of words only *returns as a guest* that pales by comparison with the dashing simplicity of the built structure itself. These simple praises, uttered by four users of the pavilion (an architectural historian, the namesake of the pavilion and its patron, an architect and professor, and a former Rice president), resemble what Bruno Latour termed "infralanguage."[13] While the unadorned words may lack in precision worthy of academia, they nevertheless serve as witnesses to the agency of the architectural object. Contemporary architectural parlance often appropriates architecture's agency as the architect's intention:

8 Ronnie Self, "Brochstein Pavilion at Rice University," *Cite* 76 (Fall 2008): 30.
9 Stephen Fox, "A Review of the Brochstein Pavilion," Rice Design Alliance, December 19, 2008.
10 "Raymond Brochstein," interview with David Bucek, June 26, 2015, William R. Jenkins Architecture, Design & Art Library, University of Houston, https://av.lib.uh.edu/media_objects/pr76f3513/.
11 Self, "Brochstein Pavilion," 31.
12 David Leebron, "Leebron Reflects on His Time at the Corner of Sunset and Main," interview by Tomás Russo, *The Rice Thresher* 106, no. 27 (Wednesday, April 20, 2022).
13 Bruno Latour, *Reassembling the Social: An Introduction to Actor-Network Theory* (New York: Oxford University Press, 2005), 30, 77.

1. Design decision A *allows* favorable result A'.
2. Design decision B *provides* space for preferred function B'.
3. Design decision C *fosters/cultivates* agreeable ideology C'.

To move away from this mode of thinking that sees the object's agency as nothing but the architect's built-in intention, one must step back and attend to Latourian infralanguage: the banal or sometimes meaningless utterances by the very users of architecture. In this sense, language is not the starting point or instrument of architectural criticism, but language testifies to a Built Criticism, the reverberations and resonances of an architecture that critiques.

fig. 6
Brochstein Pavilion and the gentle slope towards the west. Photo: Yifei Zhang.

fig. 7
Brochstein Pavilion and the back facade of Fondren Library. Photo: Yifei Zhang.

Brochstein Pavilion as Built Criticism

What, then, does the Brochstein Pavilion critique? Before the pavilion's inception, its site—the Central Quadrangle—was a monotonous grass plain, a "lost space" which fell prey to the mid-century ethos of the suburban United States that "truncated . . . and misunderstood" a monumental square, turning it into a "soggy backyard."[14] The pavilion's critique of history comes in its complete reconstruction of this "phantom court"[15] into a bustling gathering space for students, faculties, and visitors alike. The success of its critique is manifested in its popularity, which extends to the outdoors—the grassy, vague terrain of yesteryear is today a cheerful space for concerts, frisbee, and club events ***(fig. 6)***.

[14] Fox, *Rice University*, 108–9.
[15] Fox, 108–9.

fig. 8
Brochstein Pavilion and the landscape to the west. Photo: Yifei Zhang.

fig. 9
Academic Quadrangle framed by Lovett Hall. Photo: Yifei Zhang.

For newcomers who did not experience the Central Quad before the pavilion, the Brochstein offers a louder critique towards the Academic Quadrangle. Across from the library, the Academic Quadrangle conceptualizes the Gulf Coast climate to claim legacies of the Mediterranean via its eclectic buildings and formulaic French gardens ***(fig. 9)***. Yet the physical experience of this climate was largely left unaddressed. Despite its exuberant visuality, the sunbaked plaza produces undeniable discomfort. In the scorching sun there is no shade other than shadows of monuments, architectural or statuesque—the Academic Quad admonishes loitering and demands veneration. Here, the division between solid (architecture) and void (the quadrangle) is absolute. The Academic Quad is picture-perfect—it can be appreciated only by its instantaneous visual power recreated ad infinitum by promotional merchandise, webpages, and professional headshots. A notable phenomenon is its popularity among Houstonians as a backdrop for photos of weddings, engagements, and quinceañeras.[16] The dignified monumentality endorses only the most ceremonial occasions, the most ritualistic attires, and the most enduring commemoration, yet one cannot live beyond the shutter speed, in a fraction of a second.

The Central Quadrangle, on the contrary, produces something other than photogenic moments. The glaring radiance is transformed into dappled vibrancy under the shade of elms and oaks, and is reinterpreted architecturally as the pavilion's brise-soleil canopy ***(fig. 10)***. The total transparency of the Brochstein's glass cladding and its generous span blur the line between interior and exterior, dissolving architecture's solidity within a leafy landscape ***(fig. 11)***. The brightness outdoors is carried indoors through angled skylights and the perforated ceiling. The pavilion's openness can also be felt in its accessibility. Brochstein's transparency recalls Farnsworth or the Glass House, but it sits on no podium and can be accessed from all four sides. The transparency prepares those entering by displaying the code of conduct—coffee-drinking, book-reading, laptop-staring. Without an ID reader at the entrance (omnipresent

[16] "Portrait Photography at Rice University," Rice University, accessed September 22, 2023, https://portraits.rice.edu/portrait-photography-rice-university.

among campus buildings), the pavilion soothes Rice non-affiliates with a refined form of control presented as a gesture of scholarly hospitality. The insalubrious Texan climate has been alleviated at the Central Quadrangle by the diffused effulgence and the refreshing breeze, allowing prolonged sojourns and "impromptu gatherings."[17] The atmosphere here is temperate and jovial. The experience in the Central Quad has been intensified through the richness of sensations, arousing the auditory (swaying trees and the falling water of the fountain), the haptic (the variegated ground texture of the landscape), and the olfactory (the smell of coffee and pastry inside the pavilion), a "polyphony of senses" to its counterpart's "ocularcentrism."[18]

fig. 10
Brochstein Pavilion in the shade of oak trees. Photo: Yifei Zhang.

fig. 11
Brochstein Pavilion with Fondren Library in the background. Photo: Yifei Zhang.

The pavilion's critique of the Academic Quad was felt as early as fall 2008, less than a year after its dedication: "An unintended consequence of the project, however, is that the landscape of the [Academic] quad, for example, now appears harsh in comparison. Likewise, in relation to this new, crisp pavilion, the architectural approach adopted for the campus over the last several decades seems lackluster."[19] Indeed, the "unintended" nature of this critique was manifested in Brochstein architect Thomas Phifer's intention to respond to existing campus architecture, specifically the iconic Cram and Goodhue buildings.[20] Similarly, the claim that the pavilion and landscape follows the model of the Tuileries Garden seems extraneous to its success.[21] The operation of the Brochstein Pavilion has made it into an essential part of life on campus. In addition to a place for meetings and classes, it became the default space for many regularly scheduled campus events, such as study-abroad fairs and small-scale art exhibitions. "Broch N Talk," the casual conversation between students and visiting lecturers to the architecture school, inscribes the physical location as an indispensable part of the gathering.

The Brochstein perhaps responds less to the Rice architectural vernacular. It creates a vernacular of its own. James Turrell's skyspace *Twilight Epiphany* was built in 2012 along the same central axis as Brochstein. Located outside of the music school, the small structure has an atrium that often functions as a micro-orchestra pit and a

[17] "Portrait Photography at Rice University."
[18] Juhani Pallasmaa, *The Eyes of the Skin: Architecture of the Senses* (Chichester and Hoboken, NJ: Wiley-Academy, John Wiley & Sons, 2005), 19, 41.
[19] Self, "Brochstein Pavilion," 33.
[20] Thomas Phifer, "Current Work: Thomas Phifer, Thomas Phifer and Partners," The Architectural League, recorded on November 12, 2013, YouTube video, 5:05, https://www.youtube.com/watch?v=rxuM8vJxlJ4&ab_channel=TheArchitecturalLeague/.
[21] Barry Moore, "Everyone Loves Raymond," *Cite* 76 (Fall 2008): 33.

fig. 12
James Turrell, *Twilight Epiphany* skyspace. Photo: Yifei Zhang.

higher level with additional seating. Visually, the skyspace resembles the pavilion in its bold white color, while formally it also sports an ethereal canopy that floats like a cloud ***(fig. 12)***. Working with Phifer to create the skyspace, Turrell was explicit about his inspiration: "I wanted to do a piece that offset [the Brochstein Pavilion]—something that had a certain lightness, because [Phifer's] structure has this elegant lightness."[22] Surely, one can draw some conclusions from Turrell's words and connect them to Phifer's, or to Renzo Piano's Menil Collection to the north of campus, or to several of Thomas Phifer's museum projects that employ similarly ethereal skylights. What remains of interest in a pragmatic approach to Built Criticism in this contingent context is that Turrell's skyspace joins the Brochstein Pavilion to render the nearby heavy, earthy buildings loaded with meaning "lackluster" and "harsh in comparison." The skyspace gave the community on campus all the more reason to leave the air-conditioned interiors and venture into the landscape.

The Brochstein Pavilion and its landscape thus fosters a new communal life. To speak in Walter Benjamin's language, the pavilion is perceived "gradually by habit"—along with the landscape it exerts quotidian influence on a distracted public that uses it in the *longue durée*.[23] Such a new life is staged and conditioned by the built elements and is put on most conspicuous display—it is a life that is much more genteel, much more refined and light-hearted, much less provincial, much less self-ingratiating and self-righteous, much less anxious about identity and meaning.

[22] Beth Broome, "Light Craft," *Architectural Record* 200, no. 7 (July 2012): 86.
[23] Walter Benjamin, "The Work of Art in the Age of Mechanical Reproduction," in *Illuminations*, ed. Hannah Arendt, trans. Harry Zohn (New York: Schocken Books, 1969), 240.

Perhaps a ramification of the critique, the production of a new academic life was to lay bare the message so eager to be read—the occidental iconography was instrumental to an institution that was founded upon slave capital and black labor, for the exclusive benefit of white Houstonians. Architecture and landscape in this way only "put a veneer of culture on a fortune," transforming slave capital to academic capital.[24] Thus the Italian cypress, St. Joe brick, and marble columns weave into a continuous semantic web culminating in the glorious bronze statue of William Marsh Rice, a slave owner. The monumentality of the statue made it the physical locus of sustained protests in 2020 and 2021, and its removal became the central demand from student activists. As a result, an independent study on the statue was published by the university's Task Force on Slavery, Segregation and Racial Injustice, detailing its history and symbolism.[25] A year later, the university removed Rice's statue, and is now rebuilding the Academic Quad after a new design, undoing much of the formulaic symmetry while rehearsing many of the strategies seen around the Brochstein Pavilion: outdoor seating, tree-lined paths, perforated canopies.[26] Those living a new life can no longer sustain even the most desperately diluted and secularized idolatry. It would be difficult to make the case for a strict causality between the pavilion's success and the revamp of the Academic Quad. And of course, it would be even more absurd to suggest the Brochstein Pavilion as a critique of the founder's cruelty, or the institution's disputable early years. The effectiveness and scope of a Built Criticism is undoubtedly limited. Nevertheless, the chain of events that surround the Founder's Statue, the Academic Quad, and the distinctly different character across the Fondren Library is surely one of the many turns of history that were set into motion in the late 2000s after the pavilion's initiation, whose ripple effects are still felt today. The critical power of architecture is attested by Aldo Rossi: "When one goes to a charitable institution, the sadness is almost something concrete. It is in the walls, the courtyards, the rooms. When the Parisians destroyed the Bastille, they were erasing the centuries of abuse and sadness of which the Bastille was the physical form."[27]

Biography

Yifei Zhang (He/Him) is a Chinese writer and designer based in Cambridge, MA. Zhang received a BArch and BA in Architecture and French Studies (Cum Laude, Tau Sigma Delta) at Rice University; and an MDes from Harvard GSD, where he worked as a research assistant and an editorial assistant at the Harvard FAS CAMLab. Zhang's design and writings were published on the occasion of the Venice Architecture Biennale 2021, the Association of Collegiate Schools of Architecture, and in *The Avery Review, Scroope: Cambridge Architecture Journal,* and *Yale Paprika*! Zhang's research centers around the Blue Humanities, and the urban and architectural history of 19th century England and France.

[24] Dell Upton, *Architecture in the United States* (New York: Oxford University Press, 1998), 264.

[25] See "Update on the Founder's Memorial," Task Force on Slavery, Segregation and Racial Injustice, Rice University, June 2021, https://taskforce.rice.edu/.

[26] See "Academic Quadrangle Redesign," Rice University, accessed January 28, 2024, https://www.rice.edu/quad/.

[27] Aldo Rossi, *The Architecture of the City*, trans. Diane Ghirardo and Joan Ockman (Cambridge: The MIT Press, 1982), 101.

Tactical Reflections between Architecture, Criticism, and Politics: Towards a Comprehensive and Alternative Thinking of Architectural Practice

Maria Valeria Bernabei

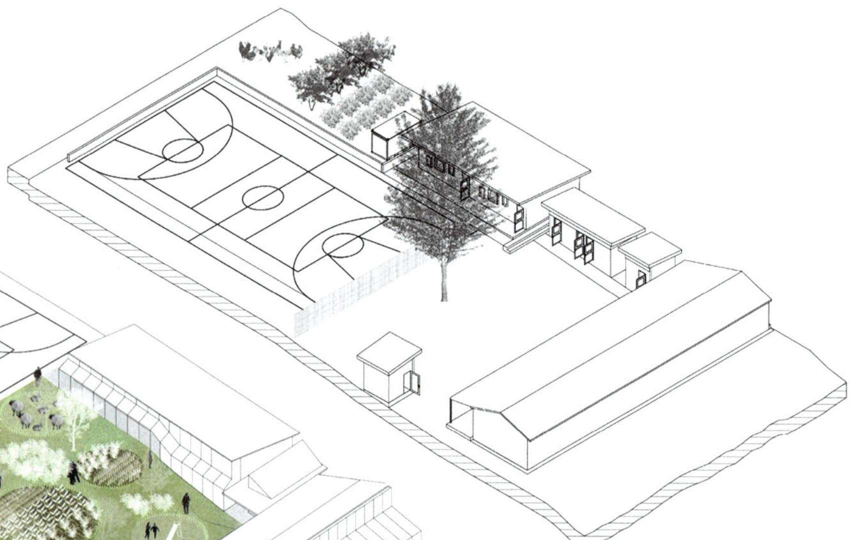

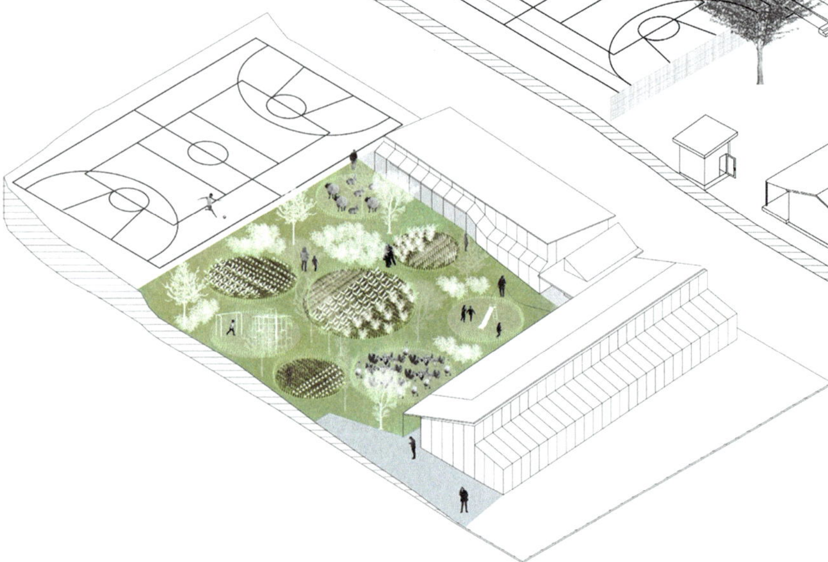

fig. 1
Al Borde architects. A sustainable school in Chile (2019). Isometric of the school before intervention. © Al Borde architects, 2019.

fig. 2
Al Borde architects. A sustainable school in Chile (2019). Isometric with the proposed intervention that is later modified by adding the multipurpose room in the center of the playground, as can be seen in the floor plan of figure 4. © Al Borde architects, 2019.

This research is a tactical reflection on the relationships between architecture, criticism, and politics, relationships that are evident and unfold from the study of the first sustainable public school in Lo Zárate, Chile, designed by Al Borde architects and managed by the NGO Tagma within a public network of sustainable schools for Latin America. The complex framework revealed by the project allows us to perceive that architecture should not be understood as an isolated discipline since it comprises multiple layers and levels, which in turn highlights the importance of relationships and their various degrees. However, depending on each project, some ties manage to prevail over others, transcending the mere pragmatism of construction to assume other meanings.

keywords:
school, sustainability, Al Borde, participatory architecture, politics

Introduction

In studying the first public sustainable school in Chile, managed by the NGO Tagma and designed by Al Borde architects, it becomes possible to review the links that are interwoven in our architectural practice. The project displays a tactical reflection about the relationships between architecture, criticism, and politics that questions established conventions, suggests the possibility of being different, and proposes changes within a conception of architecture that is usually considered immutable. The work reflects, structures, and highlights these ties, while considering three variables: the educational institution, participatory architecture, and collective need.

Architecture as Built Criticism implies a conscious political act extending over time and made manifest by necessity in specific forms and materials. This act involves taking a position, forming a resistance towards both an other and implicit subjectivity. It also means rendering visible everything that is absent from that category, among other issues, making common sense[1] visible while simultaneously questioning it. Furthermore, architecture can merge into a political operation where a set of previously excluded particulars come together to universalize a demand that is transformed, thus becoming valid for the entire community. The work at Lo Zárate seeks to recover the social meaning of architecture and the importance of the territory. But it also aspires to reconnect public and private actions and to rethink the role of architects in their discipline.

The First Sustainable Public School in Chile

The school is in Lo Zárate, a rural community[2] of three hundred inhabitants in the Valparaíso region. As a rural school, its basic educational system follows current educational policies by having multigrade classrooms from first to sixth grade. Significantly, the schoolteachers developed a contextual environmental pedagogy that began as an extracurricular project. The region's climate is conditioned by a large temperature range and advanced desertification that limits access to drinking water. Additionally, Chile is part of one of the most seismically active regions in the world. During the 2010 earthquake, the school was destroyed and had to be reconstructed. This building ***(figs. 1–3)*** consisted of two joint classrooms, a psycho-educational farm, an orchard, rooms for the school principal, a service area, and a small school canteen.

1 Common sense refers to Gramsci's concept. Santiago Castro Gómez explains that Gramscian common sense does not have a rational character but rather one of faith, which is why it becomes a strategic field of dispute. See Santiago Castro Gómez, *Revoluciones sin sujeto. Slavoj Žižek y la crítica del historicismo posmoderno* (Mexico, DF: Ediciones Akal, 2015), 223–379.

2 It is a region that has horticulture as one of its main economic activities, with lettuce and strawberries being the most important products.

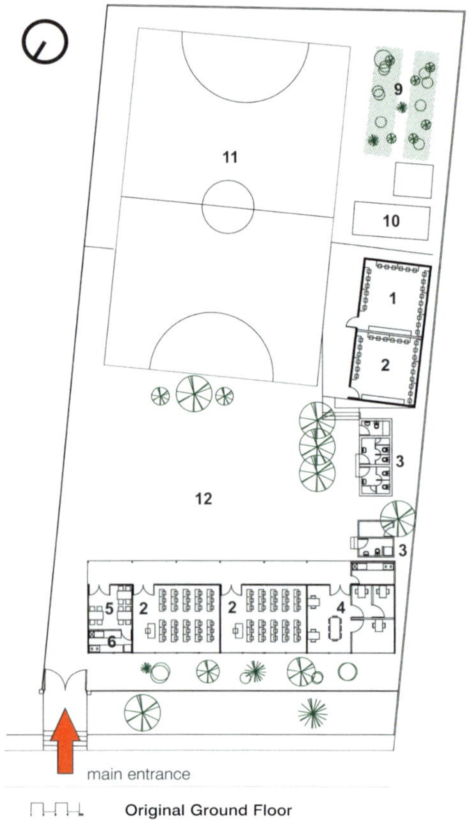

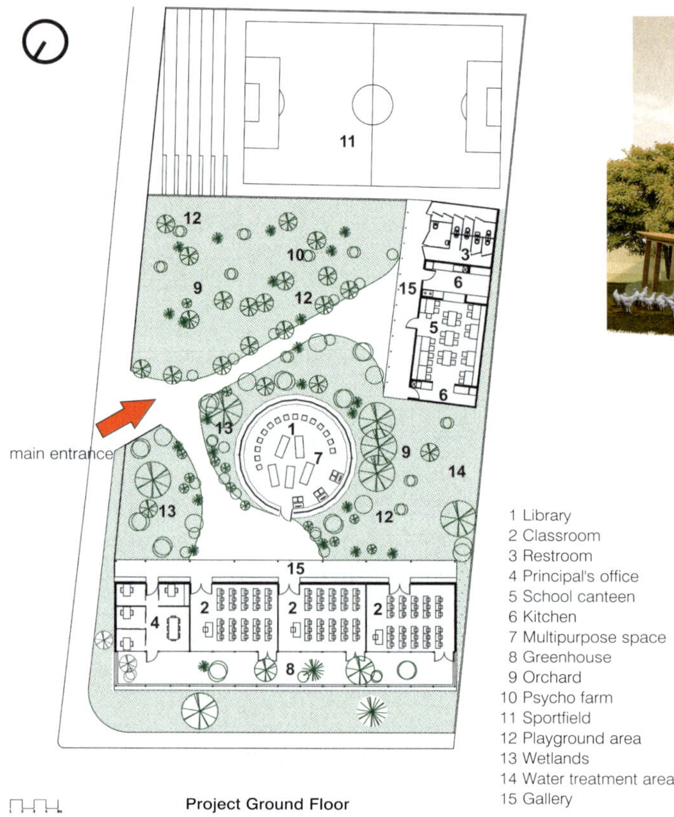

fig. 3
Al Borde architects. A sustainable school in Chile (2019). Floor plan before commencement of the new project, with specifications of my own. © Al Borde architects, 2019.

fig. 4
Al Borde architects. A sustainable school in Chile (2019). Executed project plan with specifications of my own. © Al Borde architects, 2019.

The program for a network of sustainable public schools in Latin America was developed by the NGO Tagma.[3] They seek to construct sustainable and self-sufficient schools in vulnerable locations to meet various needs, from adequate facilities for teaching in environmental education classrooms, as well as the development of a training process helping builders to become self-sufficient, to the reactivation of the local economy through the use of materials from the region. The Lo Zárate project ***(fig. 2)*** started in mid-2019 with participatory workshops to learn about the requirements and conditions that influence the design. Subsequently, at the beginning of 2020, the construction process began. In forty-five days, 270 m^2 of existing buildings were renovated, 225 m^2 of new useable floor area were built, and a total of 1,800 m^2 were redeveloped in the surrounding area.

The project ***(fig. 4)*** articulates and expands the two existing blocks—one to the north and the other to the southwest—that delimit the edges of the property and serve as a framework for the central sector where the open recreation spaces, the orchard, the psycho-educational farm, and the central volume with its circular plan are organized. This central volume functions as a multipurpose building, generating a family–student–teacher recreational area in relation to the natural areas and the surrounding landscape. It also emphasizes the idea of communal centrality with the library and computer room, forming a pedagogical center for the whole village.

The 120 m^2 north building was partially dismantled, leaving only the metal structure. A greenhouse with an attached orchard was built to the north. Classrooms and

[3] https://www.unesco.org/en/articles/tagma.

fig. 5
Al Borde architects. A sustainable school in Chile (2019). Perspective section from the classroom and greenhouse sector. © Al Borde architects, 2019.

fig. 6
Al Borde architects. A sustainable school in Chile (2019). Diagram of thermal gain in winter and ventilation in summer. © Al Borde architects, 2019.

fig. 7
Al Borde architects. A sustainable school in Chile (2020). On the left (with a yellow wall), wetlands in relation to the multipurpose building. © Maria Valeria Bernabei, November 21, 2023.

fig. 8
Al Borde architects. A sustainable school in Chile (2020). On either side are two wetlands located near the main entrance. © Maria Valeria Bernabei, November 21, 2023.

the administrative area were relocated to receive more hours of sunlight, reducing the use of electricity. The classrooms are separated from the greenhouse by adobe walls to provide thermal mass. These walls are built on foundations of tires and have double-glazed windows at the top.

The interior walls are made of OSB panels and lined with oat root mattresses, wool from domestic sheep, and polystyrene waste. In this way, the classrooms can be thermally insulated and opened to the north to benefit from the solar gain from the greenhouse ***(figs. 5-6)***. The thermal comfort system is complemented by Canadian wells. The kitchen and school canteen were relocated to the south, as they do not need thermal gain.

A mix of construction techniques was employed that used conventional materials such as cement, iron, glass, and wood. Besides traditional dry construction, innovative research has been carried out in Chile on building with wood in seismic regions. Local materials such as adobe, timber logs, straw, and recycled waste (for example, old tires, plastic bottles, and beverage cans) also found an application. The greenhouse reused windows from buildings with a significant local history.
The water system is based on two sources: (1) a combination of mains water and rainwater, and (2) a combination of water from purifying wetlands ***(figs. 7-8)*** that treat gray–black water and sewerage. Water derived from the latter source is used for agricultural irrigation, while toilets and urinals are supplied with water from the first source, thereby halving water consumption. The building is designed to constantly process, recirculate,

and reuse the main resources, that is to say, its facilities are in constant operation so that the cycles are optimally completed.

Twelve solar panels on top of the greenhouse ***(figs. 9–10)*** produce 3 kW, charging the batteries for about a week, while they are in use, enabling the school to be self-sufficient for four days. The electricity-generating system is also connected to the main grid so that any surplus can be fed into it, thereby turning the institution into an electricity supplier. At the same time, the solar panels provide shade for the greenhouse.

fig. 9
Al Borde architects. A sustainable school in Chile (2020). Placement of solar panels in greenhouse. © Lorena Presno, 2020.

fig. 10
Al Borde architects. A sustainable school in Chile (2020). View of the panels in place. © Maria Valeria Bernabei, November 21, 2023.

Al Borde Architects

Based in Quito, Ecuador, the Al Borde team has been developing a collaborative and experimental approach since 2007. It consists of David Barragán, Pascual Gangotena, Maríaluisa Borja, and Esteban Benavides, all graduates of the Catholic University of Quito. Their projects demonstrate an empathetic understanding of people's needs; they review real problems in specific contexts to find possible solutions. With this comprehensive perspective, Al Borde work with local materials, limited budgets, and participatory design and construction processes. The principle of sustainability as an intrinsic part of life is at the center of their actions. The goal is to generate a common-sense architecture with an ethical base as an aesthetic and political way of situating oneself in the world. This position emerges from the edges of conventional architectural practice, even though Al Borde insist they are not on the margins of what happens in the discipline. In the beginning, the team experienced the difficult economic, political, and social conditions existing across Latin American countries, and they are also trying to work in a way that respects the varied cultural contexts present. Thus, they developed a way of building from "doing more with less,"[4] leading to an architectural language in which the aesthetic of the common, the austere, and the reimagined local prevails. Two

[4] Al Borde made a documentary called *Do More With Less* that is about the postcrisis generation of newly founded architecture studios in Ecuador, as they were the ones who had to focus their paradigm towards the role of the architect in society. See https://www.albordearq.com/hacer-mucho-con-poco_do-more-with-less.

important aspects of Al Borde's participatory process are the investigation into suitable materials for the project and getting to know all the project's participants in order to establish a relationship of complicity. Architecture, Al Borde maintain, is a vision that can be built, but for a vision to be realized it needs the commitment of all those participants so that everyone understands the difficulty and complexity of the process; in other words, it is indispensable to comprehend the diversity of layers that make up a project so that everyone is prepared to go beyond the limits of their own discipline.[5] While their theoretical approach is based on "thinking with our hands,"[6] they also maintain contacts with colleagues such as the mentor and architect José María Sáez from Ecuador and the architects Solano Benitez from Paraguay and Mauricio Rocha from Mexico. They are also interested in the work of the Spanish architect Santiago Cirujeda, since he understands architecture as a device for debate and criticism, realizing architectural projects to explicitly criticize canonic architectural works, as Barragán states.[7]

Most Al Borde projects are designs to further public interest. As antecedents in the educational field, three works can be mentioned: the Nueva Esperanza School in Puerto Cabuyal (2009), the Wagon of Knowledge (2012), and Yuyarina Pacha Library in the Ecuadorian Amazon (2023). These projects radicalize teaching; they understand that education must be accessible and flexible in order to reach all social groups and that they must establish relations with the context and not the other way around. Their architecture reflects the team's way of life: they take collective decisions, buy organic food, use public transport, participate on building sites, teach at universities, and work in their studio.

5 David Barragán, personal interview with the author, October 30, 2023.
6 Barragán, personal interview.
7 Barragán.

Participatory Architecture

Lo Zárate School is the third realized project built by the NGO Tagma. Starting in 2016 in Uruguay, their approach has reached different parts of Latin America. The construction of self-sustainable buildings is based on Michael Reynolds's (US) seven principles of sustainability: (1) water collection, (2) treatment of gray and black water, (3) production of agro-ecological food, (4) production of renewable energies, (5) passive conditioning of the building, (6) use of recyclable materials, and (7) inclusion of the human factor in the process. These principles comply with different Sustainable Development Goals as proposed by the 2012 UN Conference on Sustainable Development in Rio de Janeiro for the 2030 agenda. Buildings are conceived as Earthships: just as a ship must adapt to and take advantage of the climate and the sea for good navigation, a building must be in line with its context and natural phenomena to create good architecture.

The school was selected from Tagma's call for applications on the basis of its rural surroundings, the needs of the inhabitants, the school's environmental pedagogic program as an extracurricular activity, and the profile of the actors, given that almost half of the pupils have special educational needs. Tagma commissioned Al Borde to coordinate the design and realization of the project together with the cooperative Caminantes, a team from Argentina that specializes in sustainable construction; Bioantu water eco-engineering company from Chile; and Cíclica, a local architecture studio. In addition, the program was supported by a number of NGOs and private companies, as well as government agencies at different levels. It was important to gather the best from the public and private sectors, creating an allied team.

The first stage consisted of participatory design workshops and classes on bio-construction. The second stage took on construction itself. The design workshops ***(figs. 11-12)*** took place in mid-2019 and construction began in February 2020, between a period of social unrest in Chile and the beginning of the global Covid-19 pandemic,

which delayed the inauguration. Al Borde, with Maríaluisa Borja leading this project,[8] developed the architectural design and were in charge of the participatory design workshops. Tagma supervised a team comprising architects, educators, artists, teachers, and students, who, together with the community, contributed their perspectives to the design development of the project. The work on the transformation of the school was structured with course modules through which participants acquired knowledge that could be transferred to their own contexts; it is therefore in itself a pedagogical process, with additional open workshops for the entire community. One hundred students from twenty-two countries were involved in the educational design process and construction course. Along with an additional one hundred volunteers, these students formed a participatory and horizontal design and construction team. In addition to this, an artists' residency program was offered under the guidance of the conceptual artist Luis Camnitzer.

The school day begins at 9:00 a.m. Children with learning or behavioral difficulties occasionally go to the farm to interact with the animals first, so they can relax and socialize better. They then begin their classroom activities. Although the children live in a rural context, the teachers demonstrated that they have become disconnected from that context because the official government education program is devised for urban settings. As a result of this observation, the teachers implemented a paradigm shift in the curriculum by introducing contextualization learning, whereby children begin by observing the nearby and familiar to subsequently expand to more universal perspectives. For this reason, the designed spaces help pupils to interact with their context ***(figs. 13-14)***, thereby enabling knowledge to be acquired by using architecture and the environment as a frame for learning and subsequently bringing the experience gained in the field to the study of textbooks on natural sciences, mathematics, and other subjects. Sustainability calls for the need to be close to nature in order to learn from its processes and thus gather knowledge, developing respect and a desire to care for it, as Rivero, one of the Tagma representatives in charge of the project in Chile, explains.[9]

fig. 11
Al Borde architects. A sustainable school in Chile (2020). Design workshops led by Maríaluisa Borja with teachers. © Al Borde architects, 2019.

fig. 12
Al Borde architects. A sustainable school in Chile (2020). Participatory work on site. © Lorena Presno, 2020.

8 Al Borde planned three visits before construction. During the first, Maríaluisa and Pascual oversaw the participatory workshops with the teachers. During the second, Maríaluisa and Esteban presented the new design according to the school's needs to seek confirmation and to integrate possible changes. Information updates obtained by Cíclica architecture studio (the local contact architects who liaised between Al Borde and the community) were also taken into account. Finally, during the third visit, Maríaluisa and David arranged approvals, suppliers, logistics, etc. After that, Maríaluisa was in charge of the project and advised on the construction. See Barragán, personal interview.

9 Paso Sustentable—Gustavo Bertrand, "1° Escuela sustentable en Chile (Bioconstrucción, Energía solar, huerto, biolfiltros) Lo Zárate," YouTube video, 12.30 minutes, accessed November 21, 2023, https://www.youtube.com/watch?v=2xWZGd7OXlw.

fig. 13
Al Borde architects. A sustainable school in Chile (2020). Children at recess playing near the orchard. © Maria Valeria Bernabei, November 21, 2023.

fig. 14
Al Borde architects. A sustainable school in Chile (2020). Children at recess saying farewell to the year by dressing up and taking part in playground activities. © Maria Valeria Bernabei, November 21, 2023.

Tactical Reflections

Experience is associated with sensations of novelty and surprise, tracing a path towards a risky, non-manipulable, and impressionable otherness. It is also possible to embrace the experience of others, to view phenomena from others' perspectives and to absorb the social effects that are generated, as the philosopher Diego Fonti states.[10] The school's architecture offers a reflection on and a critique of conventions. Architecture functions as a Built Criticism[11] and as a political act when it renders the act of decision-making conscious. These choices are translated into space and matter by the architects, thereby generating palpable experiences and meanings, but also making visible postponed situations. In this way, Lo Zárate School questions contemporary architecture's conventions. Such a conscious assessment and positioning of the designer and the user takes place, with the built object thereby affecting the entire image of the "polis," where polis is understood as the symbolic space in which the conflicts between the different representational systems of itself that a society builds are played out.[12] The term is linked to the Gramscian version of "common sense," when a social formation leads to the construction of a hegemony.[13]

On the one hand, the Built Criticism translates into a physical–spatial materialization that takes into account the location, the design of the project, and its realization. On the other hand, from the point of view of social practices and their embodiment, the building is a critique of systematized teaching methodologies, where individuals and their diversity are made to conform to conventions, nullifying their ability to transform what might be a stigma into a strength. The Lo Zárate program proposes a human-centered pedagogy put into practice one day at a time, while at a communal level other universal problems, such as the environmental crisis, social inequality, or functional systems for the development of economic capital, are rendered visible.Given the construction materials that were found in the vicinity, the project's location allowed the school to develop a rural character, also implying that pupils, teachers, and residents do not need to move into a city, as innovations and possibilities no longer emerge

[10] Diego Fonti, "Hacia la tierra sin mal. Hacer experiencia," *Hoy Día Córdoba. Year XXVII N°6474*, September 15, 2023, 6.

[11] Criticism, in this sense, is understood as individual assessment, as aesthetic, ethical, and interpretative judgment, following Josep Maria Montaner, *Arquitectura y Crítica*, 2nd ed. (Barcelona: Gustavo Gili, 2000), 7.

[12] Michel Foucault (author), Eduardo Gruner (preface), *Nietzsche, Freud, Marx* (Barcelona: Editorial Anagrama: 1970), 14.

[13] Castro Gómez, *Revoluciones sin sujeto*, 223–379.

fig. 15
Al Borde architects. A sustainable school in Chile (2020). Architect Maríaluisa Borja chooses the windows that will be used in the greenhouse, to be purchased from a demolition house. © Al Borde architects, 2020.

fig. 16
"Playa Chica in Cartagena", Chile, c.1930. The castles are located at the back of the image. © Colección Museo Histórico Nacional. Photo: unknown photographer.

fig. 17
"Walk on Chica beach in Cartagena", Chile, c.1920. © Colección Museo Histórico Nacional. Photo: unknown photographer.

fig. 18
Al Borde architects. A sustainable school in Chile (2020). Greenhouse and adjoining classrooms. © Lorena Presno, 2020.

from large urban areas. The school's architecture generates a dynamic that adjusts to natural cycles and programmatic change, both understood as processes and not as finished products. The project proposes a design that is based on the intelligence of the commons. The austere, local, experimental[14] aesthetics of the complex are focused on the individuality of the parts that make up a complete project. The choice of materials, the reuse of components, and the adaptation of construction systems mean that elements are not subject to standardization but become individualized, since some are used in an unconventional way, for example cans and tires. In addition, the variously sized recycled windows ***(fig. 15)*** that are now part of the main facade of the greenhouse were part of the local heritage, thereby helping to preserve and keep alive some of the history of the region. These windows originate from the end-of-nineteenth-century "castles"[15] that were designed for the Chilean upper class, when Cartagena was a fashionable seaside resort ***(figs. 16–17)***. With the arrival of the railroad, the previously exclusive beaches came within reach of people from other social strata, so wealthy families from Santiago de Chile moved to other destinations nearby, such as Viña del Mar.

These local stories are narrated in schools and are part of the region's identity. The teachers of Lo Zárate School assembled an extracurricular program for the recovery of intangible heritage based on urban legends, oral history, poetry, and songs. While in most schools the greenhouse is located either away from the teaching areas or in residual spaces, at Lo Zárate it is attached to the classrooms ***(fig. 18)***, thus fulfilling several functions: capturing heat, growing plants, and serving as a pedagogical space. The greenhouse forms the new facade to the street, mediating between it and the classrooms ***(fig. 19)***. Previously, classrooms faced directly onto the public space and curtains were used for privacy; this provided neither good lighting nor natural ventilation.

Contrary to conventional practice resulting from odors associated with waste or animal feed, the farm and orchard are connected to the densely populated areas

[14] Al Borde's notion of experimental means getting to know local products and working with them, ensuring that they can be used in a given context. This knowledge is acquired by researching the materials, construction techniques, and professionals' or other actors' experience, and by performing laboratory tests. The term does not refer to a merely playful situation, given the need to assume technical responsibility for the built work. See Barragán, personal interview.

[15] The large luxury mansions that wealthy families in Santiago de Chile built on the seashore to spend their vacations in were dubbed "castles."

because of their important social function within the pupils' pedagogic development. The classrooms and the recreational open areas are designed comprehensively to assure a continuity of indoor–outdoor activities according to specific pedagogical criteria ***(fig. 20)***.

In Tagma's third project, the collective of actors invoked their own knowledge from the Latin American context, deconstructing Reynolds's typology and method to adjust the school to the needs of the community. For example, in terms of materials, tires are not considered waste (unlike in the US); however, this creates problems for collection. The construction of a cylindrical building also departed from architectural norms. The idea was not to limit the search for solutions to the community of Lo Zárate given that it was the first project to start from an existing building, thereby revaluing the contribution of the existing. The collective focused on reorganizing, repairing, and reusing as many existing things as possible, rather than designing a new building.

In the final design, Al Borde emphasized the school's distinctive aspects, notably

fig. 19
Al Borde architects. A sustainable school in Chile (2020). Main facade formed by the greenhouse. © Lorena Presno, 2020.

fig. 20
Al Borde architects. A sustainable school in Chile (2020). Children in the new classrooms during school hours. © Maria Valeria Bernabei, November 21, 2023.

fig. 21
Al Borde architects. A sustainable school in Chile (2020). The orchard and the psycho-educational farm occupy the central sector of the property. © Maria Valeria Bernabei, November 21, 2023.

fig. 22
Al Borde architects. A sustainable school in Chile (2020). Simulation of a natural wetland. © Maria Valeria Bernabei, November 21, 2023.

the extracurricular environmental activities established by the teachers, and the playground as another pedagogical space, together constituting the heart of the school, allowing these activities to be visibly at the center of the design. It is these that differentiate the school from other public educational institutions. At the same time, this view coincides with Tagma's sustainable and pedagogical goals. The farm, the orchard ***(fig. 21)***, and the landscape are linked to the multipurpose room by their social character. Given the region's water scarcity, the teachers are reinforcing awareness of its use, demonstrating how it can be recycled. A wetland, simulating natural conditions, has been annexed to the playground area ***(fig. 22)***.

In the context of social practices, while the incorporation of environmental education is no longer a challenge (since the activities and the building are explicitly manifested), their articulation within conventional education is. Teachers have recounted that the school building has empowered them to promote environmental education even more, especially now the children are motivated through the architecture in a way they were not by the previous building. Taking advantage of orientation, optimizing natural light, and generating natural thermal comfort through natural means are factors that have influenced students to be more active, attentive, and perceptive in the learning process.

At Lo Zárate, the pedagogic institution and its architecture, usually functioning as a symbolic space and an instrument of power of the state apparatus, have been reformed and managed by Chilean citizens with the help of actors from different countries. Conventional schools should learn from the community of Lo Zárate and its extracurricular activities.

Architects assume that their role is changing from that of a facilitator and mediator to that of a project manager. This transformation requires the profession to look beyond architecture as an isolated discipline,[16] implying that our specific skills and interests should not be separated from everyday life. No architect works alone and the profession's raison d'être is not only generated from the discipline but also determined by humanity. Barragán affirms that Al Borde are trying to devise their own modus operandi to relate to those people who are looking for alternative processes, because Al Borde understand that there are other ways of living.[17] In addition, concepts from pre-capitalist Latin American societies, such as reciprocity and complementarity,[18] are inscribed into this project, thereby reconnecting with knowledge from aboriginal roots. Given the type of project and the community, these concepts are familiar; they are implicit in the Andean world. Barragán argues that "they are already there, in the DNA . . .. The only thing we do is activate those 'genes' when they are 'turned off,' it is another layer that responds to the territory."[19]

Artist Luis Camnitzer emphasizes that the work constructs not only a building but also a culture and a pedagogy. He sees the program expressing a self-confession of what we, as a society, failed to correct.[20]

In its various dimensions, the project for Lo Zárate School challenges the notion of common sense[21] dominating the world and architecture. The different elements of the school's program were adjusted through a participatory exchange, thereby anchoring them to the needs of the people. By allowing this type of common sense to prevail, the professionals have ensured that the work benefits the entire community. Each space that has been designed is proposing an alternative and diverse vision, even though it was generated from the same field of everyday planning. The intention has been to render visible all the layers of the process, whether human, material, political, or economic, contrary to the conventional view that prioritizes the evaluation of the final object.

[16] In an interview, Pascual Gangotena explains that, sometimes, colleagues reject Al Borde's way of working; they accuse Al Borde of moving away from the discipline, and affirm that architecture has to work by itself, without involving other arts or sciences. See Club de Crítica Arquitectura Udep, "Pensando con Al Borde. Entrevista," YouTube video, 41 minutes, accessed November 24, 2023, https://www.youtube.com/watch?v=6MKVRbmhIGM&t=2458s.

[17] Barragán, personal interview.

[18] Reciprocity—"I give to you, you give to me"—is the exchange of labor or comparable goods that occurs in balance and with mutual understanding. Complementarity refers to the fact that opposites should not generate conflicts with each other, but rather integrate and understand each other in pursuit of the common good.

[19] Barragán, personal interview.

[20] Tagma—Una Escuela Sustentable, "Luis Camnitzer sobre su participación en Una Escuela Sustentable, Chile" YouTube video, 1.47 minutes, accessed November 21, 2023, https://www.youtube.com/watch?v=WybSE8eu3ME&t=108s.

[21] Santiago Castro Gómez, following Gramsci, affirms that it is necessary to change the "common sense" that structures daily practices, in order to open cracks in the "vision of the world" that the ruling class has imposed. This is achieved through the influencing of popular opinion by intellectuals, the true ideological supporters of the masses. See Castro Gómez, *Revoluciones sin sujeto*, 383.

fig. 23
Al Borde architects. A sustainable school in Chile (2020). The multipurpose building and the volunteers who participated in the construction of the school. © Lorena Presno, 2020

The ability to differentiate and the acuity to observe reality from another perspective are often questioned. While conventions can offer safety, they also make us dependent on a system that is external to us. The collective work leading to the realized Lo Zárate School was part of a broader cultural criticism that has not only questioned the values established in current common sense but also allowed the revaluation of Andean common sense as a way of opening up diverse visions of the world and as a significant and intrinsic contribution to our society. In the context of the first quarter of the twenty-first century, Al Borde are an unconventional architectural practice in that they engage with regular everyday life, offering critical resistance from a vantage point of local technology, history, and popular culture to explore the capacity for new forms of collective agency. In the case of Lo Zárate School, the broad coalition of individuals—professionals such as architects, engineers, educators, and artists, as well as the inhabitants of the town, including the schoolchildren and their families, and public and private organizations—has transcended the passive to assume a collective form ***(fig. 23)***.

Biography
Maria Valeria Bernabei received her master's degree in Housing Management and Development from FAUD-UNC. She is an instructor and researcher at the School of Architecture, Urban Planning and Design of the National University of Cordoba (FAUD-UNC); Assistant Professor to the Chair of Introduction to History of Architecture and Urban Planning A, and Assistant Professor for the elective course named: "The Project as Research"; as well as Assistant Professor to the Chair of Theory and Methods A. She is currently studying for a bachelor's degree in Philosophy from the School of Philosophy – Faculty of Philosophy and Humanities at UNC at the National University of Cordoba. She is a member of the SECYT Research Project (Secretary of Science and Technology)-UNC entitled: "Metropolitan fabrics: public space and architecture in peri-urban territories. Reading of forms and modes of production of urban extensions from the approach of sustainable quality in the Metropolitan Region of Cordoba" (1990–2020).

You Make Me Worry . . . And That Is Good Building Criticism

Al Borde
David Barragán, Pascual Gangotena,
Maríaluisa Borja, and Esteban Benavides

fig. 1
Al Borde, Sacred Forest, Quito, Ecuador, 2021.

When we shared with Santiago Granda—a fellow Ecuadorian architect and a partner in the architectural practice ESE Colectivo—the eucalyptus tree perimeter wall we designed for a cemetery at Valle de los Chillos,[1] his reaction was one that could easily define our work in one sentence: "I must admit that when I see what you are doing, you make me worry . . . and that is a good thing."

keywords:

emotions as ambitions, clients as partners, architecture as a collective act, local production

The feeling of excitement that comes from facing the unknown, the unthinkable, and the seemingly impossible is what drives us to tackle the challenges of each project. This excitement is what motivates us to come to work every day. Without this almost childish emotion, Al Borde would not exist. Indeed, we intentionally trick ourselves into perceiving work as a constant challenge, where the challenge is the gasoline that fuels the flame of our conversations, forcing us to push the limits of scenarios that we consider unique and specific to each situation.

The cemetery *(fig. 1)* is in the rural part of Quito, Ecuador, on land used previously for cattle pasture; therefore, all trees had been removed, leaving only a few eucalyptuses on the perimeter. Eucalyptus is a species that was introduced to Ecuador in 1865 and is currently one of the predominant trees throughout the highlands, especially in the area where the project will be located. As a very aggressive species, it restricts the growth of others around it and consumes a lot of water; thus, it is not the best tree to plant if the goal is to improve soil quality. So, replacing eucalyptus forests with native forests is a good idea. The problem is that killing a eucalyptus tree is not an easy task. It has been proven that the best and most efficient technique is to pull them out by the roots.

Building the perimeter wall became the first action in creating this cemetery. Our goal was to use the minimal amount of energy in the construction of this two-hundred-meter barrier; in other words, to find the easiest way of assembling it with the least environmental impact. What could this simple action be?

The wall was made through the primitive act of uprooting the remaining eucalyptus trees, dragging them a few meters, and piling them up on the perimeter. The decision to take this approach, like the result, was visceral and arose from a response to the specific conditions we found on the site. This design strategy would be absurd in another context, because our decisions were not based on the quest for a form or an aesthetic result; they were based on the pursuit of coherence with the territory, such that the formal and aesthetic result responds to that specific condition.

We like to think that what is striking about Santiago Granda is that when he thinks of a perimeter wall, he thinks within the possibilities of what has been seen or known as a perimeter wall, never of the possibility of piling up trees, which is not just a functional or constructive strategy but a sustainability choice that, once it takes the form of a design, is easily perceived as something logical and even obvious—so obvious that it is overlooked as the first design option. Each project is an opportunity to renew the excitement and, if possible, push the limits a little further.

The Best Project in the World

Now to talk about the conference that is the subject of this book. In our last conversation with Wilfried Wang, in the lobby of a hotel in Shanghai, we talked about the research he was developing to objectively define the quality of a building. One of the

[1] This project is under construction, and its biggest intervention is in the landscape. It seeks to convert a cattle pasture into a native forest, where the spiritual connection of those who visit is enhanced by nature.

points that resonated most was the "intellectual ambition" with which an architect approaches a project, and how that can be synonymous with its quality. It is striking how something so seemingly subjective can be translated into the concrete, and ways of measuring it sought. And how this ambition can be read in a plan, in a construction detail, and in the building itself. So what we call "emotion" can easily be synonymous with the "ambition" that Wilfried was talking about.

fig. 2
Al Borde, Entre Muros House, Quito, Ecuador, 2008. © Raed Gindeya, 2008.

fig. 3
Al Borde, Entre Muros House, Quito, Ecuador, 2008. © Al Borde, 2007.

When we approach a project, there is a joke (every joke has some truth in it) that we keep repeating: How can we make this "the best project in the world"? We don't know exactly where it comes from, but we have some hypotheses: Could it be that this vision comes from living in an unstable environment? Somehow, in Latin America, we never know what will happen tomorrow. A president can change from one day to the next, and the apparent progress of a country can be reversed and go back ten years. Our situation as a country has always forced us to think in the present. The board on which we move is constantly changing, so our way of working is rather to flow with what we have, with what we can do, and to look forward for the best answers, to think that the project in our hands must be the best in the world. This instability has always made us feel that opportunities are unique and that we may never have another chance to do something.

Or, is it the nature of architectural projects, where most of them never see the light of day because they are long-term processes? Out of twenty people who call us for a project, we accomplish one. Most of them give up early in the process, but it also happens that when everything is ready to start construction, the project gets postponed or canceled. So in that one chance that a project becomes a reality, not giving it our all would be a complete waste, a privilege we can't afford.

We try to remember where this phrase came from. The truth is that this idea of "the best project in the world" has been with us since our first project in 2007. We

had not even established the office; we were just friends from the university who got together to do a project that would eventually be called Casa Entre Muros ***(fig. 2-6)***. To continue with the speculation, one reason for approaching this project in this way was that it seemed too difficult to imagine a future. If we thought that this would be a project without risks or ambitions, in which we would learn and gain experience so that the next projects would be good, we were putting our hope in a further opportunity that might never come. In the reality we live in, it is almost utopian to think that there will be continuity. This was the first project we were doing, and it would probably be the last.

We also had the ambition to believe that we could handle a project, that we could take the idea as far as possible and build it. To want to prove to ourselves that a client could trust us and that we were capable of shouldering that responsibility. And to respond to a budget that was tight and that could not be used as an excuse for not achieving the ideal project. Also, to understand that in our context there are people who are very good at building in a certain way and very bad at building in another way, and that these human and technical resources must be aligned to enhance the ideas.

But something that was always in the back of our minds was the desire for intellectual independence, to be able to do what we believe should be done, to structure our own statement, and to decide how to invest our time.

The idea that every project we work on has to be the best project in the world has to do with the fact that life goes by quickly and that, in the end, every project involves an expenditure of energy and, above all, time. The Entre Muros House took two years of our lives, but after that we had projects that we developed in three, four, and even one that took ten years. We don't see the point of going into something if we don't start with the premise that it's going to be "the best project in the world."

As we have been thinking about "the best project in the world," words have taken on a subtext, a meaning in another language, a collective language that we

fig. 4
Al Borde, Entre Muros House, Quito, Ecuador, 2008. © Raed Gindeya, 2008.

fig. 5
Al Borde, Entre Muros House, Quito, Ecuador, 2008. © Raed Gindeya, 2008.

fig. 6
Al Borde, Entre Muros House, Quito, Ecuador, 2008. © Al Borde, 2007.

have developed in our digressions over so many years together. Let's start with the word "world." Our world is the one we want to inhabit with our heroes, the world of Emil Cioran and Felipe Gangotena,[2] of Violeta Parra and Facundo Cabral, of Richard Buckminster Fuller and the anonymous architects of vernacular architecture, of José María Sáez and Fadhila Mammar, of Zaida Muxi and Solano Benítez, of Rita Segato and Santiago Cirugeda, and of so many others. Of those who have done something that we admire, in a world where we want to be, in a world where life and architecture have something to say. Regarding the word "best," we believe it has the sense of taking the position of protagonists of a circumstance, of giving oneself the possibility of thinking about how this world should be, of imagining what one could do if one had the power, of even thinking that one has it; it is about the reason why one does things, because it is the possibility of thinking about what we are and where we are. For us, "project" is an opportunity to do something. If we are commissioned to build a staircase, we are making a plan to think about the world. Of course, the staircase has to be a staircase and fulfill its function, and in a way it is nothing more than a staircase in itself, but in another way, at the same time and above all, it is a manifesto about humankind.

Partners in Crime

Again and again, we heard the same comment: you can do what you do because your clients are not normal; with clients like yours you can do whatever you want. For a long time, we wondered just how maladjusted our clients are, and if it is true that they are peculiar.

Years ago, in a conversation with Solano Benítez, we asked him about his clients, and we identified very much with his answer. First of all, he clarified that he does not have a commercial relationship with them in the sense that someone pays for a service and on the other side that service is delivered. This type of relationship establishes a hierarchy that does not allow for horizontal dialogue. Rather, he prefers to create a relationship of complicity. He even goes so far as to call his clients accomplices. In this way everything changes, because a relationship of trust is established instead of a commercial one. In this vision, both parties work to achieve "the best project in the world," as opposed to having a relationship in which the architect must try to convince their client to cross over to their side of the shore. From this point of view, there is no madness or weirdness in the client. It is the way in which the bonds are established with the other that generates complicity, which realistically implies that it will not be possible to establish this relationship with all clients.

To start working with a new client, the first thing we look for is that we like each other. We want to work with people who are curious, who are dissatisfied with the injustice of our society, who are rebellious in the face of environmental problems. In this sense, we have realized that our name is strategic.[3] Secondly, the appearance of our workspace also serves as a filter. Normally, there is no middle ground: when someone arrives and sees our old house in the historic center of Quito—always in a process of change, always under construction, a kind of laboratory in constant evolution—that person either connects with us or never comes back.

Having got through these filters, the next thing to do is to explain how we work. Compared with other firms, we are very slow. This slowness is due to the fact that our design process tries to build each step together with the client. We try to establish a deep collaboration with them, to be a team that decides on every part of the development, and to go back as many times as necessary. This means there are no bad surprises at the end, and we don't create something that neither they nor we expected. We know the limits of our ideas and our strength. And by approaching each challenge

[2] The head teacher of the Nueva Esperanza school.

[3] Al Borde translated into English means "On the Edge." It is the state of mind with which we face life: never in the comfort zone, always on the edge.

as if it were the best project in the world, new ideas come and strength is renewed. That is why it is important to identify the commonalities between the client's philosophy and ours, to develop them, and to push them together to their maximum limits. This relationship of complicity that we establish eases the burdens, because the risks and mistakes are shared, so we are much stronger to take on challenges and risks.

fig. 7
Al Borde, Garden House, Quito, Ecuador, 2020. © JAG Studio, 2021.

fig. 8
Al Borde, Garden House, Quito, Ecuador, 2020. © JAG Studio, 2021.

This complicity dilutes the authorship of the projects to the point where it is often impossible to tell whether the idea that pushed the limits of the project was ours or the client's. Understanding this way of making connections with the other, where we are all "partners in crime," enables an understanding of the bathroom in the Garden House ***(fig. 7, 8)***: a glass cubicle in the middle of the countryside. José—the client—was involved in the entire design process and, not only that, he plunged headlong into the construction process; this bond he created with his house led him to understand better than anyone else the potential of each space.

José had decided to build his house in the countryside because he wanted to be more aware of the cycles of nature that run through us all and that urban life has disconnected us from. He wanted to experience them firsthand (which we were very excited about). The big question was whether this relationship he was looking for should be direct as an actor or indirect as an observer. To which he replied, if there is no direct relationship, there is no point. The next thing to understand is: How direct should this relationship be? His ideal was to have the possibility of daily contact, even several times a day, to feel nature—if it is raining, if it is sunny, if it is night, if it is windy—and to be able, for instance, to find a bee and watch its trajectory, which flowers it goes to, if it goes up, if it goes down, if it rests (something that moved us again). The fact that each answer leads us to more specific questions is a clear symbol of how the limits of the project are pushed. The next thing was to understand if what he was looking for was "the possibility of doing it" or "being obliged to do it." At that moment, it was he who got excited and asked us to continue digging, clearly in a game in which we didn't know where we were going, but had the excitement of discovering something.

fig. 9
Al Borde, Raw Threshold Pavilion, Sharjah, UAE, 2023. © Pinxcel, 2023.
fig. 10
Al Borde, Raw Threshold Pavilion, Sharjah, UAE, 2023. © Pinxcel, 2023.
fig. 11
Al Borde, Raw Threshold Pavilion, Sharjah, UAE, 2023. © Pinxcel, 2023.
fig. 12
Al Borde, Raw Threshold Pavilion, Sharjah, UAE, 2023. © Pinxcel, 2023.
fig. 13
Al Borde, Raw Threshold Pavilion, Sharjah, UAE, 2023. © Pinxcel, 2023.

The first conclusion, and the one that will define the project, is that the house will be split and that the spaces will be located a considerable distance apart, so that the way to them allows José to have that direct and literal contact with nature. In the frenzy of the conversation, together we proposed a completely open bathroom in the middle of the field, but after the excitement of the moment, the project evolved into a glass cabin, with some natural elements that surround it for privacy.

Already in the construction stage, once the glass was installed, we were developing the designs to set up some fabric between the trees that would allow a vine plant to grow and thus achieve privacy for the space, but when José was faced with the experience of having a bathroom in total contact with nature, he immediately decided that the vine was not necessary.

No Freedom Please

That we think opportunities are unique, understand the client is an accomplice, and seek to solve projects with seemingly radical simplicity is perhaps the best way to explain how the construction of our Raw Threshold Pavilion in the United Arab Emirates was possible. In 2022, when Tosin Oshinowo invited us to take part in the Sharjah Architecture Triennial, to be held in November of the following year, the challenge she put on the table was to understand how our design approach, which is based on local production, could be translated into the exhibition she was curating under the title *The Beauty of Impermanence: An Architecture of Adaptability.*

Our work is based on the use of local materials and labor, whereas that society is characterized by importing everything from all corners of the planet: we are literally at the antipodes. Working with what is available sets limits on the territory, while having access to everything gives the illusion of infinite abundance.

How do you decide what kind of project to develop when you can literally do whatever you want? This apparent state of freedom is not where we feel most comfortable: we need limits, and it is within those limits that we are able to generate an answer. Since the limits had to be set by us, our pragmatism led us to look for a problem and think about how we could contribute to solving it.

[4] The shade is created using palm tree mats, a material available in the area. They are used in various applications, from the floors of houses to the ceilings of the souks, and even in enclosures. These mats can be easily acquired in any bazaar, offering a variety of types, sizes, shapes, and textures.

The Sharjah Architecture Triennial *(fig. 9-18)* is a very new event: this was its second edition. Its organizers had earmarked two buildings in the city as venues: the old vegetable market and the former Al Qasimiyah Primary School. When we visited these venues, it was clear that they were projects under construction, and as the triennial matured these spaces would also take shape. The opportunity was there in these half-baked processes for something we designed to contribute to the debate about the use of these buildings.

A master plan had been developed for the use of the exterior spaces of Al Qasimiyah School; one of its phases was to be executed for the opening of the triennial in 2023. The master plan had a very clear strategy: in its eagerness to open the school up to the neighborhood as a cultural space, it created two new accesses, which converge in a plaza in front of a restaurant. The master plan ensured the new connection with the neighborhood, but not the use of the space. The strategy was apparently very simple and consisted in creating a shadow, because in a climate like that of the Arab Emirates, it is the shadow that makes the space habitable. To create a shadow in this place was to create a meeting point, and to turn this place of passage into a welcoming space.

This approach of transforming our exhibition into something bigger and of interest beyond the event made the triennial immediately commit to the installation; they stopped being clients to become accomplices and pushed the project to its realization, with all the difficulties that implies. We found an opportunity and we took it to the maximum, without fear, knowing that there were many risks, and also knowing that we were not running them alone: the project was no longer just our project.

These kinds of projects for an exhibition are inherently temporary, something we have always questioned. We decided to make a project whose materiality is rooted in the local, with an easy-to-understand life cycle of materials. The palm mats[4] can slightly degrade over time and

return to nature; the logs can return to the SEWA[5] warehouse and find another life, or they can degrade as well.

The fascinating thing about doing a project in this kind of context is that it allowed us to test the place and exceed our expectations about the uses that the organizers could create for it. During the course of the triennial, we saw photos on Instagram that people shared about outdoor lunches that had been organized there, something that was impossible to imagine when we first visited this place because it was an extremely wild location. Its life extends beyond the triennial; it has earned its place as a welcoming space in the school. The project has multiplied the possibilities that were imagined for the place. It is in the hands of the organizers how long it will stand, and when it fulfills its cycle, the project has a programmed "death" so it will leave a minimal impact.

Architecture is a collective act in which the visible part is the built project that, when able to unite the ambitions of all those involved in the project, reaches a dimension beyond the realized work to become a manifesto capable of building criticism.

Biography

Al Borde is an architecture practice, founded by **David Barragán** (b.1981), **Pascual Gangotena** (b.1977), **Maríaluisa Borja** (b. 1984) and **Esteban Benavides** (b. 1985) in 2007 and is based in Quito, Ecuador. The four partners graduated from the School of Architecture, Design, and Arts at the Pontifical Catholic University of Ecuador. Al Borde questions certainties as to what architecture should or should not be. Their ideas develop with greater precision during the construction process.

Al Borde's practice has received significant recognition including the 2021–2022 Donghia Designer-in-Residence by The Environmental Design Department at Otis College of Art and Design in Los Angeles, listing among the 100+ Best Architecture Firms 2019 by *Domus Magazine*, finalist for Design of the Year 2015 at the Design Museum in London, winner of the Lafarge Holcim Award Acknowledgment for Latin America 2014, the Global Award for Sustainable Architecture 2013 in Paris, the Schelling Architecture Prize 2012, and the Bicentenary Medal for Cultural Merit by the Ministry of Culture and Heritage of Ecuador 2012.

Al Borde's work has been included in landmark exhibitions such as *The Beauty of the Impermanence* at the Sharjah Architecture Triennial 2023, *Crossroads* at the Seoul Biennial of Architecture and Urbanism 2021, *Reporting from the Front* at the 2016 Venice Architecture Biennial, *Share and Exchange* at the Kultursymposium (Weimar, 2016), *The State of the Art* at the Chicago Architecture Biennial 2015, *Think Global, Build Social! Architectures for a Better World* (Vienna, 2014), *Réenchanter le Monde* at the Cité de l'architecture & du patrimoine (Paris, 2014), and *Ways to Collaborate* at the São Paulo Architecture Biennial 2013.

Al Borde partners are engaged in teaching, lecturing, conducting workshops, and serving as jury members and reviewers at various universities, institutions, and conferences across the Americas, Europe, Asia, and the Middle East, such as professor at Columbia University in New York, USA; professor at UCAL in Lima, Peru; lecturer at Tonji University in Shanghai, China; lecturer at Cité de l'Architecture & du Patrimoine in Paris, France; jurist at Solar Decathlon Latin America and Caribbean in Cali, Colombia; and jurist at Quito Architecture Biennial in Quito, Ecuador.

fig. 14
Al Borde, Raw Threshold Pavilion, Sharjah, UAE, 2023.© Danko Stjepanovic. Courtesy of Sharjah Architecture Triennial 2023.

fig. 15
Al Borde, Raw Threshold Pavilion, Sharjah, UAE, 2023. © Shahbaz Ahmed, 2023.

fig. 16
Al Borde, Raw Threshold Pavilion, Sharjah, UAE, 2023. © Danko Stjepanovic. Courtesy of Sharjah Architecture Triennial 2023.

fig. 17
Al Borde, Raw Threshold Pavilion, Sharjah, UAE, 2023. © Danko Stjepanovic. Courtesy of Sharjah Architecture Triennial 2023.

fig. 18
Al Borde, Raw Threshold Pavilion, Sharjah, UAE, 2023. © Ahmed Osama. Courtesy of Sharjah Architecture Triennial 2023.

[5] The Sharjah Electricity, Water, and Gas Authority (SEWA) has initiated a process of replacing wooden poles with metal ones, which has resulted in a hundred preserved wooden poles being stored in their depot. The best ones are selected, the damaged ends cut off, and a package of logs of various sizes is obtained, tall enough to assemble a structure which can provide an area of shade.

Al Borde's work has been widely published. The Mexican periodical *Arquine* published Al Borde's monograph titled *Less in All* in 2020. Additionally, Al Borde edited *Las Tres Esperanzas* in 2020, a book that tells the story of a decade-long collaboration with the community of Puerto Cabuyal, focusing on a long-term project centered on community participation.

In 2017, Al Borde co-produced the documentary film *Do More With Less*, which explores the practices of the post-bankruptcy-crisis generation of young architecture studios in Ecuador, highlighting their innovative approaches to the role of the architect in society. In 2023, they co-produced the short film *Building with Living Trees*, the first episode of a documentary series that explores Al Borde's works, unveiling the social, environmental, political, cultural, and human contexts surrounding these projects. The series aims to foster a deeper understanding of architecture and its societal impact.

Sound of Silence: Chinese Architects Rediscovering Classical Gardens

Jin Qiuye and Chang Tao

fig. 1
Helou Pavilion in the Square Pagoda Garden. Photo: Chang Tao, 2023.

The classical courtyard garden is a paradigm of traditional Chinese architecture. Numerous Chinese architects of the early twenty-first century have been incorporating their interpretation of the design sensibilities of classical Chinese courtyard gardens into their architecture. The environmental, spatial, and cultural characteristics of these gardens are summarized. The history of the study of classical courtyard gardens and the translation of their design principles into the twenty-first century are reviewed systematically. Case studies demonstrate how contemporary Chinese "garden architecture" has transcended the boundaries between traditional gardens and modern architecture by exploring the classical design principles and de-symbolization, giving rise to new formal languages and indigenous architectural design theories. This broadly shared approach can be seen as both a critique of and a complement to rationalism.

keywords:
classical Chinese courtyard gardens, modern translation, locality, architectural theory, garden architecture

Introduction

"Great sound is silent."
—Lao Tzu, *Tao Te Ching*

Powerful ideas are wordless. "Form" communicates in more direct and powerful ways than written discourses such as "architectural criticism." In a world filled with theories, the way to clarity could be found by embracing the "language of form." Any honest architecture embodies comprehensive judgments on the discipline's history, the local environment, practical constraints, and the human condition; it inevitably involves a critical dimension. In the context of China, the disconnection from ancient architectural traditions and the problems brought about by modernization manifest the lack of a conscious mastery of architecture's formal languages. Over the past decade, some Chinese architects have sought answers within tradition, revaluing the relevance of the design sensibilities expressed in classical Chinese gardens and engaging in a series of interpretations and translations.

Contemporary "garden architecture" in China is neither landscape architecture nor the study of architecture within gardens. Garden architecture is a unique genre and practice focused on classical Chinese gardens. It combines the theories, methods, and research of modern architecture to explore the universal value of classical gardens. It seeks to integrate the ideals of living with gardens and their creative possibilities into modern architecture.

The Characteristics of Classical Chinese Gardens

Chinese garden making and house building are both related to issues of "space design," but according to modern academic classification, they belong to the disciplines of "landscape architecture" and "architecture" respectively. However, from the perspective of garden architecture, this boundary does not exist. Compared with other ancient Chinese books on construction, the design strategies, construction methods, and detail patterns revealed in Ji Cheng's *Yuan Ye*[1] (The Craft of Gardens) all address

[1] Ji Cheng , *Yuan Ye* (1582–1642), originally published c.1634, late Ming dynasty.

real architectural problems. Furthermore, the book expands the spectrum of construction materials to include natural objects, extending the purpose of construction from quotidian life to spiritual cultivation.[2] The rise and development of Chinese garden architecture in the twenty-first century are closely related to the rediscovery and interpretation of *Yuan Ye* by some visionary Chinese architects.

Yuan Ye distinguishes itself from other architectural or garden treatises in that its design philosophy or environmental thinking is rooted in Taoist philosophy. One aspect of this is the aesthetic ideal of design "created by humans, as if created by nature," and another aspect is the design method of "borrowing." The borrowed objects are diverse, allowing *Yuan Ye* to encompass various aspects of the natural and the artificial world. It integrates personal gardening activities into a broader "architecture," achieving a phenomenological sense of "dwelling." The humanistic aspect of *Yuan Ye* is also reflected in its subtlety and thoughtfulness. This elevates it beyond being a mere technical manual for a specific time and place, reflecting humanity's universal pursuit of nature. In Ji Cheng's design philosophy, the world (as the background of construction) serves as a rich historical and cultural system. As part of this system, "nature" is not an objectively neutral external environment but a cultural condition that must be acknowledged and integrated. Consequently, architecture is not an inward logical structure dependent on mathematics and geometry. Instead, it is a subsystem residing in a larger context that constantly exchanges information with the external environment. The external conditions must be carefully considered, and architecture has to participate in a system alongside nature to form the overall environment and cultural construction. "Construction" thus becomes a matter of "environmental relationship," viewing all new constructions and renovations as forms of "renewal" with natural–historical significance. Through ubiquitous "borrowing," it embodies a dual respect for history and the future. This philosophy holds significant implications for contemporary urban renewal.

Since the Ming and Qing dynasties, Zhang Nanyuan (Zhang Lian, 1587–c.1671), Ji Cheng, Ge Yuliang (1764–1830), and many unknown garden designers have left us with rich legacies. Despite centuries of modifications, this heritage has retained its essence and can be found throughout China. Chinese gardens provide a unique living environment, situated between reality and idealism, sensibility and poiesis. They bear profound cultural imprints while being universally appreciated. Classical Chinese gardens are a convergence of poetry, calligraphy, painting, seals, plaques, inscriptions, plants, and rockeries, and a comprehensive set of construction techniques have been accumulated for their creation. They embrace a closeness to nature while fully considering human comfort and hygiene needs. Gardens have served as the backdrop to many traditional Chinese operas, stories, and poems throughout history, thereby becoming deeply ingrained in the hearts and minds of the Chinese people. It can be said that gardens represented a level of personal freedom that was extremely rare to attain in ancient China's strictly hierarchical society, serving to counterbalance the compulsory aspects of daily life. Undoubtedly, gardens are perhaps the only spatial type closely related to individual experience and free consciousness in the long history of ancient China.

Theoretical Background of Garden Study

During the Second Sino–Japanese War, Tung Chuin (Tong Jun, 1900–1983) was one of the first scholars of the modern era to rediscover the spiritual values and spatial meanings of Chinese gardens. He single-handedly visited and surveyed the classical gardens of Jiangnan and authored the highly influential garden classic *Jiangnan Yuanlin Zhi* (Record of Jiangnan gardens).[3] This book accurately documented the existing

[2] Chen Zhi, *Yuanye Zhushi*, 2nd ed. (Beijing: China Architecture & Building Press, 2017), 75.

[3] *Jiangnan Yuanlin Zhi* was completed in 1937 and published in 1963.

conditions of gardens in eastern China. From a modern perspective and architectural standpoint, Tung Chuin raised a series of garden-related issues, such as the three spiritual realms of Chinese gardening: "density-varying, path-winding, scenery in view."[4] This goes beyond mere aesthetic judgment; it is a methodology for garden making. Tung Chuin's rediscovery and critical examination of Chinese gardens opened the door to garden architecture.

In the 1980s, architects such as Mo Bozhi (1915–2003), Wang Dahong (1917–2018), Ge Ruliang (1926–89), and Chen Qikuan (1921–2007) all engaged in valuable research and practices from the perspective of combining modern architecture with traditional gardens. Two events in particular deeply influenced later garden architecture. The first was Feng Jizhong's (1915–2009) creation of the Square Pagoda Garden (1978–82, Songjiang, Shanghai), which is quiet, spacious, and of an ancient elegance, unlike the narrow and complex gardens of the Ming and Qing dynasties. During the 1980s, there were no tangible examples of Tang and Song dynasty gardens; the Square Pagoda Garden made people aware of more possibilities in the artistic range of gardens. In terms of construction technology, the Helou Pavilion provided a simple yet diverse indigenous construction ***(fig. 1)***. It is a modern and interpretable creation that transcends common rational systems, holding groundbreaking significance. The concept "Join the Past, Become the New" is fully manifested here, and Wang Shu (b. 1963) regards the Square Pagoda Garden as "a measure of modern Chinese architecture."[5] The second event was I. M. Pei's (1917–2019) design of the Beijing Xiangshan Hotel (Fragrant Hill Hotel, 1978–82), which sparked extensive discussions about the relationship between tradition and modernity at the time.[6] The Xiangshan Hotel, as an attempt to translate Jiangnan gardens, was completed amid controversy, leaving many unresolved questions.

It seems that the only consensus is that the application of simple forms is not the path to traditional revival. In the 1990s, the collective abandonment of the "big roof" style coincided with a large influx of foreign architects. Chinese architects lacked a distinct language, lacked profound reflections with a contemporary spirit, and lacked a strong voice within the international architectural community. These issues were suddenly magnified as Chinese architecture became part of the global context. It was during this time that classical Chinese gardens once again attracted people's attention.

In 1997, Chang Yung Ho (b. 1956) published the book *FCJZ*, in the preface of which he explicitly outlined his views.[7] He discussed topics ranging from the perspective of traditional Chinese painting to the visual and physical experience in the Master of Nets Garden. Looking at gardens from a modern spatial perspective, he raised new questions. Under the guidance of Wang Mingxian (b. 1960), the editor-in-chief of the magazine *Architect*, architects like Chang Yung Ho and Wang Shu engaged in dialogues with artists like Sui Jianguo (b. 1956) and Wang Jianwei (b. 1958).[8] In 2000, the Architecture Research Center of Peking University was established as one of the cradles of contemporary Chinese architectural thought. The modern transformation of classical Chinese garden design gradually became one of the many topics of interest. Dong Yugan's (b. 1967) research direction also shifted towards garden design. Seizing this opportunity, the Architecture Research Center of Peking University organized two garden seminars, bringing together scholars and architects like Wang Shu, Tong Ming (b. 1968), and Ge Ming (b. 1972). At this time, after completing the construction of the Bird's Nest, Li Xinggang (b. 1969) also began to develop a growing interest in classical Chinese gardens. The environment in which to discuss garden architecture was essentially formed.

4 Tung Chuin, *Jiangnan Yuanlin Zhi*, 2nd ed. (Beijing: China Architecture & Building Press, 2014), 16.
5 Wang Shu, "To Recollect Fang Ta Garden," *World Architecture Review*, no. 3 (2008): 57.
6 Gu Mengchao, "Discussions on Xiangshan Hotel," *Architectural Journal*, no. 3 (1983): 57.
7 Chang Yung Ho, *FCJZ* (Harbin: Heilongjiang Science & Technology Press, 1997).
8 Rao Xiaojun and Yao Xiaoling, "Experiments and Conversations," *Architect*, no. 10 (1996): 80.

The first garden seminar directly focused on the theme "Garden and Architecture," while the second one concerned "Body and Architecture." This was not only because "body" is a primary subject of phenomenological discussions and a crucial tool in contemporary architectural theory but also because the first-person, subjective experience is a primary characteristic of Chinese gardens. In modern times, objective and rational scientific thinking dominate, treating humans as unified analytical samples and emphasizing commonalities. The subjective experience of first-person perspective, on the other hand, implies starting from the individual and emphasizing human diversity. By emphasizing the importance of "bodily experience," contemporary Chinese discussions on gardens not only bridged phenomenology and traditional culture but also, for the first time, highlighted the significant position of classical garden spaces within the framework of modern architectural knowledge. This laid a theoretical foundation for later explorations in practice.

fig. 2
Xiangshan Campus (Phase II). Photo: Chang Tao, 2013.

fig. 3
Tiles Hill. Photo: Jin Qiuye, 2014.

Modern Translation of Classical Gardens in Contemporary China

Around the year 2000, Wang Shu was commissioned to design the Xiangshan Campus of China Academy of Art and completed the construction of Phase I in 2004 and Phase II in 2007 ***(fig. 2)***. The Xiangshan Campus is the result of Wang Shu's long-term contemplation on Chinese gardens and urban settlements.[9] Wang delved into various aspects such as history and reality, East and West, urban and rural, and theory and practice. These issues became particularly pronounced at the turn of the century with the progress of urbanization in China, the introduction of foreign architectural trends, and the influx of overseas architects. Despite being fundamental problems, they were seldom seriously discussed. When these buildings materialized in real form, their theoretical significance surpassed mere hypothetical plans or textual discussions. Wang Shu's solutions carried a strong experimental flavor. Unlike Chang Yung Ho's gentle heuristic criticism, Wang can be said to have thrown many issues directly in people's faces, sparking intense discussion. This discussion became more widespread and profound after Wang won the Pritzker Prize in 2012, providing different perspectives for the reevaluation of gardens.

[9] Wang Shu and Lu Wenyu, "Xiangshan Campus of China Academy of Art," *Architectural Journal*, no. 9 (2008): 51.

Wang Shu's designs are based on a thoughtful look at Chinese traditions, especially gardens and landscapes in the form of Chinese Shanshui (mountains and water) paintings. The ideal world reflected in ancient landscape paintings not only forms the basis of traditional gardens but also shapes the way people observe and contemplate the world. Wang reminds us that the way people perceive the world is historical and cultural, and the modes of representation not only are related to materials and tools but also reflect different individual life consciousnesses. Many of his works can find similar painterly foundations, employing modular assembly to seek the "propensity" of landscapes and the perspective of wandering.[10] These methods date back to the pre-garden state, reconstructing architectural design principles from a more basic stance of "observation and representation." These are topics that Chinese architects have not previously explored.

Wang Shu thinks buildings should be like the mountains in paintings—rugged, with nonlinear folded exteriors and deep interiors, stretching endlessly and offering different views at different points ***(fig. 3)***. This gives the architecture a spatial richness and romantic form, much like natural mountains. Wang's goal is not to create a "mountain-like" building but rather a "world filled with differences." This concept originates from typology, describing internal features of primitive human settlements or forms in nature, like a forest: similar everywhere, yet different everywhere. He thinks it is important not to make things too simple or too abstract, but instead to connect with our real experiences. Wang employs a richly diverse typology to compensate for the absence of the "body" in modern architecture. He uses "ways of seeing" to achieve a "vision of Shanshui" and "natural narratives," believing that the "method of gardening" serves as a means of translation between Shanshui painting and modern architecture. At the core of Wang's realization of a "Shanshui world" is the creation of differences. His architecture is a critique of uniformity and standardization.[11]

Dong Yugan's Red Brick Art Museum, completed in 2012, reflects his interest in the singular use of material and commemorative space. By the time of the construction of Xiaozuo Art Museum (2017) and the renovation design of Wind H Art Center (2019–20, ***fig. 4***), he had developed a new approach using a collage of new and old materials to pursue the aesthetic of traditional gardens. Dong created an introspective spatial perspective, then used simple and authentic modern materials (such as steel and concrete) in conjunction with the original buildings to form a binary and mutually reinforcing internal tension. In both projects, the juxtaposition of the lightweight steel

[10] Jin Qiuye, "A Gaze and a Glance," *Architectural Journal*, no. 1 (2014): 18.
[11] Wang Shu, "Constructing a World of Difference," *World Architecture Review*, no. 12 (2011): 112.

fig. 4
Interior of Wind H Art Center. Photo: Jin Qiuye, 2019.

fig. 5
Xishan Garden. Photo: Chen Hao, 2023.

structure and the substantial concrete creates a strong contrast, suggesting the intertwining of plants with rocks in a garden. The collage of diverse materials and the fragmented management of paths at different elevations are deeply connected to the nuanced and balanced layout of classical gardens. Dong's pursuit of the sense of remoteness represents the profound and poetic meaning of Chinese garden spaces. It gradually sheds the symbolic language, returning to a simple, vibrant, and natural essence. Using the courtyard's in-between character to blur inside and outside provides a beneficial strategy for contemporary urban renewal, fitting with the Chinese garden principle of "appropriate volume and borrowing." From form to meaning, these works comprehensively transcend the boundaries between classical gardens and modern architecture.[12]

Dong Yugan explores a type of "courtyard garden architecture" closely linked to "living." It is known that Chinese living spaces have moved far away from nature. Dong not only attempts to bring back a way of life centered around courtyards but also follows the path of ancient gardeners, creating layers and depth in confined spaces to evoke feelings of seclusion or vastness. Dong's designs emphasize the body's experience. Walking through them, your senses are constantly activated, with frequent changes in direction and views. The sequences are rich with details, much like walking through a garden. Almost every visible spot is accessible, with endless exploration possible and an added touch of poetry. Dong has studied the spatial features of Chinese gardens in depth, and from these studies has created an open design approach. Like ancient gardeners, he uses artificial elements as well as natural features like stones and trees. He intertwines these elements, giving the composition a high level of complexity and natural poetry. In a featured case called Xishan Garden **(*fig. 5*)**, modern elements are predominant, but due to the inclusion of natural elements a mountainous feeling is evoked.

[12] Dong Yugan, "Making Courtyards In-Between—Design of Wind H Art Center," *Architectural Journal*, no. 9 (2020): 62.

fig. 6
Songyang Three-Temple Cultural Communication Center. Photo: Jin Qiuye, 2020.

fig. 7
Dongxian Garden. Photo: Arch-Exist, 2020.

Liu Jiakun (b. 1956) excels in "dealing with reality." His West Village·Basis Yard squeezed various elements into a vast modern concrete structure, encompassing local life, flea markets, sports fields, bamboo groves, and ponds. Here, history and reality converge, delicacy coexists with roughness, creating an urbanism of unique locality. Liu's Suzhou Imperial Kiln Brick Museum uses a winding walkway to connect different buildings. The handling of "introverted space," especially through the combination of modern and traditional materials, creates a distinctive atmosphere that is neither ancient nor modern. This recalls the architectural explorations of the 1980s by architects like Feng Jizhong and Ge Ruliang, who integrated classical gardens with modern forms in landscape architecture. For the Culture Neighborhood·Songyang Three-Temple Cultural Communication Center project, Liu Jiakun used a continuous corridor. However, this time the connected buildings are located throughout the neighborhood, seamlessly embedded with irregular boundaries into the interior of the urban block, breaking the clear linear spatial sequence and blurring inside and outside ***(fig. 6)***. This design strategy establishes a symbiotic relationship between gardens and urban textures.

Liu's approach is similar to the core idea in classical Chinese gardening: to borrow or utilize the given situation. When things do not fit as planned, instead of fighting against them, one should go with the flow, making the best use of the opportunity. The goal of design is to work with the natural forces of reality, showing strength and following trends, becoming a part of the flow of time and space. Architecture and nature should not be in a hierarchical or antagonistic relationship. They should neither harm nor protect each other, but rather engage each other in harmony by combining forces to reveal the presence of the other. In the renovation of Tianbao cave district in Erlang town (Dongxian Garden, ***fig. 7***), nestled between high mountains and a river, Liu Jiakun scattered a series of buildings to adapt to the terrain. The composition

fig. 8
National Sliding Center. Photo: Jin Qiuye, 2021.

creates the illusion of overhanging eaves, emphasizing the contours of the landscape. Simple weathered steel is used to generate a soaring gesture, while concrete and stone form a sturdy foundation. Through the contrast of light and heavy elements, the design pays tribute to Song dynasty Shanshui paintings, showing a remarkable romantic spirit. While Liu does not specifically emphasize how his design ideas are derived from classical gardens, what he expresses in his design strategies and explores in architectural forms align with classic garden designs, and even traditional architecture in a broader sense. That is the concept of "borrowing" from all existing conditions. Whether they are found in urban or natural, positive or negative situations, by ingeniously applying these ideas and absorbing them into new environments and rejuvenating them with fresh vitality, Liu's architecture showcases a deep understanding and flexible application of Chinese garden design.

The study of classical Chinese gardens, starting from the initial documentation to the exploration of their history, gradually became integrated with Chinese architectural design practice. By the first decade of the new century, studies had expanded to various aspects related to gardens, including natural concepts, the life of the literati, mountain imagery, social psychology, and material systems. Beyond the material entities and artistic imagination, technical research on gardening methods, such as the formation of rockeries and the assembly of timber structures, has gradually developed in depth. However, following in the footsteps of ancient "garden making" is far from a dominant present-day practice, and the association of gardens with the life of the literati has no foundation now, meaning even imaginative reconstructions lack an existential basis. In the context of modern architecture and landscape architecture, interest in garden architecture should be of a more fundamental and broader character. The understanding of Chinese gardens themselves should also break free from the limitations of "vernacular" forms, exploring universal spatial theories and methods without losing their unique characteristics.

In 2018, Tong Ming translated his grandfather Tung Chuin's English work *Glimpses of Gardens in Eastern China* into Chinese, with Tung Chuin's words printed on the title page: "Taste counts here much more than mere know-how." In the preface, titled "Just for Taste," Wang Shu pointed out that "taste" is fundamental to garden making and the life within gardens: "Because gardens are not just visual objects, but also physical experiences. The former owners of gardens spent years living in them, time passed and life acquired a flavor."[13] Taste is the praise of life itself, and the subject of praise is the individual who views nature from a civilized perspective. Gardens represent the collective imagination of the Chinese literati regarding individual freedom. They are both historical and transcend time and space, capable of being appreciated and admired by modern people. Tong Ming borrowed Foucault's terminology, referring to the Chinese garden as "heterotopia," believing that people utilize gardens to create an "illusory space": "Different from the completely hierarchical and ordered spaces in real society, the Chinese garden is a world where reality and illusion coexist, a world interwoven with proximity and distance, the present and the future, closure and openness, rupture and continuity. . . . People reflect upon themselves in an environment full of vitality, experience the flow of life, and derive spiritual pleasure from it."[14] Gardens are a tribute to individual life.

In 2013, Li Xinggang completed the Jixi Museum, creating an inward-facing layout with multiple courtyards and undulating roofs that echo the mountains. Li Xinggang proposed the concept of "Geometry and Poetic Scenery," which refers to the scenery in one's heart, representing cultural aesthetics through subjective experiences. Geometry is closely associated with modern architecture, approaching nature through rational operations from an external-to-internal perspective. This concept reflects Li's professional ideal of bridging the gap between subject and object, aiming to achieve a unity of architecture and its surroundings. The National Sliding Center designed for the 2022 Beijing Winter Olympics ***(fig. 8)*** aptly demonstrates how geometric forms can harmonize with mountainous environments, striving to shape a new and experiential natural "garden." This building is not only a modern spectacle but also an inward-focused garden that offers a deeply immersive experience.[15] The designer considered the climate and topographical features of the south-facing ridge, the movement and body postures of the bobsleigh and luge, and the complex flow and management requirements of large-scale events. By weaving a winding pathway through the interior and exterior spaces, centering the individual "view," the design seamlessly integrates modern sports competitions into the natural mountains and forests of the north.

Ge Ming, as one of the main participants in discussions on classical Chinese gardens, has demonstrated his knowledge of them in his designs for the Ru Yuan Garden, the Wei Yuan Garden, and the Spring Garden, all of which explore the relationship between architecture and gardens. Traditionally, the architecture is a part of the garden. But in Ge Ming's designs, the garden is accommodated within the architecture, or the architecture incorporates the imagery of mountains. His "Six Approaches to Garden"[16] are essentially design principles to achieve garden-like qualities in modern architecture, rather than creating gardens in urban spaces or imitating classical garden layouts with modern architecture. The design of the Spring Garden is about "half garden, half house"[17] and involves shaping a winding garden through the terrain beneath a unified roof ***(fig. 9)***. Ge Ming keenly recognizes the relationship between the Loosian "Raumplan" and the spatial complexity of Chinese gardens, providing a new perspective for understanding the abstract forms of gardens.

[13] Tung Chuin, *Dongnan Yuanshu*, trans. Tong Ming (Changsha: Hunan Fine Arts Publishing House, 2018), 6.

[14] Tong Ming, "The Gardens in South-Eastern China as a Concept of Heterotopia," *Architectural Journal*, no. 12 (2017): 103.

[15] Li Xinggang and Jin Qiuye, "The Fitting of Nature and Sense," *Architecture Technique*, no. 12 (2021): 40.

[16] Ge Ming, "Notes on the Design of Ru Yuan Garden," *Time+Architecture*, no. 2 (2011): 94.

[17] Ge Ming, "Notes on the Spring Garden," *Architectural Journal*, no. 1 (2020): 55.

Conclusions

fig. 9
Interior of the Spring Garden. Photo: Jiang Menglin, 2019.

In 2006, with the completion of I. M. Pei's Suzhou Museum, it seemed that there was a standard answer for the modern translation of classical Chinese gardens. However, during the same period, works like Wang Shu's Ningbo Museum and Phase II of the Xiangshan Campus proposed entirely different approaches. The discussions on garden architecture centered around the Architecture Research Center of Peking University and the China Academy of Art in Hangzhou have also flourished, influencing a generation of scholars and inspiring many young architects to embrace this as their professional focus. Blindly copying ancient ways is not advocated; instead, the goal for today's Chinese architects should be to draw nourishment from classical Chinese gardens, translating what has been derived from studying them into modern architectural expressions and construction systems to shape an ideal living environment.

From a contemporary perspective, Chinese gardens possess rich physical scales and extremely high spatial density, emphasizing design methods based on borrowing and on following the natural flow. They form complex systems comprising artificial and natural elements. Their asymmetrical layouts and decentralized forms represent the pursuit of spiritual freedom. The Chinese architectural community has continuously studied classical Chinese gardens throughout the past century, but the vast difference between ancient gardens and modern architectural expressions has hindered direct appreciation and application. Chinese architects are facing a modern world that feels very regular and streamlined, lacking natural touches and subtle experiences. Since 2000, Chinese architects have studied the formative ideas expressed in ancient paintings and classical Chinese gardens, and have used their design imagination together with local building conditions to fuse memories with new creations in their respective modern architectural language. These buildings may not be a direct link to the past, but they carry a deep sense of appreciation and thus human connection that the modern era sometimes lacks. The forms provide a genuine critique of rationalism, saying a lot without even speaking.

Biography

Jin Qiuye, MIT Research Scholar; PhD from Tsinghua University; member of the Comité International des Critiques d'Architecture (CICA); member of the Architectural Society of China; professor at Beijing University of Civil Engineering and Architecture (BUCEA); architect, scholar, and critic. Founder of Jin Architects Studio. Research fields include the translation of Chinese traditional design language into modern architecture and contemporary experimental architecture in China. He is the author of more than ten academic books including *A House is also a Garden* and *Foreign Body Sensation*, and the editor of journals such as *Arcadia: Painting and Garden* and *Readers on Chinese Architecture and Criticism*. He is also the Chinese translator of more than thirty architectural theory books including *Transparency* and *Luis Barragán: Search and Creativity*. His design works include the Wind H Art Center 751, the Folding House, and the Hexagonal Court.

Chang Tao PhD. Candidate at Beijing University of Civil Engineering and Architecture, member of the Student Association of the Architectural Society of China.

Construction as a Critique

Wang Shu

fig. 1
Buildings constructed for the 2008 Olympic Games.

This conference has a special significance in that it focuses on the question of whether construction can be a medium of critique. This is an important discussion. For our studio, architecture has the capacity to bear memory. For us, buildings often include materials that can be recycled and reused to carry forth memory—that is the way we connect the physical with the metaphysical. But why do we do this? Because China has a special context.

keywords:
continuing tradition, recycling resources, vernacular crafts, respecting nature

As almost all architects in the world know, China has been building fast, especially in its cities, mainly in the last thirty years. If, for example, I showed you some images of a city and didn't tell you that it was Beijing, you would not know where it was. This kind of city means the future for some people: a huge new city. It has very good infrastructure, highways, high-speed train systems, and high-rise buildings usually built of concrete. The concrete forest is interspersed with some trees in the middle, known as landscaping. People usually think all this heralds a very bright future. Another example is this typical and famous swimming center in Beijing, which was built with completely new materials for the 2008 Olympic Games ***(fig. 1)***. It has absolutely nothing to do with the cultural traditions of the area. There are other strange forms of high-rise buildings. Some say that these forms are bearers of traditional Chinese cultural meaning, but they are so unusual that this so-called relationship is just a fabrication.

Lu Wenyu and I have our Amateur Architecture Studio in Hangzhou. Hangzhou is to the south of Shanghai. The journey takes an hour by high-speed train. Why are we based in Hangzhou? Because we think that Hangzhou is the most special city among all metropolises in China. The most beautiful thing about Hangzhou is that the mountains and the water are present in the city center. It is unbelievable that even in the city center there is still a lake and a surrounding landscape. This view has not changed in the last thousand years, as can be seen when an ancient painting from the Song dynasty is compared with the contemporary view ***(fig. 2)***. However, if one turns around to look in the other direction, one will find that context has been altered considerably ***(fig. 3)***. Nevertheless, given this combination of old and new, it is still possible to claim that many memories and buildings remain. In other cities of this scale, new and old buildings are usually mixed together ***(fig. 4)***. The blending of memory and reality is discussed in a similar way. Architects usually talk about different methods of urban planning, urban design, basic concepts of architecture, about different forms, different archetypes, or about different ways of landscaping. But in fact, when looking at this mix of new and old, of buildings and landscapes, in my experience as an architect, it means that there is implicitly an architecture that is closer to nature.

To me, large and small mean two different worlds. A world full of small things is sustainable. It does not just mean tradition. It means a sustainable world. But a huge modern building usually means that it is unsustainable. It is simply too big. In real life, a common-sense way of living is where memories are still present in trivial realities, but people can choose to ignore them. When I was carrying out research in rural Hangzhou, I found that almost the same things we can see in this painting from a thousand years ago were still there; very beautiful ***(fig. 5)***. Such villages have existed sustainably for over a thousand years. I saw these incredibly beautiful things that embodied the skills of those who built them ***(fig. 6)***. All these things were made by common people, but each one looked like a masterpiece of some kind. Villages are usually like this.

fig. 2
(Top) Southern Song dynasty, Li Song, *West Lake*, scroll. (Bottom) Hangzhou from the same perspective today.

fig. 3
Looking from the West Lake towards the present-day city.

fig. 4
A mix of old and new buildings in Hangzhou.

fig. 5
Northern Song dynasty, Guo Xi, *Old Tree, Level Distance.*

fig. 6
The countryside of Zhejiang, which is almost unchanged and where very beautiful things can still be found.

fig. 7
Corridor bridge spanning thirty to forty meters in the mountains of southern Zhejiang province.

fig. 8
Hand-ramming earth in Hangzhou, 2000.

We like to conduct research in these villages. This does not mean that we favor the traditional, it means that we want to look for a different understanding of the basic concepts of architecture. For example, the materials used in the villages are small, very small. However, in ancient China, there were also large-sized materials. For example, two thousand years ago, bricks were enormous. Tiles were also huge, similar to those used in ancient Rome. But in the last thousand years, the traditional Chinese construction system has changed a lot.

Over the two to three thousand years of China's history for which there is physical evidence, many environmental crises have been encountered. For example, according to documents from two thousand years ago, emperors built so many huge houses that eventually there were no trees left on the mountains. Thus, people had to change their materials and building systems. Gradually, they developed a system that used small-sized elements. This meant smaller materials that were more accessible and easier for ordinary people to handle could now be used. The construction process thus became more civilized and generalized, resulting in better-quality buildings. It was a completely different idea. Even a thousand years ago, it was already possible to build bridges across creeks and rivers with these very common, small wood elements via a special weaving process. The largest spans were between thirty and forty meters ***(fig. 7)***. This is truly ancient high technology. But in the last thirty years, in the name of building modernization, we ourselves have destroyed this old tradition, this material and construction system, very quickly.

For example, twenty years ago, there were forty thousand villages in the province of Zhejiang; now, there are only thirty thousand of them left. About 10 percent of their traditional houses still exist. The traditional building method has been destroyed by the modern system of professional architecture, including construction technology. That is why we call our office an amateur building studio. Amateur means ordinary people. They know how to build a house. The professional system is actually a very bad system in relation to tradition and nature, as it is abstract and not in touch with reality. So we began to change our thinking, and this decisive change began with thinking with our hands ***(fig. 8)***. Using your hands does not just mean a particular human experience.

fig. 9
Tile Garden, 2006; the first Chinese Pavilion at the Venice Architecture Biennale.

fig. 10
Tile roof, tree shadow, bamboo bridge.

Building by hand is a completely different way of building. In one of our early experiments in 2000, my wife and I rammed earth together for the first time. It meant that two architects could build something. It was only a small thing, but important to us. Even more importantly, it was the first time that we used recycled materials from an abandoned site. Some critics talk about our architectural style; they think we're more into traditional styles, implying that I am a traditional architect rather than a contemporary architect, but the truth is, I'm not interested in the past: I'm just interested in the differences between traditional and contemporary styles.

It is from this small difference that we can think about how to reshape rural culture in contemporary China. But it is not just rural culture; it means something that really touches the future and is equally important for cities. It means a different view of the future. For us, the first thing we usually think about is recycled materials, and that does not just encompass the physical aspect of materials. It also includes recyclable memory and recyclable time. Very few contemporary architects have a sense of time. They don't care about time. They just want to get the construction done as quickly as possible. We have carried out many little experiments in this area. For example, in 2006 we designed the first Chinese National Pavilion at the Venice Architecture Biennale. We did this installation in Venice, and it was set against the backdrop that everywhere in China, from the cities to the countryside, there were sites with demolished traditional buildings. In order to build cities, it seems that the countryside has to be demolished, that traditions have to be demolished. Is there any other choice? We are also faced with a huge amount of discarded material. Before we started to recycle this material for our buildings, it was similar to the waste that is discarded everywhere in China. The materials have lost their meaning; they have lost their identity, their value, and their dignity. For this installation in Venice, on the shaded lawn of the original site, we designed a garden of eight hundred square meters, entirely in an architectural way. As we were not allowed to alter the ground, it meant that we had to install a substructure. This we built with five thousand pieces of bamboo and sixty thousand pieces of small recycled Chinese green tiles ***(fig. 9)***. We had six studio members and three artisans. Working together, we built this eight-hundred-square-meter tile garden

fig. 11
Wooden theater construction site, House of World Cultures, Berlin, Germany, 2012.

fig. 12
Very light system, no base, gently placed on a platform.

in half a month, fifteen days. It was interesting to notice that this tile garden became almost like a living thing. It looks like a creeping animal breathing there, like a huge mirror reflecting the shadows of the big moving trees. We also built a bamboo bridge on which people could walk ***(fig. 10)***. When people walked on it, they realized that all structures are flexible. It was a place with which people could engage. It was very close to being a real building. For us, this fact is very important because we did not make a sculpture, but a building.

We were invited to rebuild this tile garden in Berlin for 2012; however, we designed something new, but with memories from Venice. We built an open-air theater using wood, with the help of five or six German artists. There was not much work available for artists at that time, so they were able to join our project. Some of them were landscape architects, some of them were sculptors. In fact, it was a very large-scale construction. We finished this wooden theater in a week ***(fig. 11)***. Importantly, we had a very clear idea of the whole construction process. The context is very special. It is called the House of World Cultures. Originally, it was a gift given to Germany by the United States after World War II for use as a conference hall. It is a very large and heavy reinforced-concrete building. In contrast, we built this very light system without foundations. It is resting gently on the hall's platform, creating a stark contrast with the main building ***(fig. 12)***. It is clearly a different system for the future.

We have also designed and built museums. To us, a museum is more than just a building. It stores memories and time. A typical case is the Ningbo History Museum. The site is at the center of a huge new city. Architects in China are often faced with very scary situations. When we started to design this new museum, we realized that it was in an empty place. The city demolished thirty old villages in this area to generate a completely empty area. Then architects were invited to design a museum here without any context, without history, without a cultural lineage; it was like being asked to design something on the moon or on Mars. So how does one rebuild a context? It is not just about what is around you, because everything has disappeared. That is why sometimes one should start using one's imagination to think about the old craftsmanship and the context of that area, to think about the

fig. 13
Traditional broken-tile wall construction of the Ningbo region.

fig. 14
Ningbo History Museum, near completion in 2008.

fig. 15
Details and memories.

fig. 16
This is a place of memories.

difference between the remembered living world and reality. On the other hand, we found something very interesting. We traveled around the historical countryside near the site and discovered the local way of recycling materials. Given that in this region typhoons make landfall every year, causing buildings to collapse, locals knew that they needed a very fast way to rebuild houses. They gradually developed a method that mixes eighty to ninety different materials. However, usually the buildings are not very tall, two floors at most, but they are very beautiful ***(fig. 13)***.

We wanted to build this museum with recyclable materials, but the new building was to be very tall, far beyond the traditional typologies. Therefore, we had to develop new methods. In fact, the construction was fast. Speed has a special meaning in China. Speed also means some special necessities. On the other hand, speed can also mean cost savings. This museum is very large, more than thirty thousand square meters, and it was completed in two years. We can see its mixed appearance, recycled materials with the texture of bamboo set in smooth concrete. It is clear that it has a radical look, but the construction was carefully considered, with the recycled material built vertically and the concrete parts sloping ***(fig. 14)***. When I visited the museum again, I noticed that many of the visitors were elderly people whose houses had been demolished. They came here to retrace their memories. They found many familiar details. They said that they felt acquainted with this place, these walls, the yards, the house ***(fig. 15)***. Some of the older people come here maybe four or five times in a year. They come again and again. They are not interested in the exhibition. They are just interested in

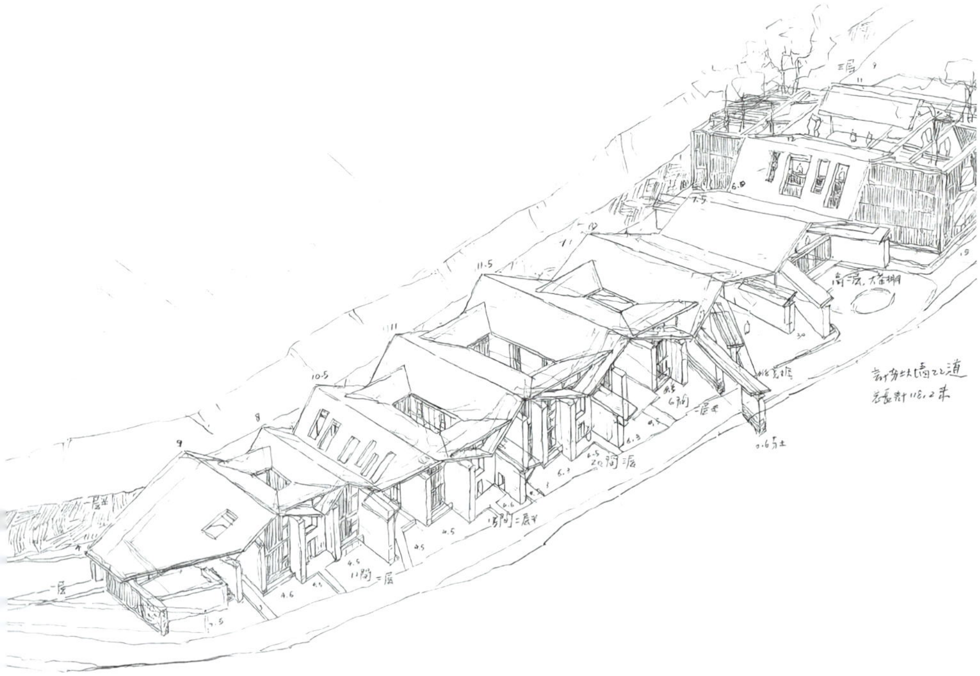

the memories of this place. Sometimes you see an old woman just standing there, like a philosopher thinking, because this is a place about memory ***(fig. 16)***.

"Tile Mountain" is another project. The challenge here was how to construct a large modern building using the traditional small-scale approach. Small things can easily coexist with elements in nature. My sketch shows that it is a large building of about ten thousand square meters ***(fig. 17)***. In fact, underneath the big roof are a number of small buildings. The whole composition is more like a village under a single roof, like a secret hive. We used recycled small green tiles, bamboo, and rammed-earth walls to form a new construction system. Usually, we will prepare some perspective sketches of the design ***(see fig. 18)***. For us, it is not just a rendering. It is a means by which we reorganize collective memories. So for us, memory is like a design element. For example, we once visited a small Buddhist temple in a remote mountainous area, and we realized that it was completely integrated with nature. The locals used a special method to respond to the hot weather and to control the interior temperature. It was possible to see very clearly the intersections of each part and the way the building is constructed. We learned a lot from these vernacular buildings.

The ability for many different things to talk and mix together to form a diverse system, similar to nature or to a garden, has always been an important goal in our work. In our Hangzhou Branch of the National Archives of Publications and Culture (HNAPC; 2020–22), while it is a huge building of one hundred thousand square meters, it essentially consists of a diverse garden structure that directly echoes traditional architecture, though in a completely new way.

In fact, the materials used here are not extraordinary; on the contrary, they are all commonplace: brick, bamboo, wood, concrete. From a construction point of view, our focus was on the creation of a new circulation system. We were not interested in special materials or special techniques. With this approach, we offered a strong critique of

fig. 17
Sketch of Wang Shu's "Tile Mountain" program, 2010.

fig. 18
Painting, architecture, how to reorganize memories.

fig. 19
Hangzhou Branch of the National Archives of Publications and Culture (HNAPC), summer 2019.

fig. 20
Sketch of Wang Shu's HNAPC, 2019.

fig. 21
Architecture is like a garden.

conventional construction systems in China. Here, the common way of designing and building is not about architecture, it is about construction companies wanting to save money, which means that they design and build in very simplified ways, very fast with lots of mistakes and no details. At the end they apply interior and exterior decoration. This has nothing to do with architecture. It means that building is reduced to decoration and advertising. Quick to realize, quick to abandon, and very wasteful.

However, if one has to build quickly, is there any possibility of realizing a high-quality building? The HNAPC is a new project that we have completed in a short period of time. We carried out all stages of this work over the last three years during the Covid-19 pandemic. The building serves as the national archives of the publishing culture and includes exhibition galleries. It is worth noting that the site has almost been destroyed by modern humans. The former mountain provided aggregates for the production of concrete to be used in the construction of the city. Nature has been reduced to this, almost obliterated ***(fig. 19)***. With our studio's design approach, if the task is to build such an enormous modern building here, the first thing we should consider is how to make the building coexist with nature, or how to repair the troubled relationship between man-made creations and nature with the help of the opportunity offered by the new building.

Our guiding principle is: do not destroy nature. We did not permit construction companies to destroy any natural topography or trees. As my sketch shows ***(fig. 20)***, all the new buildings were decomposed and precisely determined, and they were integrated with the mountain. This meant that the heights of the buildings were strictly controlled; we used a very sensitive method to dimension them. Indeed, we can see that the building complex is like a garden, where many different archetypes are brought together and mixed, achieving a vibrant state of diverse things coexisting ***(fig. 21)***. Of course, materials are very important. For example, we used local ceramic crafts in a way that gives a new feeling. This also engaged local artisans. The ceramicists had the opportunity to be involved in the construction of large buildings ***(fig. 22)***. Of course, we also used reinforced concrete. But we gave its surface a special quality using

fig. 22
New celadon technique developed in a collaboration between architects and artisans.

fig. 23
The special surface quality of concrete with a more natural texture.

fig. 24
The large-span steel-and-wood structure on top of the main study of the HNAPC.

fig. 25
Bronze-tile roofing on the HNAPC.

bamboo formwork. With precise control, we obtained a more natural texture ***(fig. 23)***.

The roof consists of new timber structures that appear to have a traditional feel. However, on close inspection, one will notice that nothing directly mimics tradition. It is an entirely new approach. The wooden structures span some thirty meters ***(fig. 24)***. We experimented with this frame in Venice and Berlin, and after more than ten years of continuous exploration, we developed it into a truly modern architectural structure. This building complex is a place for important national cultural events, and we were keen to draw people's attention to this innovative construction. The roof's profile has a curved form similar to traditional architecture, though with a subtle natural texture and bright sheen, thanks to the special treatment of the metal that was developed together with local coppersmiths ***(fig. 25)***. It poetically re-expresses the way we translated traditional styles into contemporary practice.

Biography
Wang Shu (b. 1963 in Ürümqi, Xinjiang, China) is the first Chinese architect to win the Pritzker Prize (2012). He studied architecture at Nanjing Institute of Technology (MSc 1988) and at Tongji University (PhD 2000). Two years later, he and his wife, Lu Wenyu, together established a practice, Amateur Architecture Studio, in Hangzhou. From 2000, Wang Shu taught at the China Academy of Art and served as head of the architecture department, and in 2007 he became dean of the architecture school. Wang Shu is a scholar, calligrapher, craftsman, and architect.